# WHO'S BLACK AND WHY?

The Sugar Mill.

The Sugar Works

The Sugar Canes.

T. Beckington Sculp.

# Who's Black and Why?

## A Hidden Chapter from the Eighteenth-Century Invention of Race

EDITED BY

## Henry Louis Gates, Jr., and Andrew S. Curran

THE BELKNAP PRESS OF
HARVARD UNIVERSITY PRESS

*Cambridge, Massachusetts*
*London, England*    2022

Second printing

*Library of Congress Cataloging-in-Publication Data*

Names: Gates, Henry Louis, Jr., editor. | Curran, Andrew S., editor.
Title: Who's black and why? : a hidden chapter from the eighteenth-century
    invention of race / edited by Henry Louis Gates, Jr. and Andrew S. Curran.
Description: Cambridge, Massachusetts : The Belknap Press of Harvard University
    Press, 2022. | Includes bibliographical references and index.
Identifiers: LCCN 2021036013 | ISBN 9780674244269 (cloth)
Subjects: LCSH: Académie royale des sciences (France) | Racism in anthropology—
    Europe—History—18th century. | Scientific racism—Europe—History—
    18th century. | Black race—Color—Europe—History—18th century. |
    Black race—Color—Europe—Public opinion—History—18th century. |
    Europeans—Attitudes—History—18th century. | Racism—France—
    Bordeaux (Nouvelle-Aquitaine)
Classification: LCC GN27 .C38 2022 | DDC 305.8009409/033—dc23
LC record available at https://lccn.loc.gov/2021036013

*For Karen C. C. Dalton and Sheldon L. Cheek*

# CONTENTS

## PART II

# Who's Black and Why?

I promised you some returns for your favors, by sending you my Essay on
that strange *phenomenon* in Nature, the cause of the colour of Negroes . . .
but I am afraid that this will come too late for a solution of the Prize-
Problem proposed by the Academy of Bordeaux.

Letter from Dr. John Mitchell, of Urbana, Virginia, to Peter Collinson,

Fellow of the Royal Society, London, April 12, 1743

IN 1739, the members of Bordeaux's Royal Academy of Sciences met to
determine the subject of the 1741 prize competition. As was customarily the
case, the topic they chose was constructed in the form of a question: "What
is the physical cause of the Negro's color, the quality of [the Negro's] hair,
and the degeneration of both [Negro hair and skin])?" According to the
longer description of the contest that later appeared in the *Journal des savants*,
the academy's members were interested in receiving a winning essay that
would solve the riddle of the African variety's distinctive physical traits. But
what really preoccupied these men were three larger (and unspoken) questions. The first two were straightforward: *Who is Black? And why?* The third
question was more far-reaching: *What did being Black signify?* Never before
had the Bordeaux Academy, or any scientific academy for that matter, challenged Europe's savants to explain the origins and, implicitly, the worth of a
particular type of human being.

The Bordeaux competition on the source of blackness did not occur in an intellectual vacuum, of course; it emerged in tandem with the ever-growing dependence of European economies on African slave labor throughout the New World. It is important to note, in fact, that in 1741—the year when the essays arrived at the Royal Academy—62,485 African captive men, women, and children are estimated to have boarded ships in chains along the long west coast of Africa, destined for plantations in Brazil, Central America, the Caribbean, and North America. As was invariably the case, a disturbing percentage of these humans died before spotting shore—9,454 in this year alone. Although the trans-Atlantic slave trade had not yet reached its peak, the number of Africans who had been forced to make this dreaded voyage already totaled well over four million. By the end of the eighteenth century, the era we have come to know as the Enlightenment, another 4,500,000 Africans were forced to leave their home continent for a life of brutal enslavement in plantations on the other side of the Atlantic. (See https://www.slavevoyages.org/assessment/estimates.)

The imperatives and advantages of France's slave-based colonies in the Caribbean were patently obvious to every member of the Bordeaux Academy in the 1730s. Yet the question they ultimately decided upon for the prize-problem of 1741 centered solely on black bodies themselves, as if the reality of Africans' enslavement in the Caribbean (not least in the city of Bordeaux) was not pertinent. This competition format, in short, not only obscured the city's and France's relation to New World slavery, it also hid the fact that the color of sub-Saharan bodies had become synonymous with human bondage. Lurking behind the framing of the academy's competition were thus two metonyms: in addition to the fact that the color black was a metonym for Africans, Black Africans themselves were undoubtedly a metonym for slavery and the trans-Atlantic slave trade.

To a large extent, the Bordeaux contest was only the latest iteration of a two-thousand-year-old fascination with dark skin. When the ancient Greeks, Romans, and Arabic peoples first described the black-skinned inhabitants of Africa, it was inevitably Africans' color that was the most striking takeaway. Over the centuries, African "blackness" had grown into an all-encompassing signifier that substituted itself for the range of reddish, yellowish, and blackish-brown colors that the skin colors of Africans actually express. Indeed, the notion of blackness had even become synonymous with the land itself: a number of the geographical names that outsiders ultimately assigned to sub-Saharan Africa—these include Guinea, Niger, Nigritia, Sudan, and Zanzibar—contain the etymological roots of the word "black."

The most telling example of this darkened-inscribed geography is the word *Ethiopia*. Derived from the Greek, *aitho* (I burn) and *ops* (face), this term not only became one of the most widespread labels for the entire sub-Saharan portion of the continent until the late seventeenth century, it even hinted at a theory about the original cause of blackness itself.

The members of the Bordeaux Royal Academy of Sciences had obviously become puzzled by the mishmash of conflicting explanations for African pigmentation. To begin with, they were well aware of bioclimatic accounts dating from Antiquity that maintained that the heat, sun, and humidity of the Torrid Zone not only had darkened African skin, but may have thrown African bodies out of equilibrium, introducing humoral imbalances that produced an excess of black bile and melancholia. These naturalist explanations existed alongside sacred history or what we might call European biblical "anthropology": both the Old Testament–inspired belief that all humans descended from Noah's three sons and the notion that Black Africans were actually an ill-fated branch of the family, the result of a curse that not only "marked" them but sentenced them to slavery. In addition to both climatological and biblical explanations, the Bordeaux Academy members had heard about new scientific discoveries and theories related to Africans: anatomists were sending back reports of anatomical dissections of slaves from the colonies; naturalists were putting forth secular histories of human mutation; and taxonomy-minded thinkers had begun proposing human classification schemes that separated the world's peoples into *races* for the first time.

All of these trends are found in the Bordeaux essays. Ultimately, sixteen men—a varied group of biblical scholars, anatomists, gentleman naturalists, and climate theorists—took up the Bordeaux Academy's challenge. The written traces of this unpublished, by now 280-year-old contest, which elicited responses from as far away as Sweden, Ireland, and Holland, are now housed in the municipal library of the city of Bordeaux. That these manuscripts have survived the ravages of mice and moths, humidity and fire—not to mention the French Revolution and two world wars—is nothing short of miraculous. Seemingly trapped in amber, the essays submitted to the academy constitute the rarest of treasures: a *sui generis* artifact in the history of ideas, a set of texts that, taken together, help us understand the larger context in which the concept of race took shape.

*Who's Black and Why?* is designed to be of interest to eighteenth-century scholars and anyone else concerned with the history of medicine, the history of science, and the history of race. Indeed, we hope that this book will help its audience understand how Enlightenment-era naturalists

The first page of Essay 2 (now renumbered as Essay 9), as submitted by the author. The announcement of the contest on Black skin and hair appeared in Europe's most prestigious literary and scientific periodical, the *Journal des Savants,* in 1739. Essays could be submitted either in Latin or French.

progressively transformed the alleged cognitive and physical differences existing among the world's peoples into normalized categories—taxonomical schemes that positioned white Europeans at the pinnacle of a fixed *racial* hierarchy.

In order to provide the widest context for the 1741 contest, the Introduction in Part I begins with a short history of Bordeaux's Royal Academy of Sciences before moving on to a longer examination of the involvement of the city's merchants and magistrates in the lucrative exploitation of Africans' free labor on New World plantations. This section of the book also provides a snapshot of life in Bordeaux, including an assessment of the Africans and Caribbean-born people of color who had been taken to the city during the eighteenth century. Our discussion of the academy and the city of Bordeaux is followed by a more pointed presentation of the essays themselves. The editors have also added an extensive chronology of the history of race at the end of this book to further contextualize the 1741 contest.

While preparing *Who's Black and Why?* for publication, the editors also became fascinated by a second prize-problem related to African bodies that the academy announced in 1772. In stark contrast to the contest of 1741, however, this competition no longer concealed or mediated the wider context of slavery that was generating interest in black bodies in the first place. Reacting to the shifting political climate of the 1770s, by which time Enlightenment philosophers had begun to draw attention to the suffering of African captives on European slave ships and in the colonies, the members of the academy decided to organize a very different and supposedly more righteous type of competition, namely: "What are the best ways of preserving Negroes from the diseases that afflict them during the crossing to the New World?" Emblematic of the academy's belief in both philanthropy and practicality, this improbable contest was ostensibly designed to promote a more "humane" crossing for the slaves who were enriching Bordeaux's economy— by helping ship captains and their owners simultaneously decrease mortality and thereby increase profits. Excerpts from the three entries submitted to this contest, along with a short introduction, are included at the end of this volume.

*Who's Black and Why?* casts light on these revealing (and sometimes unsettling) blind spots: moments in which Enlightenment-era thinkers made use of the rhetoric of progress and humanitarianism in order to rationalize human bondage; moments in which the scientifically based quest to improve the human condition seemed perfectly compatible with the economic imperatives of African chattel slavery. Such were the limits of the

era's universalism—in many cases, the benevolent ideology of Enlightenment simply did not apply to non-Europeans, especially Africans. Looking
back at the complex and hidden history of the competitions found in this
book not only helps us understand how the notion of race came into being
at mid-century; it provides insight into the insidious relationship between
science and enslavement in an era—to paraphrase W. E. B. Du Bois—that
was the dusk before the dawn of race. *Who's Black and Why?*, in short, allows
us to begin to fathom how sub-Saharan Africans and their descendants
became "a people seen, but not seen," as the African American artist Kerry
James Marshall has so eloquently put it.

# NOTE ON THE TRANSLATIONS

THE CONTESTANTS SUBMITTING essays to the prize contests of the Bordeaux Royal Academy of Sciences had the choice of writing in either French or Latin, the two scholarly *linguae francae* of the day. Eleven of the nineteen essays appearing in this volume (eight from the 1741 contest, three from that of 1772) were written in French; the other eight were composed in Latin.

To translate the submissions from this pan-European contest into English, the editors worked with a team of four translators. Karen C. C. Dalton, director and curator of the Image of the Black Archive and Library (a project of the Hutchins Center for African and African American Research), and Susan Emanuel, a veteran professional translator of numerous works of French scholarship into English, undertook the translations of the French essays. Translations of the Latin submissions were provided by Sheldon Cheek, also with the Image of the Black Archive and Library, and Rosanna Giammanco, the principal at Verbum Linguistic Services and translator of more than thirty books from Latin and Italian into English. Additionally, Ben Lee, professor at Oberlin College, provided valuable consultation at an early stage of the Latin translations.

Reading and transcribing the often idiosyncratic script of the essays posed one of the greatest challenges to the translators. Several essays are written on both sides of relatively translucent paper, producing a vexing double image. There were also occasional lapses in the text produced by illegible characters as well as fragments hidden within the gutters of the bound volumes.

Our goal was to produce a version of the essays in readily accessible, modern English. Thematic titles and headnotes have been added to the essays in the interest of clarity. Some of the essays have been redacted. Much of the rambling and repetitive arguments made in Essay 6, for example, required significant abridgment. Such edits are noted within the text by an ellipsis between brackets: [. . .]. The texts of more cogently argued essays, on the other hand, have been retained in their entirety.

The last sentence of each of the translated essays from the 1741 contest reflects a stratagem designed by the Bordeaux Academy to maintain the anonymity of the essay contestants. Each author was told to append a relevant aphorism to his submission. At the close of the contest, these edifying sayings were to be matched with a list of authors' names kept secret from the jury. Some essayists chose passages from the Old Testament of the Bible. Two of these directly relate to the subject of the contest. The author of Essay 12, for example, quotes a phrase from the beginning of the Song of Songs, one of the most eloquent books found in Holy Scripture: "I am black, but beautiful." Equally apropos is the selection from Proverbs chosen by the author of Essay 7: "Can the Ethiopian change his skin?"

After the assessment of the essays by the jurors, Jean Barbot, secretary of the Royal Academy, recorded the status of each essay. All of them were deemed unworthy of a prize, or had arrived too late to be considered by the jury. Their rejection by the academy is succinctly stated in the upper left-hand corner of the first page of each essay: "read, examined, and rejected from the competition" or received "outside the time of the contest." The essay sent in by Eric Molin numbers among these late arrivals. Docketed "at Amsterdam, 15 February, 1742," it was received well after the contest had ended. The reasons for this are found in the manuscript of his essay. He reveals that he had not seen the original announcement of the contest in the *Journal des savants*. Rather, he had learned about the competition more informally through some "scholarly gentlemen of Amsterdam."

This small anecdotal detail, revealed within Molin's candid though unsolicited biographical sketch, suggests the broad character of the ongoing Enlightenment debate over what it meant to be human. In addition to taking shape in the era's scientific journals, the idea of what would soon come to be known as "race" was the product of an expansive European conversation occurring in prestigious national academies, anatomy theaters, royal palaces, as well as in the more informal environment of the public café.

# I

# INTRODUCTION

# The 1741 Contest on the "Degeneration" of Black Skin and Hair

Louis XIV, king of France, signed the *lettres patentes* that formally established Bordeaux's Royal Academy of Sciences in 1712. Much like the other French scientific academies that came into existence during the seventeenth and eighteenth centuries—all of which were abolished during the French Revolution—the Bordeaux Academy functioned as an exclusive and high-minded social club whose culture was one of intellectual inquiry, exchange, and public edification.[1]

To a large degree, provincial academies such as Bordeaux's were created in response to the Continent's more conservative universities. Whereas the primary purpose of the University of Bordeaux was to educate the country's priests, doctors, and lawyers—handing down scripturally compatible truths while doing so—the Bordeaux Academy saw itself as far more enlightened and humanistic: its stated objective was advancing scientific truth as part of a larger desire to promote "mankind's happiness." This latter principle was perhaps best exemplified by one of the academy's earliest members, Jean-Jacques Bel, who donated his sumptuous townhouse and impressive library to the Bordeaux Academy in 1739 on the condition that his books be made available to the city's inhabitants.[2]

Reaching out beyond the limits of the academy's own walls was an integral part of the institution's mission. On a local level, the academy invited Bordeaux's citizens to attend an annual conference in September. More

Early photograph of the former home of the Royal Academy of Sciences, Belles-Lettres, and Arts at Bordeaux. Constructed in the early phases of the monumental renovation of the port and its fashionable neighborhoods, the Bordeaux Academy was located on the fashionable Avenue de Tourny, named after the superintendent of monuments responsible for much of the city's transformation.

famously, however, the academy also organized one or sometimes two essay contests a year that they publicized throughout Europe. All of these competitions came with significant cash prizes.

The contests announced by the Bordeaux Academy during the institution's early years reflected an interest in the natural sciences: there were "prize-problems" related to the nature of air, the fluidity of bodies, the formation of kidney stones, the source of earthquakes, the movement of muscles, and the origin of natural springs and rivers. Toward the end of the 1730s, one also detects an increasing interest in proto-anthropology, in particular a concern with the distinctiveness of non-European and, especially, African anatomy.[3]

In 1737, Bordeaux's Royal Academy of Sciences announced a competition on the effect that "breathed air" might have on human blood. While this contest might now seem innocuous, such a competition would have been seen as an open invitation to speculate on the perceived liabilities of a non-European climate, and in particular how the hot air of the Torrid Zone, bounded on the north by the Tropic of Cancer and on the south by the Tropic of Capricorn, might adversely affect African plasma.[4] Two years later, when the academicians announced their contest on the origin of blackness, the academy's fascination with African anatomy had become far more explicit.

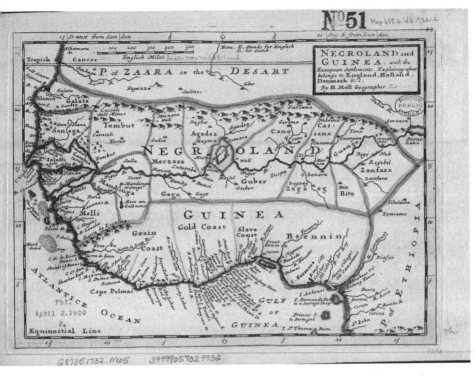

*Negroland and Guinea with the European Settlements . . .*, Herman Moll, geographer; Thomas and John Bowles, publishers. *Atlas minor* (London, 1729). The French slave port of Gorée appears in the upper left section of the map. Along the southern shore, according to this map, lie the so-called Grain, Gold, and Slave Coasts. On French maps, one finds also the "Ivory Coast," which is located between the "Grain Coast" and the "Gold Coast."

This call for essays promised the winner a gold medal worth 300 *livres*, roughly the annual salary of a common worker at the time.

By spring of 1741, sixteen submissions had arrived at the academy. Several of the essays were obviously written by profoundly religious thinkers, who explained the origin of blackness by referring to the Old Testament story of Noah and the Curse of Canaan. The majority of the submissions, however, attempted to put forward more "scientific" explanations. A number of these essays affirmed that the climate of the Torrid Zone had transformed both the physiognomy and physiology of sub-Saharan Africans, perhaps producing an overabundance of bile that led to a darkening of the skin and hair. Several others hypothesized that African mothers communicated blackness to their children through the power of the maternal imagination, imprinting physical traits to their fetuses at conception. There was also one "empirically based"

Native life in Negroland, from Olfert Dapper, *Description of Africa*, 1668. The image depicts a domestic scene in the land of *Insoko*, a region lying along the Gold Coast of West Africa. The name seems to refer to the topography of the area rather than to a specific ethnic group. The domestic scene gives a composite impression of native life in sub-Saharan Africa.

submission, an essay written by a French anatomist who had conducted autopsies on the corpses of enslaved people while serving as a doctor in Guiana; he claimed that African blood was blacker than that of Whites.

In May 1741, after the submissions had arrived, the academicians met to discuss the manuscripts in the academy's headquarters.[5] After a lengthy debate, which was so shambolically recorded by the institution's secretary that the resulting manuscript is virtually unreadable, the group ultimately decided that they were in no position to choose a winning essay.[6] While the members of the academy themselves did not know what the right answer to the question was, they surely knew what the answer was not. According to a short note that appeared a few months later in the *Mercure de France*, the academy members had been disappointed with the submissions; some people surely found that the essays were not *scientific* enough; other members presumably realized that there was no possible way to solve—once and for all—the riddle of black skin.[7]

One of the more insightful contestants actually underscored how difficult the question of blackness itself was; as he put it, whoever took on this

*Les quatre complexions de l'homme* (The Four Temperaments of Man), by Charles Le Brun, 1670s, pen and ink. One of several sculptural projects for the *parterre d'eau* at Versailles, commissioned by Louis XIV in 1674. According to the Roman physician Galen, the psychological trait of melancholy was caused by an imbalance of black bile excreted by the kidneys. Anatomists from Antiquity extended the association of bodily humors with human physiology to account for the origin of black skin color. For some naturalists and anatomists, the substance was likewise to be found in the blood and brains of people of African descent.

subject was venturing into a "land of conjecture." This was certainly an apt description of the state of knowledge regarding Black Africans in 1741. And yet, all over Europe, often within scientific academies not unlike Bordeaux's, the methods used to study the human species, particularly its non-European members, were shifting dramatically.[8] As naturalists and *savants* freed themselves from the imperatives of Scripture, they increasingly attributed the origins of human phenotypes to purely material or physical causes. That these explanations were completely spurious is not important. What is significant is that this new "scientific" orientation was opening the door to the increasing racialization of the human species.[9] This is precisely what we see in this varied collection of sixteen essays: in many ways, this is a focus group of sorts, a cluster of thinkers who, while debating the origins of African

*The Conception of Chariclea,* by Karl van Mander III, 1640, oil on canvas. Kassel, Museumlandschaft Hessen. The accomplished Dutch artist produced a cycle of paintings drawn from the ancient adventure tale *Aethiopica,* by Heliodoros of Emesa. The rambling story recounts the picaresque misadventures of the Ethiopian princess Chariclea and her Greek lover Theagenes. It begins with the conception of the princess by her mother Persinna. Normally, Chariclea would have been black like her parents. In this case, however, Persinna gazed at the image of the white-skinned Andromeda, the daughter of another royal Ethiopian couple. Due to the power of maternal imagination, Persinna produces a white child. The principle of maternal imagination in the determination of race preoccupies the author of Essay 3.

blackness, were defining human variation in terms of hierarchy and fixed categories.

## WHY BORDEAUX?

Why would a provincial scientific academy find the question of blackness so compelling? In addition to the general fascination with what we might call *proto-anthropology* and *proto-ethnography* during the era, there were also a number of reasons that have to do with Bordeaux's status as one of Europe's major seaports.

A fluvial city with direct access to the Atlantic, Bordeaux was ideally situated to export its legendary wines to the Iberian Peninsula, the Netherlands, Ireland, and the city's onetime owner, England. Yet the majority of the wealth that flooded into Bordeaux during the later seventeenth century ultimately came from its ventures in the Americas, especially from its commercial relationship with the three major French colonial islands, Martinique,

*Vue d'une partie du port et de la ville de Bordeaux, prise du côté des Salinières* (View of a part of the port and city of Bordeaux, as seen from the wharf of Salinières), Joseph Vernet, 1758, oil on canvas. Paris, Musée national de la Marine de Paris. Bordeaux established itself as a major player in the colonial trade at the end of the seventeenth century. Some of these ships were specially outfitted *négrières* [slave ships] that left the city's port laden with goods used to purchase captives along the West African coast. The human cargo was traded in the French West Indies for cane sugar and other commodities.

Guadeloupe, and Saint-Domingue; this latter colony would become the independent republic of Haiti in 1804.

Bordeaux's *négociants* or wholesale merchants not only dispatched barrels of wine and spirits to these islands, but shiploads of flour, lard, beef, ham, rolls of iron, paving stones, copper utensils, pottery, roofing materials, wood, hardware, tools, fabrics, textiles, leather, slippers, shoes, and clothing. The city's exporters also supplied the weapons and ammunition used to control the islands' Black populations.[10]

At the time the contest on blackness was announced in 1739, Bordeaux's relationship with the Caribbean had transformed its port into the busiest and most important anchorage in France.[11] Approximately thirty ships were already fully dedicated to trade with the Caribbean; half of this fleet went back and forth between Bordeaux and Martinique, the only French island with the capacity to refine its own sugar at the time. The other merchant ships traveled to Guadeloupe and, increasingly, Saint-Domingue. After the ships had unloaded their merchandise at island ports, these same vessels filled

*Une sucrerie dans une habitation à Saint-Domingue* (A Sugar Mill on a Plantation of Saint-Domingue), engraving from Père Jean-Baptiste du Tertre, *Histoire générale des Antilles habitées par les Français* (Paris: Thomas Jolly, 1667–1671). The many sugarcane plantations of the French West Indies were often the final destination of slaves brought from Africa by French slave ships. Surgeons were assigned to the colonies in order to tend to sick or injured slaves. The engraving depicts the structures and operation of the plantation, with illustrations of local flora in the foreground.

their holds with a wide variety of colonial products, among them achiote spice, clayed sugar, cocoa, coffee beans, cotton, ginger root, leather, and turtle meat. Once these commodities had cleared Bordeaux's customs house, they were either directly dispatched to the rest of Europe or transformed into other saleable goods by the city's burgeoning manufacturing sector. This was especially the case for the tens of millions of pounds of raw sugar processed annually in the city's refineries, much of which was sent to Southern France, Holland, and northern Germany.[12]

Over the course of the century, most of Bordeaux's direct investments in the Caribbean centered on Saint-Domingue.[13] By the 1770s, this comparatively new colony had become something of an extension of the city's economy; in addition to the fact that the city's wholesale merchants had a virtual monopoly on the goods passing through the island's ports, most of the colony's 792 sugar plantations, 3,097 indigo plantations, 2,810 coffee plantations, and 705 cotton plantations were owned by families from Bordeaux.[14] Indeed, fully 40 percent of the island's white population, a total of approxi-

An African *mascaron* stares out from the former Place Royale, now Place de la Bourse, facing the esplanade along the Garonne River. Images of Black heads are among the immense repertoire of fanciful heads seen on the façades of Bordeaux's elegant administrative buildings and townhouses. In the case of the African *mascaron*, the visage was not necessarily intended to represent an actual slave, but the long-established trope of an idealized African. These heads are nonetheless a reminder of the source of much of Bordeaux's wealth during the eighteenth century.

mately 30,000 people in the 1780s, had come from Bordeaux and Southwest France.[15] Even more telling, of the 346 slave-trading expeditions that left Bordeaux's port in the eighteenth century, approximately 78 percent ultimately were destined for Saint-Domingue, whereas only 4 percent went to Guadeloupe and 9 percent to Martinique.[16]

The colony-derived affluence flowing back from the phenomenally profitable sugar plantations on Saint-Domingue and the other French islands helped transform Bordeaux during the eighteenth century. In addition to all the new businesses and manufacturers that came into being, Bordeaux's downtown became home to shops featuring the latest luxury items for its wealthy citizens: there were jewelers, silversmiths, goldsmiths, furniture makers, clockmakers, wig makers, merchants selling rugs and tapestries, and purveyors of the latest fashions. The period's affluence can still be seen in Bordeaux's stunning cityscape, which added some 5,000 stone buildings, apartments, and townhouses during the city's so-called "Golden Century."

The most telltale vestiges of Bordeaux's colonial involvement in the Caribbean are found, however, on the façades of several buildings near the old customs house on the banks of the Garonne River. Looming above the massive *portes cochères* or covered entryways of these former townhouses, *mascarons* (sculpted stone faces) with African features look down at the passersby below.[17] These *bas reliefs* are a reminder that the city's *armateurs* (shipowners) organized roughly 500 expeditions to Africa, which resulted in the deportation of approximately 150,000 Africans to French plantations between 1672 and 1837—approximately 13 percent of the 1.2 million enslaved Africans who arrived alive in the French colonies.[18] To put this figure in perspective, it is useful to note that the total number of African captives taken from Africa to the Caribbean by Bordeaux slave traders far exceeded the total population of the city itself in 1789 (c. 110,000).[19]

Compared to the other cities involved in the slave trade, Bordeaux was a minor player for much of the eighteenth century. In the years prior to the 1741 contest, slaving expeditions represented perhaps only 10 percent of the capital invested in maritime ventures, a fraction of Bordeaux's total colonial trade.[20] Despite this fact, the number of such voyages had begun to rise significantly at the precise moment that the Bordeaux Academy was asking Europe's naturalists to hold forth on the subject of black skin. Indeed, between 1739 and 1740, the number of slaves carried to the Caribbean on Bordeaux's ships increased by a factor of five, rising from 353 to 1,841.[21] Although there were further downturns during times of war, this trend intensified during the second half of the century. By the 1780s, Bordeaux's participation in the slave trade had reached a point where the city's ships were transporting between 4,000 and 8,000 slaves annually to the colonies.[22]

Slavery, slave-trading expeditions, and the constant flow of "ethnographic" information coming back from the Caribbean transformed the subject of Black Africans into a major preoccupation during these years. And yet, there was a far more concrete reason why the question of blackness had become so intriguing for the Bordeaux Academy: the city itself had become home to an increasing number of sub-Saharan Africans, Caribbean-born Black people (often known popularly as *nègres creoles* in French), and a growing group of the offspring of Black and white parents.

Most of the enslaved members of Bordeaux's Black population labored in or near the port, often for short periods of time before returning to the islands on merchant ships or, on occasion, escaping. Others had been taken

*Prospect of the Coast from El Mina to Mowri*, from John Green, comp., *A New General Collection of Voyages and Travels*, vol. 2 (London: Thomas Astley, 1745–1747), facing p. 589. In this panorama of the slave-trading coast, captive Africans are being taken to European ships anchored offshore. The vessels were also reprovisioned with fresh stocks of water and local medicinal remedies.

*Africa: A European Merchant bartering with a Black Chief,* from a series of the *Four Continents* by Jean-Baptiste Oudry. 1724, oil on canvas. This highly romanticized tropical scene introduces the subject of the African slave trade into the European imaginary. A richly attired European merchant bargains with his African counterpart over the sale of two children. Possibly commissioned by a wealthy French maritime trader, the painting forms one of a set of four scenes depicting commerce among the world's continents. Each may have once crowned the doors of an elegant room within a sumptuous residence, perhaps located in the large seaport of Nantes.

to the city by rich merchants or ship captains to work as house servants in some of the city's great townhouses. There was also a small population of enslaved people who had sailed to Bordeaux from the colonies to be trained as cooks, valets, or porters. Some of the youngest Africans to come to the city spent their early years as so-called *négrillons,* often represented in European art as devoted, even beloved extended family members hovering expectantly around their masters as living emblems of their owner's power and opulence.[23]

Several categories of elite, mixed-race visitors also passed through Bordeaux. A number of these were the illegitimate (but free) children of French planters who were sent back from the islands for a proper education. Rich merchants who had settled in Senegal also returned to the city on occasion

Louise de Keroual, duchess of Portsmouth, by Pierre Mignard, 1682, oil on canvas. London, National Portrait Gallery. Born in France, the sitter became the mistress of King Charles II of England in 1671. Here she shelters a young Black serving girl in the crook of her arm. By the time this portrait was painted in Paris, so-called *négrillons* or *little negroes* were very much in vogue. Louis XIV's wife, in fact, had been given an African dwarf as a present. These people were living symbols of the elevated status of the ruling elite.

with their mixed-race children. The most famous free Black people to live in Bordeaux were Placide and Isaac Louverture, the sons of the Haitian general and revolutionary, Toussaint Louverture (1743–1803). It was the revolt under the leadership of Toussaint, ironically enough, that ultimately led to the destruction of Bordeaux's economy.[24]

The actual number of enslaved Black people and free people of color in Bordeaux during the eighteenth century probably numbered in the hundreds at any given time. By 1777, the first year in which an official census of the

Black population was carried out by the newly established *Police des Noirs,* there were some 400 people of color living within a city of perhaps 90,000 inhabitants.[25] In all, it is estimated that some 4,000 Africans or Caribbean-born Black people passed through or lived in Bordeaux during the eighteenth century.[26]

### THE BORDEAUX ACADEMY AND SLAVERY

Bordeaux's participation in the slave trade drew Frenchmen of all classes into numerous trades and professions. Along with the investors who underwrote the voyages in the first place, there were shipwrights, ship chandlers, sail-makers, rope makers, coopers, stevedores, merchants, wholesalers, customs officials, and warehouse workers, not to mention all the people working in the industries that supplied departing ships with the guns, iron, tools, dishes, textiles, and alcohol that were manufactured for ships purchasing slaves in Africa.

The forty exalted members of the Bordeaux Academy generally avoided soiling their hands *directly* in the slave trade. This is not surprising since the academy did not admit merchants, even rich merchants, to its ranks. And yet, as was the case with many of the city's elites, it was not rare for academy members to have significant contacts with and financial interests in the French Caribbean. Some of the academicians belonged to aristocratic dynasties whose flagging fortunes had been revived by the royal allocation of plantations in Martinique or Saint-Domingue.[27] This was the case for Alexandre de Ségur (1695–1755), Louis Charles Mercier Dupaty de Clam (1744–1782) and his brother, Jean-Baptiste Mercier Dupaty (1746–1788), the latter who was actually born on his family's estate in Saint-Domingue. The Bordeaux Academy had also welcomed François-Armand de Saige (1734–1793) and Pierre-Paul Nairac (1732–1814), both of whom came from families with ties to the slave trade. Nairac had actually been directly involved in the business himself; indeed, along with his two brothers, he and his family's company had deported more than 8,000 African captives to the French colonies, above and beyond any other syndicate or individual in the city.[28]

There are also numerous examples of Bordeaux Academy members with other personal links to the islands. The cash-poor aristocrat, academician, and military officer Antoine de Ricouart d'Hérouville (1713–1782) married into the family of a bourgeois sugarcane planter, effectively trading on his aristocratic pedigree for access to the sort of huge fortunes being made on the other side of the Atlantic.[29] Other less direct associations abound as well;

one academician had a brother who owned a coffee warehouse; a sister married a banker in Martinique. All of these peripheral links to the Caribbean dovetailed with the academy's larger "scientific" interest in developing knowledge related to French colonies, generally, and, more specifically, to the enslaved peoples on those islands. It was with this in mind that the academy would admit the Martinique-born botanist, colonial administrator, and plantation owner Jean-Baptiste Thibault de Chanvalon (1723–1788) to its ranks in 1748.

To understand the academy's complex relationship to its overseas colonies—as well as the question of chattel slavery—one needs to examine the social makeup of the institution itself. During the eighteenth century, the Académie Royale des Sciences, Belles-Lettres, et Arts de Bordeaux was generally referred to by its abbreviated title, the Academy of Sciences. This is somewhat misleading given that the majority of the academy's members were not what we might today consider "scientists." While a dozen or more of the forty academicians were trained as doctors, engineers, botanists, hydrographers, and mathematicians, those members with actual expertise in such fields held the subordinate title of *associates*. The far more important group in the academy—from which the president was always elected—was comprised of *membres ordinaires* or regular members. These academicians were nobles and, in the vast majority of cases, magistrates with lifetime membership in the city's most important legislative and judicial body, the Parlement of Bordeaux.

The members of Bordeaux's parlement—approximately forty-five men who had either inherited or purchased their positions—had two major roles: in addition to the fact that they effectively ruled over the entire Guyenne region as a type of supreme court, they also functioned as a check on royal power, either ratifying (registering) or rejecting the royal edicts and proclamations that were dispatched for approval from Versailles.[30] It was in this capacity that the dozen or so academicians who were also serving in Bordeaux's parlement at any given time sometimes found themselves directly implicated in passing judgment on the city's trade practices and even on the question of slavery.[31] One such instance occurred in 1738, when the parlement was asked to take up the question of the legal status of the city's Black population.

Prior to 1716, enslaving a person in France, at least theoretically, was illegal. According to a longstanding royal principle dating from the fourteenth century, any enslaved person who set foot on French territory was immediately freed.[32] Indeed, in 1571, Bordeaux's parlement had famously upheld this principle when a Norman slave trader arrived in the city and attempted to sell his cargo of African slaves. The Parlement of Bordeaux, citing the principle that "no one is a slave in France," issued an order that both freed the slaves and ordered the owner taken into custody.[33]

The status of the so-called "Free Soil" principle was first called into question during the Regency (1715–1723), the interim between the reigns of Louis XIV and Louis XV. During this era of rampant colonial expansion, Duke Philippe d'Orléans, Regent of France, countermanded this policy by proclaiming in 1716 that enslaved Africans from the Caribbean—they were technically considered *meubles* or property according to the 1685 *Code Noir*—were no longer automatically emancipated when they arrived on French soil. After three hundred years, the regent had once again recognized the legality of slavery (specifically the enslavement of Black people) in France.[34]

In the two decades after this decision, an increasing number of enslaved Africans were taken to cities, including Nantes, Bordeaux, Saint Malo, La Rochelle, Orléans, and Paris. As these Black populations became more numerous and hence more visible, Louis XV felt compelled to issue a "declaration" clarifying their status in 1738. To avoid "problems" (he was surely alluding to a fear of miscegenation that was already a legal and social concern in the Caribbean) and the "spirit of independence" that might develop among Africans living in France, he limited the term of slaves' stays to three years.[35] He also stipulated that enslaved Africans in France needed to be registered and engaged in either religious or technical training. Owners who violated either portion of this decree were to be fined the sum of 1,000 *livres* and have their slaves confiscated and returned to the colonies. The ostensible goal of this statute, theoretically, was to control or even limit slavery in France. Its effect, however, was to further codify the legality of human bondage in the country, and quash the principle of Free Soil.

In 1738, provincial parlements including that of Bordeaux were called upon to ratify or reject this declaration. Paris's parlement, which was both far from any port and somewhat contrarian, refused to vote on the validity of this new royal decree. The parlements of the slave-trading cities of Nantes and Bordeaux, however, backed the king's proposal, effectively endorsing the existence of enslaved Black people on French soil. It is certainly noteworthy that those members of the Bordeaux Academy who were also seated in the city's parlement were very much involved in determining the political status of Black Africans in France only months before the competition on the causes of blackness was proposed.

TWO ACADEMY FIGUREHEADS: MELON AND MONTESQUIEU

By the 1730s, Bordeaux had entered an era of tremendous prosperity, in part thanks to its links to the colonies. Unsurprisingly, the academy's members, many of whom benefited either directly or indirectly from the port's activity, tended to be champions of the city's manufacturing and maritime businesses. Perhaps the most telling example of the overall commercial positioning of the academy occurred in 1726. More than a decade after the institution announced its first scientific competition, its members decided that, in those years when the academy did not award a prize, they would reallocate the money and purchase shares in the *Compagnie des Indes* (The Company of the Indies).[36] This French trading company, which had been awarded the monopoly on slave trading in the French islands, had been involved in the deportation of approximately 38,000 Africans to the Caribbean by the time that the contest was announced in 1739.[37]

The academy's archives reveal very little about what individual academicians thought about slavery and Africans in the 1730s. Yet the published writings of two of the most prominent members of the academy provide some insight into the complex links among Bordeaux's commercial interests, African chattel slavery, and the era's proto-science in the 1730s. The first of these academicians is the economist Jean-François Melon (1675–1738), who was both a member of the Parlement of Bordeaux and one of the academy's founders. Melon was a household name in Bordeaux during the first decades of the eighteenth century. In addition to occupying the lucrative position of superintendent of tax collection—*inspecteur général des fermes*—in Bordeaux itself, Melon had also served as advisor and secretary to the regent, the Duc d'Orléans, at the very time when he authorized slavery on French territory in October of 1716.

Melon published his views on chattel slavery in his best-selling 1734 book, *Essai politique sur le commerce* (A Political Essay upon Commerce). Echoing the point of view of Bordeaux's merchant class, he proclaimed that "equality among mankind is an illusion" and that African chattel slavery posed no moral problem; not only does it save souls, he implied, but Europeans should embrace this trade since it is necessary for the economic success of the colonies.[38] So besotted was the economist with the advantages of African chattel slavery that he actually advocated replacing French domestics with African slaves in cities like Bordeaux. Melon also provided one of the best examples of how economic, racial, and scientific concerns tended to crisscross in people's minds in the eighteenth century. After sharing a fear of miscegenation—a common preoccupation at the time—he wondered aloud about the effect of the climate on Africans' bodies. This is, of course, the exact type of "scientific" question taken up by the academy a few years later.

The other notable Bordeaux Academy member to write on slavery was Melon's colleague and friend Montesquieu. Today this philosopher is remembered as one of the forefathers of classical liberalism and a leading light of the French Enlightenment. Montesquieu's fame as a writer began a few years after he joined the Bordeaux Academy, when he published one of the greatest satirical novels of the eighteenth century, the *Lettres persanes* (Persian Letters), in 1721. His most significant work, however, was his multivolume treatise on political philosophy, the 1748 *De l'esprit des lois* (The Spirit of the Laws), a book that ultimately had an enormous effect on the evolution of political thinking in Europe, including the legality and morality of the ongoing slave trade.

Montesquieu's interest in the "dark-skinned peoples" living in the Tropics (and Bordeaux itself) had actually begun before he started his career as a writer. In his second year at the academy, in 1717, he delivered a paper entitled the "Dissertation on the Difference of Intelligences," which speculated that harsh climates, be they too hot or too cold, might ultimately give rise to cognitively and morally inferior humans.[39] Though we only have an incomplete manuscript version of this speech, the notes he left behind reveal what would become two of his lifelong convictions: the first was that extreme temperatures acting on the body's "fibers" can have a ruinous effect on human beings, especially their drive and ability to process complicated ideas.[40] The second was that climate not only explains the character of a given region, but it also determines the most appropriate form of political system for these same people.

Montesquieu refined his understanding of the supposed relationship between climate and the ill-fated populations of the world over the course of two decades, ultimately incorporating these thoughts into *The Spirit of the Laws*. Though he avoided singling out Africans as a *type* during his discussions of different environments, Montesquieu nonetheless asserted that those who live near the equator have "distended or relaxed fiber endings" and are consequently lazy, pleasure-driven, unthinking machines with "no curiosity, no noble enterprise, no generous sentiment."[41] Even more problematically, Montesquieu also stressed that people in the Torrid Zone are deficient in the capacity to reason and, therefore, have such difficulty thinking that a life of rough treatment and servitude is perhaps easier for them to withstand than their inherent lethargy. As Montesquieu put it: "the majority of punishments [for the inhabitants of hot countries] are easier to endure than mental exertion; servitude is also more tolerable than the force of mind necessary for human affairs."[42] That Montesquieu was, in fact, talking about Africans is made quite clear when one considers an unpublished note he jotted down in 1750 about emancipated Black people living in Saint-Domingue. He described them as "so *naturally* lazy that those who are free do nothing."[43]

Montesquieu's racialist assertions regarding the indolent, warm-climate body stand in stark contrast to what he asserted about slavery elsewhere in *The Spirit of the Laws*. Although his environmental relativism did lead him to admit, reluctantly, that slavery might *reasonably* exist in "a few particular countries on Earth," he was also the first Enlightenment thinker in the 1740s to condemn the institution of slavery on the basis of natural law. Far more famously, he also provided a highly ironic and often-quoted list of nine reasons that he, "if compelled," would use were he *forced* to justify slavery. Some of these presumed justifications underscored the absurdity of the era's mercantile argument for slavery, e.g., we must enslave (and kill) Africans or "our sugar will be too expensive." Others unveiled how increasingly racialized arguments served to desensitize Europeans: "These slaves are black from head to toe; and they have such flat noses that it is almost impossible to pity them." (The phrase about Africans being "black from head to toe" would be repeated by Immanuel Kant in 1764.) The penultimate reason in Montesquieu's ironic list was arguably the most pointed: it demonstrated how Europeans created taxonomical categories that insulated Christians from their grotesque hypocrisy: "It is impossible for us to suppose these creatures to be men; if this were truly the case, it would follow that we ourselves are not Christians."[44]

Though he was later criticized for his flippant tone, Montesquieu's ironic criticism of his era's justification of slavery lived on in French thought far longer than his proto-raciology. In the decades after his death, which occurred in 1755, French philosophes including Voltaire, Helvétius, and Diderot all recognized Montesquieu's role in underscoring the fundamental evil of slavery.[45] This concern ultimately manifested itself within Bordeaux's Academy of Sciences as well, particularly after the pressure to address the suffering of Africans finally became a subject of national concern in the mid-1770s.

## SLAVERY AND THE LAST YEARS OF THE ACADEMY

The Bordeaux Academy responded to the first antislavery rumblings by proposing two competitions having to do with African slaves, both in 1772. The first was an open contest on the treatment of diseases from which enslaved Africans suffered. The second competition solicited essays on a more disquieting aspect of the same question, the "best ways of preserving Negroes that we transport from Africa from the diseases that they contract during the crossing." The motivation behind this latter contest reflects a forgotten and appalling trend at the dawn of the abolitionist era: the notion that, through science, slave traders and planters could reform, rationalize, and "improve" existing enslavement practices, moving the colonies toward a form of bondage that was supposedly more benevolent.[46] The three essays that were submitted to this later contest are found in Part II of this book and described in the Part II Introduction.

The 1772 contest was not the final time that the academy members took up the question of slavery, however. Sixteen years later, on August 26, 1788, the academician André-Daniel Laffon de Ladébat (1746–1829) read a polemical speech, entitled "Discourse on the Necessity and the Means to Destroy Slavery in the Colonies," at the one academy session of the year open to the general public. Ladébat began his sermon by citing Montesquieu's condemnation of slavery from *The Spirit of the Laws*. He then went on to recommend a progressive emancipation that would include a small piece of property for each liberated African, claiming that "the work of a free man" would be more economically advantageous for everybody.

Unlike the far more incendiary abolitionists writing in the late 1780s, Ladébat was careful not to blame Caribbean planters or, implicitly, Bordeaux's own slave traders for the horrors of slavery: it was a fact, he admitted, that the "most respectable men . . . have had slaves, and have bought and sold them." Ladébat also explained how this came to pass, how even "the most fair-minded man" might fall into the trap of selling or exploiting other humans. In his opinion, this was not a personal moral failing; indeed, he believed that the existence of slavery should be attributed to "the vices of legislation," in other words, to the French laws that did not reflect a pure "expression of justice."[47]

That Ladébat sought to rationalize the past's unenlightened understanding of slavery was not surprising: his own father, Jacques-Alexandre Laffon de Ladébat, had been among the most successful *négriers* in Bordeaux during the 1760s, sponsoring no fewer than eleven expeditions to Africa and even

*André-Daniel Laffon de Ladébat,* Suzanne Caron, 1763, pastel. Musées de Bordeaux. This delicate half-length rendering of the youthful Ladébat captures him at the beginning of a long and varied career. A distinguished member of the Bordeaux Academy of Sciences, Ladébat's father enriched himself as an *armateur,* an owner of ships involved in the slave trade. The younger Ladébat, however, went on to become an abolitionist and an active participant in the French Revolution in Paris.

purchasing a large sugar plantation on Saint-Domingue. The irony did not end there, however; it had been the colonial wealth that his father accrued that had allowed the Ladébat family to be ennobled, and therefore, for the son to become a member of the city's elite, including being worthy of the Royal Academy.

Ladébat's assertion that the shame of African chattel slavery was the result of governmental failings now seems patently and inexcusably self-exculpatory. And yet, this committed abolitionist was not only implicitly addressing his family's legacy, he was speaking for all of Bordeaux in 1788—hoping to encourage the city to abandon African chattel slavery without getting bogged down in the moral implications of the city's prosperity during the previous century. This speech, according to contemporary accounts, was greeted first by a stunned silence, and then by a sudden burst of overwhelming applause.

Though Ladébat did not yet know it, much of the world that he and his fellow academicians knew in 1788 was coming to an end. A year after the academy member and abolitionist gave his impassioned speech, France's revolutionaries had restricted the political authority of the monarchy, established representative government, and issued the Declaration of the Rights of Man and of the Citizen. By 1793, after both Marie Antoinette and Louis XVI had been executed, the Revolutionary Government also began abolishing institutions that they felt were bastions of aristocratic privilege and power, among them Bordeaux's Royal Academy of Sciences.

The shuttering of the academy paled in comparison to other events affecting Bordeaux in 1793. In the aftermath of the 1791 slave uprisings in the sugar plantations of Saint-Domingue that caused great uncertainty about the colony's future, France declared war on England, suspending the city's indispensable colonial trade with the Caribbean for the subsequent decade. Even more unsettling, from the perspective of Bordeaux's merchant sector, Saint-Domingue's new revolutionary civil commissioner, Léger-Félicité Sonthonax (1763–1813), had believed that the only way to save the colony was, paradoxically, to decree that all the slaves in the rioting north province of the colony be set free. At the end of 1793, more than half of the remaining colonists on the island returned to France, most of them to their native Bordeaux region.[48]

Bordeaux's Golden Century was coming to a close.[49] Although the city's wholesalers, shipowners, and storekeepers briefly held out hope that, after Napoleon came to power in 1801, France would restore order on Saint-Domingue and Bordeaux might once again enjoy its privileged relationship with the colony, this prospect faded in 1803, when the combined forces of the Black revolutionaries Jean-Jacques Dessalines (1756–1806) and Alexandre Pétion (1770–1818) defeated Napoleon's expeditionary army at the Battle of Vertières. On January 1, 1804, Dessalines signed the country's declaration of independence, announcing the creation of the new independent Republic of *Hayti*. The irrevocable loss of what had been the most profitable colony in the history of the world was the first of two crushing blows to Bordeaux's economy. At the same time that Bordeaux's special connection with Saint-Domingue came to a close, France entered into a prolonged war with England that resulted in a decade-long blockade of the port. By

1808, fully 15 percent of Bordeaux's population had fled the area for lack of work, and the once-thriving "Port de la Lune" was generally devoid of ships.[50]

## HOW TO READ THE 1741 CONTEST ON BLACKNESS

To understand what was at stake in the Bordeaux Academy contest on the causes of the blackness of skin, one must remember that scientific culture in 1741 is a fascinating example of the exoticism of the past. Among other things, the contestants who wrote essays for the academy did so during an era when belief in short biblical timescales continued to exert an enormous influence on the understanding of the world; even educated persons would have balked at the spans of time that we now use to describe the long process of human speciation and development.

Even harder to grasp would have been the generally accepted truth that modern humans appeared in Africa first, and that these ancient populations contributed the lion's share of genes and DNA to humankind's current genetic makeup.[51] One marvels at how difficult it would be to explain the implications of this scientific fact to Europeans in 1741: 1) that all hominids, including *Homo sapiens,* originated in Africa and could only have been black-skinned; and 2) that white Europeans themselves were

*4*

*EPOQUE pour l'Année 1741.*

ON compte depuis la création du Monde jusqu'à la venue de Jesus-Christ, 4000 ans.
Depuis le Déluge universel jusqu'à présent, 4085 ans.
Depuis la Naissance de N. S. Jesus-Christ, 1741 ans.
Depuis la correction du Calendrier Grégorien, 159 ans.
Depuis l'origine de la Monarchie Françoise, 1321 ans.
Et du Régne de Louis XV. du nom, Roy de France & de Navarre, 26 ans.

Chronology for the year 1741. From the *Almanach royal* (Paris: Veuve Houry, 1741), p. 4. The privately published *Almanach royal* first appeared in 1683. At the beginning of each edition, one finds a full contextualization of the year in historical time, beginning with the Genesis account of the beginning of the world. The biblical narrative is thus considered an inviolable account of the age of the earth, calculated to be 5,741 years old in 1741. The same authority was accepted by some of the authors of the Bordeaux contest essays.

the fortuitous result of migration, mutation, and natural selection among vitamin D–starved bodies.

The writers who contributed their (anonymous) essays to the Royal Academy's contest nonetheless had their own explanations for the "origin" of black human skin. Indeed, one finds a staggering range of possibilities scattered among these essays, including the following:

1. Adam or Eve was black, or Adam was half black.
2. Blackness is a mark of God denoting sinfulness.
3. God made all people white, but some unknown exterior causes generated blackness.
4. Black skin is a God-given gift allowing people to live in the Torrid Zone.
5. God transmits ethical proclivities to people, who then advance these principles toward glory or toward degeneration. A moral defect in parents, a "perverse disposition of the mind," leads their progeny to be black.
6. Since the sun is the hottest in the Torrid Zone, it follows that Africans have the darkest skin. Likewise, their noses and mouths have been swollen and flattened by the heat.
7. A huge shift in climate after the Flood led God to protect Africans by giving them darker skin, which is resistant to the climate.
8. White women produced a black child when they thought about or saw an African or the color black during conception.
9. Based on Newtonian optics, blackness results from the absorption of light.
10. Blackness arises from vapors emanating from the skin.
11. Africans have darkened semen.
12. Blackness results from the blood, and Africans have darker blood, because of the effect of air.
13. There is a specific liquid—black bile—in the black body. This hereditary feature is passed down through the soul of the father, who "impresses" blackness on the fetus through the mother.
14. White skin has a greater number of "tubes" filled with transparent liquid near the surface of the skin, whereas Black people have far thicker blood that cannot nourish the tubes, and thus they have drier, darker skin.

A similar range of theories was proposed to explain textured "Black" hair or "wool," among them: 1) the presence of "special particles" in the follicles that were curled as opposed to straight; 2) the fact that African heat twisted the hair as did a curling iron; 3) a critical lack of "vegetative" humidity; 4) the curling process that black hair undergoes as it grows through smaller pores; or 5) the presence of a black humor or coloring matter that tinted and curled hair.

How can we make sense of all this speculation that, today, strikes us, at worst, as racialist or, at best, as nonsensical pseudo-science? The first thing that one notices in examining the often-conflicting notions related to African skin and hair is that a number of these "naturalistic" theories existed in perfect harmony with the idea that some form of divine providence (or the power of the soul) had helped contribute to the creation of hair types of different hues.[52] Indeed, many of these conjectures had obviously been advanced by scripturally minded contributors, be they ecclesiastics or devout laypeople. For many of these essayists, the reasons for participating in the competition probably had little to do with determining the source of black skin or hair; the real goal was putting forward a theory of human difference that was compatible with scriptural authority.

It is difficult to overstate the importance of religion in French debates on human diversity in this era. Religiously oriented thinkers who engaged in speculative "anthropology" generally did so in ways that were perfectly compatible with three truths related to the Creation story. The first was the belief—based on a literal reading of the Bible—that God had created the earth precisely 5,741 years before the 1741 contest. The second was the status of Nature itself. For the most literal of biblical scholars, Nature could not have an autonomous and dynamic history; it was unchanging and *providentialist*. It was, in other words, dependent entirely on God's will and his actions at the moment of Creation. The third and most important concept related to the Christian history of humankind was the idea that, according to Scripture, all the world's peoples not only were created by God, but were God's children, members of the larger family of humankind.

This belief in human consanguinity remained one of the most powerful features of European thought during the eighteenth century, even among the more medically or anatomically oriented essayists. Several of the contributors who sent in submissions, in fact, referenced the Bible's evidence of shared human origins, the canonical Old Testament parable recounting how Noah's three sons split up and populated the earth after the Ark had come to rest in what is now the Caucasus.[53]

Virtually everyone who had been raised in Christendom, generally, and in the Roman Catholic Church in France, more particularly, had learned about the aftermath of the Flood as if it were historical fact. According to

*The Drunkenness of Noah,* Luca Giordano, second half of the seventeenth century, oil on canvas. Madrid, El Escorial. The dramatic tableau relates the biblical account of the betrayal of Noah by his son, Ham. While Ham callously mocks his father's nakedness, his brothers Shem and Japheth piously walk backward to place a cloth over Noah's genitals. Upon awakening, Noah curses not Ham, but Ham's own son, Canaan. The alienation of Ham from his kin alludes both to his personal guilt as well as to the lasting stigma of Black Africans supposedly descended from his lineage.

this account in the Book of Genesis, which was written sometime in the sixth century BCE, Noah drank too much wine one night and lay naked and exposed for all to see. Two of his sons, Shem and Japheth, quickly covered their father's naked body so as to preserve his modesty. His third son, Ham, however, indiscreetly glanced at his sleeping father, an act of filial impiety that ultimately led Noah to curse Ham's only son, Canaan. Canaan, as the story goes, was thus sentenced, along with all of his descendants, to a life of slavery as a "servant of servants."

The "Curse of Ham"—especially its relationship to the Black peoples of the world—has a long and complex history. Although much of the "postbiblical" history of this fable is fragmentary, to say the least, it is clear that both Talmudic and Christian scholars, the latter from North Africa and the Middle East, began adding direct references to the "blackening" of Ham alongside the curse of eternal bondage at least as early as the third century CE.[54] Medieval theologians in Europe revived these ancient rabbinic and Christian writings related to the myth a millennium later, asserting that the so-called Hamites were not only destined for all time to be slaves, but had become darkened by God in the process. The "Curse of Ham" or, alternatively, "the Curse of Canaan" echoed in European religious and secular thought for centuries. And well into the nineteenth century, proslavery writers (especially in the United States) pointed to the blackness of people of African descent—a supposed malediction—in order to argue that it was the Africans' destiny to serve the descendants of the other (non-Hamitic) branches of the human family.

Most of the Bordeaux essayists tended to disregard this biblical story. And yet, the vast majority accepted the proto-*biological* notion embedded within this parable: that humankind shared one single origin, a so-called *monogenesis*. This concept is behind the precise language that the Bordeaux Academy used in constructing its question for the *Journal des Savants:* "What is the source of the *degeneration* of black hair and black skin?"

### THE KEY TO THE BORDEAUX CONTEST:
### HUMAN DEGENERATION

Human degeneration was a critically important idea throughout the eighteenth century. Today, the term *degenerate* connotes someone who has somehow morally declined from what is customarily expected in society—from our moral norms. This same basic concept functions on the level of the human *species* in the Royal Academy's question. In asking contestants to identify the causes of African degeneration, the Bordeaux academicians were unambiguously asserting that Black human beings were somehow debased and corrupted, albeit members of the human species.

The belief that all nonwhite branches of the human family tree had undergone some form of deleterious degenerative process is far more than simple xenophobia: it is one of the first proto-scientific expressions of racialized thinking, since it provided both a genealogy and a tiered rationalization of humankind. Consider the remark of the contestant in Essay 15:

> There is no doubt that the first species (the one we ourselves are from) is the primitive and legitimate one, so to speak. All the others have degenerated, but diversely according to [their particular] susceptibility. If you want to know in which order I place them in this respect, I put the Americans in second place; next, the Lapps and the inhabitants of the Isle of Dogs; finally, I put the Negroes in last place because of their general stupidity and the almost bestial barbarity of some of them. (Part I, Essay 15, p. 174)

As vile as the notion of species degeneration is, however, the academy's contest was actually framed in such a way as to exclude entries that might posit an even more powerful (and heretical) notion, polygenesis: the idea that the most "extreme" examples of humans—Africans and Laplanders were favorite examples—actually constituted distinct *species* of humans who had come into being separately and independently from white humans.

Like many anthropological notions dating from the early modern era, polygenist theory was discussed in the context of the era's religious debates. As early as 1520, the Swiss physician and alchemist Paracelsus had challenged the traditional Genesis story by claiming that there were not one but *two* Adams: a white one, who had come into existence in Asia, and a Native American one, who had been created in the New World after the Flood. Several decades later, in 1591, the Italian philosopher Giordano Bruno followed Paracelsus's lead, but pointed to Africans as obviously stemming from either a Black "Adam" or a separate pre-Adamite race.[55] As Richard Popkin has written, "In considering the differences between Ethiopians (Africans), the American Indians, and various special or mythical beings . . . Bruno felt that all of those beings [could not] be traced to the same descent, nor [did they spring] from the generative force of a single progenitor."[56]

Several decades later, the French theologian Isaac La Peyrère published the most influential book theorizing a *polygenetic* explanation of humankind in his 1655 *Praeadamitae*. Much as Bruno had done before him, La Peyrère claimed that God had actually created humans on multiple occasions. Based on scrupulous biblical exegesis, he claimed that, before God created the Jews, he had given life to the tribes of Gentiles (Native Americans, Eskimos, Africans, South Sea Islanders, Chinese, Europeans, etc.), all of whom initially lived in something akin to Hobbes's state of nature. While the intention behind La Peyrère's book was simply to resolve one of the thornier problems associated with Scripture's "anthropology"—the existence of physically dissimilar people who are not mentioned in the Bible—the unintended effect of *Praeadamitae* was to spur new polygenetic explanations for the physical, cultural, and geographical differences among humankind's many varieties.[57] Not surprisingly, the next generation of polygenists abandoned La Peyrère's belief that Whites numbered among the pre-Adamites. Henceforth, Whites became the descendants of Adam, whereas Blacks and Native Americans became the brutish pre-Adamites.

Two of the Bordeaux essayists (Essays 13 and 14) mentioned either Black "Adams" or pre-Adamite races, but they carefully avoided developing these highly unorthodox ideas. In Essay 15, however, the writer found the related theories of one of La Peyrère's freethinking friends, François Bernier, to be far more compelling. Like La Peyrère, Bernier had traveled extensively and was also attempting to grapple with the existence of different human phenotypes. In 1684, Bernier decided to submit an anonymous article on this subject to the *Journal des Savants*.[58] In an essay that is now generally regarded as the first published instance of racial classification, Bernier argued that humankind could be organized into four or five distinct races or *species* (he hesitated about Amerindians) based on physico-biological criteria.[59] While Bernier's so-called *New Division of the Earth* did not put forward polygenism per se, he certainly encouraged people to think of the human species as composed of fundamentally different groups.

The threat of polygenesis loomed large over the Bordeaux contest. Only a few years before the competition, the most famous French philosopher of the eighteenth century, Voltaire, was claiming that the anatomy and intelligence of Ethiopians differed so much from those of Whites that it was clear that Blacks were members of an entirely distinct species with distinct origins: "It seems to me," he wrote, "that my belief that there are different kinds of men, just as there are different kinds of trees, is well-founded; pear trees, fir trees, oak trees, and apricot trees do not at all come from the same [kind of] tree, and the bearded Whites, the wool-bearing Negroes, the horse-haired yellows, and the beardless men, do not come from the same [species of] man."[60]

The Royal Academy, whose bylaws expressly forbade putting forward any views that would be "contrary to religion," understandably did not wish to encourage any such answers to the question of the causes and origins of blackness. By forcing their essayists to explain how black skin and hair had come about—that is to say, how they were examples of "degeneration" from a norm of white skin and straight hair—they were predetermining the type of essay that would win the contest: one that was compatible with a biblical understanding of the unity of humankind, but that would also explain in a rational manner how the Black peoples of Africa could be the degenerated descendants of Europeans.

Most of the essayists who attempted to explicate the African's skin color and hair texture understood this perfectly. Though the truly religious contestants restricted themselves to arcane interpretations of the Book of Genesis, several of the essayists either sidestepped or alluded quickly to the Bible before moving on to more naturalist explanations of blackness that were not divine in origin: these included climatological theories, humoral explanations, moral observations, and anatomical "discoveries."

### CLIMATE AND CLASSIFICATION

By the time that the Bordeaux Academy had announced its 1741 competition, twenty-five centuries of competing explanations related to the causes of African skin had been widely and continuously circulating. To the extent that these theories had one thing in common, it was the basic idea that dark skin had something intrinsically peculiar or perhaps pathologically wrong with it.

Various environmental or climatic explanations of African skin were the most compelling. These can be traced, at their origin, to the writings of the Greek physician Hippocrates, especially his "Airs, Waters, and Places," which he wrote around 400 BCE. Hippocrates's belief that there was a causal relationship between extreme environments and the minds and bodies of peoples living under such conditions was passed on to Plato and Aristotle in Ancient Greece, to Lucretius, Ptolemy, and Galen during the Roman era, to Afro-Arab philosophers such as Al-Jahiz and Ibn Khaldun, and finally to virtually every early modern thinker grappling with the origins of human diversity.

Bioclimatic theories of humankind were an appealing choice for many of the Bordeaux essayists for several reasons. More religiously oriented contributors used environmental theory to render the story of Noah's children slightly more *scientific* by adding material or naturalistic explanations to the scriptural account of humanity's forebears. Climate theory also allowed numerous thinkers to identify the temperate European climate as the source of white cognitive, esthetic, and ethical preeminence. As the writer of Essay 9 put it: "it is only in intermediate regions, especially the warmer ones, that we find fertility and agile minds, an agreeable activity in external manners, and a delicate sensibility in pleasures" (Part I, Essay 9, p. 110). Overall, the seductive power of climate theory among eighteenth-century thinkers cannot be overemphasized; among other things, the belief that a given environ-ment determined the type of people who inhabited a certain land, coupled with the power of circular reasoning, effectively positioned white people as humankind's original and superior prototype. What was more, it could also be used to explicitly justify the French, Spanish, and English slave codes that determined the relationship between a society of masters and a society of enslaved Africans in the New World.[61]

Climate theory also became an effective tool among a new group of sec-ularly minded thinkers, many of whom were envisioning a far more fluid understanding of human history than had been the case in the past. This explains the surprising concept of racial reversibility that one finds in several of the essays. According to this theory, the physical traits that allowed Euro-peans to identify sub-Saharan Africans as "African" (color, thickness and shape of lips and nose, hair textures) were understood as little more than temporary characteristics brought about by the region's food, drink, climate, and the custom of applying oily unguents to the skin. Remove these causal factors, the idea went, and the color of Africans will revert to their default whiteness over the course of several generations.

The author of Essay 8 actually proposed himself as a living example of this phenomenon. Explaining that one of his ancestors was Black, and that his own pigmentation showed no traces of this coloring, he claimed Ethiopians who moved to colder climates would, over several generations, not only lose the blackness in their skin, they would

> show the same color of the rest of the inhabitants of their land (from experience). Indeed, I can prove this by the evidence of my own family line. That is to say, although my color is the same as that of my people, I am nevertheless the distant descendant [lit., the great-great-grandson] of an Ethiopian who was brought from Africa to Germany by Emperor Charles V during the war in Mauritania, and whose children gradu-ally turned from a black to a white color.
>
> Therefore, the truth is confirmed: the color of the Ethiopians is not inherent. (Part I, Essay 8, p. 102)[62]

Similar statements were also made about the potential mutability of white populations during the era: transport a family of Englishmen to the Congo, it was commonly asserted, and over the next 200 years or so their descen-dants will degenerate and become Black. In stark contrast to what fixists, bib-lical scholars, and strict providentialists were asserting about the history of humankind, a new generation of thinkers proclaimed that natural forces acting on matter could produce accidents—including human accidents— that were clearly outside of God's jurisdiction.

The belief in human mutability that appears (briefly) in several of the Bordeaux essays quickly gained traction in the years after the contest. In 1749, the most important naturalist of the era, Georges-Louis Leclerc, comte de

*Georges-Louis Leclerc, Comte de Buffon (1707–1788),* François-Hubert Drouais. Musée Buffon, Montbard. Buffon's formal academic training consisted of a thorough grounding in mathematics, botany, and medicine. After pursuing his own investigation of calculus and probability at his country estate, he was appointed curator of the Royal Botanical Gardens in Paris by Louis XV. During this period Buffon embarked on the ambitious task of assembling a comprehensive, forty-four volume study of natural history, including his seminal chapter entitled "Varieties of the Human Species."

Buffon, synthesized many of the climatological ideas that were scattered pell-mell in the Bordeaux essays into a coherent narrative. The result—a dynamic and degenerative chronicle of the human species—had a profound effect on the understanding of the nature and history of the human community for decades to come.

Buffon was well placed to realize such a project. In his capacity as Keeper of the King's Garden, he had pored over an enormous amount of "ethnographic" pigmentation data sent to him from around the globe. Like many people who adopted degeneration theory, Buffon concluded that a white prototype had morphed into the world's different human varieties over time as a function of climate and various other causal factors. A simple examination of the world's pigmentation, in his view, not only refuted the theory of polygenesis; it told a story of progressive mutation:

> As soon as mankind began to move around the world and spread from climate to climate, its nature was subject to various alterations; these changes were minimal in temperate regions, [lands] that we presume to be the place of its origin; but these changes increased as man moved farther and farther away and, once centuries had passed, continents had been crossed, offspring had degenerated due to the influence of different lands, and many [people] had decided to settle in extreme climates and populate the desert sands of southern lands and the frozen regions of the north, these changes became so significant and so apparent that it would have been understandable to believe that the Negro, the Laplander, and the white constituted different species . . . [But] these markings are in no way original [or distinct]; these natural alterations, these differences, being only on the exterior are only superficial. It is [in fact] certain that all humans are nothing more than the same man who has been adorned with black in the Torrid Zone and who has become tanned and shriveled by the glacial cold at the Earth's pole.[63]

Buffon's account of humankind's origins cuts both ways, of course. On the one hand, the naturalist forcefully asserted that differences among the world's varieties were only skin deep. On the other, his version of the human story suggested both the ancestral and qualitative supremacy of a white prototype race, a race that, "having multiplied and spread across the surface of the globe, in time produced all of man's varieties."[64]

Far more than any other thinker before him, Buffon processed the era's ethnographic prejudices into a coherent proto-racial chronicle of the human

| Human variety | Skin color, humoral tendency, and posture | Defining physical traits | Temperament | Clothing or skin treatment | Political orientation |
|---|---|---|---|---|---|
| Americanus | Red, choleric, straight | Straight, black and thick hair; gaping nostrils; freckles on face; beardless chin | Unyielding, cheerful, free | Paints himself in a maze of red lines | Governed by customary right |
| Europaeus | White, sanguine, muscular | Plenty of yellow hair; blue eyes | Light, wise, inventive | Protected by tight-fitting clothing | Governed by rites |
| Asiaticus | Sallow, melancholic, stiff | Blackish hair, dark eyes | Stern, haughty, greedy | Protected by loose garments | Governed by opinions |
| Africanus | Black, phlegmatic, lazy | Dark hair, with many braids; silky skin; flat nose; thick lips; women [with] elongated labia; breasts that lactate profusely | Sly, sluggish, neglectful | Anoints himself with fat | Governed by caprice |

Carl Linnaeus, *Systema Naturae*, 1758. In the first edition of the *Systema Naturae*, published in 1735, Linnaeus divided humankind into four varieties based on color. For the tenth (1758) edition of the book, he added two new categories to what he was now calling *homo sapiens*, namely, *homo sapiens ferus* (wild man) and *homo sapiens monstrosus* (monstrous man). Most importantly, as seen above, he supplemented his original classification of Africans, Americans, Asians, and Europeans by specifying 1) humoral tendencies; 2) physical traits; 3) temperament; 4) clothing or skin treatment; and 5) political orientation. Although Linnaeus used the term *variety* as opposed to *race* in the *Systema*, his categorization of the so-called *Homo africanus* was withering; among other things, he not only identified Black Africans as flat-nosed and thick-lipped, but lazy, phlegmatic, and having women with elongated labia and profusely lactating breasts. He also claimed that, whereas European society was based on law, the governing principle of that of the African variety was *caprice*.

species. Be this as it may, Buffon's particular version of degeneration theory was also designed to combat two other racializing tendencies that we can also see in the Bordeaux essays. The first trend was reducing "Black" Africans to a monolithic *scientific* category. This was precisely what Buffon's nemesis, Carl Linnaeus, had done in 1735 in his *Systema Naturae*. Following in the footsteps of François Bernier's somewhat imprecise breakdown of the human race fifty years previously, Linnaeus produced a far more serious taxonomic scheme in which he separated what he called the genus *homo* into four smaller categories, including the *Africanus niger* rubric for Black Africans. (Essay 8 cites Linnaeus's breakdown of the human species.) Such taxonomies represented a real challenge to the more fluid understanding of humankind that was taking shape (simultaneously) in works such as Buffon's *Natural History*. To put it bluntly, thinkers like Linnaeus were substituting category for continuity.

### ANATOMY, THE ACADEMY, AND THE BIRTH OF RACE

Explaining the source and meaning of blackness during the eighteenth century occupied three groups of distinct but mutually influencing thinkers. There were, first and foremost, traditional natural historians primarily interested in describing nature (including humankind's varieties); taxonomists who broke the species down into conceptual categories; and anatomists who sought out clues to an essential blackness within the cadavers they dissected.

The anatomical study of the supposed differences in African physiology entered a new phase shortly after (and in part because of) the Bordeaux contest. Yet the first attempts to locate the anatomical specificity of blackness had really begun in the seventeenth century. Most famously, in 1665, the Italian anatomist Marcello Malpighi announced that he had found a third and separate layer of dark epidermis located in African skin. Before Malpighi published these findings, most Europeans had simply assumed that Black skin was, in fact, black. In his careful description of African dermal layers, Malpighi demonstrated that Africans' epidermis was as white as that of a European. Blackness, he showed, was located in the basal layer of skin, in a netlike stratum covering the true skin, or dermis. This soft layer of tissue soon became known as the *rete mucosum* [mucous net], or Malpighian layer. What was more, Malpighi also described a dark, similarly viscous coloring material, the mucous liquor, that exuded from hollow nerve endings under the *rete* and spread across its surface, thus creating a uniformly dark zone between the epidermis and the underlying dermis, or true skin.

Today, such a small anatomical discovery might seem inconsequential. And yet, generations of early modern anatomists and natural historians considered the Malpighian layer to be far more significant than other more visible "African" traits, such as "flat" noses or "wool-like" hair. While African features were understood as distinct from those of white Europeans, they were also considered versions or *degenerations* of originally white characteristics. The *rete,* on the other hand, was a singular physical feature that Europeans purportedly did not have.

The era's awareness of this supposedly distinctive anatomical characteristic can be measured by the number of Bordeaux essayists who alluded to it. Writers of Essays 2, 8, 9, 11, 12, 15, and 16 all mention the *rete* in their arguments, though they disagreed wholeheartedly about its import. The author of Essay 16 fleshes out the most complete theory involving the reticular membrane. This essay was written by Pierre Barrère (1690–1755), a Perpignon anatomist whose name is known to us thanks to his decision to publish a book-length version of his essay in 1741, something he claimed to do at the urging of some of the Bordeaux academicians.

Unlike all of the other contestants, Barrère had actually studied "Black" anatomy in his capacity as a doctor (and botanist) in the French colony of Guiana. Going far beyond what the other essayists had said about the *rete*— that this may or may not be the seat of blackness—Barrère claimed to have found the secret to blackness while dissecting cadavers of African slaves. As was often the case when early modern anatomists hunted down specific anatomical features in Black bodies, Barrère found what he was looking for, even though it did not really exist.[65] In the published version of his contest submission, the *Dissertation sur la cause physique de la couleur des nègres* (Dissertation on the Physical Cause of the Color of Negroes), Barrère announced to the world that he had discovered that Africans' bile was "as dark as ink" and that their "blood was a reddish black." Blackness, as he saw it, was far more than the simple effect of the sun burning the skin; it was a pathological, jaundice-like problem within the African body itself that was caused by an excess of a black substance in the blood that was "analogous to bile"[66] (Part I, Essay 16, p. 185).

Despite the fallacious nature of his anatomical discoveries, Barrère's sweeping claims regarding the overall pathology of the Black body echoed in European thought for decades. In many ways, the Bordeaux contest had found its winner in Barrère, even though the anatomist did not collect the prize itself. Even Buffon, who read Barrère's twelve-page essay while preparing a section on Africans for his *Natural History* in the late 1740s, recognized the anatomist's discovery as significant, though he also claimed that such anatomical discoveries remained little more than a footnote to his overall theory of degeneration.

Other savants were far more intrigued by Barrère's book and the budding field of African anatomy. By the mid-1750s, a number of anatomists followed Barrère's lead and began seeking out the deeper, supposedly organ-related structures of "Africanness." In 1755, the German anatomist Johann Friedrich Meckel (1724–1774) announced that his dissection of a Negro man had revealed that Africans had bluish brains and darkened pineal glands; ten years later, Claude-Nicolas Le Cat (1700–1768), a French anatomist working in Rouen, claimed that his own dissection studies had allowed him to identify an elemental black fluid, which he called *aethiops*, that purportedly coursed from the African's brain through to the nerves, the organs, the skin, and even Africans' sperm.[67] These "breakthroughs," which were generally received as fact, provided a new generation of European classifiers—particularly Germans—with the raw material for an increasingly essentialized, or racialized, category for Africans.[68]

Spurious anatomical ideas crossed the Atlantic as well. In his 1787 *Notes on the State of Virginia*, Thomas Jefferson marveled at the range of anatomical explanations related to black skin. While he himself was unsure which of these causes was the "actual" one, he was also convinced that, whatever the source, blackness meant that people of African descent were in a category of their own: "The first difference [between Blacks and Whites] which strikes us is that of color. Whether the black of the negro resides in the reticular membrane between the skin and scarf-skin, or in the scarf-skin itself; whether it proceeds from the color of the blood, the color of the bile, or from that of some other secretion, the difference is fixed in nature, and is as real as if its seat and cause were better known to us. And is this difference of no importance? Is it not the foundation of a greater or less share of beauty in the two races?"[69]

### THIRTY YEARS AFTER THE CONTEST: THE BIRTH OF RACE AS A TAXONOMICAL CONCEPT

Thirty-five years after Bordeaux announced its contest on the source of blackness, the increasingly pseudo-scientific concept of race had come into its own. This new era had begun in earnest in 1775 when Johann Friedrich Blumenbach (1752–1840) published the first edition of his groundbreaking *De generis humani varietate nativa* (On the Natural Varieties of Mankind). Ironically, despite his role in helping to advance a science of race, Blumenbach himself was actually among the most benign and progressive proto-anthropologists of his era. Recognizing the mounting threat of polygenesis in the 1770s, the German naturalist repeatedly emphasized the unity, continuity, and common origin of humankind when discussing the human race, paying particular attention to Black Africans.[70] And yet, despite his overall generous treatment of Africans—in later years he became an ardent abolitionist—Blumenbach repeatedly referenced his era's anatomical discoveries during his classification-oriented study. In speaking about the so-called Ethiopian category, in particular, Blumenbach not only cited details related to skin color, shape of nose, and hair texture; he underscored the Ethiopian variety's supposedly distinctive anatomical features, including "dark blood and an ash-colored brain and spinal marrow."[71] By drawing attention to these "unique" characteristics, some of which came directly from Barrère's and Meckel's fallacious anatomical studies of African cadavers, Blumenbach opened the door to a far more insidious form of racialized classification, one where specific biometric information could give heft to increasingly rigid human categories. This was particularly true in the third edition of his *On the Natural Varieties of Mankind* (1795), where his comparative examination of human skulls— he described the African head as "narrow and compressed," with a knotty, uneven forehead and protruding malar bones—allowed him to divide the human species into five generic races: Caucasians, Mongolians, Ethiopians, Americans, and Malays.[72]

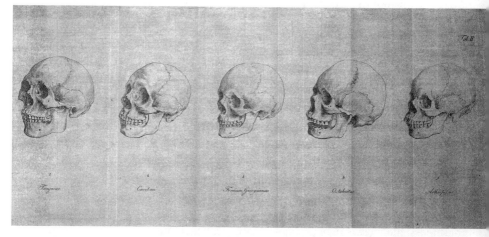

*The Five Races of the World,* Johann Friedrich Blumenbach, *De generis humani varietate nativa* (On the Natural Variety of Humankind). 1795 edition. After the assiduous observations of physical difference among his universal collection of crania, Blumenbach distinguished five principal races within the human family. From left to right, they are: Mongolian / East Asian, American Indian, white Caucasians, Malayan / South Asian, and the black Ethiopian.

The taxonomists who followed in Blumenbach's footsteps lacked his comparatively noble intentions. This was certainly the case for Blumenbach's German colleague, Immanuel Kant (1724–1804). Kant, it goes without saying, was and continues to be a towering figure within the Western philosophical tradition; it was he, after all, who defined the Enlightenment era itself by challenging humankind to dare to know, to free itself from its religion-inspired blindness in a process leading to illumination. There are, indeed, a number of powerful *emancipatory* currents running through Kant's thought, in particular, his internationalism and cosmopolitanism, and the corresponding belief that universal democracy could lead to an era of perpetual peace. These tendencies, many of which are at the core of classical liberalism, come into stark relief against his excoriating treatment of non-Europeans, especially Africans.

Kant drew his convictions regarding the African "race" from the same basic assortment of travelogues and anatomical works that Blumenbach had. Yet the foundation for Kant's career-long vilification of the African actually stemmed from the brutal and deterministic understanding of the "Negro" put forward by David Hume. In 1753, in an infamous footnote that the Scottish philosopher had composed for the revised edition of his "Of National Characters," Hume sharpened an earlier racist screed on the subject of Africans, whom he described as a distinct and "naturally inferior" species. From Hume's point of view, one could travel across the entire African continent and not find any trace of "arts" or "sciences" among black-skinned peoples. In so doing, Hume indicated that Black Africans lacked both the ability to evolve toward civilization as well as the capacity to reason itself. To further this last point, he belittled the free Black poet from Jamaica, Francis Williams (1702–1770), who had become well known in London for his Latin-language odes. Though Hume had never met Williams, he reduced the poet to a "parrot who speaks a few words plainly."[73]

Kant responded directly to Hume in Section IV of his *Observations on the Feeling of the Beautiful and the Sublime*. Echoing Hume's breakdown of the world's people based on national character, Kant put forward a typology of moral and esthetic aptitudes based on what he believed was a clear hierarchy in the cognitive abilities of the world's peoples. In particular, Kant claimed that Africans were incapable of the higher esthetic reality that defines Europeans since, as he put it, they lacked any "feeling that rises above the trifling."[74] Several pages later, Kant cemented this idea with an anecdote that he borrowed from a travelogue written by Jean-Baptiste Labat. Commenting on a story told by the French missionary, who described how his "Negro carpenter" had criticized white men for indulging their spoiled wives, Kant initially found value in the enslaved man's criticism, before reminding himself that this observation had come from someone who was "quite black from head to foot, a clear proof that what he said was stupid."[75] Compared to Montesquieu's use of the expression "black from head to toe" that Kant seems to have been quoting from *Spirit of the Laws,* there is little or no irony here: from his perspective, dark skin was no longer simply a matter of pigmentation; it was clear proof that Africans were, by definition or a priori, "stupid."

In his subsequent anthropological writing, Kant continued to assert that black skin corresponded to a lower cognitive potential, a lack of reason, and an inferior and unchanging moral character—all of which prevented Africans from reaching the state of civilization. These views became the foundation of his 1777 "Of the Different Human Races," where Kant provided the first philosophically rigorous definition of *race* in history, one that not only asserted the biological permanence of racial categories (Whites, Negro, Hunnic [Mongolian], and Hindu), but positioned the "Negro" as seemingly less than fully human, a type of person whose fundamental liabilities were "unchanging and unchangeable."[76]

Kant's anthropological breakdown of humankind in this seminal text relied on several key concepts. First of all, he claimed that each of the four races he identified could be characterized by their heritable adaptations to the climate, changes that were obvious on the physical level. These characteristics were stable over time and manifested themselves, from generation to generation, through a form of heredity transfer, which he identified as transmissible *germs.*[77] The most significant aspect of his taxonomy, however, was asserting that the notion of race, which he defined as a *deviation* from a single lineal stem stock, had a real conceptual value by dint of the fact that race mixing between pure racial categories (such as between White and Black) produced so-called "half-breeds," sub-categories that proved the existence of the antecedent classes.[78] In so doing, Kant became the first monogenist to reconcile the tension between the muddy theory of degeneration—the process of mutation that he believed produced humankind's varieties—and a logical basis for racial classification. This was no longer the dusk before the dawn of race; it was the first light of scientifically rigorous racism: an era when the ability to *reason* was being painted white; an era when naturalists and taxonomists began dividing the world's peoples into discreet subspecies; an era where skin color and category became synonymous with racial destiny.[79]

Kant was but one voice in what would become an increasingly larger chorus of taxonomists asserting that Black people, Whites, Asians, and

Native Americans belonged to irrefutable, discreet subspecies that were both naturally occurring and irreparable. Over the course of the late eighteenth and nineteenth centuries, these classification schemes not only proliferated throughout the world, they also became the intellectual infrastructure allowing Europeans (and their descendants in the New World) to pass on centuries of misinformation and propaganda about Africans and people of African descent in a much more structured and understandable way.

It would be a stretch to assert that the Bordeaux Academy's failed contest on blackness was directly related to these sweeping trends. Indeed, the only person of note who actually alluded to the 1741 competition in subsequent years was Voltaire, and he did so in order to mock it as a perfect example of the intellectual bankruptcy of this type of contest. That he, a corresponding member of the Bordeaux Academy, inserted a satirical presentation of the contest on blackness in the most famous short story of the era, *Candide,* must have made his fellow academicians wince. The scene in question takes place when Candide, who is traveling with an enormous red sheep that he had acquired in the utopian country of El Dorado, arrives in Bordeaux on his way to Paris. While in the city, Candide realizes that he can no longer take care of his exotic pet, and donates the animal to the Bordeaux Academy of Science. The academy, according to Voltaire's story, saw the sheep's unusual color as an excuse for yet another contest, and quickly "proposed a prize competition for that year on the subject of why the wool of this sheep was red." Unlike what happened to the essays submitted in 1741, however, in Voltaire's story the Bordeaux Academy actually awarded a prize to a man whom the narrator jeeringly describes as "a scholar from the North who demonstrated by A *plus* B, *minus* C, divided by Z, that the sheep had to be red and would die of the mange."[80]

Voltaire's humorous jab notwithstanding, the Bordeaux Academy's long-lost competition on African skin color remains a telling reminder of a critically significant moment in proto-anthropology. While Voltaire was indeed correct that such a contest would ultimately teach Europeans very little about the riddle of blackness, he failed to understand that the academy had actually helped bring about a new era, one in which science would claim the right to provide compelling anatomy-based explanations for humankind's many varieties. These new methods and discoveries would, of course, have another function as well: vindicating the ongoing dehumanization of people of color in the Americas.

# I

# Blackness through the Power of God

This short essay written in Latin examines the origin of human diversity in relation to a seminal event recounted in the Bible. Indeed, the primary preoccupation of this author is actually the power of God to make miracles, not the question of blackness. Nonetheless, he reasons that as diverse groups of people settled in certain lands, they became distinguished from one another by what would be today considered their own characteristic phenotypes. The most curious part of this essay comes at the end, when he proposes that someone conduct a generations-long experiment in which Blacks would be moved outside Africa and adopt the living habits of the native population, including diet, to see what effect this would have on their skin. Any resulting changes in color and hair could then be compared with a control population, presumably to ascertain the influence of climate and diet. The author advances no opinion on the outcome.

I HERE SUBMIT my thoughts, such as they are, on the subject of the color of those men whom we call *Nigri* [Black].[1] These thoughts also apply more broadly to solving similar questions concerning other peoples, such as [their] particular skin color or facial characteristics.

These traits can persist broadly and equally within lineages among Europeans, indeed even in those living far from other Europeans. Europeans differ from all or most of the peoples of the Americas; similarly, distinguishing features are easily apparent in other clans, a subject on which I could expand if there were more space here.[2]

Here are my thoughts. In Genesis 11 our Lord said, "Let us confound their languages, that they may not understand one another's speech. So the Lord scattered them abroad from thence upon the face of all the earth," etc.[3]

Wise people understand that there is something over and above the usual order of nature in this divine action. [Some] interpreters of the Holy Scripture, however, have tried to explain this text by asserting that this phenomenon [the dispersing of humankind] was the product of natural causes, thereby affirming that no miracle took place.[4] Hereafter I use the term "miracle" to refer to an event that, by God's will, is outside the normal order of nature. Nothing else is worthy of the word "miracle."

The miraculous event [referred to in this selection of Scripture] led those men and women who had been endowed by God with the same language to come together and found different settlements and nations. The Bible has described this as a prodigious event. To this I add, for good measure, the following probable hypothesis: that in order to form a community quickly and easily, the people so scattered saw it necessary to be united by the same language.

At the same time, God altered the color of their body and made them white, black, red, and other intermediary colors between white and black so that in a short time afterward all men and women whose skin was covered with the same color understood the same language that had been infused in them.[5] Fellowship arose right away among them, marriages took place, and in this way many different settlements of clans and peoples were established.

In His all-knowing providence, God arranged matters in such a way that each group chose to settle in the region that would be most suitable for preserving their skin color. He also endowed their bodies with the essential physical qualities whereby their offspring would unchangingly maintain a given skin color and certain facial traits, bodily shape, type of hair, etc., unless with the passage of time one nation mixed with another. In His providence God, the all-powerful Maker, was able to provide for these things without a new miracle. I admit here that several objections to my argument are possible.

**First Objection:** If we are seeking a physical cause of the problem, this argument assumes another cause, one of a higher [divine] order.

**Answer:** If the physical cause is to be sought solely in a system of physics [natural science] or in anatomical principles, or in a similar source, my argument does not offer a physical cause. But if we understand by physical cause what is indeed the true cause, so far as we can understand it with a nearly certain inference, then I am clearly offering a physical cause.

**Second Objection:** In the absence of historical records, a prodigious event can be adduced or fabricated without providing an explanation.

**Answer:** I have not suggested a definite miracle other than the confounding of languages. I admit that no historical records exist. This is not surprising, since no records from the age immediately following the Deluge have come down to us.

And yet, whoever reflects on this issue will reasonably conclude that a prodigious event did occur. This hypothesis suitably explains all the varieties of the diverse nations, and a claim is made that it was miraculous. On the other hand, even if one could prove that a prodigious event did not transpire in this specific case, it remains that this would still be a lesser-known miracle being added to a better-known one. The final reason why [we can consider this a prodigious event] is because so many people have attempted to explain [the mystery of blackness] in many ways, yet all have failed to win the approval of scholars. It was for this reason, though many dissertations have been published recently on this subject, your academy has selected it again for investigation.

Nevertheless, if someone were to suggest that the Lord so arranged physical causes without a miracle, in a manner unknown to us, so that the first generations born after the Deluge were allotted different colors, and in accordance with the different colors and the shape of their limbs, etc., God also bestowed upon them different languages, I will not object, nor will I judge that hypothesis to be different from mine.[6]

The academy poses another question: namely, as to black people brought to other lands from their native regions, to what evident degree does the darkness of their skin and the structure of their hair recede, generation after generation. Indeed, I believe that up to now no experiments have been performed with the following method, which would be required to establish anything with any certainty.

It would be necessary to relocate not just a few, but clearly many pairs of black couples in different, even distant locations in Europe and also in regions outside of Europe. Those couples living in the same area would be prescribed different diet, work, or leisure plans under equal and different circumstances. Then one would observe a sufficient number of generations born from this experiment in order to compare how those who lived in the same region but who followed different regimes were affected. What is more, we would also observe in turn female slaves in different, even distant locations. Until such exact experiments are conducted, so as to confirm the laws of natural science, it behooves us not to issue any conclusions.[7]

"Iron sharpeneth iron; so a man sharpeneth the countenance of his friend."

Proverbs 27:17[8]

# 2

## Blackness through the Soul of the Father

This long essay written in Latin begins with pages and pages of anatomical and humoral notions culled from Antiquity and more recent "discoveries." In the first part of the text, the author attributes skin color solely to an internal process of *generation,* which we now call *reproduction.* He then delves deeply into a religious view of embryology where he affirms that the characteristics of Black persons are communicated to an embryonic soul "through the soul of the father," as well as through the power of the maternal imagination. Toward the end of the essay he refutes the notion that Africans came about as a result of chance, or the climate. Blackness, in his view, is a part of God's plan and, therefore, Ethiopians are a specific species of men. This seemingly *polygenetic* (separate species) explanation is followed by a biblical digression where he speculates, somewhat paradoxically, that Blacks descend from Noah's son Ham, followed by Ham's son Chus. Proof of this theory, he asserts, lies in the etymology of this name, "black."

### THESIS 1

What physical cause explains the color of the black peoples of Ethiopia?[1] This question has been debated often among scholars. Yet as much as scholars have exerted their talents in investigating this subject, they have not been successful in identifying a cause based on valid arguments. Nor have they been able to overcome the obstacles separating them from the truth. This is the most difficult challenge. We cannot realistically hope to find one single explanation of this phenomenon that might free us from all doubts, as there is a lack of history about the earliest origin of the black peoples. If we must make a guess, then, the cause could be the result of numerous possible historical circumstances: in reviewing them, we must draw a conclusion that would be subject to the fewest possible doubts.

### THESIS 2

The following preliminary observations are paramount:

1) Not all the people who reside in Ethiopia are the same color black. Instead, we notice that they differ by shades, such that some are truly as black as coal, some are a pale black or a brownish black, and some instead are brown. In the same way, many Europeans are lighter skinned than others.

2) The territories where black Ethiopians mostly dwell are located between the Tropics, some at the equator and some below it, where they are subjected to the most intense rays of the sun. Indeed, no region in the Americas or in India which is similarly located at the Tropics or at the equator receives the same fury of the blazing sun so as to produce men of this type of blackness. One exception is the vast peninsula contained between the Ganges and the Indus Rivers, where travel diaries tell of black men that differ from the Africans only in their hair. However, due to a lack of historical records, we cannot ascertain whether these black inhabitants of India are indigenous to the region or were transported there from Africa at some point in time, just as Arabs relocated to Africa and Europeans to America, occupying territories larger than what they had possessed up to that point.

3) Regarding other Blacks, many of them are found in the vast American territories; we know for certain that they are not native inhabitants but that several thousands of them were transported there from Africa as slaves by Europeans to be employed in many kinds of labor.

### THESIS 3

Another observation no less worthy of note is that men of other nations never become black in Ethiopia, the land of the Blacks, even after spending their entire lives there, or even if they were born there. Examples from Europe prove this, of men who moved their homes and families to Guinea and other regions of black men and begat children there: neither they nor their offspring ever changed their native color or turned black.[2] The opposite has also been observed, namely, that Ethiopian Blacks who are transported to northern regions and grow old there never lose their black color. In the same way, their offspring, even if born in distant provinces, do not lose their blackness as long as both parents are of that same color.

### THESIS 4

After examining the two foregoing propositions, it unmistakably follows:

1) That the climate and the unique position of the sun in the Tropics and under the equator in no way produce the blackness of the Ethiopians. Otherwise, due to clearly the same position of the sun, the peoples of the islands of St. Thomas, the Maldives, the Moluccas, [illegible], Sumatra, Java, Borneo, Malabar, and of the mainland, Guiana, and the Amazon region clearly would also be the same black color.

2) Neither the excessive force of the sun, nor the peculiarity of the air or the soil, nor the location in which they are born, produces blackness in the inhabitants of these regions. For indeed, those Europeans who have settled in the regions of Ethiopia never become black, nor do their offspring born there; however, if they spend a long time under the sun they are affected by a brown color, just as in our regions [Europe] those who are continually exposed to the sun's rays will turn dark. Still, when winter returns, the brownness fades, while the blackness of the Ethiopians does not change even after being transported to northern provinces, for it is permanent. This is clear evidence that blackness is not caused by the sun.

### THESIS 5

I am not unfamiliar with the general opinion of natural philosophers who maintain that the diversity of climate has a variety of effects on the native inhabitants of a region. For example, the peoples of the North are usually of a more robust physique, with lighter complexions and hair, as well as a more phlegmatic temperament and duller wits, the very opposite of peoples who inhabit more southern regions.[3] Take, for example, the Italians: they have a more slender build, tend to be dark in complexion and hair, tend toward a choleric temperament, and are more clever. Scholars believe that the reason for this difference must be sought only in the different climate, and consequently, they believe the same thing is true of the blackness in Ethiopians.

In point of fact, however, the extent of these effects does not correspond to the extent of the alleged cause, since general causes must produce general effects. In fact, everyday experience offers not a few examples from each region that present exceptions to the rule. Thus, even in the southern regions we find men with athletic builds, lighter hair and skin color, a phlegmatic temperament, as well as dull wits; and conversely, in the northern regions we find men of softer build, with brown hair and brown skin, a choleric temperament, and more clever wits.

For this reason, such phenomena are inadequately attributed to the climate, since climate influences each and every one equally. These same results should be more correctly attributed partially to education and habits, and partially to hereditary acquisition. For it is a well-known fact that those living in northern climes are accustomed to a harsher and more toilsome life, as their bodies are exposed to the harshness of their native air. Southerners instead become sluggish due to the heat, and are more disposed to leisure. Hence, it is no surprise that northerners enjoy a more robust build.

In the same way, we note that many Ethiopians, though they live under the hottest sky, still yield nothing to northerners in their strong, massive physique, especially if they exercise strenuously by working or hunting. Any observer that pays attention to the children they propagate, both in the South and in the North, will see that offspring very rarely stray in type from their parents; instead, it is most often the case that even over time they closely follow the color of their bodies, their hair, their temperament, and quality of mind.

### THESIS 6

Whether a different idea can be entertained, namely, that diet causes the blackness of the Ethiopians, is indeed an incorrect question to pursue; for if we consult trustworthy travel diaries, this idea is ridiculed and has no merit at all. For [European travelers] partake of the same food, roots, grains, seeds, and game of the villages where black people live, enjoy the same type of drink, and share water fortified with the sap of palm trees, and yet they do not grow black; therefore, it follows that food is not responsible for blackness.

Although we find some cannibal tribes among the Ethiopians, nevertheless the unusual custom of eating this type of meat cannot cause blackness.[4] This is proven by the fact that American cannibal tribes, many of whom reportedly are found in Brasilia, are not similarly black. And I need not mention the power of the stomach's digestive faculty that can transform any food of any color it receives into a uniform, white-colored fluid, the chyle.

### THESIS 7

Another remarkable observation that merits close scrutiny is the following. If *in commercio* [enslaved] black Ethiopians unite with spouses of a different kind, we note that the children born from this union will have a different type of blackness.[5] Obviously, if black men have children with white women, or black women with men of another color, their immediate offspring will have a dark yellowish color, mulatto [*mulâtres,* as the French say], by analogy with the procreation of mules. For just as mules, born from the union of a horse and a donkey, share the form of both those species, so do the children of parents of different colors: they are neither white nor black, but take on a middle color, part black and part white, that is, a tawny color.

Nor does it matter where such a union of different colors takes place, whether in Ethiopia or in the farthest edges of the world—the resulting effects will always be the same. This is another indication that the blackness of the Ethiopians is not due to any external cause, but depends upon their very bodies; and further, that the explanation must be sought in that *nationem* [people] itself.

### THESIS 8

It is now clearer to us that the formation of blackness is a phenomenon that takes place within the body. Père [Jean-Baptiste] Labat calls attention to this in his history of Western Africa, vol. 2, p. 266 [*Nouvelle relation de l'Afrique occidentale*], and I myself have it on the direct authority of the Ethiopians themselves that, of course, their children are born the same color as our own, with one exception: their genitalia are already tinged with black from the mother's womb, and are marked at the time of birth by black rings around the roots of the nails of the hands and feet.[6] Their bodies, however, do not turn black all over at the time of birth but one month later, and more often in the second or third month.

If, therefore, infants already have some body parts colored black from within the mother's womb, and these newborns grow more richly black soon after birth (in the first place, to protect the newborns from the air and shield them from injury), it surely must follow that blackness is innate and proceeds from an intrinsic, not extrinsic source.[7]

## THESIS 9

Thus far, this point has been clearly demonstrated, namely, that the physical cause of blackness is internal or intrinsic, that is, produced in the body, and is not conjoined to any external cause. It now remains to determine what the proximate cause is, and then discover the principal cause. On this subject, the earlier anatomists had declared that it was to be found in the epidermis but not the *cutis,* as it is called today.[8] It was first the Parisians who, after dissecting and inspecting [Ethiopian cadavers], and, as confirmed repeatedly by other autopsies, discovered that the proper subject of the cause of blackness among Ethiopians is not the epidermis but a thin layer [*tunica*] lying between the cutis and the cuticle [*cuticula*] that is found in Ethiopians. This tunica is called the Malpighian layer; others call it a reticular tissue [*corpus reticularis*]; it is of a marked, silky softness, and its color is soft black.[9]

This is confirmed by two further observations, the first being that when an Ethiopian develops blisters from a mild burn where the cuticle has lifted, he has no white scars on the site, which would be the case if the epidermis were the locus of blackness.

The second observation is that, if the blisters were to penetrate more deeply, as with smallpox or deep sores or even fierce burns, the cutis and the above-mentioned reticular tissue would be destroyed and, I would say, after healing, some pale whitish scars would remain that would rarely return to black, particularly if the leftover scars are thick and tough and embedded much below the blackness, even though the cutis might have regrown.[10]

This is confirmed by travel accounts about slaves employed in burning sugar [cane]. If they happen to sustain major burns to their limbs, as often happens, the burnt areas always remain light-colored. In fact, both the epidermis and the cutis are easily repaired, unlike the thin membrane, or *corpus reticularis,* which has an extremely soft texture.

## THESIS 10

The proximate cause of blackness, by which the aforementioned *corpus reticularis* is colored, is a dusky yellow or brown fluid, which is distinct from the blood, that has penetrated the *tunica reticularis.* In this thesis, I prove its fluidity; in the following thesis, I will prove its dusky yellow color, and in the twelfth I show that it originates from the blood. Clearly, this dark color must be a fluid, otherwise it would not be able to pass beneath the extremely soft fibers of the *tunica reticularis,* imbuing and penetrating it deeply with color, for this dark color is not located outside. Second, the fluidity of this blackness is proven by the changes that have been reported during an illness.

Worth recounting is the well-known and consistent phenomenon that whenever Ethiopians fall ill, in all cases the blackness fades and they grow pale; on the contrary, as soon as they regain their health (or if they die) the pristine blackness returns intact. This changeability of color not only indicates that the matter [*materia*] of this blackness is liquid and mobile, but also points to the specific manner by which it comes about. If we care to take as analogy what happens to our own bodies with the passage of time, we will learn how the fluid nature of blackness comes about.

As we know, when our bodies start to become sick, our vivid color fades and the lips, the cheeks, all external body parts grow pale, sag, and become frail. The closer we approach death, the more these conditions are exacerbated. But if we recover our health, our vivid complexion is restored. If we die, a short time after death the appearance of the face, which was clearly unchanged at the point of death, reverts to some of its original color, and the fleshy body parts regain some of their fullness.

The cause of these changes is the reversibility of tonic movements in the external parts of the body. Now when an illness attacks the body, the fibers are slightly drawn tight and constricted, the blood and lymph from the interstices of those parts are pressed back toward the internal organs and simultaneously prevented from flowing back to the periphery.[11] This causes paleness in the limbs, repeated shivering, and a frail condition—the so-called Hippocratic face [of illness].[12] But once the illness is over, the tonic tightness of the fibers relaxes, the pallor gives way, and a vivid color returns. Or, if death has induced a complete relaxation of the fibers, that part of the blood that is still liquid again fills first the watery surface of the body and the flesh regains its fullness.

Clearly, the same process is at work when pallor overtakes Ethiopian bodies, when they are sick, and leaves once their health has returned or death follows upon an illness. From this, it also follows that the substance that blackens the part of the body subjected to it must be fluid, otherwise a reciprocal motion of this kind, and in such a brief span of time, would not be possible—that is to say, compressed toward the interior at one instant, and driven toward the exterior the next.

## THESIS 11

And now it is time to prove that the fluid that tinges the bodies of Ethiopians with blackness is initially dusky or brown. The following phenomena will be considered: as mentioned in Thesis 7, not all Ethiopians are completely black—some are a dark golden-like [tawny] color, some are brownish-black, and others truly black. This makes it clear that shades of color are given to them by degree, hence, black is the dominant color, then in gradation a tawny dark and brown that are closer to black. Brown hues usually follow blackness in a descending line, and a swarthy or tawny color follows brown, as we can see, for example, when a recently cut log is at first bright white, then in a short time turns tawny brown, and finally darkens to brown.

A second fact is that the blackness of a child begins as a darkened brown. Again, the blackness of an Ethiopian child does not cover the child's body all at once; it does so gradually. Here Nature always works by employing the same method, never working by leaps, but gradually, and we plainly see a similar coloring process in the newborn babies of our own color. After a while—not immediately at birth but after the first month and in some cases later—the [Ethiopian] infant takes on a brown color, which soon turns swarthy, then finally becomes very dark.

[...]

From these phenomena, we deduce that Nature, in forming the blackness of the Ethiopians, follows the same mode and method it uses when it imbues flowers, leaves, and fruits with color, always over time and by degrees, starting with intermediate, softer hues and gradually progressing to the principal, more intense colors. Hence, the production of black begins with a swarthy or tawny-brown color, or, if the phenomenon follows a reverse order, the color recedes from black. The same process is at work when the color is determined by impression on the [mother's] imagination, in which case it is halted and remains dusky. This phenomenon will be explained in Thesis 20. In the absence of such [maternally] determined factors, the color would tend toward complete blackness.

Moreover, coloring is achieved through either aggregation or concentration: in the former case, many particles of the substance [*materia*] that constitute the color brown are gathered and collected together into one; this necessarily gives rise to a dark color verging on black, just like a line drawn with a painter's brush that has been dipped in brown liquid, when the same color is painted on the line several times. Or, just as a brown liquid, when poured into a slender glass, usually colors the glass container holding the brown color as if it were truly black. Now in the case of concentration, blackness arises from brownness when dissolving watery particles are expelled and the remaining dark particles become compressed—as we see, for example, when an herbal extract has been diluted with water—the more particles become concentrated and escape through evaporation or condensation, the darker the extract. Nature can act in either of these ways, though aggregation seems to me to be the more likely process.

### THESIS 12

Next, I prove that, indeed, the coloring fluid discussed above is obtained from the blood, since the blood is the universal source of all the humors or fluids in our body; it is the common repository of the substance [*materia*] needed for the body's formation and nourishment.[13] From the blood arise bile, pancreatic juice, lymph, saliva, serum, etc. In fact, blood contains particles of different kinds, hence humors of varied color and taste are secreted from it, such as for example milk, bile, urine, and earwax.

If indeed the vital principle of life [*principium vitale*] has the power to separate particles that are yellow-green or dark green, such as bile, or yellow, such as earwax, from this ruddy liquid, why could it not likewise produce particles of some other, darker color? To whoever might have doubts, I offer for consideration the choroidal coating of the eyes, or uvea, which is acknowledged to be clearly and conspicuously black; I will not mention those black birthmarks induced by the mother, which are often found on people's bodies.[14] And so, the active force that tints the choroidal coating, the uvea, and the hair and eyebrows with black, and which is capable of producing black birthmarks on the body, can, with the same ease, color the entire surface of the body black; and it can separate from the blood the particles that are suited to forming that color (which particles, as I said above, are the source of blackness), especially if a quantity of dark yellow particles is present in the blood, as proven by the existence of bile.

[...]

### THESIS 13

Since I have now discussed the proximate cause of blackness in Theses 9, 10, 11, and 12, in this section and those that follow I will discuss its principal cause. It has now become clear that this primary cause or active principle [*principium activum*], which I mentioned in the preceding thesis, is our vital spirit or soul.[15] It is this which proves to be the source of remarkable effects in the body and is, in fact, the primary cause that forms the blackness in the bodies of Ethiopians.

When God the Highest Creator, the Spirit of all living beings, had determined that the soul should have a body joined to it, the body was thereby instantly joined to it, in order that the soul build its dwelling there, as it were. Hence, the soul was endowed with the knowledge [*gnosis*] essential to forming and maintaining the specific body; indeed, that knowledge would be necessary in order to constitute and form a machine of such artful construction.[16]

The soul begins to apply this innate faculty or knowledge [*notitia*] as soon as it finds the threads [*stamina*] or initial stages of the body already preexisting in the mother's egg: it [the soul] finds them once the father has communicated the act of procreation. All of this is well known and confirmed by manifold examples from Nature, so that I need not indulge in lengthier demonstrations.

Further, since this spiritual substance is transmitted from the father, and consequently is a propagation of the father's soul, it follows that it necessarily employs the same manner and method in forming and nourishing its own body as the one employed by the father's soul (of which it is an offshoot) in forming and nourishing the father's body; and that it works in accordance with the same order of ideas, and builds the parts of its machine according to the same type and pattern as the father's. This representative faculty dwells in the soul, from which arises the children's similarity to their fathers as they reproduce their fathers' shape, appearance, height, hair, temperament, habits of mind, and even diseases.

Since each and every one of these things depends upon a certain arrangement and growth of fibers, as well as a specific mixture of humors and a specific proportion of solid elements, it follows that the soul of the embryo acquires the coordinating knowledge from the soul of its father, whose offshoot it is. Hence, inasmuch as blackness is the most conspicuous characteristic of Ethiopian bodies, by necessity their children will replicate the color that was native to their fathers, and hand it down to the bodies of their own children.

THESIS 14

The embryo's soul—in addition to its innate ability [as arranged by God] to construct and conserve its own body [the embryo's soul being derived from its father's soul of whom it is an offshoot]—also acts according to certain impressions acquired by the father externally [*extrinsecus*] through sensory perception.

I understand these impressions to be ideas that the father had formed by gazing at the external form of his own body, as well as at the body of his spouse. The embryo's soul imitates these ideas in the structure of its own tiny body and adapts its external form according to the father's impressed ideas, as if it [the embryo's soul] were modifying and also refining a certain model [*exemplar*]. The result will express the likeness [*effigiem*] of both mother and father so that both parents are represented, though one may be stronger than the other, or both equally, depending on which impression was first imprinted on the father's soul, and then retained in the soul of the embryo.

The above assertion is supported by the evidence of egg-laying animals, where the chicks take after the external shape of either the hen or the rooster, but more often of the hen. If the eggs are separated from the mother shortly after fertilization and are heated only by an external source, still the embryos within develop to perfection. From this it appears that this resemblance from which the chicks repeat the external form now of the father, now of the mother, or of both parents, must solely arise from the father's impression. We can apply the same reasoning to the subject of resemblance in viviparous animals, whose young imitate the form of their parents, namely that resemblance is transmitted from the father by the very impression of his form, than by that of the mother.

The idea of the father's form is innate [*innata*] to the father; the idea of the mother's form is impressed [on the father's soul] by his looking [at her]. Having established this, it becomes clear that the idea of blackness, partly innate [*inhaerentem*] in the Ethiopian father, partly impressed [on the father's soul] by his looking at the mother, disposes the soul of the engendered embryo [as it were, the father's offshoot] to transmit such color to its own offspring at a later stage.[17]

THESIS 15

[The author defends himself against the possibility that his theory of blackness also opens the door to the possibility that the embryo's soul can be divided.]

## THESIS 16

[Adapting the theses of Nicolas Malebranche and his successors, the author affirms the idea that the mother's imagination can influence the embryo, in some cases, coloring it according to the idea that had been received by the mother.]

## THESIS 17

So then, the infant's soul sets in operation the formation of its body according to the same ideas, the same form, and the same impetus from which it originated, following Nature. And it receives the idea of the external form from both the father and the mother, both coming from the father's soul, with which it [the infant's soul] exists essentially as one and the same. It also receives the rudiments of its body from the mother, formed like the mother's soul and one with the nourishment arranged specifically for it.

If the embryo is still hidden in the uterus, in intimate communication with the mother's soul, and follows the mother's method and mode of action, and does not receive from the mother any ideal external impressions applying them to the body, as I explained above, then by necessity the embryo will carry its native color to its body, in this case, the specific black of the Ethiopians. In the same vein, if the soul of an embryo generated by white parents colored its body black, it would be a deviation from the customary process of Nature, and would definitely constitute a monster or prodigious birth.[18]

The fact that the soul knows how to extract the color black from the blood will not seem paradoxical to anyone upon careful examination, since the same soul produces a variety of colors from the blood: yellow-green in the bile; black in the ocular choroidal tunic; white in the sclera [the fibrous membrane that forms the outer covering of the eye]; diaphanous in the cornea; and gray and cerulean in the iris. It also produces birthmarks and hair of different hues, and can convert the whitest chyle into red blood, or form from it the whitest parts of the body such as the brain, the bones, and the bright white skin of baby girls.[19] And who will deny how much cleverness our soul possesses when we realize that the active principal (*principium activum*) that builds the bodies of plants, with open joy paints so many colors from the same juice? And this *principium* is a form lower than ours!

## THESIS 18

The formation of blackness in Ethiopians proceeds from the same principle by which a similarity of form normally is carried on from parent to child. The fact that men cannot bear horses, nor horses produce men, and the fact that children imitate the form of their parents in height, gesture, temperament, etc., does not depend by any means on the material itself as much as on its specific disposition and arrangement.

The embryo's material is not only arranged according to an exquisite order and perfect symmetry, but also appears to be formed according to a specific, defined pattern. From this, it follows clearly and correctly that a certain active principle is at work, which takes joy in its power of representation, ordering and forming the underlying material according to fixed ideas of its representation, some of which are indwelling and inherent in it, others impressed from a different source. Indwelling or inherent ideas include specific facial features, the temperament, the way of acting and the characteristics of the individual soul; foreign ideas are the forms of external objects that have been impressed upon the soul.

In Thesis 16, I presented a notable example of the latter type of idea, in which a woman, due to the visual impression of her own body burned by gunpowder, impressed the idea of this artificial blackness on the soul of the embryo inside her, in such a way that its body also became colored black.

Another example of color conveyed by maternal impression is reported by Paullini in *Observat. Med.* Cent. 4 Obs. 85.[20] A pregnant woman was overcome by such a violent appetite for saffron that she refused all food unless it had been prepared with it. She finally gave birth to a child that was entirely suffused with that color. Another such example is found in Amatus Lusitanus, *Cent. 5 Observ. Thed.,* regarding the origin of all birthmarks: it is well known that their sole cause is from the mother.[21]

If, then, the soul is able to transfer foreign ideas of external objects to its body, and similarly block corporeal ideas, how much more powerfully will it impress inherent ideas upon its body? From this, it is sufficiently clear that a purely ideal impression can cause the soul of the fetus to color the body black. Furthermore, this causal action is sufficient to render an impressed idea bodily, and can also fashion any type of fluid from the blood in the same way in which the vegetal principle forms nutrition from the juice of its own plant.

### THESIS 19

The soul does not release the dark tint of the body in the uterus, however; rather, as stated above, it does dispose that Ethiopian infants will come out of the uterus not yet colored black but for their genitals, and with black rings that have been observed around the base of the fingernails. This is hardly surprising, as Nature follows the same method in our own children, namely, that she waits to finish her work on the external parts of the body that pertain to shape and grace, until the child is outside of the mother's womb.

That only the genitals of Ethiopians are colored black in utero does seem to have a moral cause, because Nature wants to imprint the most prominent characteristic of the destiny of these men on the natural parts through which reproduction takes place. In truth, the likely physical cause of this phenomenon probably lies underneath, in that the parts just mentioned have a particularly soft and loose texture when compared with others, to such a degree that they provide access and secondary channels to a larger supply of blood; consequently more of the dark fluid that I discussed above in Thesis 12 separates itself from the blood, and on account of the denser aggregation, swiftly colors the parts exposed to the fluid.

[...]

### THESIS 20

Now that I have demonstrated the above propositions, it will not be difficult to individuate the cause of the change in blackness that occurs when an Ethiopian has relations with a mulatto. Everyone knows that the color of Blacks, once nature has tinted them, never changes or dies out, even if they are transported to the extreme polar regions. However, should they have relations with partners of a different color, the blackness of children born of these mixed relations changes at once. When a black man couples with a white woman, or white man with a black woman, their children are born of an intermediate color, a dark tawny or tawny brown color. The French call them *mulâtres* since mules, born from a horse and a donkey, take their form from both parents. We know from experience that this also occurs in the mating of birds of different species.

If then a black man unites with a white woman, the soul of the fetus thus produced will, in forming its own body, primarily follow the mode and method of action of the father's soul. For example, the resulting offspring will express the father's blackness in its own body, unless the [blackness] is retracted by the impressed idea of the white mother. For after the mother's whiteness and the different traits of her face have made an altogether vivid impression on the father, the following could happen: the soul of the fetus, immediately eager to imitate the mother's form, produces something in-between, so that the body color becomes intermediate white and black, such as a golden brown. Similar changes occur in the hair and lips, which are features that distinguish Blacks from other peoples, and we know that in the case of illegitimate children, they always retain some vestiges of the form of both parents. The same rationale applies to children born of a white father and a black mother.

### THESIS 21

I have demonstrated in the foregoing that the soul of the fetus acts according to the impression of ideas as it strives to complete the external form of the body, and that it does so in the same way one strives to paint or to write following a manifest pattern. First, it forms to itself exact ideas of the lines of the picture as if they were letters, then strives to express them on its own corporal canvas, as it were.

The external form presupposes a fixed and definite material quantity, as well as a fixed position or arrangement of fibers and pores that underlie the production of color for the figure. And yet, the moving cause [*causa movens*] of both is the imagination and the acting cause [*causa agens*] is the soul's adherence to this or that idea, the latter of which has been offered freely for imitation, as it prepares the material and orders it varyingly so as to produce the intended result.

[. . .]

### THESIS 22

A particularly strong impression from foreign objects upon the soul can render [such] ideas, transferring them into bodily form and making them exactly the same. (Examples abound of such images created in desire and play. Pliny, in his *Natural History,* reports an example of the power of the imagination: "The case of Nicaeus, the celebrated wrestler of Byzantium, is a well-known and undisputed instance. His mother was the product of an act of adultery, committed with a male of Aethiopia; and although she herself differed in no way from the ordinary complexion of other [white] females, he was born with all the swarthy complexion of his Aethiopian grandfather.")[22]

This child represents a double aberration from the normal method we find elsewhere occurring in nature: first, because the mother of Nicaeus was white despite the fact that she had a black father; and second, that Nicaeus, instead of taking after his mother, took after the color of his black grandfather.

In his *Relation historique de l'Ethiopie occidentale* (Historical Account of West Ethiopia), Père Labat discusses the case of an Ethiopian woman who was born from completely black parents, but was herself white, married another black Ethiopian, and nonetheless gave birth to children who were perfectly black. But in neither of these cases is there any mention of any prior incidence of maternal imagination [having an effect on a baby]. Still, we cannot doubt that it [the mother's impression] must have been the *causa movens* in both cases, for we know for certain that exceptional aberrations of this kind always arise from the same basis.[23] However, even assuming that no such violent impression had preceded the pregnancy, we must conclude that both cases were engendered by the play of the imagination. This is because the soul equips its body with a scheme of matter and form, so it follows that an extraordinary aberration of this kind must stem from the same principle.

### THESIS 23

From the foregoing arguments I conclude as follows. If, in the process of arranging the external form of the body, the soul of the fetus applies the ideas determined by the form of its parents (as I showed in Thesis 14 and 18); and if, at some time, according to Thesis 21, the soul imports into its body ideas of foreign objects; and if sometimes, according to Thesis 22, as a result of a different imagined image, the soul recedes from its normal course, then, assuming all these things to be true, we must inevitably conclude that the soul brings about the change in the blackness of children born from the marriage of black Ethiopians with spouses of different peoples.

In fashioning the body's external form, it must be the case that the soul intends primarily to imitate the image of its father in its own body, following nature. But when a form is impressed in the mother's imagination, and this impression is more vivid that it would customarily be, then the soul transfers that idea to the body and does so eagerly, and starts to produce an admixture with the form of both parents.

If the father was black, the child begins to imitate him in his own body, which becomes colored with a dark tawny color, the first gradation of blackness. The color white is determined by the impression of the mother's form, as intended. From this mixture results an intermediate color. If, on the other hand, the father was white, then he impressed the primary color on the baby's body. But if the color is determined through the idea of the black mother, as the body develops the first rudiments of blackness, the innate idea of the father's form is retained and blocks blackness from developing further: from this comes the intermediate color that I mentioned. It can also happen that an idea fastens on the infant's soul, stronger and more vividly than either the mother's form or a clearly foreign object, such as an impression of desire or fear. In this case, it conquers the color inherent in the father's form. These sorts of aberrations deviate from the normal course of action of the soul, as I showed in Theses 21 and 22.

### THESIS 24

What I have shown to be the principal cause of the mutation of black skin also determines the mutation of the hair among the Ethiopians. We know that they normally have black hair, which is of a woolly consistency, soft and frizzy. As this pertains to blackness, the cause must be physico-mechanical, since all the Ethiopians that we see have hair of this same perfect color; accordingly, the cause must be universal and mechanical. We thus affirm that the blackness of the hair must arise from the same black *tunica reticularis* that makes Ethiopians black. Those mucus globules, from which the hair grows, are fixed as we said above, and the hair receives the dark color from them. On the other hand, Ethiopians who are of a tawny-brownish hue do not always have black hair; it is sometimes swarthy or reddish brown. As far as the softness of their hair, it comes from the fine texture of the matter from which they are made.

The fine texture of their hair depends for the most part on the greater division of the matter from which it is made; this is because Ethiopians have a greater amount of hair than others, hence it grows shorter and more even. The fine texture of the hair arises from the delicacy [*teneritudine*] of the molecules from which it is made. Moreover, as we know from autopsies, this more handsome blackness is given by the exquisitely pliable black substance that also colors the uvea of the eyes, the skin, and the *tunica reticularis* of the Ethiopians. There must be a different explanation for the frizziness typical of Ethiopian hair since it cannot be derived from the hot climate or from the blackness of their bodies since their children are born with frizzy hair even in distant lands.

[. . .]

The physical manner in which black hair becomes frizzy, at least as far as can be gleaned from exact microscopic examination, consists in the special particles that form the hair, which are uneven, as opposed to straight hair in which the particles are arranged in a straight line. It is also entirely likely that the body's fatty molecules, which lend black hair its frizziness, are in turn arranged according to their natural line; and when they are deprived of aqueous particles through evaporation, the hair is fully exposed to the corrupting effect of the air. Since they are more tightly coiled, this contraction affects the line in which the coils are arranged, and the bending of the hair creates the curls.

### THESIS 25

From what I have stated and demonstrated up to now, it follows that the blackness of the Ethiopians arises solely from an internal, not an external cause. I have shown that this internal and principal cause is the soul, which is accustomed to correctly determining [the form of] its own body and depositing the particles from the blood that are apt to cause blackness into the *tunica reticularis;* and that the aggregation of these particles produces blackness.

Earlier I proved that the imagination is the *causa tollens,* or *causa movens,* by which the soul forms a color of this kind. The [role of the] imagination [in the instance of the normal propagation of black children] is not as unstable and transitory as what arises in the soul of pregnant mothers; it is deliberate, firm, and consistent. On the other hand, if an Ethiopian woman bears white children, that extraordinary phenomenon would have to be attributed to the effect of her imagination. This would also be the case if European women were to bear black children.

Likewise, I proved—citing examples—that it is a simple matter for the soul to transmit images of external objects when engaged in the formation of its own body; and it does so with the same ease with which it impresses in the body whatever color it sees fit. I also proved that, just as easily, the soul is able to express images in its body derived from the mother through the intimate communication that occurs *in utero.* Finally, I proved that changes in blackness and hair turn out not to derive from men themselves, but from the maternal imagination, which affects these features to varying degrees.

After discussing everything concerning the form and the causes of black Ethiopians, I ought to conclude with a brief description, namely that black Ethiopians are a particular and definite species of man that differs from the other human species in the blackness of the body and in the hair, which is woolly.[24] The properties [*proprietatis*] of the ancestors of this species owe their origin to no external cause, but rather to the imprinted [*impressa*] and innate [*ingenita*] nature of the Ethiopians, such that the children are born from their parents according to the law of heredity and its processes. This takes place as the soul transfers to the body ideas about blackness and hair received from the parents by the power of the imaginative faculty, rendering those ideas corporeal. They never recede from this type of formation, except in cases of a mixed parentage with a different species, and consequently, a change in the ideas of the imagination.

### THESIS 26

When I use the term "determined species" for Ethiopians, I expressly mean to assert that this class [*genus*] of man was destined to come into existence by the design of divine Providence, not by chance or accidental existence. Just as God desired to manifest the infinite wisdom of his Majesty in the innumerable diversity of species in both the vegetable and mineral kingdoms, this is also the case for the animal kingdom, and most especially in the wonderful diversity of the subjects of the human species. For here, He desired to create an exceptional model, all to the greater glory of His name.[25]

If the lineage of black men owed its origin to chance, it certainly would not have continued to exist over such a long time, nor would it have continued so consistently. Indeed, since everything that is born by chance is also disordered, such an eventuality would result in deformities such as birthmarks and the like that would be transmitted across generations.

In sum, we must concede that no definite documentation survives from the authors of both sacred and secular history as to how Blacks might have evolved from the first origins. Nonetheless, from a variety of writings and records from remotest antiquity, it would seem that in the early age of the Deluge, the Ethiopians also suffered a disaster of similar proportions.

And there is a well-accepted tradition among [the Ethiopians] that claims that in fact they owed their origin to Ham, son of Noah, through their parents and ancestors, all the way back to the first progenitors, almost as if transmitted by word of mouth. In particular, Ethiopian priests add the following:

that Noah had three sons, one white, the second brown, and the third black; that the wives of each of them imparted to their progeny the same color as their husband's, so that the wife who coupled with her equally black husband gave birth to black Ethiopians.

Putting these considerations aside for the moment, there are two questions we must ask that would prove the truth about the blackness of the Ethiopians. The first question is about the first men after the Deluge. We should note first that Hebrew proper names often have meanings: the word Ham (the name of one of Noah's sons) also means "hot" or "burnt" and by analogy denotes "black." The name Ham probably reflects the color of his parents. Secondly, both lay and religious authors involved in these studies derive the origin of the Ethiopians to Cush, the son of Ham.

Thus in his *Geographia Sacra,* Samuel Bochart writes about the ancient Greek author Eupolemus who listed the Babylonians as follows: Belum (i.e., Noah) was first, and Noah's sons were Belum and Ham; Ham gave birth to Canaan, who is the progenitor of the Phoenicians; and he gave birth to another son, Abraham, who is the progenitor of the Egyptians; and thirdly, he gave birth to Cush, father of the Ethiopians, who in Greek are also called *Asbalos,* or "soot."[26]

Doubtless, the Greeks employed this designation to signify the color black, just as *Aithiopia* in Greek means "burnt-faced." In the Sacred Scriptures, the Ethiopians are always called Cuschim, that is, sons of Cush, or Cushites, while Ethiopia itself is called Chuschi. Thus from the Sacred Scriptures we learn that dark-colored men existed and inhabited Ethiopia. Hence, the Song of Solomon, ch. 1, v. 5, if I may paraphrase the Hebrew, reads: "I am black, but comely . . . as the tents of Kedar"; and Jeremiah 13:23 says: "Can the Ethiopian [ever] change his skin?"

There are other examples I could cite. Bochart, in particular, devoted much time to this topic in order to prove with deserving arguments that the sons of Cush, with the exception of Nimrod who migrated to Babylon, inhabited the Persian Gulf region; that in the first days after the Deluge they occupied the rocky and the fertile parts of Arabia; and that the Arabs were called Moors and even Saracens because of their color.[27] With the passage of time, continues Bochart, overwhelmed by overcrowding, or lured by the fertility of Africa, nothing would have prevented them from crossing the Red Sea and penetrating into Africa, and hence also into Ethiopia, as Leo Africanus confirms several times in his description of Africa, to wit, that the Arabs almost completely inundated that continent, and likewise settled there.[28]

From these facts I conclude that Ham was the father of the Ethiopians, and in his line the sons of Cush followed, Cush seemingly having the same body color as his father, and they propagated this stock [*genus*] of black men. The children of Mizraim, brother of Cush, also entered Ethiopia and began to settle there, as Bochart demonstrated. Hence, it is indeed probable that the difference in color of the Ethiopians, which I mentioned above, clearly and necessarily owes its origins to intermarriages with the descendants of Cush.

He beseeches:
Horace
"So I'll play a whetstone's part,
which makes steel sharp, but of itself cannot cut."[29]

# 3 ⌒

# Blackness through the Maternal Imagination

This compact Latin essay attributes the origin of black skin and textured hair to the ability of white women to produce black children through the power of the maternal imagination during pregnancy. The author begins his argument with the oft-repeated story of the biblical patriarch Jacob, who transformed pure white sheep into spotted and speckled varieties of the species by exposing mating sheep to the brown branches and white pulp of poplar and almond trees. From there the author moves on to the much more complex process of somatic transfer as it occurs in humans. The second part of his argument involves the complementary action of maternal impression and maternal imagination to reproduce the unique features of the black body. The curious highlight of the essay comes when the author takes the reader through an elaborate step-by-step "thought experiment," through which a black baby is born to a white woman and a simulated black man. At this point, his scientific argument has become pure fiction.

A FTER THE PATRIARCH JACOB had spent fourteen years toiling under his uncle Laban [to pay for his wives Leah and Rachel], Laban asked Jacob to serve him for six more years. Jacob consented to this as well. When it came time to set his wages, he in fact asked for the multicolored sheep as his wages. In truth, Jacob asked to have only the animals marked with spots or speckles.

Laban granted him the animals, and Jacob departed. He placed rods that he had peeled, revealing white streaks, in the water troughs where the flocks would go to drink. It was during the time when the ewes were ready to conceive. Once this had transpired, he saw that, through the process of [imaginative] imprinting, the lambs that were born were spotted with many colors.

The above episode is recounted and narrated in richer detail in the Book of Genesis, chapters 29, 30, and following. Now, if an impression or the imagination could provoke this result in animals, including sheep, could the same not happen, indeed happen more easily, with rational creatures, especially with humankind of course, in whom imagination is more vividly perceived?

The same experience also occurs in our time also, and we even notice it every day. A pregnant woman is fully capable of picturing something to herself; indeed, should she see a black sheep or a lamb with frizzy wool it is well known that by the same logic the child thus conceived will similarly be born with black, frizzy hair. This is inevitable.

Therefore, Ethiopians, Africans, i.e., black people, propagate through the process of imprinting, until it becomes customary in nature.

Mnemonic verses, or declaration:
My hope grows that by thought and meditation
the Ethiopian genus will be revealed to me
by the word of God.

### EXPERIMENT

A chaste virgin, fit to bear children, is to be selected for this type of experiment; she will be told that she must lie [have sexual intercourse] with an Ethiopian. And a young [white] man is to be chosen for this purpose. This man should be of utterly normal size and shape, with large white eyes, a hooked nose, thick lips and, finally, white teeth. His whole body is to be covered with odorless black paint. His head is to be shaven, and he is to wear a wig made of black, crispy wool, such as to suggest and indicate the shape of an Ethiopian's head.

Once this is done the young man, dressed as an Ethiopian, is to be brought to the woman at night by the light of a candle or a shining lamp, so that neither might know the other either by their shape or speech. Then [illegible] by him indeed, but not in a choleric temperament.

The counterfeit Ethiopian and the woman sit at a table, and in the presence of a witness he offers her a glass filled with wine, on the bottom of which is painted the image of a recently born Ethiopian baby. After she has drunk all the wine, emptying the glass, she is to be asked what she sees. She is to be reminded carefully to look at the image, so that again and again she will examine it in detail and properly reflect on this image of an Ethiopian.

The man should be instructed beforehand about everything. When all this has transpired, the candle is put out. To be sure, he is to be left alone with the woman, but afterward, when the night is over, he is to be separated from her. And the woman is to be brought into a closed room and left alone, the walls being hung with several panels depicting Ethiopians. And an Ethiopian woman is to minister to her up to the birth. Finally, after she has given birth, the counterfeit Ethiopian is to take the woman in marriage.

# 4

## Blackness as a Moral Defect

This essay begins with an interesting autobiographical note. Although the Latin essay was submitted from Amsterdam, the author—Eric Molin—was a native of Sweden. He seems to have been associated with dissenters from the state-sponsored Lutheran church, which ultimately led to his exile.[1] In his essay, he proposes a survey of the suggested causes of blackness. His view is that this condition can only be the product of internal processes, such as the force of the maternal imagination. He avows that "Moors" are not created black, either by divine intervention or by climate; on the contrary, blackness in his view stems from a moral defect, which produces a permanent state of depravity. Molin's essay was clearly influenced by two famous Swedes. The "scientific" component related to heredity within this theory suggests that he was familiar with the work of Carl Linnaeus (1707–1778), the Swedish doctor, zoologist, and botanist who was at Uppsala University concurrently with the author. The first edition of Linnaeus's groundbreaking work on taxonomy, his *Systema Naturae*, appeared in Latin in 1735, a few years before this essay was written. The second and far more metaphysical half of Molin's essay, which deals with "vital force" and the need for God's mercy to overcome sin, reveals the spiritual influence of another great Swede, the scientist, theologian, and philosopher Emanuel Swedenborg (1688–1772), nicknamed the Leonardo da Vinci of the North or the Aristotle of Sweden, who constructed a theory of the correspondence between the material and spiritual worlds.

To Your Illustrious Lordship

[. . .] Should your most honorable colleagues truly desire to learn who I am, they ought to know that I am from the Swedish nation and that, when I was able, I immersed myself in studies since my earliest childhood. Poverty, however, prevented me from progressing in these endeavors since, from the age of twelve, I was forced to take on various duties to earn my living.[2]

In the year 1725, at age sixteen, with the aid of some citizens I was sent to the Academy of Uppsala where, shortly thereafter and until 1735, I began to give frequent lectures during the academic year. In my seventeenth year a particular concern for divine truth and God's will grew in me, and I could not help but fall prey to the envy of many.

Therefore, in the year 1734, I was summoned before three Consisto-
ries [ecclesiastical courts] and in the same year appeared before the
High Royal Council. In the following year, I was summoned before
the Royal Swedish Senate. Since the High Council showed me great
favor, the Senate treated me no less favorably. In the time that I was
held in captivity, I held debates with several clergymen whose work
was not customarily regarded favorably or fairly by the High Council.

As such, the Senate, which at this time was protecting my work
from my bishops as part of its duties, was greatly troubled. Despite
their wishes, they were effectively forced by the Supreme Judicial
Council to have the bishops publicly issue a judgment [regarding my
views]. Two members of the court were appointed and the hearing
took place on the seventh of [illegible]. When it ended, the High
Council, after considering the matter, ruled that my adversaries had
undeservedly and strenuously harassed me and that their case against
me was less substantial than they had claimed. Yet they [nonetheless]
remained hostile to me, and ruled at once against me, ordering me to
leave the kingdom.

[. . .] The judgment of the Senate was executed: in the year 1739,
after four years in prison, I was taken by ship to Stralsund and placed
under the extraterritorial custody of the royal government. [3] Now I live
in Amsterdam and earn my bread preparing commercial accounts for
the merchants Anthon and Johan [illegible: *Grills*?], who are now
writing a letter [of recommendation] on my behalf.

I place Your Illustrious Lordship under God's guidance and protection, humbly entrust myself to your benevolence, and remain, Your
Lordship, with great submission,

Your most humble author

Ericus Molin

Done at Amsterdam

On the 15th day of February 1742

THE ORIGIN OF BLACKNESS IN THE MOORS, EXPLORED BY
PHILOSOPHICAL INQUIRY INTO THE NATURE OF MAN AS FOUND IN
EVERYDAY EXPERIENCE

## BY ERICUS MOLIN

*Banished from Sweden for having confessed the truth*

[. . .]

While by its very nature the question of the color black in the Moors could be answered superficially in just a few words, such a response would be unable, of course, to take everything into consideration. This is because in order to be unassailable, the arguments on which the question rests would require a more extended treatment, first of all because the investigation and knowledge of nature and its extremely powerful forces are a subject of no small difficulty that needs to be properly and seriously weighed. Our Creator [God] would have demanded nothing less.

May the benevolent reader forgive me, if my method of reasoning will be somewhat encumbered, as truth, not eloquence, is my goal. Indeed, I have frequently opted to value truth more than eloquence. Given the time that my work, which is in fact dedicated to inquiring about the truth, necessarily demands, the short time assigned does not allow me to be concerned with a more accurate examination of language. Since I am thus bound and hindered by this weakness, I nevertheless beg the reader to seek thoughts, not words, and to indulge my faulty and fevered language.

Thus moving on to the subject itself, it is first necessary and lawful to set aside and eliminate the false theories about the blackness of the Moors. I plan to do this in the following way. If I were to say that the Moors were founded such as they are, either by God's will or by His operation, we would have solved the Gordian knot with Alexander's sword; this said, in so doing we would have engaged in a faulty line of reasoning.[4]

Many obstacles stand in the way of this theory, and these [problems] begin with a fundamental reality; we find not only black-colored Moors that differ from those of other nations [nationes], but also whitish [albicantes] nations that differ from each other in that they either tend toward black or toward white, with black hair or whitish hair, brown or cerulean eyes, tall or short height, round faces and flattened noses or oval faces and moderately upturned noses. This being the situation, one might conclude based on these differences and, in particular, the blackness of the Moors, that several kinds [genus] of men were created at the beginning, and not just one kind.

This belief contradicts both reason and the Sacred Scriptures, both of which maintain that humankind comes from just one blood, not from a plurality of men and women created at the very beginning. The Scriptures also testify that all living souls were extinguished [intersecta] by the waters [the Deluge] except for Noah and the surviving tribes [tribus] of his sons. You will not find in history anything older than the Sacred Scriptures, so that no evidence exists about the origin of this blackness from the beginning of creation.

And if you were to say that some of [these original men] were black, you would [also] be mistaken, since they came from one and the same father. On the other hand, if you were indulging more in superstition and said that Ham was made black by the curse, you would be denying different progenies whose origin leads back to one and the same man, because they existed before us in the color white.

And if you were to say that this difference [*discrimen*] among nations [*gentes*], whatever it is, was found to have come about by specific divine direction and operation, you would indeed have stated something.[5] However, first of all, you would have to concede that it happened after Noah and with the passage of time; and second, we would need to interrogate the reasoning that led to this conclusion, because indeed nothing of this nature has been discovered.

Neither do I hold that the difference [of the Negroes] is derived from the different climates, or indeed that we see this contrast recede [in different climates]. Rather, I add that we see different kinds of men being born by the law of heredity on this or that shore of the world because the first inhabitants or their descendants by emigration (having subjected this or that shore to their rule) had this or that nature [*indolem*].[6] For one does distinguish the Jews from the Batavians or from men of other nations from their lively white color, because even in that part of the world they [the Jews] maintain black hair and eyes.[7] Should this be otherwise—should these nations mix among themselves—either blackness or whiteness would lose its primacy, as we will make evident in what follows.

It will be enough to demonstrate here that the diversity of colors does not come from the climate or the characteristics of any other region. This is because white people and those who enjoy that general type of appearance, although they may emigrate to the lands of black nations or to the lands of different kinds of natives, still preserve their own characteristics in their progeny, unless they mix with other peoples [*gens*] through indiscriminate sexual unions, in which case eventually this or that distinctive [feature] would be eliminated. Thus the Gauls [*Galli*] living in Sweden, since they keep themselves bound in marriage within their own kind, always remain distinctive in face and body height from the native people [of Sweden]; it would be different if they allowed themselves to marry with the indigenous people.

As we have briefly demonstrated, this diversity owes its origin neither to divine creation, nor to the different climates and characteristics of the different regions of the earth. Accordingly, it follows that the cause cannot be ascribed to anything external such as water, food, medical remedies, cold, or the varying heat of the sun. From this we may extrapolate, and this you will see, that any specific particular effect originating from the above [factors] is not transmitted to the descendants, but dies with the individual in which it resides: fully in the individual that was affected by it.

Thus, when people are turned dark by the sun's raging heat and made stout by hard work and nourishment, these coarse, hard humans [nonetheless] give birth to white, delicate children. [What is more], the children may later escape from either their delicate or stout state depending on the method of their upbringing. I will not say that they can escape their shortness or their tallness, or the external shape of their limbs, because those must be ascribed to the parents' nature and not to how the child was raised.

It is true that if you were to say that diseases provoked in the parents by an external cause will very often occur in their children, I might acknowledge your point. And yet, I do not [entirely] agree, since those external causes (or more probably the strong poisons of the disease) might excite the parents' nature, but much less so their children's. For instance, is it not the case that abuse of wine and women produces gout in some people but in others only intermittent or durable aches in the limbs? And that the effects vary in different people, and thus also in other, different situations?

Even if we were to acknowledge that the cause [of Negroes' blackness] is external, its effect would always remain one and the same, similar to itself; instead, we find that some things bring conservation and life in some individuals and death in others. It is absolutely worthy of mention that if you were to amputate someone's hands and feet, there is no doubt that their children would not be born with the same amputation. Were it otherwise, if in one generation someone were blind, deaf, or mutilated, this defect of nature would usually extend to only three or four generations, as if the more perfect nature of one spouse struggles with the utmost effort to correct [the defect] in the future. I have observed with admiration the nature of one or the other [spouse] alternatively prevail in their offspring.

Yet I fear I have already said enough to the wise about these insights. From what appears above, it seems quite clear at this time that the nature, form, and innate characteristics of men, and the singularities of this or that people [gentes] [. . .] are preserved to them through marriages with equals. Just so Jupiter couples with Juno, Mars with Venus, and it is the same with others also, such as Pluto who kidnapped Proserpina to make her his bride.[8] And truly, it is sufficiently clear that all nations propagate their innate characteristics in this manner, and if in some cases the usual order is broken in this or that individual through marriage with opposites, that characteristic will recede in the ensuing generations over time.

We have already spoken about the reproduction of the form and the innate characteristics of the parents in their children and of how they are passed on in the ensuing generations in the same way, or on the contrary, of how they change or disappear. One can easily see how this reasoning can be applied to the blackness of the Moors, if we consider the half-black form of children born from white and black [parents], or of how it recedes to this or that extreme in the ensuing generations if [male] children born from this or that type of union join again with women [of that color]. Our greatest concern is the main cause of this difference, which indeed can be determined by looking at the previous generations.

[. . .]

There are different types of faculties, characteristics, and forms among humans: some people have a shallow and dull intellect, others a broad and deep mind, some are quick and penetrating or fleeting and reckless, or of an easy and careless will, while some are strong and persistent and indeed others again are inclined to think contrarily, something that is often ascribed to people having different tastes in their senses. Some people are delighted in certain things that others find wearying or irritating, and some people have differently shaped limbs as well as a different color of hair, eyes, and skin. There are specific reasons for these differences: one finds the greatest diversity of these features in one people (*gens*) more than another, or in one clan (*familia*) more than others. Indeed, as we stated earlier, features are regulated and modified through the marriage of dissimilar spouses, until finally a people will preserve a characteristic more strongly than another, either as its own, or as pertaining to several nations.

Further, everyday experience teaches us how persistent are characteristics as well as mental defects or bodily form or defects, so that, should they insinuate themselves into a given lineage [*stirpes*], they will scarcely be eliminated after the fourth or fifth generation born from disparate unions, and indeed given the least opportunity, they might reappear even after long permutations.

But if we were to hurry through the origin of all these fortuitous, not general, matters, what offers itself for consideration is that, however much history leaves us in the dark, the origin of blackness among the Moor is abundantly confirmed by the Bible, since [they] were present already in the time of Moses. Reasons are brought forth about the origin of this and other specific properties of various peoples [*gentes*], though many others are denied to us.

As everyday examples teach us, pregnant women, if suddenly coming before some object, may at first be flooded by panic or admiration and receive such a great impression that very often a substantial change will occur in the fetus. Thus in the time of pregnancy, if [the mother] should intensely desire, or deeply fear or detest, a certain something, we shall not fail to find those same characteristics in the fetus. Thus a baby will carry a form similar to that of a certain man that the woman had looked upon with pleasure or admiration.

I believe, given the above, that it is often the case that some children are born without resembling anyone in their family. And it is not rare to see blackish [*subnigricantes*] children issue from parents who are whitish [*albicantibus*]. I believe that this happens not always from gazing at that [color] of man [during conception], but also from frequent conversations about matters and clothes that are specific to black people. In the same way, wild animals living in the forest are not greatly subjected to a diversity of colors, with the exception of bears, wolves, foxes, and hares that are established in habitats where much snow falls and stays [frozen] for a long part of the year, so that some white birds and hares are often white because of the whiteness of the land.

On the other hand, the external cause of this should only minimally be ascribed to the cold, since cold weather accompanied by snow always provides more nourishment for growing things and, among others, for the hair of beasts, than dry cold without snow. In the latter case, food is supplied by resinous trees and also serves to protect them from the cold, while wild forest animals that live in regions where little snow is to be found, and where their food comes from trees and water plants, are made weaker against the punishing returning cold.

Indeed, you see them keep their own colors in the customary greenness of the forests, while on the contrary horses, dogs, chickens, cows, and many other kinds of animals that spend their lives amidst men, take on many different colors and are subject to a diversity of colors undoubtedly conceived by impression during pregnancy. The Patriarch Jacob, having knowledge of this phenomenon, exposed his pregnant sheep to varicolored rods, which made the entire flock give birth to varicolored lambs. Because of this, it will be neither incongruous nor improbable to conclude that the color black in Moors is of the same origin, especially because looking for a different origin will be an eternally vain task as all the aforementioned varieties that we observe in men and wild beasts belong to their nature.[9]

However this or that came about, [it is clear] that when a pregnant woman is excessively flooded by the impression of black color or indeed by fear, she gives birth to a fetus that is predominantly blackish [*nigricans*]. And, if the woman and the husband are medium-black, and her nature [*indolem*] is not thwarted, she will give birth to black offspring. This departure from the norm could in the end strengthen over time if due to a scarcity of men who had left [their native region], there will be unions with strangers. Now, once a characteristic nature has been established, it will be passed on undisturbed to the descendants, to which one might add that at one time marriage between brother and sister [or first cousins] was quite common. It may also be that this same characteristic [of blackness] will recede in people living in caves without any light. They will receive such an intense impression that it will have an impact on their offspring, thus increasingly strengthening [the new characteristic].

Now, to end this section, I submit three considerations. (1) The first one is from the examples we presented up to this point. We find white men, with hair almost as white as snow, who cannot abide the daylight but see most clearly in the dark. We may infer from this phenomenon, which has been passed on, that those material characteristics were eventually contracted with the passage of time, in deference to the usual state [of whiteness]. Still, I hold that whiteness coming from a specific impression of their own fundamental nature has a different origin than darkness does.

That notwithstanding, the children of Blacks are also born white, but after an intervening lapse of fourteen days they gradually achieve their blackness. This is because recently born babies will equally have the interior parts of the mother, which are not black, because it is the innate quality of their nature to predispose the blackening material in the extremities of the skin. We observe the same phenomenon in horses and other animals whose newborn do not boast the same color that will later adorn them. By applying the latter reasoning to the former, we say that their fundamental idea is impregnated during their generation [i.e., reproductive process].

[. . .]

(2) As to the second consideration, it is fitting to remind you here of how much free will and power are found in man, such that his vital essence could be impregnated by such impressions.[10] Here we see that the power of human will is clearly a part of the design of God the most wise. And I ask, up to what point did humankind stray from his general condition, quality, and nature, if anyone, being free, can either raise or destroy characteristics in himself and in his progeny?[11]

[. . .]

(3) As to our third consideration, we note that it will be impossible to change propensities once they have originated in the same manner in the

parents (their bodily features and structure being already stable and fixed); they will be reproduced in the bodies of their children even before they are formed. This is so because the parents' thoughts, deliberations, and judgments as they affect their heart—what we call the direction of nature—will arouse a certain proclivity of the vital force, which will be communicated and passed on to their progeny through the features of face and body, which are signs of the mind and will also be reproduced in their children. Therefore you should not wonder if by some circumstance some people will deviate from the external form of their parents. And lest anyone should offer a conjecture about this, we must recall experience once again. In addition, I am aware that some men have acknowledged, about children born to them when they were in a certain moral state, that instead of inheriting the same quality and features of the father, they had absorbed the features of the father in his altered state.

Given all of the above, in which we have brought forth the signs of nature inferred from everyday experience, we do not hesitate to set forth the following summary:

1. The Moors are not created black.
2. Nor are these people made so by divine direction and command.
3. Their blackness does not derive from the climate.
4. Nor from food or drink or any external means.
5. The general forms and faculties of humankind cannot be changed in procreation.
6. Only certain more specific qualities can change, and color is among them.
7. Hence the blackness of the Moors must have the same origin.
8. Certainly not by sexual intercourse with beasts.[12]
9. It is not given to man's free will to be able to arouse in himself, by his will, an impression or feeling that might produce an innate quality or form in his progeny.
10. But by such impressions as are induced by sudden causes, as they more strongly arouse this or that feeling in the mind.
11. Sometimes by extended usage and practice, the deliberations and judgments of our reason will eventually be changed into a strong proclivity of the heart and of our vital force.
12. Similarly, innate qualities [*indolem*] eventually pass through by propagation to the progeny.

[Number 13 is missing from the list.]

14. The external form and features, which are signs of the mind, will transmit themselves.

15. Lastly, we observe how persistent are innate qualities, and how an agreeable form that was once an external appearance will, except in a few more sensible men, be adopted by most men, who will lead their lives as if it were an innate quality, only rarely upset by an unexpected event or by untiring pursuit.

We trust that the above claims have been confirmed by these very clear examples and signs of nature, and I have no doubt that they will meet with the approval of the Illustrious School of Scholars at Bordeaux.

In truth, an earthly matter cannot be said to have been properly investigated unless it has been found to provide manifold usefulness and real erudition. On the other hand, knowledge [*Scientia*] about the nature of things, over which vain men are accustomed to boast, will not eschew the reputation of being deceitful wisdom [*sapientia*], unless it be applied to its real use. [Accordingly,] we have fully performed our duty in that, having first explained the nature of the matter, we now shall speak of our infirmity.

### ON THE MEDICAL, MORAL, AND SPIRITUAL USE OF
### THIS SCIENTIFIC KNOWLEDGE

*1*

It is now time to inquire about the use of medical science, first of all for the Physician, whose concern will be to aid a suffering man, whether the illness be caused by an impression received or by the predisposition [*constitutio*] of the soul [*anima*], or according to us, by a sickness in the vital force [*potentia vitalis*], whether originating from birth or from some specific accident.[13] For, in the former case, generally all remedies will be applied in vain unless one finds the connection to the mind [*mens*] on which the patient's fundamental disposition is laboring. In this case, he will be relieved by means of different remedies, [specifically] by an untiring effort of the patient himself and by wise conversation. But we have rarely seen such defects of nature give way to improvement.

In the former case, when the offending [sinning] concept [*conceptus peccans*] originates in a person after birth, it is not always so strongly governed by those root causes. And so you will see the sick person trust the physician and by the same token conceive the form and image of the desired-for health, which will most certainly be the sign of a good outcome. On the contrary, treating the sinning matter [*materia peccans*] with material powers or good medications to restore the sick body will accomplish nothing, and other remedies will be applied in vain; [indeed,] the entire physician's work will be frustrated unless the impression of the soul in the sick man is altered [*convertatur*].

Truly, in respect to the sinning matter, or the body's broken machine, a third solution might be considered: [this might involve] the sour and bitter material forces [of sin] struggling to upset and destroy the body's structure and its fluids on which health depends, by living a disorderly life and by abuse that pushes them to their limit. Indeed, [this way of life] will affect the endurance of the vital force that works continually to correct and remove [those unhealthy forces] but which nevertheless may be forced by them, in the end, to succumb.

If therefore, as they say, the damage is not so deeply rooted that the sinning matter has become fixed in the structure of the body, nor has the body succumbed [to this effect] for too long, the soul will not lose all hope of reinstatement; or perhaps, in fact, it will have already received a concomitant awareness of the defect. Now this will not be a task for a physician, who would resort to physical powers or medications, because the sinning matter is totally resistant to repairing the fault, which the vital force, according to its disposition, had so quickly attacked.

Indeed, medications produce an agreeable and exhilarating effect in our lives according to one's inclinations and custom, but more often with respect to the senses [i.e., pleasure] rather than [actual] usefulness. Now since [our sinning predispositions] are attracted to many of the sweeter things in inexperienced people, this alteration, which is fermented by human passion, will be changed into burned and rotten material because in them are many elements hostile to a healthy life. For this reason, the physician must employ the greatest care in his treatment, correcting [the defect] with remedies or preparations for the [blood] vessels and in doing so, making sure that they do not mix with the blood and corrupt it.

Moreover, it is not at all true that [medications] can arouse new ideas and operations in our vital forces; rather, they should be employed according to one's own disposition [*indolem*] and course of life or endeavors to remove negative forces. However, if there should occur a sudden, excessive attachment, or some other chance event, another outcome would prevail, so that one is forced to desist from the effort.

This has been a concise examination, for medical use, of our life and nature, so that those who are in charge of the temporal health of men might easily transform it into use for themselves.

## 2

[From this point on the essay is a discourse on Swedenborgian theology and the need to convert; spiritual change will affect the body, including blackness. One central tenet is that each one of us must cooperate in repentance, reformation, and regeneration, taking Jesus Christ as our example.]

[...]

### I PRAY TO GOD!

[The overall conclusion is that "if a perverse disposition of the mind can be transmitted to our descendants, the blackness of the Moors can also be transmitted, for it was not created in them but was contracted through a flaw of the parents and is similar in the descendants as it is in the parents." This is another version of the sins of the fathers being visited on the sons.]

# 5

# Blackness as a Result of the Torrid Zone

This long essay, written in French, is an example of the analytic method and is highly structured into Research Topics, Phenomena, Corollaries, Remarks, and so on. This can be quite tedious to follow, so we have streamlined it. Among other things, the author cautions his readers that there is no need to attribute black skin to any biblical curse, or to assume that Blacks are a race apart from all others. His view is that, since Africa lies in the hottest part of the Torrid Zone, the skin of its inhabitants is logically the darkest in the world. He is unsure about the exact location of this darkness in the skin, however, and states that determining the essence of blackness would require a black body to dissect. The author of Essay 16, as we will see later, would undertake this exact experiment.

FIRST RESEARCH TOPIC: IN WHICH COUNTRIES DID THE
NATURAL AND NATIVE NEGROES LIVE?

The term *natural* corresponds to the inhabitant of a land who is born there; someone who is both natural and native is not merely born there, but whose ancestors also lived there.[1] I not only call the peoples of Nigritia Negroes, but also all those who are black, as in Guinea, Nubia, etc. Some Blacks are blacker, have flatter noses, have wooly hair, and others less so.[2]

Travelers and geographers assure us that our continent [Europe] is hotter than America, that the same latitude in France is hotter than the corresponding latitude in Canada, and that Spain is hotter than Virginia. The Torrid Zone in our continent is therefore hotter than the Torrid Zone in America. [ . . .]

SECOND RESEARCH TOPIC: WHAT IS THE CAUSE OF
THE BLACKNESS OF NEGROES WHO INHABIT THE LOWLANDS OF
THE MIDDLE OF AFRICA?

I use the term *hale* to designate the sun's heat and its rays' intensity.[3] I attribute the sun's heat to the effect of its indirect rays, which are broken and reflected and reduced to turbulent [radiation], whether this radiation is still specific to these rays or is communicated to the air. In a word, what I call the sun's heat is the heat from a cloudy sky, and the sun's intensity is the direct heat under a clear sky.

The degree of hale is proportional to the degree of blackness. Accordingly, Negroes of the lowlands in the African Torrid Zone (who are the blackest in the world) inhabit the hottest lands in the world; they are also the most burned by the sun's rays. The peoples of the Asian Torrid Zone (whose skin shade is less black than that of the Negroes of Africa) inhabit a country that is less hot than the African Torrid Zone. The peoples of the American Torrid Zone, who are merely swarthy or reddish, etc. and not as totally black [as Negroes], live in a land that is less hot than the Asian Torrid Zone. On our continent the half-blacks similar to the Egyptians live in a land that is less hot than the Negroes do; finally, Whites live in a land that is less hot than the half-blacks.

Since blackness corresponds to the quantity of sunburn, i.e. the heat and intensity of the sun's rays, this already points in favor of this being the cause of blackness, since when two things constantly come after each other—one after the other—one must be the cause of the other. The degree of heat constantly corresponds to the degree of blackness, and since one cannot say that blackness is the cause of heat, hence heat is the cause of blackness.

[. . .]

Whites who travel and are in the sun for a long time are swarthier than those who are long in the shade. The former become tanned and swarthy. But this swarthy skin shade is nothing other than half-blackness [. . .] especially in the long run and after several generations.

The color that is given by the sun to the skin of tanned Whites is merely a layer. It cannot be removed by dint of washing or rubbing; and it is not derived from a black liquor, as some say about the Negroes. We cannot find either the vessels that might carry this black liquor, nor those that might filter it. Bearing this in mind, a particular arrangement of the parts of the skin is necessary for blackness, similar to what heat produces in wood, in parchment, and all combustible bodies. A greater degree of heat will produce a larger arrangement and a greater blackness in Negroes than that of sun-tanned Whites. [Blackness in the lands of Negroes] is caused by greater sunburn than in the country of Whites.

Every day we see that Negroes who are transported to the country of true Whites, as in France, lose a little of their former blackness. I have never seen Negroes arriving from Guinea, but I have seen some arriving from the Antilles. And I have seen some long settled in France, and I have noticed a big difference in their colors.

Consequently, if these Negroes in France marry other Negroes and their children do the same, each generation will lose a little of the blackness acquired by their forefathers. Ultimately the children will become white, and so we must agree that the forefathers were black only because of the heat in their native country.

[. . .] It is true that Negroes transplanted to the country of half-blacks do not degenerate after several generations, but this does not disprove the last consequence, because the country of half-blacks is too hot for the Negroes there to degenerate and not hot enough for the naturals of the country to become completely black. Similarly, our lands are warm enough to let certain plants and animals live here but not hot enough to have them originate here.[4]

If you put meat on the fire it blackens. We see this every day. The same thing happens if you put meat under the rays of a magnifying glass. Why wouldn't the intensity of the sun['s] rays at the equator in Africa not have the same effect over time after several generations, at least on people in the countryside [who are] always exposed to the sun?[5]

[. . .]

### THIRD RESEARCH TOPIC: WHETHER GOD'S CURSE ON THE CHILDREN OF HAM IS THE CAUSE OF THE BLACKNESS OF NEGROES

God does nothing useless; it would have been useless for God by himself to blacken immediately the children of Ham to punish them for the perfidy of their father, for only the heat of the African Torrid Zone would have made them black independently of any other cause.[6] So it was useless for God to make them so by this or some cause other than the heat and intensity of the sun's rays. Moreover, the children of Ham spread only in Africa and there are still Blacks in Asia, and no proof they came from Africa.

Negroes transplanted to the lands of the true Whites lose their blackness and Whites transplanted to the lands of Blacks lose their whiteness. If Whites marry Whites in the lands of true Blacks and their children do not interbreed, they would become black in several generations, since each generation would lose a little of its whiteness. Reciprocally, the children of Negroes transplanted to the land of true Whites would become white, for the same reason. Consequently, this blackness of Negroes has nothing to do with a curse on Ham's children, since if this were the cause of their blackness, the curse would continue in the country of Whites, and the color would remain the same.

[. . .]

## FOURTH RESEARCH TOPIC: WHETHER NEGROES ARE A SPECIES OF MEN DIFFERENT FROM WHITES

God never does anything useless. [. . .] Now it would have been useless for God to have created Negroes black since, independently of this creation and this immediate operation, they would have become black via another process [also engineered by] God, meaning secondary causes, the force of the heat and intensity of the sun's rays. Therefore, the Negroes are not a species of men different from Whites any more than the swarthy and the olive-skinned are.[7]

[One should note that] it is not heat alone that blackens, it is also the intensity of the sun's direct rays as well as the different quantity of calm skies that contribute to the different quantity of blackness in the skin. Here are a few phenomena that prove this proposition:

I have observed that the women of the southern provinces of France who take care to keep themselves in the shade have a whiter skin tone than peasant women in northern provinces. The former women in fact absorb a greater and longer heat although they almost always stay in the shade, while the latter women, though often exposed to the [direct] sun in lands where the sky is clearer although less hot, ought to acquire a darker tint than those who live under cloudier but indirectly heated skies.

One darkens more as a result of having been a single day in the sun than for having absorbed the heat of a whole summer in the shade. The intensity of direct sun rays therefore contributes to darkness as much as the heat of a covered Sun.

[. . .]

## FIFTH RESEARCH TOPIC: HOW DOES THE SUN'S HEAT AND INTENSITY PRODUCE HEAT?

When I refer to skin, I mean the first four envelopes of the human body that so tightly adhere to one another that they seem to be only one. These four membranes are: a) the most external, the Epidermis, a thin and transparent membrane; b) the dermis, or skin properly speaking, a membrane made by a sort of net, so it is called reticular; c) the Papillary body, which has an infinity of small protuberances formed by the nerve endings; d) the fourth is the hide, which is composed of an infinity of tendon and nerve fibers formed by vessels that are mostly lymphatic.

The Epidermis or outer skin of a Negro seen alone and backlit appears reddish like burned horn. The dermis or skin seen alone and backlit appears much blacker than the Epidermis or outer skin. Any transparent body that is dark in color and seen alone and backlit appears dark, and when seen against an opaque background and a dark color appears black. [. . .]

Thus it is certain that the blackness of Negroes is: 1) in the Epidermis; 2) in the dermis or skin properly speaking; 3) uncertain whether it is in the third and fourth membranes since these membranes are a tissue of nerves that are white by themselves and moreover are protected from the heat and intensity of the sunshine by the two first membranes, so they might be able to keep their whiteness. On the one hand, the heat and intensity of the sunshine that pierces the outer skin might indeed penetrate the skin and even reach the innermost membranes. To be sure of this, one would have to dissect a Negro, see these two membranes against daylight, and if they appeared dark then conclude that they are as black as the others. But it is not in my power to do this operation at present.[8] [. . .]

Negroes have a finer and oilier skin than Whites. Under the skin there is a fifth envelope over the human body, and this is fat. Their fat must be softer and oilier, and the darker parts must be inserted more into the pores of Negro skin because of the great heat. In Whites by contrast, the fat is more solid and less inserted into the pores of their skin, making it less soft. It even seems that the skin of Whites is softer in summer than in winter, apparently because the heat softens the fat more in summer and makes parts glide into the pores of the skin.

The heat and intensity of the sunlight thus forms the blackness of Negroes in two ways, the first by digging into their skin (as into wood) pores that receive light and do not give it back, the second by wrinkling their skin into rolls and thus forming pores that do not give back light. [. . .]

### SIXTH RESEARCH TOPIC: WHY DO THE CHILDREN OF NEGROES WHO ARE NOT BORN BLACK IN THE LAND OF THE WHITES BECOME BLACK AFTER SOME TIME?

In children born either black or white, the tissue of the skin is very thin. It is transparent, the links in the tissue are large, and the body of a newborn is like flayed flesh. Nature is wise and does not give a thick skin in the mother's womb, where it is not needed.

The skin tissue is transparent, and so we cannot see its own color but only that of the flesh that is underneath and that of the fat (if the latter is thick enough). Since the flesh is not itself transparent, it is not surprising that Negroes at birth are not black; some time afterward the skin thickens and becomes opaque, and then we see the proper color which is black.

In every country newborns possess the qualities inherent in their parents. A blond child comes from a blond, a white comes from a white, a swarthy from a swarthy, a tall from a tall, a short from a short, a handsome from a handsome, an ugly from an ugly—such are the admirable but unknown laws of Nature's author to do with generation [reproduction]. *Nec mortali fas et propius accedere ad divos* [No mortal is permitted to approach the gods].[9]

So we should not be surprised that Negroes are not born at all black in the land of Whites, and even in their own lands; they become black only a while after their birth. Black skin is a quality inherent in the father. This skin is transparent at birth; this is why it does not give its own color, but rather it lets that of the flesh show through, or of the fat (if the latter is thick enough not to be itself transparent). This skin thickens for a period of time, loses its diaphanous quality, and assumes that of skin tissue and the pore quality of the father, and thus gives its own color, which is black.

[. . .]

### EIGHTH RESEARCH TOPIC: WHAT CAUSES THE NATURE OF NEGRO HAIR?

I put some hair on a hot shovel and put some near the fire. In both cases the hair curled. Wig makers put their wigs in ovens covered with hide to make them curl.

In our country straight hair is naturally oily and humid while kinky hair is dry—which is a sign of more heat in the latter.

We know that Negroes inhabit the hottest and driest (due to sunburn) lands in the world. And since hair is turned kinky by great heat, and since kinky hair among Whites is drier and therefore hotter than straight hair, and since Negroes' hair is kinky, it appears that this frizziness results from heat acting on the hair of Negroes from father to son, making them kinkier and frizzier.

Other qualities of Negro hair result from its curliness. Their hair is like sheep's wool and it is short. These two properties follow naturally from the first; when it is put in the fire at great heat it twists and becomes frizzy. I discovered this in the following way: I put a little wax at the end of a strand of hair close to a candle flame and I noticed that the wax turned about as the hair became frizzy. The hairs could not fail to thicken and get shorter. A rope that is twisted gets thicker and shorter. Hair in twisting does much the same thing, i.e., it gets thicker and shorter.

Hair should get shorter for another reason: nourishing sap does not enter into twisted fibers as easily as into straight fibers. A twisted tree does not grow as well as a tree whose fibers are straight. Overly strong heat brings dryness, and the dryness deprives it of nourishment. A dry land bears only malnourished plants. A head that is dry and too hot will have only malnourished hair.

### NINTH RESEARCH TOPIC: WHAT IS THE CAUSE OF THE DEGENERATION OF THE COLOR OF NEGROES AND OF THE QUALITY OF THEIR HAIR?

By identifying the cause of the color of Negroes and of the quality of their hair, we have simultaneously identified the source of their degeneration. However, it is clear that if the cause is removed, then the effect will also be removed. The cause of the color of Negroes is sunburn (due to the heat and intensity of sunshine in the Torrid Zone of Africa) and since this is passed on from father to son, it makes the skin of Negroes full of pores, able to receive light rays without reflecting them. In twisting their hair it thickens and shortens it. It follows that if this cause were removed the effect would also be removed—not all at once, because this is a permanent and not a fleeting effect, but afterward [it would] gradually decline, a little in each generation. The consequence of the cessation of sunburn (of the heat and intensity of sunshine) is the degeneration of the color of Negroes and of their hair quality, which happens when Negroes are transplanted to lands of the true Whites, as in France.

**"The wise man does not subordinate Nature's effects to his own opinions, but the other way around."**[10]

# 6 ～

# Blackness as a Result of Divine Providence

This author, who is from The Hague, wrote his essay in French. He begins by dismissing the validity of both sacred and secular explanations for blackness. And yet much of his overall understanding of the source of blackness stems from Moses's account of what happened to Noah's descendants. The writer then turns his attention to what today we call geography, and speculates that huge shifts in climate after Creation obliged God in his infinite wisdom to protect those tribes who ventured into the Torrid Zone by changing their skin. Revealingly, his examples of Torrid Zone lands all come from Dutch colonies in Africa and Asia.

I WILL NOT BROACH the question debated between doctors and anatomists about whether Negroes have three skins while Whites have only two, or whether blackness acts in the epidermis or elsewhere. [Anatomists and doctors] have had many opportunities to perfect their knowledge while studying Negro anatomy, and it is surprising they cannot yet agree nor instruct us with certainty about the essence of blackness. Now I will explain my opinion on the physical cause of this color, and flatter myself that those who read this dissertation attentively will be satisfied.

Some authors have imagined that Blacks descended from Cain and that blackness was supposedly a mark of recognition, but in fact Scripture does not specify what this mark was; moreover, if the Flood was universal, then this race should have become extinct—or else we cannot believe Moses's account in Genesis or in Biblical tradition. Thus this opinion is unsustainable.

Others have believed that this blackness was a consequence of Noah's curse on Ham, but this opinion is just as equally unfounded, since this curse fell principally on Canaan, Ham's youngest son, whose descendants settled in Palestine and thereabout but who were not Black; moreover, the curse that Canaan would be the servant of his brothers' servants was meant only to convey the Israelite view, which would reduce them to Slavery when they came into possession of the land of Canaan. I conclude that Holy Scripture offers no clue as to the cause of the blackness of Negroes.

Nor does secular history offer any cause of blackness nor the time it took for these peoples to acquire it, although authorities often mention the Ethiopians, who probably were formerly as black as they are presently. [. . .]

We should not seek the cause and origin of blackness in either sacred or secular history. The explanation can be uncovered only by reflecting on the state of the world as well as the care which Providence takes daily regarding all of mankind. Certainly, the design of Providence was to populate the whole Universe: the discoveries made over the last 200 to 300 years prove that no country is totally devoid of inhabitants (except for a few islands distant from continents).

It appears, according to Moses's account in Genesis (9), 1), that Noah's descendants multiplied and extended beyond Armenia (where the Ark of the Covenant was); 2) that they penetrated as far as Babylonia, where they must have settled before erecting a considerable city and the Tower of Babel; 3) that construction of this Tower could not have been begun until long after the Flood, since they could not have acquired [in such a short time] enough knowledge to build such a huge structure; 4) that they still all spoke the same language; and hence mankind dispersed after the Tower of Babel was built; finally, 5) we cannot date the origin of different languages and the dispersal of peoples until many years after the Flood.[1]

From this, I conclude that once each tribe scattered, they sought a new territory wherein to settle outside the Canaan lands alongside Egypt, and from there, over time, they spread out all over Africa—but only when Providence had given blackness to their bodies in order to enable them to bear the extreme heat of that land. Egyptian writers claim their land belongs to Antiquity, which supports my opinion; perhaps the first kings of Egypt built the immense Pyramids more to serve as retreats in case of a second Flood than to serve as tombs.[2]

This summarizes the accepted view, but if one considers what I say here about Providence being determined to populate the whole world as He had created it, then one senses a difficulty, namely, God could not have made an error in creating lands in both cold and torrid zones that now seem almost uninhabitable, despite the fact that historians boast about the great age of these lands. I, [however], can explain this as well as the blackness of Negroes. [. . .]

To uncover the veritable cause of the blackness of Negroes, I will begin by demonstrating how Providence aided the people to settle in the cold zones and survive there, then I will look at the means used to populate the Torrid Zone.

After the scattering of tribes that originated in the temperate lands of Asia, how could people settle in such cold lands as the glacial zone? These cold lands were populated just as early as (or shortly after) the more temperate regions. While this seems like an incongruity, we can resolve this if we accept the judicious opinion of an English author who plausibly maintains that the Divinity during Creation did not create ice, but only waters, along with the property of their freezing, and it was only gradually that they became blocked off as the ice increased in size, as it currently does on an annual basis.[3]

Following this argument, we may conclude: 1) that at the beginning of the world, the lands of the glacial zones had no ice at all and could not have been so cold as they are now. The proximity of ice itself makes things cold; the absence of the Sun—without which nobody would want to settle there— produces new ice; 2) that ice fields [glaciers] gradually formed and as their vastness increased, these tribes became gradually accustomed to the cold; 3) that Providence granted them a stronger temperament to resist such climate; we see today that women and those who lead sedentary and comfortable lives have a much more delicate and white skin than those who spend their lives in the open air or in hard work and who also have more robust temperaments.

[. . .] Now I must explain how Providence peopled the Torrid Zone with inhabitants and why some of them are black, while others are white or swarthy.

We need to consider: 1) that although the sun is the first principle of heat, this heat is doubled by reflection (or else diminished) due to external causes; 2) this is why, in the Torrid Zone, the amount of heat differs in various lands, even when [they] are situated at the same distance from the equator; and 3) that in the opinion of all modern philosophes, black is the color that best resists heat.

We know for certain that heat is greater in Africa and similar regions than it is in America, though both are located between the Tropics. Various European nations have made settlements in America, where they have propagated without trouble and can maintain themselves as well as in their native countries. Although some of these settlements are at an equal distance from the equator as Africa is, the heat there is not as strong. Africa was discovered a long time before America and although various nations have become masters of certain tropical lands, they built no fixed settlements in Africa. Their conquests were made only to ensure trade; they do not bring their wives there to reproduce, they only go there to acquire wealth and then retire to their native countries.

The few Portuguese (who might be an exception) do not count because they mate without regret with Negresses, and their descendants gradually acquire the color of their maternal ancestors, which helps them resist the excessive heat.[4] So I conclude that since Africa is more virulently [hot], [...] the inhabitants destined by Providence to people these lands could not have survived had not the Divinity (which perpetually looks after the human species) imprinted them (and other peoples in similar lands) with this black color. I believe the Imprinting took place when they first settled in these lands, probably not long after the dispersal.

This line of reasoning explains various issues: 1) the glacial zones and America could become populated because the cold was not so excessive there, so it was easy to spread out and penetrate everywhere by routes that have since been blocked by ice; 2) some lands are much colder than others although equally removed from the equator; many northern peoples made long treks across Europe (they were the principal cause for the fall of the Roman Empire) and at various times explored the world. [...]

[The author here theorizes how wind blowing over the sea gradually produced the cold lands and ice associated with the far North.]

IN THESE UNFORTUNATE CLIMATES, the Divinity did not just give men the strength to help them bear excessive cold, but also placed there animals suitable to this climate that can withstand the cold and multiply extraordinarily, as demonstrated by the great quantity of pelts of wolves, bears, foxes, beavers, and sables—all animals with long fur. The inhabitants of the North send their surplus furs as far away as the temperate lands.

These lands that are too cold for the large livestock of the temperate regions have reindeer, which serve the inhabitants better than horses could when traveling, since they are able to drink the deer's milk and eat the deer's flesh.[5] However, if transported to temperate lands the reindeer would die; indeed, both the men and the animals of these cold regions are so well-suited to the climate that they would have trouble surviving elsewhere.

[...]

I believe the above is sufficient proof of the following propositions: 1) Providence took care to put the inhabitants of Arctic lands in a state to get habituated to that climate and probably took the same care for the people of the Antarctic, who are almost unknown to us. 2) Apparently, it also gave the inhabitants destined to inhabit burning climates the means to bear the excessive heat of their lands: this is blackness. No matter when this happened, they benefited from beginning to turn black; I will now list the reasons for their color.

My main proof of the cause of the blackness of Negroes will be drawn from the location of the lands they inhabit, which I must explain before going any further: why the Sun's strength is redoubled in certain lands but diminished in others.

Nobody will deny that some lands at a certain distance from the equator are hotter than others at a parallel [latitude], or that a land sitting on the equator (or very close to it) is sometimes less hot than another land at thirty-five or even forty degrees. It is an old error to believe that proximity to (or distance from) the equator is the sole cause of heat; generally, those who have lived a long time in Batavia all maintain that although this famous city is only about five degrees from the equator, it is less hot than in Bengal which is beyond twenty degrees; I could cite many examples that prove this, from Asia to Africa or America.[6]

[. . .]

The coast of Guinea, lying almost on the equator, although in general burning and unhealthy for Europeans, is less harmful to them than the Kingdom of Benin, which lies at a parallel latitude; since this difference cannot result from the strength of the sun, which is the same in both places, it must result only from the winds and the geography. Although Biledulgerid is over twenty-five degrees from the equator, the heat there is very strong, and therefore cannot be attributed to the sun's strength alone, but mostly to the sands and the deserts that fill this land, and also somewhat to the wind that blows there, which in passing over the arid desert sands becomes charged with the heat imprinted by the sun.[7]

[. . .]

I could cite many more examples taken from the four corners of the known world to prove undeniably what I have advanced, namely that different levels of heat occur in lands equidistant from the equator, for which one could give four principal reasons: First, that the arrangement of mountains contributes to heating or cooling a land, whether by preventing winds from penetrating, or because the sun shines its rays on naked rocks, which redoubles the reflection [radiation] in the plains, an effect that is missing when lands are covered with trees and plants and black earth. A second reason comes from waters that by their natural coolness and their river courses make the air move and render the terrain capable of producing plants, trees, and roots, which dig into the earth and prevent radiation. The third and principal reason comes from the winds. All travelers agree that almost the entire Torrid Zone has trade winds that blow almost perpetually and temper the piercing heat because they have not passed over burning sands where there is no shade. This is the reason for the intense heat felt in the greater part of Africa, where there are few rivers in proportion to the large extent of the land and where one sees only arid deserts in waterless areas. [. . .]

The fourth reason may also be attributed to the territory itself, for many voyagers claim that the African terrain is mostly whitish and gleaming, which vastly increases [radiation], so that Africa's inhabitants are subject to violent eye diseases, notably in Egypt, the Cape of Good Hope, and elsewhere. [. . .]

I think this suffices to prove that in some regions the sun's heat is twice as intense, particularly in Africa; I will avoid prolixity and not present further proofs of this.

In conclusion, the goal of Divinity in creating the world was to people it entirely, as experience confirms. We should infer from the command given in Genesis (9:1) in which God tells mankind to be fruitful and multiply and fill the earth, that the earth was at the time still in a state of perfection, thus even the Northern lands could be populated. Later, at the time of the earliest settlements in Africa, in order to make this terrain suitable for settlement, the Divinity imprinted this black color on the inhabitants who went to settle there. This must have marked their type.

[. . .]

The Divinity could not populate these burning lands with the same quality of men as those descending from Noah without endowing them with some necessary protection. He made them different from the rest by making them black, a color that seems to break up and diminish the strength of the sun's rays so as to resist this redoubled heat. This color was originally in them, and their bodies were disposed to adopt it. While they may seem different from the rest of mankind, that is not really so, since their children are born white and only acquire blackness gradually a few weeks after birth.

It seems that Providence assigned [Negroes] to this climate. Here are some of the reasons: 1) they are not happy and do not multiply at all in other lands, even when they live equally close to the equator, as they do in their native lands; 2) one finds no Negro at all in temperate regions unless he was transported there by force; 3) those who live in lands closest to Negroes are more or less swarthy in proportion to their proximity to them, although their color is not intrinsic as it is in Negroes; swarthiness became necessary for them only in order to be able to negotiate with both Negroes and with the inhabitants of temperate lands; 4) Europeans, either in their own lands or when traveling to hot lands, acquire this color by a simple accidental cause [e.g., tanning] which ceases when they leave, whereas Negroes remain black, as do their descendants even if they are born in temperate climates. They long to return to these burning lands, whereas Europeans long to see their homelands again and live peacefully on the wealth they have amassed at the risk of their lives.

[. . .]

The conclusion is that a few centuries after the dispersal of peoples throughout the world, Providence sent inhabitants to the burning lands and made them black so that they would be able to bear the heat. It was from these inhabitants that Negros descended, inheriting along with life itself the blackness of their first ancestors, which continued from century to century and still continues today.

[If this dissertation is approved, the Directors of the Foundation of the late duc de La Force are requested to notify Michel de Cutter, a Merchant in the Hague in Holland, who will communicate it to the Author, whose name he will give later.[8]]

# 7

## Blackness as a Result of Heat and Humidity

One can imagine that the scientifically minded members of the Bordeaux Academy would have found this short essay written in French to be ridiculous. The submission begins by emphasizing both the power and intelligence of a divinely engineered Nature. The author then puts forward his theory of blackness according to a series of curious analogies. Basing his views on the way that paper, wax, coal, and various other substances react to heat, fire, light, and humidity, he maintains that Africans are nothing more than humans whose lips and noses have been swollen or flattened by the burning heat of the Torrid Zone, and whose skin has turned black due to this same heat and humidity (which supposedly produces an overabundance of pores that do not reflect light, allowing Africans to remain healthy by sweating more profusely). This essay is perhaps less indicative of climatological submissions in this section than it is of the drifts of science and mythology that were circulating among many people during the century of Enlightenment.

N ATURE SO LOVES DIVERSITY that it is not content with making all sorts of different animal species corresponding principally to the climates that produce them. It also amuses itself by engendering an infinite variety of people, which results most notably in a wide variety of different [colored people].[1] In the case of Negroes, this cannot be considered an accident; it is an inseparable property that distinguishes them from other men.

Nature has constituted the Negro such that the heat of the sun produces an effect in him that is quite contrary to that of the sun's light. In short, light illuminates the Negro and heat darkens him. The sun's light and heat acts upon the Negro as it does on any object, since the same star that darkens the Ethiopian also whitens cloth and wax. And yet, in Negroes the [effects of] heat are increased by humidity, which one might expect. This is also how the sun affects coal, gangrene, and those parts of the human body that are struck by lightning.

If the first qualities that affected objects were to adopt a color, then cold would no doubt be white, as is seen in water, ice, snow, and the white fur of animals that live at the poles.[2] This would be particularly true at the Arctic

Circle, where every living thing is white, even though the animals, such as the bear and the hare, are of the same species as ours.

[. . .]

If heat had [one] color, it would be red, since we see that it gives this color to faces that were previously pale, and to iron and wood that are on fire. Superfluous humidity suffocates this heat, and in extinguishing it leaves the color of corruption, which is blackness.[3] And, as we see, the whitest skin is blackened by heat when traveling to the south. The opposite occurs in those who travel northward, the climates of which produce men and women who are as white as the peoples of the south are black.

All that has just been said proves that after humidity, the sun is the secondary cause of this blackness. Another proof is that everything that stays in [a] fire to the point of being burned at some point turns black, with a few exceptions. But how does the sun produce this state? In Negroes, this is due to the heat causing a greater degree of sweat than among the inhabitants of cold countries, and by multiplying the pores of their skin so that it is infinitely riddled with them, which keeps them healthy.

We may be convinced that the color black comes only from the black body being more garnished with pores, which reflects back fewer effective rays of the light than do bodies that have fewer pores. And to be convinced of this truth, merely consider with the aid of a microscope a piece of coal and you will see how prodigiously many pores it has. This is sufficiently proved by those who have shared their experiments with the public.[4]

Since the sun (and the sun's heat) is only the secondary cause of the blackness of Negroes, something other than the sun may produce more or less heat in men, and engender in them more or less sweat. These phenomena, consequently, would render them more or less black. This explains the different [levels of] blackness that are found among peoples of the same climate. The very humid temperament of some will prevent this heat of the sun acting on them with the same rigor as it acts on others. And consequently, they will not be as black as their compatriots.

Perhaps it is not necessary here to prove the opinion that the blackness of Negroes comes from the few effective rays that their bodies reflect. Nor is it necessary for me to observe that this negro-black is by no means the [pure] color black, so to speak, since some [anatomists] have tried to extract this black color from their skin [by putting it in] some water for this purpose.

How did the first men who inhabited these burning lands become black? This [process] took place gradually, with the first Negroes being slightly blackened, the second ones more so, etc., but how were their other properties formed, like their big lips, flat noses, etc.[?][5] Did something else distort them? The heat might have produced these traits by shortening certain muscles of the skin or certain nerves. This results from the pores of their skin being [subject to] so many humors that their sweat makes it hard to exit or to reach daylight easily. The resistance they find in the tissue of the tunic layer of the skin—which is tighter than elsewhere—obliges [the sweat] to seek tissues that are more open than those of this tunic. Blackness is simply caused by a body reflecting back parts of the effective rays on the light, just as is the case with Whites.

A multitude of effective rays also produces the whiteness of teeth formed by tooth enamel. And if this tissue is broken by some liqueur or bitter or corrosive humor, then the tooth becomes black. And since it appears that the temperament of Negroes is due to all sorts of liqueurs or corrosive humors, therefore dry heat also enters into this temperament.[6] The enamel of their teeth is less corroded than that of other peoples' whose temperament is not so dry. One proof that Negroes are of a very dry temperament is that they rarely spit. All this proves that their teeth are less affected by corrosive liqueurs when they drink than are those of other peoples.[7]

**An mutare potest aethiops cutem suam** . . . [Can the Ethiopian change his skin . . .]

# 8 ⌒

# Blackness as a Reversible Accident

The author of this essay asserts that the diversity of color among the world's peoples has a simple explanation related to climate and anatomy. Black Africans, red Americans, and dusky Asians, he argues, are variously affected by the unhealthy life outside the temperate zone. To prove this climate-based theory, he delves deeply into the work of the anatomists Herman Boerhaave and Jacques Winslow. In parallel to this anatomical discussion, which he developed in Latin, the essayist makes three important climate-based assertions that remained touchstones during the eighteenth century. First is the author's assertion that a "pleasant whiteness" is the original color or prototype; the second is that Africans' color is "artificial" or accidental; the final point is that the so-called Ethiopian color need not be permanent. Indeed, the writer offers himself as proof of this theory, claiming that he had an "African" great-great-grandfather, and that traces of this blackness have all but disappeared in his own skin. The original form of the essay was a series of numbered assertions with interspersed references to various scholars and scientists. It has been streamlined and made more discursive for ease of reading.

[. . .]

### THOUGHTS ON THE CAUSE OF BLACKNESS IN THE ETHIOPIANS:
### OBSERVATIONS ON THE EVIDENCE FOR JUDGING THAT
### CLIMATE IS THE CAUSE

The human body contains a large amount of blood vessels: from these originate the watery [*serosa*] vessels; from these the lymph vessels, etc.[1] This is proven by anatomy, and substantiated by analogy.

In some of these vessels red blood circulates in a perpetual circle; in others, yellow fluid [*serum*] circulates; in others again, white lymph [*lympha*] circulates. These vessels are either arteries or veins.

[The author goes on to describe the circulation of sweat in "sweat arteries," his understanding of the lymphatic system, and finally how the skin is changed when various anatomical liquids are pushed toward the surface of the body.]

The color of human skin varies, so that according to common observation and to Linnaeus, Europeans are called white [*albus*], Americans reddish [*rubescens*], Asians dusky [*fuscus*], and Africans black [*niger*]; infinite other variations can hardly be expected, since all human varieties obviously proceed from the same source.[2]

Every anatomist agrees that all this difference in color must reside essentially in the Malpighian reticular membrane, and anatomical experiments confirm it.[3] And indeed, Ruysch always found in the Ethiopian man a completely black reticular membrane; in the semi-Ethiopian he found a more diluted black; in the European, yellowish in those exposed to the sun [by working] in the fields, but white in those not much exposed to the harshness of the sun; and the corpses of European men are so white that the membrane can hardly be detected.[4] As to its blackness, Heisterus explained that in Ruysch's study, in order for the external face of the membrane to be black, it should also appear extremely black inside.[5]

Therefore, based on this point, there is a greater distribution of the humors between the skin [*cutis*] and the Malpighian membrane, than between the membrane and the epidermis [*epidermida*].

Although this physiological truth may not bring about the cause of blackness from within, it nevertheless proves by its liquid nature that liquids can certainly become condensed, so as to tinge the Malpighian membrane with different colors.

Therefore, the material cause is to be sought in the humors inside our bodies, insofar as it is easier for the humors to reach the internal surface of the Malpighian membrane than the external surface. And if Santorini had a material cause in mind, it can be explained by our own findings.

Should a cause acting from within not be sufficient, there should be another that can reconcile the presence of so much blackness in the reticular membrane, so as to last for an entire human life; nay, so as to be maintained by a fixed law for many successive generations of children.[6]

For if this cause were to be rejected due to some [physical] law, there ought to be another cause by which subcutaneous arterial liquids can become concentrated so that, the healthy circulation of the humors being maintained, only the smallest lymphatic and serous molecules are carried to the Malpighian membrane. Having chased away their extremely limpid and moist medium, the molecules can dry to an intense yellowness, or even to blackness, which will impress itself most firmly on the walls of the [Malpighian] membrane and fill all its thinnest little holes. This blackness will be found not only in the Ethiopian man: the change in color is also present in all men.

I have inferred this familiar experiment from the actions of the chemicals in the preceding paragraph, whose agent left behind a certain amount of serum, [which when] heated by an external fire evaporated to the point of dryness, leaving a black earthy dust which when distilled produces an oil, dual in nature, both light and heavy, etc.[7]

Again, from my own experience in anatomy, and supported by the indisputable experiments of the celebrated Leeuwenhoek and Boerhaave, I similarly theorize that the humors of the human body separate from each other to a very great degree, with the blood providing material to all of them.[8] The blood, restricted to such a degree in its smallest passages, so that not even one globule can cross through the narrowest arteriole, gives origin to the serum. On the other hand, the serum-carrying arterioles having been now reduced in diameter, they more fully block free passage to the serous globule, and the lymphatic globules created by the broken-up mass of serous globules spread throughout their own channels. Any that remain will pass gradually through the smaller ducts of the human body up to the nerves, while others will reach the most distant vessels that supply the cheeks.

And so serum and lymph, and the oily humor of the small subcutaneous cells as well, warm up their molecules, which, once their fluids have been driven off by some unexpected cause, become compacted and take the form of a dry powder. Therefore, if we have shown that a desiccating force exists, the same could also apply to the Malpighian membrane moistened by fluids. Therefore, I have demonstrated the truth of the proposition.

Some time ago it happened that the skin of an exceptionally white man, exposed to the bright sun, was changed after becoming saturated with a yellowish color in all its naked parts, but still retained his native color (based on experience).

This change occurs more quickly just before and after the summer solstice and during the same, than in winter, spring, or late autumn (based on experience).

The same man [when exposed to] the intensely bright sky during the [summer] solstice, when the air is calm (especially when it threatens to rain and the rays of the sun flow together ever more through refraction), feels the blood flowing even more on his bare skin, a very gentle, prickly tickling or if you prefer, a subtle lacerating heat (based on experience).

That color, the same color that people of the North acquire in summer, during the winter tends to gradually fade away (from experience).

The reason why the color of the body's covered parts does not change during that period, unlike the color of the naked parts, must be sought externally. It must be attributed to a force that moves subcutaneous fluids and excites the skin by prickling, expelling liquid molecules through the sweat arteries serving perspiration and leaving the denser, earthy residue fixed to the Malpighian layer by [the action of] the oily, fatty, and sticky properties of the cellulose membrane, until it colors [the skin] with a yellow color, which is proper to serum. This efficacious force is due to the rays of the sun.

In the summer, in our climate, the sun is nearly perpendicular, but in winter it is extremely oblique: therefore, when the cause ceases, the effect also ceases.

Therefore, the more perpendicular rays the sun emits, and the longer the rays' action continues with sustained strength, the greater will be the effect of heat and warmth on the human body, and the quicker and more lasting the coloring of the Malpighian layer.

By the same token, when the sun's rays fall on our skin more obliquely or nearly horizontally, for a shorter time, and less forcefully, the action of our fluids is diminished and there is less change in the color of our skin.

Since the changing of color ceases at different times, it must be artificial. This means that it is a variation, not a kind [species], hence it is neither [inherently] natural nor established by God from the beginning of the world.[9]

The Ethiopian, when brought to a temperate or frigid climate, begets swarthy children by a white European wife. These children are either minimally black or not at all black like their father. The color changes gradually from the original blackness among successive generations [born in] the same frigid climate and from white mothers. Grandchildren, or certainly the distant descendants, will have no blackness in their skin but will show the same color as the rest of the inhabitants of their land (from experience). Indeed, I can prove this by the evidence of my own family line. That is to say, although my color is the same as that of my people [nationis], I am nevertheless the distant descendant [lit., the great-great-grandson] of an Ethiopian who was brought from Africa to Germany by Emperor Charles V during the war in Mauritania, and whose children gradually turned from a black to a white color.[10]

Therefore, the truth is confirmed: the color of the Ethiopians is not inherent. This is also proved by the fact that the closer the region is to the equator, the blacker the inhabitants become; likewise, the farther from the equator, the more people are of a more diluted tawny color, and, ultimately, become white.

On the other hand, where people experience the greater heat of the sun and the perpendicular fall of its rays throughout the year, since more parts of the body are bare or at least only very slightly clothed, they are more exposed to the sun (by experience), hence the more effective the action.

Although a variety of colors exists in man, God indeed created only one true kind [*species*] of man.[11] It follows that in the beginning the first men were of one color. Evidently, the fluids of their healthy bodies, undisturbed by any foreign cause, favorably disposed the [Malpighian] reticular layer. This is also found in the Holy Scriptures, and sound reasoning avers it.

A healthy man, rarely exposed to the solar rays, and living in a place receiving only oblique sunlight, has a whitish [*albicans*] color: therefore, this is the color of creation. Hence, in primeval times white men [*albidi*] came first, and they lived their life exposed to the [oblique] rays of the sun. Therefore, the color of the Ethiopians and the many colors of the other nations suggest that they are artificial.

In this way, the fourth or fifth generation living under temperate and frigid skies would turn from the Ethiopian color into a pleasing white. Hence, we can suppose that a sixth or tenth generation living under a torrid climate would make people Ethiopian, which agrees with experience and with theory.

Therefore the sun, almost constantly sending down perpendicular rays in regions near the Torrid Zone, and said situation continuing for a long series of years, is responsible for the changes in the Malpighian layer.

Undoubtedly, the number of generations thriving under the perpetual action of the sun, imbued with the same color by their parents, with their offspring eventually more uniform and equal also under the covered parts [of the skin], did bring about blackness [*nigredinem*]. Nor is there any cause other than the sun: therefore truth is more clearly brought to light from contrasting examples.

To this we should add other secondary [lit., remote] causes. For example, the sandy soil scarcely absorbs the sun's rays, instead reflecting them back; and we see every day that sailors who have been on sea voyages (because water likewise reflects back the rays) are more colored than those who are left on land. Hence, the greater the action of the sun, the faster and more abundant evaporation of certain fluids through the arterial outlets, and the condensation of the residual earthy particles, produce a gradually richer color.

And anything at all can produce the same effectiveness of external fire, if only its desiccating power could be unleashed with equal strength over a sufficiently long period of time. This is analogous to the blackness of the gangrenous parts. Therefore, it is also clear that those parts of the body covered by light clothing would be colored in the same way as if the limbs were affected by the close perpetual heat of the sun.

The circular path of the humors under the skin being compressed, the system of vessels near the skin is affected by the same increased stimulus, and preserves residual sequelae in such a way that the same sharp tool of judgment will be able to assess its impact only over a long period of time and over the course of generations.[12] I will not mention the effect of the heat, also heightened by the sun under the clothes, that opens wide the arterial outlets of the skin, and the fluid having dissipated, the residual oily and earthy part impresses itself more deeply on the reticular membrane, etc.

It is obvious, therefore, which parts above others affect the black brilliance to a greater or lesser degree, which parts blackish [*nigricantis*] with oil and earth heat the abundant glands and the thick, oily fattiness.

Therefore, neither the dense whitish coating of the eyes nor the structure of the Malpighian layer that lacks oily fluid can be tinged by this blackness.

Even the short and crisp hair of the Ethiopians is derived from the same burned glandular fattiness dense with fluid; a meager but effective nourishment that feeds the hair's narrow elastic tubes.

[The essay stops here, without a conclusion or a signature.]

# 9

## Blackness as a Result of Hot Air and Darkened Blood

The author, a military man writing in French, opens his essay by affirming that all humans descend from the same ancestors. He then rejects the idea that there is an essential anatomical source for black skin that might suggest a separate origin for Africans, since this would contradict Scripture. Having made his viewpoint clear, he then arrives at his theory: that the hot air of a tropical climate affects the color of African blood, which affects the skin color; he also stipulates that different climates can affect human behavior and quality of mind. This point allows him to assert one of the foundations of European climatological theory: that the human race has reached its full potential in the temperate zone, and that Europeans surpass all other human varieties from cold and hot climates in mind, body, and joie de vivre.

Gentlemen,

I made only a very superficial study of Physics [natural sciences] in my youth, and then I spent a number of years engaged in military service; applying myself [to this competition subject] has thus given rise to a study that does not attempt to decrypt the nature of the created world in any way. Indeed, it is with both impulsiveness and temerity that I am presenting my conjectures on the subject proposed by your Royal Academy, a group of men with both fair and refined judgment. I have nonetheless been emboldened for a reason that will not displease you, Messieurs: I do this for the sake of the Holy Revelation, which is under siege by nonbelievers who have outdone themselves in a book entitled *Voyages and Adventures of Jacques Massé*. Spawned in England, this book questions the truth of the story handed down to us by Moses [in the Old Testament], namely the creation of a single man, father of all humankind. Indeed, this book insinuates that the body of a Moor has a different structure [. . .] and that his blackness comes from a web [of sorts], from a thin membrane that forms an envelope under the epidermis that indicates that he is a creature completely distinct from others.[1]

[. . .]

Our world is inhabited by men whose skin varies by an infinity of shades ranging from white to black. The peoples who inhabit cold lands, where the air and earth are moistened by frequent and abundant rains and snowfalls, have lands that are full of forests, and where the abundance of pastures procures nourishment of sweet and flowing sap. These are the lands, all things considered, where we generally find the most white-skinned people. On the contrary, the peoples who are placed in the hottest climates, exposed to an air charged with dry exhalations or bitter vapors attracted by winds or the closeness of seas, who are nourished by beasts and plants of a more quintessential sap, are the blackest. And it is reported that between these [extreme] climates we discover the variety of skin color that reigns in mankind. This is also the case regarding the quality of minds, if not in the same proportion, then at least with very noticeable differences.[2] This being so, it seems to me we have to attribute the color of Negroes to two causes, one internal and the other external. The internal one is the quality of blood, and the external one is the nature of the air. To be clear, the quality of the air is the sole determining principle of this phenomenon, since it establishes the nature of the blood.

[. . .]

Skin color varies of course due to our state of health. Our state of health depends on the smooth functioning of our body and all the parts that compose its mechanism; our body certainly functions like a hydraulic machine, since it is by the circulation of the blood that everything is fed or [by the lack of circulated blood] that everything dies. Thus, it is in the blood that we should seek the differences among men.[3]

The human body branches into innumerable vessels of an infinity of different sizes, such that there are some so thin that they admit only a lymphatic part of blood and not its red part. According to anatomists, red blood consists of an assemblage of a certain number of globules that compose the liquids of the human body. Vessels of this tiny dimension are located primarily on the surface of the body, where it is easy to sweat a transparent liqueur starting with the surface of the skin. These tubes full of their transparent liquors might no doubt contribute to the whiteness of the skin.

The color of the skin varies perceptibly by the quality of the blood, since an inflammation of bile gives an entirely yellow tint.[4] A doctor even sometimes judges the nature of the blood from a flushed face and the dark red of a sick person he meets. Thus the blood contributes to coloring the skin.

I remember when I was working in military architecture, I reduced the dark color of carmine ink and Chinese ink by diluting them with water. In a similar way, it might not be ridiculous to assert that blood might be of a darker color due to the lesser quantity of aqueous particles that maintain its fluidity. If blood color is darker, the skin's color must be affected by it even more because it will be less lined with vessels that contain a transparent liquor, which necessarily softens the color of the blood vessels that they must govern.

The less the blood is charged with aqueous particles, the less it will be able to supply the tiny vessels that are too small to allow red particles to circulate. So these vessels must be less swollen, and may even become desiccated due to the quality of the air outside. Thus the skin must lose part of its whiteness.

The hotter a climate, the more it causes the dissipation of liquids from all bodies, such that there are only the most solid parts [of the body] that can endure [this phenomenon]. Thus, the lymphatic vessels [in hot countries] are more liable to be impaired because they have fewer food resources. The warmer a country, the more human bodies are exposed, since they cannot bear adjustments [i.e., clothing] that might hinder imperceptible transpiration. The outside air always predominates, and consequently the skin of inhabitants must deviate more from the color white, as can be noticed. But it is essential to point out that people who are closest in color to either the most extreme examples of Whites or Negroes try to increase the radiance of their complexions in one direction or the other. The Moors, I have been told, even apply ointments from birth to give themselves the most beautiful black skin. Similarly, our Europeans use *balm of Mecca* to give their complexion a dazzling whiteness.[5] Therefore it is [a combination of] the quality of the climate, the quality of the blood, and the quality of the food—aided a little by artifice—that causes the blackness of Negros. There is also variation between persons who lead a delicate life and those who work cultivating the land or at heavy labor.

[. . .]

The blood of the inhabitants of hot lands has fewer aqueous particles. And yet, it does not necessarily follow that these peoples do not have enough fluidity to enjoy good health. This fluidity may continue to function thanks to a greater abundance of active and spirituous parts, just as blood does in those little birds that can survive the most rigorous winters. The blood of those who live in hot countries does not need the body's organs to be emptied by such abundant sweat. Among Whites this can produce a kind of furor, but Whites have the advantage of smaller body mass in volume and in phlegm. And they have agility to spare.

Therefore, it is the quality of the climate, of the blood, of the food, aided by a little human intervention, that causes the blackness of the Moor. This color will also degenerate [change] when they are transported outside their land according to: 1) the age at which they are taken from their country; 2) the color of the inhabitants where they go; 3) the whiteness of persons they will come to marry. And as for the change in the Moors themselves, it is scarcely perceptible because, as I have said, the lymphatic vessels of the skin will dry out, or rather, having suffered from a lack of lymph, they cannot resume their activity, or turn color. This is why if some change occurs in the color of a Negro, it will be for the worse; he will lose the brilliance of his complexion; the lack of heat in the air will make his skin less unctuous and therefore rougher and maybe even scaly.

I have asked myself why, if all my principles were carefully judged, the children of a Moor are not suddenly born the color of the natives where they were procreated. Here is why this doesn't work. First, we must make a distinction between the sexes. I am persuaded that a change [in complexion] would be more significant if a Negress married a blond man in some land in the north than if a Moor married a blonde woman, because the female's role in generation [reproduction] of the species is probably only (as is the case for females of all animals) to conserve deposits from the male.[6]

[. . .] The result is that, all other things being equal, the children must correspond more to the nature of fathers, because conception is effectively the transmission of their own substance [to the mothers]. The quality of the blood and the nature of the skin are transmitted (albeit with a certain alteration) as is the case with hereditary illnesses and physical resemblances that may be passed down. The process of generation that I have just described might also be supported by pointing to the influence of the imagination of mothers, to which has been attributed a power to make surprising impressions on the offspring they are bearing. [. . .]

I hope I have given satisfying reasons for the degeneration of Negroes. And here I must observe that this theory of degeneration negates the system of the unbelievers, since degeneration could not take place if the color black stemmed from a distinctly created black seed. This also explains the corresponding changes that occur in a European who goes to Africa.

After this it will not be difficult to explain the nature of the hair of Moors, which is short, thin, frizzy, and like a kind of wool or cotton, due to the fact that this type of hair lacks vegetative humidity. Each hair is obliged to force [itself through] a tortuous passage, so to speak, and to escape via a route that is not at all a straight line. In addition to being exposed to very low humidity, these hairs find themselves in dry and burning air; everybody knows that hair is an excrescence of the skin on the head, so if this skin is tightened and deprived of lymphatic vessels, the hairs appear to be crinkled by the force with which the humor reached daylight after a difficult passage, at which point it encounters dry and burning air. [. . .]

I can also finish by explaining the particularities of Negroes, like their huge whitish eyes, their milky teeth, their lower lip that is large and red, and their nose with its large nostrils. These singularities were not a major part of my discussion because they are of little consequence. The whiteness of their eyes and their teeth simply arises because they contrast strongly with their complexion, which would be less the case among Europeans. Food also contributes to the conservation of their teeth as well as the care one takes to keep a clean mouth. The inhabitants of mountains who eat a lot of dairy always have dazzling tooth enamel. The climate of Africans is such that African fruits ripen to a point of maturity that strips them of the corrosives that harm teeth in countries of the north. Moreover, Negroes do not need to protect themselves against the rigors of winter by the use of fire, which is very harmful to teeth. Perhaps they use less sweetness and eat fewer stews spoiled by herbs and spices.

Although the lips of Moors are red, they are not vermillion like those of northern peoples. They are not black but a dark red, the skin that envelops them is finer and more transparent, more moistened by the saliva glands of the mouth, and so they do not dry out; their lips conserve the colors of the blood vessels lining them.

We could regard the thickness of the lips and the snub shape of the nose of Moors as traits that are perpetuated at least as much by artifice as by the generation of species. I have heard it said that these are prized traits in Africa, and it is easy to produce them [artificially], just as one sees the Chinese crush the noses of their children at birth to correspond to the fashion of the country.[7] Some people may impose upon the muzzle of a newborn puppy the shape they love in dogs. [. . .]

Perhaps it was the philosopher who affirmed that the noses of this species were the only truly beautiful noses (because they opened a more splendid door to the aromatic world) who put forward a philosophy among Africans that was created in his own nose's honor!

Although it means putting forward an opinion that may raise predictable and considerable objections, I cannot conceal that it might be said of white skin that it carries with it a type of languid manner, and that vivacity belongs to the brown-skinned peoples. But this would mean that the eyes of Moors would be sparkling, whereas they have always appeared dull, if my memory of those few I have seen is right.

I am unable to speak of the natural inclinations of these people; I do not know if they are lively, penetrating, or bad-tempered. But it does seem to me that the eye of a Negress must be less sparkling than that of a brown-skinned woman in a hot but less ardent climate, because the blood of Africans must be, I repeat, less fluid and of more sluggish circulation. Consequently, there must be less activity in their minds.[8] Perhaps the white of their eye, which contrasts so strongly with their black complexion, also makes them appear duller.

It is time to conclude. I will do so by praying that you pay attention to all I have said about the quality of the blood as the explanation for the slowness of Moors' minds. I would also ask you to recall what I have said about the phlegmatic nature of northern peoples, who are more generally white than otherwise. It takes a lot to inspire these northern peoples to move; they walk at the pace of a tortoise, and are hardly inspired to enjoy the first sweetness of any pleasure to which they give themselves. There is too much humidity, just as there is too little in the burning climates. It is only in intermediate regions, especially the warmer ones, that we find fertility and agile minds, an agreeable activity in external manners, and a delicate sensibility in pleasures.

Forgive me, gentlemen, if I have exceeded the boundaries you have prescribed; I return to the deference and respect I owe you, concluding that with all possible reason that impiety has blinded those who have tried to attack the account of our Sacred Authors. Nothing is as possible and as true as that God created a single man (Genesis 1:27; Luke 3:38).

That "*God created of one blood all nations of men*" is my sentence (Acts 18:26).[9]

I have the honor of being, with the sentiment of the most respectful consideration, Gentlemen of the Royal Society, your very humble and very obedient Servant.

"Nothing is as possible and as true as that God created a single man."

# 10

## Blackness as a Result of a Darkened Humor

Matthew Hickes was an Irish medical doctor from the parish of Kilstrustan, Elphin diocese.[1] Writing to the academy in Latin, he begins his essay by making a clear distinction between the darkening effect of the hot sun on the skin in Africa and the other tropical zones of the world, in particular, America. With only a few exceptions, he continues, African skin is by far darker than in these other regions. The only explanation for this phenomenon, he asserts, lies in the combustible substances burning within the earth in Africa. Hickes argues that the classic term *Aethiops* (burned face) derives from the power of this black humor to darken the skin, rather than solely by the rays of the sun. He then proceeds to "prove" his argument through the example of an analogous, well-known chemical procedure steeped in alchemical lore.

HYPOTHESIS ON THE NATURE AND CAUSE OF BLACKNESS IN THE
ETHIOPIANS, SUBMITTED BY LORD MATTHEW HICKES, AN IRISHMAN

We have learned from our gazette that your most distinguished society is awarding a prize to the person offering the most plausible hypothesis related to the source of blackness. [. . .] In my response, I maintain that the heat of the sun and vapors from the ground simultaneously act together to produce the blackness of the Ethiopians.[2]

We know that heat is a contributing factor to blackness because those who spend their lives under a hot sky, such as is the case for those people who live under the equator, have black skin. It is obvious that exhalations from the ground also contribute to blackness because people who live under the same climate in America are not as black as Africans. The same can be said of those who live in a temperate zone: they are seldom as black as the people from the Kaffir region.[3] Allow me to explain more clearly.

I posit that the air of certain regions is subject to various specific vapors raised by the heat of the sun and of underground fires from either saltpans or bituminous areas.[4] Through breathing, the air commingles with the man's blood or with his fluids or humors.

After a certain amount of circulation, the mixture or blend with the blood tends to evaporate. The blackness, resulting from said blending or mixing of fluids, becomes visible as it is sweated out. This fluid or humor flows and runs continuously, like an imperceptible stream, through the skin's pores like so many small vents; along the way, [this fluid] deposits a certain clinging type of soot, like ashes from gunpowder, that clings within and is immediately absorbed into the skin, imparting to the skin a black color that no artifice can hide. The term *Aethiops* [burnt or red-brown face] is derived from this.

I shall attempt to prove with just one experiment out of many that the blackness of the Ethiopians most likely results from such an admixture. We found that a thorough mixing of sulfur and mercury, which are opposite in color, produces an extremely black compound which scientists call the Ethiopian mineral on account of its blackness.[5] This compound can be made both with and without fire. When made with fire, it immediately turns black. When prepared without fire, it blackens over time when particles with these inherent characteristics are discharged from deep fissures or caves in Africa. As far as we have been able to ascertain, these particles are not found in other places, or if so, not in sufficient quantity [to produce this phenomenon].

According to the observations of our era's natural historians, the truth of this process may be verified by analogy. [Indeed], these men have always noticed blackness, or a color similar to it, in the blood of men suffering from fiery passions and accustomed to violent emotional states. The reason, they add, is that the structure of the pores forces the sooty part of the blood to flow back into the body's blood, like soot falling from a chimney, and as it starts to mingle with the sulfurous part of the blood it catches fire and burns; this gives rise to the blood's blackness and to certain illnesses.

To this I add, as all the dyers also know, that no black color can be created artificially in imitation of nature without mixing particles of an opposite kind.

From all the above premises, it is clear why Africans appear to be black but not, indeed, the [native peoples of] America who live in the same climate. It is because the vapors exhaling from fissures and caves in America are neither in the same ratio nor of the same kind as the vapors issuing from Africa. Or if they are, it could be that in America the vapors are enveloped and incorporated into different particles of an opposite kind, which is not the case for Africa.

The above explains the reason why Ethiopians migrating to distant lands seem to degenerate very little after a given number of years or even after many [generations].

The vapors from the lands to which Blacks migrate do not possess, as it were, the requisite nature or innate quality that produces blackness. Or, perhaps whatever might restore the lost soot exuded from the pores is lacking [in such environments], given that the source of the vapor discharge is usually found only in Africa.

You might wonder why it is the case that, if a source is exhausted or the vapors have dissipated, the people of these other regions do not become white.

I would respond that the first coloring has been so fixed and interwoven into the skin that no technique can remove it. Similarly, in men [hit by gunfire], the blackness branded into the skin by burnt gunpowder is usually indelible.

If you ask why the embryos and babies of Ethiopians living in faraway lands are born black, I might answer as follows: from the innate imagination of the man or of the mother, which sends out a shape-forming force or other power that firmly imprints the blackness and other contingent traits in the young fetus; or by heredity, just as we can see other qualities develop when the vital principles of the parents are transferred into the child.[6]

Therefore, I doubt that after a certain number of generations these traits will vanish.

Now I proceed to explain the phenomena pertaining to their hair. First, it is extremely black because it is stained by the sooty evaporation, clearly through the same process that causes the skin to be black.

Secondly, the hair is smoother because either the pores of the head from which hair grows are narrow and almost obstructed by the soot within, or the African air is very uniform, not impacted daily by foul weather. Because of this quality, the dry, salty air produces no unevenness in their hair or skin.[7]

And their hair is frizzy because a very fine matter, activating nutrient elements, contracts their fibers to such a degree that they must curl, almost in the same way that barbers are wont to curl hair with their curling iron.

I now end this essay with the saying below, add my name and fatherland to it, and add it to the other essays.

**This has been just a brief exposition.**
**There is no harm in trying.**

# II ⌒

## Blackness as a Result of Blood Flow

This submission came from a doctor, André Nyvert, who studied medicine in the famed University of Montpellier in southern France and later worked in the important market town of Provins. His anatomical approach to the matter of blackness reveals an interesting tension. On the one hand, he asserts that the bodily fluids and secretions of all people are the same, regardless of their color. On the other hand, he also explains that tropical heat lowers atmospheric pressure, thereby increasing the flow of blood through its relaxed vessels. The skin thus seems darker, an appearance that is enhanced when humors under African skin become burned by the sun. He also believes that human categories are profoundly mutable, and claims that Africans' "degeneration" back to whiteness can be encouraged through intermarriage, or by migration to a colder climate.[1]

[. . .]

The vessels [*vasa*] of the human body, which contain fluids or humors [*humoribus*], can change color. The diseases that occur in living beings, as well as forms of anguish of the soul, prove the truth of this proposition: namely, that a person's innate color can change gradually and imperceptibly, or almost instantaneously.[2] Inspections performed with the naked eye or with a microscope on cadavers after bleaching or soaking both the simple and composite parts [of the body] indubitably show that all the vessels of the human body are whitish. Based on this, we can see the traces of nature at work, and actually and physically understand how the cutaneous vessels of Blacks [*nigritarum*], which are [filled] with dark humor, become white. Similarly, we can also see how their skin is colored.

In humankind we find a variety of colors: in the temperate zones or the cold regions of Sweden, Denmark, England, France, and Germany, a pale or rosy complexion is common. In some of the slightly hotter regions of Europe, Asia, and America, the color is red or becomes richly darker. In the arid areas of Africa where the sun continually shines on the scorched inhabitants, the color is very dark [*atrum*].

Consequently, we find in all human beings a variety of fluid-filled vessels coursing through the skin and especially through the Malpighian web. Most or all of the blood extracted from the veins or arteries and examined in a dish appears to be of the same or nearly the same color. Everyone has the same color of urine, saliva, mucus, earwax, mother's milk, as well as male sperm; in every individual, [one finds] the same internal organs, the same structure of the fluid-pumping heart, and the same mode of propulsion from the ambulatory parts.

And so it follows that there must be a different structure [*apparatus*] of the vessels that circulate, secrete, and expel [fluids] in the skin [*cutis*] and in the Malpighian web. There must be either a difference in the diameter of the vessels, or an external cause, such that it communicates to the humors new qualities [*dotes*] carried there from a common pool of blood, whether by removing, augmenting, or adding qualities. Anatomical examinations done in autopsies teach us that the structure of the skin and of the Malpighian web of the Blacks is the same as that of all other men.

Still, the skin [of black people] is slightly thicker, as we can see from their lips, for indeed everyone knows that the second and third blood received from the veins into the major arteries propels it with the force of its contractions into smaller and smaller vessels, until finally it reaches the minute, most slender, imperceptible capillaries of the skin that are farthest from the heart.

[. . .]

It is the case, therefore, that in the hotter regions where Blacks live the air is exceedingly rarefied under the influence of the burning sun and, as such, the air pressure on the surface of their bodies is lighter. From the above premises, it follows that the more dilated the vessels of the skin and of the Malpighian web, the larger and more numerous their pores and the lower the resistance of the fluids coursing through the aforesaid vessels [the capillaries]; it is this that produces the wider passage for the mass of larger blood globules.

Experiments carried out by Leeuwenhoek have shown that the blood globules are clear when they have less mass and red when they have more.[3] Consequently, the vessels that course through the skin and the Malpighian web are filled with heavier globules and will appear to be black. If you were to introduce that within less contracted vessels, then the blood turns to black. You would have thus demonstrated the natural color of venous blood.

Fiery heat affects more than the rarefaction of the air: everyone who uses his senses knows how all fluids behave under the tyranny of the sun. The cellulose membrane beneath the [true] skin is covered with all sorts of muscles and equipped with arteries, nerves, lymphatic veins, and oily cells.[4]

When the oily and lymphatic components of the humors that irrigate this membrane are subjected to the action of heat, they will expand and the more fluid ones will escape; therefore the oily and sulfurous parts (which in temperate climates are collected for particular functions in the fatty cells of this membrane) will coalesce in the cutaneous vessels and reach the Malpighian web; there, they are heated again and again until they become rarefied.

The more volatile watery components will disperse as they evaporate into the air through wider pores, leaving the fatty, suet-like parts which have a hardier and more expanded consistency. These will adhere to the epidermis or cuticle and penetrate it, and will tinge it with a dark color as if they had been almost burnt by a continuous but not very fierce heat. No method can remove this blackness from the skin, which is now stained like a paper that has been exposed to the flames of a lit candle. And the new components that have this property [indolis] and originate from the same source will make the skin surface light and lubricated, moistening and relaxing it.

From what we stated above, a thicker substance with a stickier consistency remains in the cutaneous vessels. Once rarefied, however, it is returned to the pool of the circulatory system. Meanwhile the finer, fatty particles will be absorbed in the interstitia of the fibers that make up the vessels of the skin [cutis], and will coalesce due to the heat of the place and the surrounding air, transmitting a dark color to them.

Everyone can see that the sole cause of this is the thickening of fluids and solids in the Malpighian layer where the cuticle is pierced through by thousands and thousands of pores, as Leeuwenhoek observed, exposed as it is to the burning rays of the sun.[5] Therefore, it is not surprising if the aforementioned layer takes on the color of burnt charcoal.

From all of the above, we conclude that there is no need to claim that bile is the physical cause of the color of black people. As we said, both the solid and liquid components of the skin and the Malpighian layer are produced by a serum of the blackest color, burnt to some extent to emulate nature as in candle making, when something remains in the bottom of the vase after the more liquid parts have been skimmed off. Finally, the aforesaid porous solids and liquids will reflect but the fewest rays of sunlight; from this, scientists derive the color black.

Having touched on the physical cause of the color of black people, the order of the questions to be answered requires that I next address the physical and anatomical properties of their hair. [. . .] The hair of Blacks also tends to grow white in old age, but otherwise is altogether short, curly, and coiled, and grows densely. Its natural color is the darkest black; it is oily and almost emulates the texture of wool.

[. . .]

Earlier in this treatise, we proved that the components making up the skin of black people are completely porous and loose. For this reason, nothing prevents us from concluding that those very fine strands of the roots, being separable, are expelled through the open pores into the air. As a result, the roots will produce large quantities of extremely thin and slender hair. As the fluid moistens the skin, the hair shows a very dark color, as the more fluid black humor (the finer parts having escaped through the pores and the thicker elements having been burnt), as we said above, gradually turns it black.

[. . .]

The complex question that has been posed also asks for an explanation of the degraded [*degenerata*] nature of the skin and hair of black people. Two forms of degeneration may be observed in the human species. In the first instance, one parent is black and the other white. In the second, both parents are black and the child is born in frigid or temperate zones. This latter instance of degeneration can only take place over a long span of time and across generations. In the first case, however, the offspring will immediately show the mixed colors of the parents in both skin color and hair.

The workings of nature in regard to the birth of animals are shrouded, as it were, in a foggy night, indeed in thick darkness, so much so that it will come as no surprise that three different opinions hold sway in medical schools today regarding how humans are conceived.[6] Some [i.e., ovists] maintain that the rudiments of the fetus are already sketched out in the mother's eggs, and once the life-giving breath of the male semen is added, the fetus is given life and unfolds: in other words, it begins life. After the egg has made its way down the fallopian tubes into the uterus, it is nourished in a manner that is common knowledge.

Others [i.e., animalculists] maintain that we should follow Leeuwenhoek's lead, as does the illustrious Boerhaave, and claim that a man's semen swarms with innumerable animalcules [*animalculi*] that are alive, minute, and have tails, which they call homunculi [*homoneiunculi* (sic)]. They say that the most vivacious of these homunculi, once it has been delivered with the others to the woman's ovaries, enters the egg before the others and there, the others having suffocated, obtains sufficient food and is thereby nourished, while the egg, having broken its pedicels, descends into the uterus and receives nourishment there.

Finally, a third group believes that through a certain motion of both parents, the seed is mixed and combined in the uterus, thus the fetus is formed and there starts to grow.[7] [All of these explanations have their faults.] The first group cannot explain how the rudiments of the fetus are formed in the egg; the second group cannot explain from where animalcules originate; and the third is unable to explicate the mixing of seed from which the fetus originates. I follow the opinion of Leeuwenhoek, who explains all the phenomena of generation with more probability.[8] And yet, it is beyond the narrow purview of this essay to refute the opinions of the other groups.

In the first part of this essay, I stated that the watery parts of the blood, which moisten the skin and the Malpighian layer of black people, evaporate by an imperceptible process of perspiration, with the result that the sulfurous and oily parts of the blood become concentrated and rarefied and are returned into the pool of circulation having acquired a black color, almost as if they had been scorched by the heat of fire. These resulting blood particles will be mixed with the remaining humors in the body, though their volume is now quite diminished, they can still perceptibly stain with their colors; therefore, they enter the testicles of the black male and mix with the seed becoming part of its composition.

The animalcules discussed above are partially nourished by these [humors] which stain with their dark color the vessels of the skin and the Malpighian layer (which are separated from the other parts that have a more proportionate diameter). Indeed, during coitus these other components of the black male seed will penetrate the pores of a white woman's uterus and enter into the blood's circulation, thereby being conveyed to the vessels of the fetus. Thanks to the power of attraction, they will unite with other components of the same nature in the fetus's skin. Once a certain arrangement in the vessels' diameter has become innate (since we know that the laws of nature are constant), the animalcule will resemble the father, just as an egg is similar to another egg. Such dispositions are greatly confirmed, alas!, in the hereditary diseases that afflict unlucky mortals.

In an embryo of this constitution, the skin's vessels are dilated, unfold, and become disentangled under the impetus of the circulatory system. Indeed, this cannot happen unless the fibers separate from this interweaving, leaving empty interstices in the process. The white lymphatic particles supplied by the mother's blood become wedged into these interstices. Many of them take on a black color from the nearby particles, while the rest will more tenaciously retain their own color; as a result, the colors from both parties will mix.

The blackness of the father will convey that attribute to the offspring born from a white mother; this faculty is restored to its function by the strong action of the air that invades the many pores of the black parts, dilating them further and opening new ones. For in fact, nearly all infants are born white, or more precisely, red, hence babies will never appear black at birth, because the parts that carry blackness have not yet been subjected to the action of the air. This can be seen in the head of the penis.[9]

Similarly, in the case of the animalcules of a white father's seed, the skin vessels, relaxed by the action of the circulating humors, will leave empty interstices; the particles supplied by a black mother's blood will wedge into these interstices, stained by the dark color that nourishes the vessels. These particles deposit themselves in the vessels along with other blood particles and would color the fetus entirely black, unless at this point the hereditary disposition of the father (discussed above) in part of his skin's vessels did not prevent it. And so the offspring born of a black mother and white father will yield the same faculty of producing mixed colors.

The animalcule [fetus], swarming with male seed, resembles the father, as we stated above, according to the constant and entirely inscrutable laws of nature. An exception is made for the organs that are assigned to the process of generation in female fetuses. Consequently, the animalcule will have hair that resembles the father's. But to some extent, the hair will resemble by analogy that of both parents, since it absorbs its growth from lymph produced from the mother's blood along with that of the other parent.[10]

In trying to explain this highly complex issue, we have done no more than replace one set of doubts and probabilities with another. Given the exceedingly constrained limits of human intelligence and the dense fog that covers the workings of nature, even if we have offered some correct observations, it would hardly be possible to shed a definite light on them.

Nonetheless, explaining the causes of the slow degeneration in the offspring of Blacks, both in regard to color and quality of their hair, occurring in both temperate and colder climates, is not that difficult.[11] In fact, the vessels of both the skin and the Malpighian layer, stained a dark color, preserve that color with such perseverance that it would be a waste of time to try to make them lose their oiliness and framework by subjecting them to washing and soaking. Though the blood retains its structure over a series of many years, when the small vessels of the skin and the Malpighian layer are subjected to greater air pressure, the pores constrict, and the watery parts of the humors escape in far lesser number through the aforementioned barely perceptible process of perspiration.

Consequently, the oily and sulfurous particles are retained in the fatty membrane in greater number. Those particles that reach the skin are fewer in number and more diluted since they are not subjected to the scorching action [of the sun]. Hence, the cutaneous humor, more diluted and composed of a smaller abundance of black particles, is returned into circulation and the male seed is stained by fewer black particles; hence the cutis of the animalcules is less black.

Indeed, the skin humors of black women undergo the same changes; hence, in the uterus the fetus is nourished by a humor that is of a lighter color, and once born the baby is nourished by milk that contains fewer black particles. Finally, the baby is exposed to greater air pressure. As a result of all these concurrent factors, the color of Blacks born in cold or temperate climates is reduced until it has faded. And no one will fail to understand how much more perceptible the degeneration [fading] among their descendants will be.

Now that the physical causes of the degeneration of the hair [of Blacks] in temperate and frigid climates has been adequately explained, it seems redundant to spend time in further explanation. In fact, due to the heavier air surrounding the roots of the hair, the hair strands are compressed and coalesce, given a greater resistance in the pores, and are nourished by a more abundant and somewhat thicker sustenance; for this reason, the hair of the offspring of Blacks is found to be stronger, longer, etc. It is obvious, even to those who are barely paying attention, that all of these things can be reconciled, with few alterations, to all kinds of reproductive scenarios.

From all of the above we may incidentally conjecture that it was not until later, after the Deluge, that the offspring of inhabitants first acquired a truly black skin.[12] We may also surmise that the Blacks who live in the hottest climates will give birth to black children, those living in temperate zones will have medium-colored offspring just as, legitimately, Whites will give birth to Whites. Only the descendants of Blacks who live in the so-called Torrid Zones will show that color in later generations. Hence, it is clear that all the solid particles of blackness in the skin and the Malpighian layer are white by nature, and can be altered in color from their white, or more properly, red, innate color.

**Time erases the comments men make, but never the workings of nature; for to err is human.**

# 12 ⌁

# Blackness as an Extension of
# Optical Theory

The author first explains blackness in optical terms, stating that the sap of the epidermal membrane in Blacks allows for greater absorption of sunlight, thereby darkening the skin. This belief may reflect his familiarity with Isaac Newton's treatise on optics, which was recently published in French in 1720. Other extenuating causes of blackness, in his opinion, are illnesses brought on by differences in climate, strong sun, and local conditions of soil and air. The melancholic behavior typical of black people, he states, is due to the effect of bodily humors. While this humoral imbalance is bearable when Africans are in their native land, he asserts, this temperament leads to a kind of mania under the stress of slavery.

WHITE MEN, who occupy a considerable part of the earth, have been surprised to see black men in Africa; and this is not the first time that someone has attempted to seek out a determinate cause for this seemingly singular phenomenon.

[. . .]

As we might suppose, Negroes were at first no less surprised to see white men as we were to see black men.

In his book on Guinea, William Bosman recounts that, among the Negroes, there are many people who claim that Blacks and Whites are two different species that God created at the same time, that the Lord gave them a choice between gold and the art of reading and writing.[1] The Blacks, he continues, had first choice because of their excellence and they took the gold for themselves; to the Whites he left the knowledge of letters.

If Whites and Negroes are different in Color, they much resemble each other in *amour-propre*. Considered from this aspect, they are indeed the same species. Whites are well convinced of their advantage in everything over Negroes; they consider the color white a reason for their preeminence, and never fail to give the color black to the Devil and to other hideous objects. Meanwhile, Negroes believe themselves very superior to Whites in their form and particularly in their color, on which they congratulate themselves for having a considerable advantage; among them, the devil and all terrible objects are white.[2]

Without bothering to settle this difference, we confine ourselves to seeking what might be the true cause of the color of Negroes. We cannot count much on what has been said previously on the matter, either by Hannemann in his book titled *Curiosum scrutinium nigredinis posterorum Cham id est Aethiopum* (A Meticulous Inquiry into the Black Descendants of Cham, that is of the Ethiopians, 1677), or by the scholar Pechlin in his treatise *De habitu et Colore Aethiopum,* (Of the Appearance and Color of Ethiopians, 1677), or even by any other writer.[3]

To proceed in an orderly way, we begin by examining in what part of the Negro body resides the blackness that distinguishes them from other men.

Leeuwenhoek, the great Scrutinizer of Nature aided by his Microscope, claims to have seen with certainty that the blackness of the skin of a young Negress is due to the tiny scales that constitute the outer skin, of which the newest and most interior scales make the older and outer ones fall out, and thus succeed them. But the observations and dissections of the greatest anatomists have not confirmed Leeuwenhoek's so-called discovery.[4]

One might prefer the idea that the blackness of Negroes resides in the reticular membrane that is placed between the skin properly speaking underneath and the outer skin or epidermis, since this membrane, when stripped of the skin and the epidermis, is black as charcoal, but the interposition of the outer skin diminishes the blackness in proportion to the transparency of this outer skin.

Messieurs Malpighi and Littré agree on this fact; they differ only in that Malpighi says it is a thick and glutinous black sap that this membrane holds, while Littré denies the existence of this black sap, based on [an experiment where] he soaked a little piece of this membrane in spirits and even boiled it for a long time in water, never being able to find or extract the slightest dye, but only a very clear liquor that when cooled formed a kind of transparent jelly.[5]

Based on his experiments, Monsieur Littré's reason for denying the existence of the black sap is not as conclusive as it appeared to him. In fact, he might have perceived his error if he had known of the experiments done after his death by [John] Belchier of the Royal Society, and reported in the *Philosophical Transactions* of 1736.[6] One or two pigs, turkeys, roosters and ordinary chickens became red after garance [a red dye] was put in their food for several days. Their reddened bones were put into spirits and into boiling water, but no dye could be extracted.

We may even see in Monsieur Du Fay's memorandum on the mixture of some colors [and] dyeing, *Mémoires de l'Académie* from 1737, that indeed there are some colors that can be easily and entirely removed from dyed cloth, and others that cannot be removed without absolutely destroying and removing the surface of the cloth.[7]

Therefore, Littré's experiment to disprove the existence of a black and glutinous sap in the reticular membrane of the Negro has no weight. There is no doubt that this reticular membrane in the Negro could be the seat of blackness and that the fibers or vessels that compose it are nourished by some kind of sap. It remains to clarify the singular quality of the nourishing sap from which the color black results.

Although I would like to condense what is a far vaster subject than it initially appeared, I cannot dispense with clarifying what the color black is and, consequently, I am now taking up the question of the system of light and colors. What I will say about this will be as clear as possible, but very abridged because I am addressing scholars.

In order to be brief, I will not refute the systems of three great men—of Descartes, Father Malebranche, and the Englishman Isaac Barrow.[8] Instead, I will simply declare that I am adopting the system of Newton, while nonetheless clarifying several points [of his system] that remain obscure.[9]

### ON LIGHT AND COLORS

We see bodies only because the Light that is transmitted to them is reflected back to our eyes. Corpuscles of Light fill this vast universe. They are compressed in a straight train or file of luminous corpuscles that, running from the sun to the illuminated bodies and from these bodies to us, are what we call luminous rays.

Rays are composed of luminous corpuscles of different shapes and different elasticity, but a single ray contains only homogeneous corpuscles, of the same shape and same elasticity. The shape and elasticity of these corpuscles depends on the extent of their refractability, which the prism allows us to perceive as rays of different colors.[10] The variety of these heterogeneous rays causes different sensations in the organ of sight and consequently in the various sensitive areas of our soul. Differences among colors account for the differential effect of these sensations.

What we call (incorrectly but here for the sake of ease) red corpuscles and red rays are those that give rise to the sensation of red, and [analogously] of yellow, blue, etc. There are as many differently colored or heterogeneous rays as there are different primitive colors. It has not been decided whether there are five or seven of them, or only three. I lean toward the latter view despite the opinion of Monsieur Newton.

The mass or shower of light that fills and occupies the space between us and the sun is an assembly of all the heterogeneous rays (or different colors). If the object that receives part of these rays in proportion to the extent of its surface reflects only red rays, then the object appears red to us. If at the same time it reflects yellow, blue, etc. but in such a small quantity that the number of red rays is surpassed by others, then the body will be of a less lively and beautiful red, but still, since the dominant color is red, the body will appear red.

The quantity of different rays may be found in such proportions that the result is not merely a degraded color, but a totally different color, for example comprised of an assembly of yellow-blue rays that give the color green. Green does not result from the blue and yellow corpuscles penetrating, mixing, or changing in figure or elasticity, but rather from the different continuous rays that cause two different agitations in the organ of Vision. The result is a complex agitation that gives rise in our soul to the sensation of green.

[. . .] But God has put limitations on the perfection of our Senses. We do not see objects that are too distant, and we do not see objects distinctly that are too small or too close to each other. To our eyes, they make a total representation that is clear, but the partial representations are obscure—as a new and celebrated physicist explains in Chapter Seven of her physical institutions.[11] We see a sheet of paper as white and we do not perceive distinctly the various tiny black, red, and blue spots that are really there. A greater perfection of sight would have been injurious to us. We know from experience that those who have a more perfect sense of smell than common men suffer from agitations that are too strong and too frequent; similarly, overly frequent agitations of light cause pain to our eyes.

When all the heterogeneous rays are reflected back to our eyes, then we see the color white, which is nothing other than the assembly of all the differently colored Rays. This is shown in Newton's optics. [. . .]

If no ray of light were reflected from the object to our eyes, the result would be perfect black, which signifies merely a total lack of light, and consequently pure shadow, but we must agree that then we would not see the object at all, because we only see by the Light.

If we [can] see black bodies, it is only because there are too few of each type of reflected rays for us to perceive their color. A sense of sight that was more perfect would perceive them. It has happened that I perceive as dark blue an object that one of my friends (whose eyesight is not as good) perceives only as black. Thus the Black that we see is only an imperfect black, but it is not one color, nor is it, as Father Castel says in his *Optics*, a mixture of dark colors.[12]

[. . .]

Let us return to our principal question: [the source of blackness]. Whatever part of the reticular membrane that we assume to be the site of the blackness, this tissue must have a kind of sap that moistens and feeds it, since the parts of this sap become the component parts of the solid. This sap, while moistening the membrane, insinuates itself into all its pores, its interior and exterior interstices, and consequently offers itself, so to speak, [as a medium] to immediately receive impacts from luminous rays and absorb them, without the interposition of a fragile and transparent outer skin that would be an obstacle to this process.

To proceed by degrees, let us prove that this sap could be black. After that we will prove that there are sufficient causes of the blackness of this sap in Negroes. I will demonstrate the first proposition by facts.

In animals there are saps and liquors of different colors. Bile is of an ashen white, blood is red. Sometimes we turn liquids into yellows, greens, blacks. Bile in the biliary ducts is yellow, in the gall bladder it is olive or brown. In man, there is a black bile—*atra bilis*.[13] The cuttlefish has a reservoir full of a black liquor that it spreads in the water when it is being chased in order to hide from the fisherman's net. Various authors believe that the pocket containing this black liquor is a gland and that the liquor contained there takes the place of bile.

Let us now prove our second proposition.

Nobody denies that the varying constitution of climates influences the men who inhabit them. According to the lands where they live, they are more or less tall, more or less large, more or less robust, more or less lively, more or less brave—one could even confidently add more or less intelligent. According to various countries, they are subject to different maladies. [. . .]

If in various climates we see men who are more or less white, more or less black, is it not reasonable to attribute this to the same cause? Everything points to this.

Different climates can be attributed principally to a sun that is more or less hot, and to the nature of the atmosphere, the terrain, and the various emissions the land gives off. The winds that reign there and the waters that flow there are also important. I will add other causes as I develop my argument.

The great heat of the sun in some climates contributes to blackening the skin of [its] inhabitants. It is fire that gives coal its blackness by the action that it exercises on wood, which has disposed it to extinguish and absorb the rays.

By the natural and sensible analogy that there is fire in the sun, I believe that the sun by its heat can blacken and burn; experiment confirms this, for example, when (with the aid of a burning mirror) the sun blackens and burns a piece of wood. Even without the aid of that mirror, the sun sometimes blackens trees and crops.

Aristotle so little doubted that the sun could blacken men's skin that in one of his problems he asks why the sun blackens men while fire does not.[14]

Afraid of darkening their skin, French women take great care not to expose their complexion to the sun's heat. They know that hunters, plowmen, shepherds, and those who are continually exposed to the sun's heat, all acquire a swarthy tint.[15]

The inhabitants of lands near the Torrid Zone are swarthier and blacker than those who are more distant [from it]. For example, the Portuguese are swarthier than the French, and the Africans in the Torrid Zone are blacker than the Portuguese. Those who live in the tropics are more constantly exposed to the burning heat of the sun than those who are nearer the equator, [and] are in fact the blackest. For example, the inhabitants of Malacca, who are under the Tropic of Cancer, are blacker than those of Ceylon, who are closer to the equator, and the inhabitants of Sumatra and Malaysia who live even closer to the equator are less black than those of Ceylon.

In cold climates the inhabitants are white, and in glacial climates the fur and feathers of animals acquire the color white.

These facts are accepted as uncontestable and can be advanced with confidence and without fear of being contradicted to prove that the sun's heat is at least the partial cause of the blackness of Africans.

There may be objections to this, but on close examination these concerns are more specious than solid.

**First Objection:** If the sun's heat were the cause of the color of Negroes, then the inhabitants situated at the same degree of latitude in the Torrid Zone would be equally black. However, it is known that Indians are less black than the Africans situated at the same degree.

**Reply:** This objection is not valid, unless one believes that the sun's heat is the sole cause of the blackness of Negroes; if one affirms that heat and other causes that we have already indicated [produce black skin] then the objection is without merit.

**Second Objection:** In the land of Cambaïa [Khambhat] in Asia that lies almost under the Tropic of Cancer, there are inhabitants close to white and women who surpass Portuguese women in whiteness, according to Linschot.[16]

**Reply:** Northerners spread successively closer and closer to the Tropic as a result of wars and trade, because they found transmigration was easy. This means that in the same place we find inhabitants who are more or less black. By mixing they have engendered children of even lighter shades. This transmigration is easy in Asia, but we must assume it is very difficult in Africa because of the barrier of the immense deserts of Barbary on the northern side and the sea on the southern side, a sea regarded as impracticable and in which navigation is only of recent date.

What I say here about the difficult transmigration of northerners to Africa because of the immense deserts of Barbary, if true, means that peoples who are not prevented by this barrier (like those of Nigritia) but situated to the west (for example, the Abyssinians) must be much less black than the former, and evidently this is the reason why they are less so.[17] The name "Abyssinian" comes from the Arab word *habesch,* which means a cluster or mixture of nations.[18]

**Third Objection:** Linschot reports that under the 35th degree of latitude beyond the equator the inhabitants are black, although they neighbor cold mountains (called the Moon) upon which snow is usually seen.[19]

**Reply:** The peak of a high mountain has a different climate from the valleys and plains that surround it. These mountains reflect the sun's rays onto the plains and valleys. They increase the heat produced by the direct rays. There the atmosphere is more humid and thicker. It conserves for a long time the same emissions that the earth furnishes because the heat is sheltered from the winds that blow continually and renew the atmosphere of mountains, which are always exposed to their action because of their elevation. A mountain's peak is often higher than the region where hail and snow are formed. This is a well-known fact. These mountains arrest this hail and this snow that have been transported by the winds.

[. . .]

**Fourth Objection:** The Savages of Canada are blackish although the land is very cold.[20]

**Reply:** We know that this comes from the fact that they rub themselves with fat and that they are continually exposed to smoke in their cabins, where they make fire and have no chimney.

**Fifth Objection:** In Martinique, where the inhabitants are white, [and] which lies at the 14th or 15th degree of latitude, there is a canton inhabited by Caribs. This is a species of Negro of a reddish and degenerated Black.[21]

**Reply:** The Caribs of Martinique were chased out of French colonies and took refuge in an area where they could live free. Thus we should not be surprised by their different color.

Before passing to the causes of the color of Negroes as depending on the constitution of the climate, I must observe a few things. One is that in the same land, the same town, the same family, we see children of the same father and same mother who have very different skin tones. The other is that there are tones much more susceptible to sunburn than others and more disposed to receive a brown tan by the imprinting of the sun's rays, which we can attribute to particular causes that give each individual different qualities of the blood and the excrement.

This must be true of Negroes, which answers the questions and objections, which I now close in order not to swell this essay.


### THE NATURE OF THE ATMOSPHERE INFLUENCES
### THE CLIMATE AND THE COLOR OF INHABITANTS

The atmosphere is nothing other than air charged with vapors and emissions that the sun's heat lifts from the earth. The more numerous these vapors and emissions are, the thicker the atmosphere and the less transparent it is; [. . .]

This reasoning leads us to believe that in the climate of the Torrid Zone, where the sun is stronger due to its proximity and the perpendicularity of its rays, the atmosphere must be more charged with numerous and heavy vapors and emissions; observations confirm this. According to Diodorus of Sicily, there is such an excessive heat in the land of the Troglodytes (in Egypt) that those Troglodytes who are close together cannot even see each other because of the thickness that is put into the atmosphere.[22] What allows us to believe this is that even in the temperate zones, after several days of rather strong heat we feel that the atmosphere is heavy and thick, but after a little rain, the weather makes the atmosphere much more transparent. Astronomers are well informed about this and take advantage [of this shift in climate] to observe the heavens. The atmosphere is more burning in the Torrid Zone than in the temperate zones, so it does influence the constitution of the climate. It is thus more able to blacken, since blackness is a gradation and a modification; both sun and fire blacken things before burning them.

[...]

### THE NATURE OF THE TERRAIN, ITS EMISSIONS, ITS SALTS AND SULFURS, ETC.

We know that the places where the sun's rays fall most perpendicularly are the hottest, the most burning, either because the rays are most numerous, or because arid boulders and sand reflect the light most forcefully. This is what makes the strength of the sun unbearable in the Torrid Zone.

But it is not only on account of these boulders, sands, and drought that the terrain influences the constitution of the climate. It is evident that the atmosphere we breathe, which is the ambient matter of all bodies, is crucial. The quality of the vapors and emissions with which it is charged depends on the quality of saps, on the particles of metals and minerals of salts and sulfurs that the earth contains.

The abundance of salts and sulfurs in this climate cannot be called into doubt. In order to diminish the prickles and itches that Negroes feel on their skin, they moisten it with oil and fat, as reported by Thomas Browne; these prickles and itches could only come from the action of salts. We feel the same prickles on our faces when we approach the sea.[23]

Sulfur comes to us from Quito and Nicaragua, says Pomet in his history of medicines; in truth, burning heat aids in the production of sulfur and, indeed, we can find a mineral variety that came from Mount Vesuvius.[24]

Salts are very suitable to black in subjects that have qualities that make them susceptible to the color black. The acid salts of vinegar make this liquor black when iron filings are steeped in it. Vitriolic salts in an infusion of walnut will turn it black. Trees that resist frost are blackened and burned by salty winds.

[...]

The consequence of all that is observed above is that in the Torrid Zone, the land grows trees that are as black as ebony, and black vegetables such as black beans and black rice, black fruits such as black pepper, certain plums, walnuts, as well as areca and junipaba, from which savages take the sap to blacken their faces.[25] One finds within the earth black coal, black lead, and black magnetite, which is the most prized, as well as the black soil from which Chinese ink is made.

So it is not surprising that nature, so accustomed in this climate to work in black—given the quality of saps in the earth and of the particles in the atmosphere—imprints the same color on men and animals. [. . .]

[The author here summarizes the potential of winds, water, and food to affect skin complexion]

## WINDS

[. . .]

## BODY PERSPIRATION'S INFLUENCE

The perspiration of living bodies is not only real (as we know) but very considerable. It is a major [by-product] of food that is digested. So it has different qualities according to the nature and quality of this food ingested. It is by odor that hunting dogs discover, distinguish, follow, and recognize game. In the same way Negroes in the Antilles (as described by Father du Tertre) distinguish by odor between the tracks of a Negro and those of a White, merely by smelling where they have walked.[26]

A body's perspiration thus enters into the composition of the atmosphere. Doctors are so perfectly convinced of this that they forbid convalescents to breathe the air of sickrooms. Thus it is obvious that bodily perspiration influences the constitution of the climate.

## SUMMARY AND CLARIFICATIONS

[. . .]

Men who were the first to inhabit lands exposed to the great heat of the sun must have received imprinting, and this imprinting (coming from luminous rays) must have principally been of color. As new inhabitants arrived, they must have received this same imprinting. But it must have been stronger in the first arrivals than in the later ones because of their longer residence; the former must have been blacker than the latter. From this comes several diverse shades in the color of inhabitants who were successively transplanted.

[. . .]

I end this portion of my essay with a reflection that merits attention.

Either God gave one portion of Noah's posterity the color white and the other portion the color black, or else he gave all the descendants of this patriarch without distinction the color white, in which case accidental and intervening causes produced the color black among those who came to inhabit the lands that we call the countries of Negroes.

Under the first assumption (that Noah's posterity were black and white from the onset) one could not explain why these descendants of Noah, both white and black, gradually became separated from each other while they spread over the earth, such that all the Blacks inhabited only one climate, abandoning all the others to the Whites.

1) Given the fact that God confounded the language of all the earth after the Tower of Babel, as established by Holy Scripture, we can easily understand why those of the same language gathered together and separated from those of a different language. There is a simple cause. A society includes only people who understand each other and who can communicate their ideas with each other. But we cannot conceive how a difference in color could furnish the cause of a similar separation. Men well-made and without marked defects never decided to separate from the hunchbacked and the lame.

2) Let us suppose there was indeed a cause for this separation. Why then did the Blacks take possession of the whole belt of land under the Torrid Zone to which they confined themselves, and why did the Whites decide to occupy the temperate and cold zones? We could say that the Blacks were more sensitive to the cold and Whites to the heat, and they both avoided the temperature that affected them disagreeably.

We easily imagine a new supposition that could rescue the preceding point, for men are only more or less sensitive to the cold or heat of the countries where they find themselves as a result of acquired habit; a White born and raised in Guinea would find France too cold a country, and a Negro born and raised in polar regions would find it [i.e., Guinea] too hot a country.

3) Why have black trees, black fruits, black vegetables, black metals and minerals been assigned to occur in the same climate as black men chose to inhabit? If men might have reasons to prefer such a climate, one could not say that vegetables and minerals chose this by an effect of their will!

But if we are to put forward a more reasonable theory, we have to find a cause that explains why black men [and] black vegetables and minerals gathered in the same climate. If such an explanation does not exist, we would need to find a particular cause for the blackness in each individual, which is quite unlikely given the way that Nature's mechanism functions.

Under the second presupposition, in which the color black is accidental although general to all those who inhabit the Torrid Zone, everything could be easily and simply explained. When Noah's descendants gradually spread throughout the earth, those who found themselves in countries where the heat of the sun and the nature of the terrain—emissions, food, winds, water etc.—all combine to make things black, these people became black because the human body is also susceptible to this phenomenon. Because all these causes of blackness work together in the torrid climate, we find black vegetables and minerals there, at least those that are susceptible to this blackness.

[...]

I flatter myself that there is no physicist who with a little attention would not see the justice of what has been summarized and clarified here. These general observations that we have detailed and proved were necessary as the foundation of our work. We are going to continue to build on this solid foundation by adding specific observations concerning man alone, since we are being asked for the cause of the color of the Black man.

## CAUSES OF THE COLOR OF THE NEGRO ARISING FROM HIS OWN CONSTITUTION

### First Cause

To speak precisely, we are not white. Snow and chalk are white. Paper is white, but this is only a relative concept. The particular tincture of our skin is a more or less degraded red. When portrait-painters paint human skin they use red, which they carefully dilute to a certain point [with] other colors.

This comes from the fact that our blood is red. In its circulation this liquid waters, moistens, and penetrates all parts of the body, notably those that are near the surface and so receive and reflect the shock of luminous rays.[27]

It is known that blood is darker and browner in the veins than in the arteries, where it is a bright red, a color *flammeus,* as the authors say. Leeuwenhoek gives the reason: it is more thin or watery than blood found in veins, and the less transparent or pale material there is in the blood, the more it tends to the color black. [...]

Everybody has learned from experience that the sun's warmth, fire, and heat neither diminishes nor dissipates the serous nature of solids and fluids;

so it is not surprising that in hot countries the blood tends principally to blackness and gives this tint to the reticular membrane. Between red and black there is an affinity, a marked tendency. If one puts cochineal dissolved in water on a fire, it is first tinted a lovely red, but being left on the fire, the liquor takes on a blackish tint.[28]

[...]

There is more Black in the blood than in other red liquors and consequently a greater tendency to turn totally to black.

If I cook blood over a fire or under a blazing sun, it will soon be black. But independently of the fire and sun, if I receive a blow to the hand, there will be a contusion. First the blood will amass and I will perceive its red color. But soon after it will become blackish.

If I let blood that has just been drawn rest and grow cold on a plate, I will find that it is black at the bottom, while at the surface it is still red. Other authors assure us this comes from the fact that bile and melancholic humor, both of which are part of the blood's composition, have a great predisposition to blacken. This will now be proved.

## Second Cause

Doctors believe that melancholy is produced by the thickest portion of the chyle.[29] *Crassior* [which literally means "thicker"] is muddy. *Limosa* [which means "viscous"] is similar to wine lees. As for *foeculenta* [excrement], according to Lazare Rivière in his *Institutions de médecine*, its effect is to make people sad, timid, and savage, and it is black in color.[30] As for *Coloris nigricantia* [blackish], it sometimes makes people dazed and stupid, and is then called *melancolia asinine* [foolish melancholy]. This author distinguishes two sorts of melancholy; he calls one *alimentaria* [related to food] and the other *excrementitia* [related to excrement].

Alimentaria is less mucky and less muddy than excrementitia, which is called black bile (*atra bilis*): the latter is burning and bitter and results from an excessive heat of its parts when it boils the saps and reduces them, so to speak, to ashes, but leaves it the consistency of a fluid. It is like very acrid vinegar and even akin to *eau forte* [etching acid], and it contributes to blackness as much as does excessive and scorching heat.

Doctors observe that the tongue, teeth, and excrement of sick people become black during grave fevers. Thomas Browne explains that this results from the imprinting of a heated bile.[31] Jacques Houllier in *De Morbis internis* (Of Internal Diseases) (vol. 2) attributes various causes to melancholy—and he always includes burned blood.[32]

[. . .]

No one disagrees that the quality of blood and its excrements influences our inclinations, our passions, our way of thinking; and reciprocally that sadness, solitude, and mental troubles (*peines de l'esprit*) can both cause and increase the melancholic quality of the blood. This is why doctors prescribe to melancholic patients entertainment, dissipation, the company of others—in short, pleasure and everything that might procure joy for them.[33]

It remains to be proven that the climate where Negroes live, along with their customs, their way of living, their labor, their troubles, their hardships, their worries and fears, and their continual peril, must make them necessarily melancholic. The causes of this susceptibility are readily understood.

Negroes are exposed to a scorching heat that even habit could not make tolerable.[34] They are almost suffocated by it, even in their caverns facing north that serve as refuge and shelter. The earth is so scorching in certain areas that those who walk without shoes acquire on their feet pustules that degenerate into ulcers. [A worse fate awaits] those who do not drink as soon as they are thirsty; they die suddenly, since the heat can consume in an instant all the humidity in the body. (Meat placed in water and under the sun also cooks quickly.) Their way of life is painful. They go about naked. They owe their always poor nourishment to their continual labor of hunting, fishing, and war. Always ready for their throats to be cut by their neighbors at the least expected moment, they know almost no other pleasure than that of massacre and spilling enemy blood, a pleasure that is barbarous and mixed with horror, hatred, and anger. These [emotions] cannot give rise to that joy that dilates our vessels and facilitates and refreshes our circulation, since according to all physicians, sad passions constrict the vessels and hinder circulation.

There is no Negro who does not fear that tomorrow he will be taken prisoner-of-war and sold in foreign lands as a slave for the rest of his life. Even children are at risk of being sold by their parents, with the result that slavery is regarded as the greatest of all evils by men whose only wealth and unique advantage is freedom.

Diodorus describes at length all the disadvantages of their habitation and way of life, and he remarks that they prefer death to the anguish of leaving their lands and embracing another kind of life. He adds that any native land has its own charms, and one may easily undergo the inconveniences of a climate to which one is accustomed from an early age.

Thus it is plausible that Negroes must be of a melancholic temperament. Let us prove by facts and observations that they are actually so and this is their known character. Those who are transported from Africa to our colonies are mournful, sad, lazy, mean, and have ideas stamped with mania. One often sees that even those who are treated with more humanity and are not left to want for anything, will strangle or hang themselves without anyone foreseeing that they had the slightest plan to do this.

They commonly run away. They are pursued with well-loaded guns. They are threatened with death if they do not stop. Still, they prefer to let themselves be killed, even if they know that if they give up, it is not permitted to punish them except by a few strokes of the rod.

They also often use very subtle poisons (of which they have particular knowledge) either against themselves—this is due to the effect of black melancholy—or against their comrades out of resentment, or against their masters out of malice—and to deprive them of their slaves. In certain areas of Africa, they fatten their prisoners, slit their throats, and eat them.

Diodorus of Sicily speaks of certain Negroes who eat fish and he reports that they are not angered by the blows they are given. They regard calmly the wounds inflicted upon them; they see their women and children killed without anger and without emotion.

Faced with such marked traits, we cannot prevent ourselves from diagnosing melancholy exacerbated by [a type of] mania—in other words, the black and burned bile that is manifested on the skin of Negroes . . . Sadness, grief, and mental troubles have an influence on the state of melancholy, [which then exacerbates] the effect that melancholy has on the color black that men in these burning climates have. [It is clear that] they have received a more considerable alteration in their color than all other [human] bodies.

A series of separate causes has been proved to contribute to the black color of Negroes; the combination of these causes must necessarily have increased their [respective] effects. What is more, the lack of one or more of these causes, or the diminution of their force, must produce a lesser effect, meaning less blackness, something we can witness for ourselves. If Indians are less black than Africans, although situated at the same degree of latitude, this is doubtless due to the different nature of the terrain, of the food, and the different way of living [among the Indians], which makes them less subject to melancholy. We know that in China, for example, the inhabitants are industrious, that they cultivate the arts and sciences, and that they are polite and sociable. If they have an olive color, it is plausibly because the fervor of the sun is too great for inhabitants to be whiter.

If the inhabitants of lands of Guinea from 43 to 45 degrees of latitude are very swarthy, although they neighbor towns where men are white, this is due to the fact that despite the more temperate heat of the sun's rays, it is still strong enough that they are not permitted to be more white, due to the arid sands, the terrain's vapors and emissions, their constant work in tar resin and other fatty matter, the coal smoke to which they are exposed, and the melancholy produced in them by their way of living.

I predict that someone will object that all the causes put forward [here] for blackness contribute in no way to the blackness of a child of a Negro and a Negress born in France. That these [French-born Negro] children are no less black than if they were born in Guinea, will now be explained.

### CAUSES OF BLACKNESS LINKED TO THE GENERATION OR PROPAGATION OF THE SPECIES

All systems concerning the propagation of the species acknowledge the [particular] aspect of generation that creates the resemblance existing between parents and their children. [The exception to this] is the story of Jacob's rod, where this resemblance is attributed to the imagination of the mother; I will not deign to refute this theory.

The formative property of the embryo, says Lazare Rivière, provides the parts of the new body with the form that was imprinted in the parents' parts. It grafts it, so to speak, onto the spirits that facilitate generation. Saint-André, a doctor, in his *New Reflections on the Causes of Diseases,* attributes this resemblance to several causes, of which the foremost is that the semen of the father and mother are only fertile thanks to their mixing.[35] Together, these seeds form a single body that contains an idea of all parts of the parents, from which are generated particles that form the child's [constituent parts], which begin to develop as soon as they are agitated by the spirits that animate them.

The second cause is that the dissolving sap that is found in the [mother's] stomach assumes the idea and character of all the bodily parts. This sap then imprints this idea on [ingested] food, and induces it to assume a size and shape that can enter into the pores [in the womb] where it must nourish [a new] body. Hippocrates says that the spirits that serve for generation detach themselves from the whole body, from both the solid and soft parts.[36]

[. . .]

This matter of the resemblance of parents to their children is one of the most thorny in the natural sciences; happily it is not my task to solve it. I am nonetheless discomfited because the scholars working on this subject have yet to say anything that is really satisfying. However, the major difficulty in explaining the resemblance of traits [in generation] appears less so when we turn to the resemblance of color, which is the sole subject here. This emboldens me to try to explain the cause.

According to the ovist theory, the embryo has received life from certain spirits which are particles of the father's blood. So they relate to his nature, his qualities, [and] his character. [The embryo] receives its nourishment and its growth from the mother's blood. This blood in Negroes passes through very small conduits and disengages a great number of the larger and blacker particles contained within it. But in the same species, though in smaller number, it happens that the germ (and principle and character) of blackness has passed to the extremities, which is demonstrated in newborns.

Although Africans are white [at birth], one perceives that the end of the penis and the tips of the nails are black in babies, a color that later gradually extends to the whole body. This does not result from the fact that the black parts that affect these extremities have been deposited there. It is simply because they are more sheltered from the movement of blood circulation.

Similarly, one sees the larger and more blackish parts of the blood take refuge in the extremity of the hemorrhoidal veins. Later this blackness extends to the whole body, which results from the child's blood being struck by external air. [At this point], the principles and the qualities [of the body] are developed, especially its bilious and fervent character.

Not every author agrees with Littré that the children of Negroes emerge white from the womb of their mother.[37] Riolan the Younger in his *Anthropographie*, Browne in his *Enquiries into vulgar and common errors,* and several others assert that they are born black or at least blackish—but they are wrong.[38] I have consulted people worth believing who are also perfectly instructed in the facts. They attest that [Negro babies] come into the world reddish like the children of Whites, and one can distinguish the Negro newborn boy only from the black spot at the tip of his penis, unlike the male infants of Whites and mulattoes who do not have this. We leave aside facts and opinions that are merely prejudices.

Herodotus says that the semen of Negroes is black. According to him, this is the source of their color, but who knows (or could know) the color of the liquid that serves as a vehicle. This is also why I say no more about Aristotle's opinion that supposes that the semen of all animals is white, or the opinion of Thomas Browne that the latter opinion is based on incontestable facts and observations.[39] I know (like him) that fish spawn and the semen of plants enclose a substance that is white in color within a black shell. We see in the seed of onions and peonies, etc., and in the spawn of frogs and shrimp, that they are white at first and only blacken after time.

Magini and several others attest that the Emperors of the Abyssinians (who always come from the same family) are white from generation to generation.[40] This is attributed to the privilege they have of not resembling their subjects in color, and their descent in direct line from Solomon and Macqueda, or the Queen of Sheba.[41]

With the same degree of certainty, we are commonly assured that there has never been any degradation in the color black in the descendants of a Negro and a Negress after they have been transported to lands of the Whites [where they have children]. I am far from adopting this view. All this argument has in its favor is that its proponents do not have to retreat from their position because nobody can incontestably prove the contrary. In vain, they say, one finds examples of the color diminishing over time. Those who believe that their color does not change then ask for an attestation of the mother's fidelity! They maintain that this degradation only occurred because the Negress had violated her marital vows, but this opinion cannot be rationally sustained.

[In summary,] the excessive heat of the sun in Africa, the nature of the terrain, the emissions, the winds, water, food, and the way of living of inhabitants (which has precipitated their melancholy) have together produced blackness from the start. Reason teaches us that the ardor of a temperate sun, the nature of its terrain, combined with different emissions, other winds, other waters, other foods, [and] another kind of living must successively produce, though slowly, a quite opposite effect.

[...]

To confirm my opinion, I will report the change that occurs to animals due to a change in climate. The dogs in Guinea have a singular trait: they do not bark. In Europe it is quite the contrary, but if you transport dogs from Europe to Guinea, from the third or fourth generation they become unrecognizable and no longer bark. This is a fact reported by Bosman in his *Voyage to Guinea*.[42]

[...]

## ON THE DEGENERATION OF THE COLOR OF NEGROES

It is generally agreed that in the infants born to a Negro and a white woman, or to a white man and a Negress, the color black degrades and alters. We easily conceive the reason for this from what was said above. The germ, character, and principles of black are less abundant in this case because of the mixing of that germ, character, and principles with the white. We call these children Mulattos; when the latter mix with Whites they will make children who are even less black, and with the aid of this continual mixing will manage to have a posterity as white as the Europeans.

### ON THE NATURE OF NEGRO HAIR, ITS CAUSE, AND ITS DEGRADATION

Negro hair in Guinea resembles a kind of wool. Their hair is short, kinky, and black. One is struck by this singularity, and yet we are not [taken] by the fact that our spaniels are covered with a kind of silk, while our mastiffs and basset hounds have rough hair. We are surprised by this latter difference because we easily imagine that the conformation of pores and some preparation of very different saps could produce this diversity.

The hairs of newborn [boys] are like the bristles that grow on the chin at fourteen or fifteen years of age. It is a kind of wool, which is why Latin speakers call it *lanugo*.

Upon examination, the hair of Whites does not differ more from the wooly hair of Negroes than the wool of sheep from the moors from that of the sheep of Segovia, and surely much less than the face of a man taken at random differs from the face of another man born and living in the same town. Thus this is not the effect of an extraordinary and quite marvelous cause.

A number of analogous features and affinities exist between wool and oil. Oil plausibly acts in the formation and nourishment of wool. The fleece of our sheep is brimming with this liquor. Oil is also the nutrient that suits wool, making it soft, sturdy, flexible, manageable, gentle, pliant, etc.

### NEGROES HAVE VERY OILY SKIN AND THEIR HAIR IS A KIND OF WOOL

Negroes are bilious and melancholic. Bile is part of the blood and full of oleaginous parts, as has been observed by Alexander Stuart, an English doctor.[43] This bile is badly lacking in serosity, as is proved by their temperament and by the constitution of the climate. This is confirmed by the observation that Negroes rarely spit or blow their noses.

From whatever pores, canals, pathways or conduits the hairs grow and through which they receive their nourishment, these conform in allowing the oily parts to pass. These are mixed with volatile spirits, producing the slight serosity that is necessary as a medium.

From all that, I conclude that Negroes have more oily parts than Whites, and that Whites have more serous parts than Negroes. It follows that the pores of Negroes somewhat resemble those of our sheep.

Another observation. Negroes have a cranium that is thick, compact, and hard. A forceful blow from a stick to the head of a Negro, [or] his falling on a hard rock and hitting his head, makes almost no impression.[44]

[...]

We have noticed that the skin of Negroes is oily. Oleaginous parts naturally rise to the outside of the body, but we have seen from what has just been said that these [oily secretions] tend to move principally and abundantly toward the head, where they enter into the construction of the cranium and the formation of hair.

This tendency of oleaginous parts to move upward is not singular. Nature teaches us that in all oleaginous trees, such as the walnut and the olive tree, the oil tends principally and abundantly toward the top. It gathers in the fruits that we harvest from the top of the tree.

Negro hair is short and frizzy due to a lack of serosity and internal humidity as well as to the external dryness procured by a blazing sun. The blackness of this hair comes from the internal heat [of the body], like the whiteness of the hair of our old people comes from a lack or diminution of this heat. Avicenna explains this in these terms: *Nigredo Significat Caliditatem et albedo Significat frigiditatem* [blackness means heat, and whiteness means cold].[45] The blackness of women's hair, says Antonius Ulmus [...] indicates their lasciviousness.[46] Juvenal, speaking of Messalina's lewdness, remarks that she had black hair.[47] This lubricity is known in Negroes and Negresses.[48] The same excessive heat that renders them lecherous also causes the blackness of their hair.

The length of this dissertation has turned me away from the plan for a deeper examination of the nature of hair and of wool.

It seems superfluous to extend this article to develop the cause of the degeneration or degradation of the species of wool that stands in place of hair for Negroes. This degeneration could only occur as a consequence of the principles we have established for the degeneration of color, and we know that the Caribs in our colonies in America (who are much less black than the Negroes of Guinea) have hair like Europeans.

**"I am black, but beautiful."**[49]

# 13

## Blackness as a Result of an Original Sickness

After exhaustively presenting numerous erudite references of all kinds (biblical, naturalist, geographical, climatic, anatomical, chemical, and botanical), in erudite Latin the author finally puts forward his own unique but inconsistently argued approach to the Bordeaux Academy's topic. When they came into being, either Adam or Eve was dark-skinned. "Ethiopians," according to this theory, are an offshoot of the first group of humans on Earth, who only came into being due to an inherent "sickly condition" of undisclosed cause, probably climatic. According to this theory, Ethiopians were not black at the outset; they were an unnatural, unwholesome red. Through inbreeding and other unhealthy practices, the black hue ultimately introduced itself into the population on a permanent basis.

Jehova
**You Are My Support**

A MEDICAL-SCIENTIFIC TREATISE CONCERNING THE CAUSE OF
BLACKNESS AMONG THE ETHIOPIANS [SECTION 1]

[I]t pleases me to investigate, in accordance with my modest capability, several of the arguments related to the cause of blackness, and even to look into the most probable cause.

*Chapter 1: On the Origin and Difference in Colors*

At the beginning of this treatment on the black color of the Ethiopians, I believe the reader would welcome a brief exposition about colors in general, in order to facilitate explanation of the matter at hand. Barbers and those suffering from conjunctivitis know what color is, but I would like to add a definition: color is the variation of rays of light mixed with darkness.[1] Light itself is the scattering of either fire or air, just like darkness is density, that is, the product of earth.

The different colors, therefore, arise from variations in the degree of mixture, thinness, and refraction, which can be demonstrated by several experiments. The Holy Scripture names as the first light the fire produced at the beginning of creation from the earth—the globe of land and water—and we know that fire is of a sulfurous nature, and that the variation in sulfurs affects and alters colors. And since no material thing in Nature arises without color, from this, I think, we may affirm that the color of sulfur is universal, in all its aspects, even those spread out across the whole world.

Moreover, just as light is fire, so fire is sulfur. And so it holds with darkness, which is the darkness left over in the abyss at the beginning of Creation. Darkness is a being [ens substantiale] in itself with substance, just as light has substance, in the same way that heat and cold are different beings in and of themselves. From this, it is clear that sulfur is fire that is specific to earth, and the power of this specific sulfur is to be the color of any given thing. And thanks to the separation created by God, no blackness could be present without whiteness, just as there is no length without shortness.

From this it follows that God is entirely the primary cause of colors, since He laid down such an arrangement in the beginning of creation, and it pleased Him to create for each individual thing its own particular color, which nature, as God's administrator, maintains His creation across the ages, to such a degree that, as stated in *Trifolium Hermeticum,* it is impossible to remove an innate color deeply rooted from nature and substitute it with another.[2] [. . .]

### *Chapter 2: On Arrangement* [dispositio] *at the Beginning of Creation*

Both Holy Scripture and sound reasoning confirm that all men were created from the first Adam. Since therefore we can perceive in men the two opposite colors, black and white; and just as the sun grows red and the moon shines with its white surface, nature preserves this order through all ages. And it preserves it so strictly and constantly that Whites are born from Whites, and Blacks from Blacks, and indeed colors become mixed only from a mixed marriage. For this reason, all subsequent procreation or multiplication of the first forebears is none other than the continuous reiteration of the first generation. Such is the opinion of Von Tschirnhaus in his *Medicina mentis* (Medicine of the Mind), and of the abbé de Vallemont on the propagation and multiplication of plants.[3] The latter bases his claim on a description of the fruits and animals that were created in the first six days of creation. But after the first creation was completed, we know that nothing else was newly created unless it be the product of an errant nature.

As far as I know, no monsters or the like were created at the Creation. If this had been the case, the world would be full of new animals not clearly corresponding to the earlier ones. Consequently, one would have to believe that the first species that were created had long ago perished. And if this had been the case, no one today could say what form a horse, deer, bull, or dog would have had either before or shortly after the Deluge—unless the subsequent generations of these created species had not been determined from the very beginning. Had this not been so, a deer might be mating with a she-mule, and so onward in infinite variations, creating new species to multiply and propagate. But nature has strictly preserved the GOD-given law to grow and multiply within kind and species only, without exception. This explains why it is impossible for a male mule to propagate its species with a she-mule.[4]

Moreover, we see signs [of this law] in the Ethiopian species. I suspect it happened that either Adam or Eve was dark, since nothing in the Sacred Texts expressly states that one or both were white. Thus, after the Deluge, blackness eventually sprang forth in a certain man and with time propagated. As Aristotle reports, such was the case with a woman from Sicily who lay with an Ethiopian—her daughter did not take her Ethiopian father's color, while later on the son born of that daughter did restore the [color of his] Ethiopian grandfather.[5] It is said that Moses, too, had an Ethiopian wife, though this has not yet been sufficiently proven.[6]

Still, if we were to consider the opposite case, that Adam alone was the first man created, and that Eve (along with the rest of humankind) was enclosed within Adam and produced from Adam (and so, properly speaking, not created), then necessity absolutely dictates that Adam had to be of two colors, since the product bears the form of the producer. Nor can we verify the assertion that Adam had two wives, Eve and Lilith; indeed it is demonstrated even more clearly that GOD created no black [ater] men, because if a dark man procreates with a white woman, or a white man with a dark woman, the dark color will gradually fade over time.[7] And why are there no men with spots when even today we find red men and men of other colors?

Experience, however, reveals the opposite, for if [blackness] depended upon Adam, throughout the world there would clearly be as many black as white men and also their mixture. But in fact, the opposite is true: in Ethiopia all men are black and in Europe they are all white. Paracelsus, however, claimed that there were two Adams. The first one, who was white, was located in Asia; the other one, black, was located in Africa, among the inhabitants of Guinea.[8] But if this is so, how do we explain [the presence of] red men? Should we perhaps claim that a third, red, Adam existed? We cannot agree with this theory.

### Chapter 3: On the Particular Location Approved by God for Punishment, or Some Other Cause Only Known to Him, by Which It Pleased Him to First Mark Man as Black

Some among the Jews dare to affirm that Ham, the son of Noah, was punished by God with black coloring immediately after he had ridiculed his father as he lay drunk and naked. It seems right to add the testimony of Josephus, *On Antiquities,* Book I, chapter 23, who writes that Africa was named after Afer, the nephew of Abraham, through his son Midian; and of Solinus, who believed that Africa was named after Afer, the son of the Libyan Hercules.[9] Thus Homer in the *Odyssey* 1, line 23, as well as Pliny S. 8, thought that Ethiopia was named after Aithiops, the son of Vulcanus.[10] Hence, up to this day, it has been bequeathed to us that the first king of Ethiopia was Cush or Kus, the son of Ham. Others claim Adam to have been white at first, before his sin, but after sinning, he turned black.

Whatever the case may be, no one denies that a black man was the propagator [of all Blacks]; regardless of what one says about this, there is no reliable testimony about how he became black, inasmuch as all of Antiquity is full of stories: for example, that Ethiopia was not named after a black or a burned man, but from the burning heat of the sun; or that the descendants of Ham were said to have spread up to Babylon where there was no such black color, indeed not [even] in many parts of Africa.[11] And nothing can be proved from Adam, since his descendants were not all black, and prior to sinning, he had no children.

And so we may infer that if someone is marked especially by GOD, it follows that this mark be a specific color, unsuitable for any other man, such as the case for the statue of Lot's wife.[12] After all, of what use would a mark be, if you do not need to be marked? Since we find Ethiopians not only in Ethiopia, but also in Eastern India and in the unknown Austral land, are we to believe that GOD has marked a plurality of men with this sign? He marked Cain on his forehead; why do we not find men with the same mark today?

And what would this mark be—natural, or supernatural? If supernatural, why do we not see black children born in Europe from entirely white parents, grandparents and great-grandparents? How many men do we find in Europe who are extremely black and have black shining hair? No one will deny that the blackness of the hair and the skin has the same cause, as will be made exceedingly clear in the following pages. If it is natural, why is it a mark? Let us undertake the task entrusted to us by investigating the natural causes of this phenomenon.

### Chapter 4: On the Mother's Imagination

Innumerable examples, all too common and very sad, demonstrate that the maternal imagination has a great influence on the formation of the fetus. When the mother's feelings are upset by her imagination, this affects the fetus by imprinting on it the strongly received idea and upsetting the infant's spirits as well.[13] [It must be so], since a feeling cannot influence a body without a medium, for one can reach one end from the opposite end only by going through a medium, and because a fetus, being recently conceived, lacks any imagination. (Not every sentient being has an imagination; otherwise all the plants, being sentient, would have imagination).

Hence, unlike what Georg Ernst Stahl believes, we are not talking about the soul [anima] of the infant, but its properly called spirits [spiritus].[14] Stahl, against all sound reasoning, denies that the imagination acts on the spirits. But it is the spirits that receive the idea from the mother, and since they inhabit the nerves and the nerves nourish the body, the spirits spread throughout the body in accordance with the nature or the form of the thing conceived, by pressing on the nerves here and there, extending them, stretching, bending, raising, dilating, constricting them, etc.—until they imitate the shape of the conceived idea, in such a way that the body, with the nerves arranged in such a way cannot grow any differently. In the same way a plant is compelled, even against nature, to grow following the shape predisposed by the farmer.

And since the arrangement of the body's humors and their changes depend upon the arrangement of the body's nerves, the change in colors will occur through the imagination. Still, however strong the mother's imagination may be, it cannot make such products of the imagination propagate in the species; otherwise the world would be full of monsters, particularly because the black [color] in which the image takes shape is not superficial but organic and created by nature with much effort. From this, it follows that imagination cannot be the sole cause of the propagation of blackness among the Ethiopians, though I would not deny that it might be a contributing factor.[15]

## Chapter 5: On Fertility

The egg which encloses the fetus, though it is present in the mother's ovary, cannot issue forth into the world by its own powers, unless fertilized by a masculine seed. But however the egg is fertilized, because it lacks its own procreative spirit, it neither grows nor comes to life on its own. A grain of wheat, however you handle it, neither grows nor multiplies but actually rots once it loses this spirit either because of the weather or some other accident. Hence it is impossible for a she-mule to conceive because it lacks eggs that can be fertilized, and the eggs of chickens, if born without the rooster, are unfit for reproduction, due to this absence. For this reason, these [infertile eggs] are called *upanemia* [8πϑνέμία] or "eggs of the wind."[16] Thus for a complete birth the ovum requires spiritual fertility [*fecunditas*] and spiritual fertilization [*fecundantia*]. (I would not say that this spirit is animate, but certainly it contributes to the formation of the soul [*anima*].)

Fertilization by the male occurs in conjunction with the mother's heat and nourishing juices, such that the spiritual substance of the masculine seed acts in the spiritual substance of the egg (not in its soul [*anima*], because these spirits are material, while the soul is a spiritual spirit). When the soul descends into an egg that has just been fertilized, it is as if a candle had lit another candle, indeed like kindling close at hand; for the soul is not created then, but added by God from the first creation.[17]

It is possible that these spirits, being of an intermediate nature, part spiritual and part material, are able to travel very easily through the bodily form; just as in Palingenesis the structure of the spirit represents the natural shape of the plant rising from the dead earth.[18]

From these things it stands that, since the male seed is an extract or the Fifth Essence of the whole body, it is necessary that a fetus, lacking the mother's image, develop according to the father's shape. Just so, the mule takes after its father the horse, and diversity varies the fruits and flowers of the earth, as experience bears witness. As to the question of the first black man, this has nothing to do with fertilization except that [blackness] acquired strength over a long period of time, thus almost becoming a recurring condition, just as Whites are born from Whites and so on. From here let us make a digression to the following topic.

## Chapter 6: On Geographical Location

As the saying goes, Africa produces some prodigious event every year.[19] We notice in so many other cases that a change in location has considerable effects [on various phenomena]. [...] The question we must ask ourselves here is: did [African geography] contribute to the dark color of the Ethiopians?

The Persians have long noses; the English red hair; the Tyroleans and people from Salzburg tend to have scrofula; and the inhabitants of the unknown Austral islands and lands near the strait of David are pygmies. Testimonials of giants are preserved in the Holy Scriptures; the Chinese are olive-colored, etc. And yet, since neither foreigners, though they may live all their life in Africa, are ever changed into Ethiopians, nor are their children, nor the mixed offspring of Whites and Blacks, and since [black humans] always stand out as distinct, I conclude that location, properly so-called, did not make the first inhabitant black.

## Chapter 7: On the Workings of the Earth, Water, Fire, and Air, and the Influence of the Stars

The earth constantly emits a variety of vapors, both harsh and noxious—a thing which metal miners experience in the mines, to such a degree that their clothing becomes colored, and they choke on the spot. Just as meat grows black when hardened by smoke, so we can see that the vapors of the earth can turn men black. This was the conclusion of Francis Bacon of Verulamium, in *Sylva Sylvarum, or a Natural History in Ten Centuries:* he attributes the pale green and swarthy colors of the Abyssinians, the inhabitants of Mauretania and Peru, to the dried vapors of the earth.[20] But, seeing as no foreigner is changed into an Ethiopian, he makes a massive error, inasmuch as we find vapors everywhere on the earth, perhaps even more abundant and dangerous in certain places. All of England is full of fumes from anthracite, yet no one becomes black. Moreover, nothing may be inferred regarding the peculiarity of vapors, since we know that there is only one center of the earth, and one form of sulfur only.

In the above-cited passage, Bacon alleges that water specifically is the cause of blackness among the Ethiopians. But even if we were compelled to admit that water is the vehicle for colors, it was also discovered that in Guinea drinking water will spawn worms, especially in the feet; that rain will corrode cloth; and that one must fear it and sedulously avoid it, making sure it does not touch the bare skin, since it will cause many diseases. Hence, we might find fitting the reasoning that either water or rain or semi-putrid vapors are the cause of blackness, as Celsus attests.[21] We may also consider blackness as being acquired from pain and fever. Furthermore, oils pertain to water, and Ethiopians use them quite frequently; they also use the dying juices of vegetables, just as we use dye derived from walnut peels. Hence, it might be possible that the first inhabitants smeared themselves with dyes or unguents to protect themselves from the heat of the sun (especially from smegmatic-like diseases).[22]

One might also conclude that blackness is both induced and propagated by the mother's imagination. Nevertheless, our experience related to propagation argues to the contrary (as we can see every day), since it is not only the imagination of the mother that is required, but also the uncreated habitual predisposition of the male seminal spirit, drawn not only from the outside but from inside the body as well. The weakening or absence of this spirit is also a contributing cause to the gradual fading of a dark color when mixed with white. Nor are such painted colors constant, since they fade again as the skin is shed.

Anatomy also argues [for a different explanation]. [Anatomists] have shown that the outermost covering of the body, the cuticle, is not the seat of blackness. (This structure would have to be the seat of blackness, if blackness came from an external cause.) Rather, the seat of blackness is the underlying *corpus reticulare.* What is more, to our knowledge, no foreigner has ever turned black from drinking water in Guinea or from any disease. Further, it is impossible that everyone [in a given area] should be ill at the same time [and consequently turn a specific color].

[...]

Aristotle proposes fire or heat as the cause of blackness, and in the same vein derives *Aithiopia* from *ab* άίθω and όψ, the Greek words for "burn" and "face" since, as he claims, the Ethiopians are burned by their proximity to the sun. However weighty Aristotle's authority might be, I cannot agree with him on this matter. [...]

It does not escape anyone that the heat of the sun in Persia near [the Port city of] Gameron is by far more brutal [than any part of Africa], as travelers testify.[23] Yet the Persians are not dark. Also, the skin grows red from the cold just as it does from heat. And if the intensity of the heat of the sun is one of the causes, why do we find white animals in Ethiopia? And why are there black and reddish [animals] in the cold regions of Russia? We know that ash-colored linen thickened from the moistening of water becomes white, not black, from the action of the sun. Thus the lilies of the valley grow white blossoms in Ethiopia, and the most powerful fire bakes the clay into white lime. Hence the cause of blackness must be sought not in the sun but in the body itself.

Hippocrates, in his book *On the Winds,* designates the air as the author and master of the things that happen to our bodies, a fact that accords with the rationale of health and diseases; for no doubt when the spirits of the air are shut in, they act on the spiritual sinewy [*nervea*] substance, a substance that can also resist changes in color. Consequently, his theory does not hold here.

We do see that various elements in the air are communicable through the pores, due to the thinness of the skin. This is an occurrence to which many phenomena testify, such as the white down seen flitting through the air in springtime and in autumn. [. . .]

The production of colors that can be transmitted [to one's offspring] can hardly be attributed to the air, however, inasmuch as the force from the terrestrial vapors of the water and the heat of the sun are a harmless element, as we discussed earlier. As experience demonstrates, nothing can be pushed continuously into the skin from the outside, or through the art of the dye-maker, hence I move on with good justification.

Here let us consider the influence of the stars [studied by] the astronomers (though not even two of them will agree on their principles) on the conception of the human embryo. We cannot deny that the stars', the sun's, and the moon's rays have an influence on the earth, from which we can simply infer that the heat of the sun ripens plants and trees and fodder for cattle. But the sun's rays also bring diseases, most conspicuously in the Indies. More frequently, the rays of the moon, when the chill of night draws near, overwhelm the insane, causing them hallucinations. [. . .]

Nevertheless, being so far away, it is impossible for the stars to have any influence, through the contact of their rays, on the formation of the fetus, [just as it is impossible] for it to be affected by the metals hidden beneath the earth in its innermost bowels. And even though they are constantly irradiated by the stars, we never see plants and animals, including wild beasts, grow or be born even the least unlike their previous generations. On the contrary, we note that twins of the most diverse nature and shape can be conceived simultaneously.

### Chapter 8: On Nourishment

[. . .] It is agreed that food and water give the body not only nourishment but also foster its growth; hence they seem to have a substantial influence in the alteration of bodies. This is especially true when we read the *Description des îles* (Description of Islands) of Mr. de Rochefort that the Juniper tree, which grows in the Antilles, produces a fruit that when eaten by parrots and swine tints their fat and flesh with a purple color.[24] When the fruit dies, this color also fades. In Guinea they chew the [leaves of the] plant Betel all day long, which then colors their saliva with a blood-red color.[25]

Similarly, we know that many Ethiopians eat spoiled meats, and there is common agreement that rotting meat grows black and that its putrid vapors can alter [the appearance of] bodies. Also, we know that honey inflames the bile in hot-tempered [people]. Such things are common knowledge. The wax in the Antilles is so dark that no procedure can turn it white.[26] From the foregoing, it is clear that color can be induced or altered with little difficulty. However, you might object as follows: "There is an enormous difference between flesh, which, by its nature is red in everyone, and the skin, which is usually white." [. . .]

And yet, this idea too must be rejected. [Take the following example into account.] [. . .] An Ethiopian who lived in Dresden for almost fifty years recently died. During this time, he never lost any of his color due to [eating] our food, just as no foreigner has ever been turned dark by the food [he eats] in Ethiopia. [. . .]

Neither blood—unless it is extravasated nor milk [when it is drunk] is able to transform the substance [and color] of the skin.[27] Since the entire function of nutrition is nothing but the continuous filtering of foods from the larger to the increasingly narrow, to the narrowest, almost invisible, pores [*foraminula*], we must ask ourselves: how fine must the color of the Ethiopians be? Is it like fine air or dew [*aeris aut roris*], and so able to transform the top layer of their skin (such that no technique can remove it), by passing through flesh and the skin itself, and leaving both of these intact?[28]

The dark color of the Ethiopians is more constant than the white of the Europeans, the latter of which is altered by even the slightest cause. From these considerations, we infer that this dark color must have received its predisposition or form together with other fixed parts of the body at the very instant of conception. [. . .]

### Chapter 9: On the Workings of the Solid Parts and Fluids in the Human Body

The solid [body] parts that come under consideration here are the *cutis*, the *corpus reticulare* above the cutis, the *cuticula* which covers the entire body, and the nerves; the other parts are not relevant here. The *cutis* of Ethiopians is very white, to which the anatomists attest: see Heister's *Compendium Anatomicum,* about which nothing more need be said.[29]

Indeed, the *corpus reticulare* is correctly said to be the seat of blackness, as both Heister (as mentioned above) and Pechlin have written about the characteristics and color of the Ethiopians.[30] And yet, the [dark] substance in Ethopian skin is neither membranous nor solid; [. . .] rather its color comes from the juice or sap [held] in the membrane, when properly remixed. Their hair, too, is colored in the same way, which grows grey, falls out, and becomes flat when humors are lacking.[31] And if they were pressed with [the ink of] a stylus of some sort, their teeth would not be colored, since teeth are not permeable, but consist entirely of bone. The lips of Ethiopians are swollen, on the other hand, due to this overabundant sap, which more freely fills the nose and lips thanks to the great number of secretory canals. This is made clear during fevers. [. . .]

During the day, the bodies of Ethiopians flow with sweat, and the humors are driven to the outermost edges of the cutis. Due to equinoxes, and the fact that heat gives way to sudden and bitter cold at night, the pores of the Ethiopian contract since heat relaxes and cold constricts, as Aristotle says in Book 4 of his *Meteorologica.*[32] It may also be that the humors which are shut inside the cutis break down and leave behind a sediment that can be colored by the heat of the sun, as Francis Bacon claims in his *Sylva Sylvarum,* Experim. 399.[33]

[. . .]

Pertaining to the liquid parts of the body, blood and bile alone come under examination here. No one will deny that blood is present in the smaller arteries and veins of the skin, and that it gives men their color (because the bloodless and the dead are pale), or that it is endowed with a fatty and sticky substance, as we said earlier. Since we see, then, that blood grows black when it spills from the veins, and leaves behind a dark charcoal-like sediment as it condenses, it would seem correct to say that blood extravasated from the vessels into the *corpus reticulare,* or brought there by some other accident, once it has condensed, is the cause of blackness among Ethiopians. Since, however, it is not possible for blood to extravasate in so many thousands of men, always and across all generations, blood alone can scarcely be the sole cause of blackness.

Indeed, Jan Baptist van Helmont attempts to persuade us that the blood of Ethiopians is black.[34] But if we were to believe this author, perhaps he was deceived by the blood of the cuttlefish, which is asserted to be black, though the blood of all fishes appears dark to some degree. Although many

Ethiopian men and women have taken cover in Europe, many battles having been waged, and many Ethiopian women have given birth in Europe, who has ever seen black blood in them? [. . .]

More than a few men say that bile is to blame for Ethopians' blackness, and to do so, they bring a variety of arguments to bear. But in order to offer my opinion on this matter from a well-grounded perspective, I ought, so it seems, to digress on the separation and use of bile. First of all, bile is produced from foods, through the remarkable act of digestion [*fermentatio*], imperceptible to the senses and accomplished by the power of gastric secretion, and is finally brought down into the duodenum through the *ductus chyledochus* and into the gallbladder. Meanwhile, the remaining mass is further changed and more thoroughly diluted by pancreatic juices for the easier separation of the chyle, particularly in an empty intestine.

[The author then describes at length the supposed path of bile, the role of the gallbladder, etc. before refuting those people who attribute blackness strictly to blackened bile.]

[. . .]

If bile could affect people's colors, why would not this always be the case? If this were how it inevitably happened, infants would be yellow, adolescents swarthy, and the elderly very dark. But in fact we can observe bilious old men (unless they were tanned by the sun) no darker than infants who are infected with the same disease. And where do the colors of doves and deer come from if, as Aristotle in his *Historia animalium,* Book 2, chapter 15 testifies, they have no gallbladder?[35] And if color comes from bile, why does it not disappear when the bile has been evacuated and corrected, just as it does in the case of flatulence? [. . .]

Neither foreigners nor other peoples become Ethiopian due to the presence of bile; in short, this fluid cannot cause the fixed and inheritable color of the Ethiopians. Perhaps the adrenal glands [*renes succenturiate*], which are called *capsulae atrabilariae* after the jet-black secretion contained in them, could give some credence to [the rejection of bile as the cause of blackness], if it could be demonstrated from the anatomical [dissection] of an Ethiopian cadaver that these are lacking in Ethiopians, so that the secretion contained in their kidneys, once disseminated throughout the skin, would [instead] provide the cause of blackness.[36] This might not be impossible because urine and sweat correspond so closely to each other that when one is suppressed, the other takes its place.

I hardly believe, however, that this could happen without detriment to the health, since the kidneys are larger in infants and smaller in adults; I imagine that they are destined for a different use, though it is not obvious. Perhaps their function is to purge the lymph of filth as it flows back along its lengthy path, in the same way as the gallbladder has the function of removing the foam or fecal matter that results from the first stage of digestion. [. . .]

### Chapter 10: On the Effect of the Temperaments

Among the various temperaments, I will only consider the choleric here, since most cholerics are of a blond or golden-yellow complexion, and the saffron or clayish color of melancholics corresponds to the color of cholerics, or depends on it, just as the phlegmatic and sanguine temperaments correspond to each other. These last two temperaments seem to differ from the first two by as much as the moon differs from the sun. [. . .]

[In this rather confusing portion of the essay, the author speaks obliquely about the fact that Africans are seen as melancholic. And yet, since, as he also admits, children with very opposite temperaments can be born of the same parents, he also maintains that temperaments are not transmitted solely through propagation. A given temperament, in short, does not have the power to transmit the dark color of the Ethiopians as a trait that can be propagated.]

[. . .]

### Chapter 11: On My Opinion Concerning These Matters

Since all of these explanations, after careful discussion, have been found insufficient, it behooves me to present my own opinion on this matter. But before I explain my final thinking, I am now inclined to take up several issues that merit close scrutiny.

The following fact is worthy of consideration: namely, that even compared to the Jews [who also tend to resemble each other], scarcely is an Ethiopian seen whose face and countenance did not resemble in face the others; all these faces are fixed in their specific, native land.

This simply leads us to conclude that they were all born from one propagator, by means of an extremely strong impression, which the outcome confirms. We can see this since, if Blacks are mixed with Whites, immediately starting from the next generation the dark color will gradually fade. However, if [a non-black or albino] comes from the same propagators, something extraordinary—extraordinary, not natural—is responsible, since nature preserves its preordained order.[37]

Conversely, in the case of Blacks repeatedly propagating with Whites, this would be analogous to the blending of the two great sources of light, namely, the sun and the moon. Nature is an ordered force, and the result of this coupling would be natural to the degree that swollen lips and an awkward body demeanor confirm a diseased state, which comes from natural processes.

We must regard this dark color as having arisen from either GOD or nature. And yet, the foregoing arguments for either tend to contradict each other. As such, a third possibility will win the hand: the assertion that our original state was sickly, hence neither immediately from GOD nor immediately from nature.

I now maintain that [color] depends upon neither external nor internal immediate causes, but upon predisposition in the very first formation. For where do spots on the tongues of animals, and their color come from? Why are stains on hides blotted out? Why does a scar change its color?; and so on. Undaunted, I conclude as follows: All Ethiopians descend from the same man who propagated their kind, and this first Ethiopian was not black, but of a ruddy complexion, and this ruddiness arose from a sickly condition, and degenerated into a dark color due to the influence of the sun's heat, through the effect of time, and with mediating applications of unguents that have continued uninterrupted to our own day. This color, which seems to almost have acquired its appearance through a strong impression, gradually became inheritable after a great length of time.[38]

If we consider that in the beginning the number of men inhabiting the earth was fairly small in comparison to our own day, we must concede that the procreation of every man comes from one propagator *through a strong impression,* with other weaker opposing forces intervening. Now a certain patriarch chose one specific place instead of another to establish his dwelling, as the Holy Scriptures testify. And since for many years they had no need of trading, and consequently of visiting each other, they saw no other men, other than those of their household. Hence the effect of the maternal imagination [during conception] remained undisturbed, and was able to be passed down more easily—no differently than lilies of the valley, which are white by nature, but, once they are tinted, are forever born colored.

[. . .]

Since, in the earliest days, men had the custom of marrying more than one wife, and since their offspring married while they were still children, in short a single family could easily become a large nation of people. And since brothers had intercourse with their sisters when there were not enough men to be found, an entire people was created bearing the color of that first father, by virtue of the strength of his fertile seed. We have found it reported that, if a man has intercourse with an animal, or a female animal with a man, or a crow with a white domesticated hen, the hen will yield speckled eggs. I have personally witnessed the latter phenomenon many times.[39]

And since it is not possible to go from one extreme to another without an intermediary, a white man's offspring cannot become black immediately. Rather, as experience shows, [this takes place progressively], from blond, yellow or brown colors. Indeed, not even by adding dark colors can one produce something consistently dark, especially dark skin, as the example of the waning of the moon bears witness, which is otherwise of a constant color. And except for these dark colors, no color of man except for white and red is found. Hence the irreducible conclusion is that the first Ethiopian was red. The Holy Scriptures give examples of such men; for Esau was reddish, hence he was called Edom, that is, "red."[40] The inhabitants of the unknown Austral lands offer a greater proof: up to this day, many red men live there among dark and white men.[41]

[. . .]

Suffice it to say, that the dark color of the Ethiopians is propagated from the color red, which is confirmed by eyewitness observation. Venturing beyond everyday experience, however, Fernel's medical regimen (*Therapeutices Generalis* (General Therapeutics), p.m. 28) makes it clear that even though nature may be accustomed to something, it can still change it into something of a different nature, after a long enough time.[42] Having become accustomed to one type of medication, for example, nature no longer responds to its power, and rejects it.

[. . .]

Still, the color red can also be turned into a dark [*atrum*] color in another manner: being faced with insects, the Ethiopians necessarily had to protect their bodies by covering themselves with oils, as is still their custom today; this action yielded an ugly [*teter*] color, like that of the Spanish reed, which is a deep yellow, though when cut into small rods and completely saturated with oil and hung in a chimney, it blackens. Wanting to correct such ugly color, they painted themselves dark all over; and this is why, even today, this dark color brings the greatest pleasure to the Ethiopians, and is why they consider it beautiful.

SECTION TWO

Concerning the peculiarities of their hair as well as the appearance of the Ethiopian body.

## Chapter 1: On the Color and Graying of Their Hair

In addition to what has been said elsewhere, a few things still need to be added concerning the hair of the Ethiopians. Hair color among Europeans and others, as well as in animals, was naturally ordained by GOD in the first creation, just as it is for plants, flowers, etc. In Matthew 6 Christ expressly says about these things that GOD colored the lilies in the fields.[43] Yet, as to the Ethiopians' hair I say that their blackness has the same origin and cause as the skin's (and it has already been satisfactorily treated above), being clearly created by the condition of the coloring matter. [. . .]

## Chapter 2: On the Curliness and Roughness of Their Hair

Concerning the curliness of Ethiopians' hair, they all have the same habit of oiling their hair with palm oil, as some are wont to do, although we know that they use the seeds of the Psyllium plant to make their hair curly.[44] Other Oriental peoples oil their hair to remove curliness. Most cholerics as well as certain animals have curly hair.

I declare that it [curliness] depends first and foremost on the imagination of the children of the first Ethiopian. This first man had a deficiency in the nourishing juice as well as an abundance of swollen common protuberances resulting from said deficiency. The nodes became bent due to the choleric temperament that heats the body excessively, causing it to dry.

It is for this reason that the hair of Ethiopians is short and rough. Similarly, in plants and trees a deficiency in their nourishing sap will cause them to grow laterally rather than vertically, will dry up the hay and bend the bark of trees. Just in the same way hairdressers make hair curly by applying a curling iron. It must be reckoned, however, that the habits of nature already accomplished most of its work given the great expanse of time that has passed, as we observe in animals. Similarly, observation has established that short, coarse hair is more easily curled than long, soft hair, and that hair with color is by nature coarser than white hair. Hardness is the result of many protuberances in the hair.

## Chapter 3: On the Awkward Appearance of Their Body and the Smoothness of Their Skin

In the preceding section I discussed their swollen lips because, clearly, the awkward state of their colored body is related to a disease of structure and a sign that blackness comes from a state of disease, or is caused by disease, which is then propagated through the [process of] impression. As it stands, the appearance of their bodies is more or less inbred. Ethiopians have flattened noses from the mother frequently pressing on them in infancy, while the smoothness of their skin is given by the softness of their nerves and the thinness of the pores of their skin.

### CONCLUSION

Here, benevolent reader, you have my explanation of this matter that has been investigated to its very roots, in the greatest brevity I could muster; I leave it to the judgment of more learned men.

"We should listen to the early writers indulgently. Nothing is completed while it is beginning."

Seneca, Nat. Quaest. 6.5.3[45]

[. . .]

# 14

## Blackness Degenerated

David Chaigneau, a Protestant minister of the French Church of Carlow and longtime member of the Irish Parliament, wrote this essay. Chaigneau was the descendant of a Huguenot family forced to emigrate to Ireland when the Edict of Nantes (a century-old document ensuring religious toleration) was revoked by the government of Louis XIV in 1685. His essay seemingly dabbles with biblical exegesis (from a somewhat ironic point of view) before moving on to questions related to anatomy and geography. The author refutes the pre-Adamite polygenist theory as well as ideas from Antiquity about differences in the blood and sperm of Blacks. He draws from diverse sources and synthesizes tenets from various existing theories to put forth his own hypothesis: blackness is an effect of various adjustable conditions such as diet and climate, influenced only incidentally by more fanciful forces such as the maternal imagination, and therefore reversible over several generations.

RELIGION HAS ITS MYSTERIES, and natural philosophy has its own. Despite the best hypotheses, the most ingenious systems, and all the discoveries we owe to modern philosophers, there are still many phenomena for which we cannot account. A great part of Nature is still only a land of conjectures. The subject [on blackness] that you are proposing to the public is proof of this; when one takes up this topic, it is easier to refute what others have said than to establish a solid truth [of one's own]. So, since we are in the land of conjecture, everyone can make of this topic what he wants. Accordingly, I will first examine what has already been said about Negroes and then offer what I myself think about them.

Let me begin by saying that it is not necessary to confound ourselves with the question of swarthiness. In the infancy of modern philosophy, the celebrated Mr. Boyle demonstrated that this color is acquired quite easily when one changes climate.[1] But that is not the case with Negroes, since experience shows us that their own color continues (with only slight changes) over succeeding generations wherever in the world they are transported. Several writers have suggested that the children of Negroes are born white and that they change color gradually during the first days after their birth. This appears confirmed by the proceedings of the *History of the Royal Academy of Sciences* in 1702.[2] However, one of my uncles, a man of discernment and probity who spent fifteen years on the Coast of Guinea, where he was Lieutenant General for the Company of Africa, and was attentively instructed about everything concerning this country and its inhabitants, assured me that this is not so.[3] Generally, infants are born black, or a color leaning to that of sage, and boys at birth have a black spot at the end of the penis, but the rest of their natural parts are white and these parts do not become the color of the rest of their body until five or six days after their birth.[4]

Several Ancients have attributed the color of Negroes to their seed, which they believed was black; but it is certain that the seed of Negroes differs in no way from that of other men. In ignorant countries it was also believed that the blood of Negroes was a blackish color like ink, which our everyday experience refutes. The blood of Negroes is of a red as brilliant and vermilion as that of Europeans.

This brings me to my refutation of the chimerical author of the pre-Adamite theory, who believes that Negroes are not descended from Adam but from another man who was black, and consequently that Negroes are a species of mankind quite different from ours.[5] Although this opinion has been adopted by some, it seems to me untenable if one accepts the authority of Holy Scripture.

Equally untenable is the opinion of a few people that the color black was the mark that God put on Cain to prevent anyone from killing him, and that the Flood was not universal since Negroes are descended from this older son of Adam.[6]

Finally, we may ignore the opinion of some Muslim doctors that Shem (the oldest son of Noah) was white, that Ham was black, and Japheth olive-colored; such that the inhabitants of the world retain the color of that of the three sons of Noah from whom they descended. Even mentioning these opinions does them too much honor, and they should be regarded as the reveries of a few empty minds.[7]

There remain two other opinions I should examine because they are supported by illustrious names, including Doctor Bochart.[8] One is that the color of Negroes is a mark and a consequence of the curse that Noah pronounced on Ham. The second attributes the blackness of these peoples to the excessive heat of the climate they inhabit, which is the means, says this scholar, by which this curse is carried out.

First, although one must believe in the miracles reported in Holy Scripture, it is both ridiculous and foolhardy to add them to one's own [more naturalistic] theory. Resorting to supernatural causes tends more to create difficulties than to solve them. If one is so inclined to accept miracles to make sense of everything, then one will soon have so many [miracles] that one cannot distinguish the false ones from the true ones! [. . .]

If we understand Noah's malediction as a curse upon the whole of Ham's posterity, we are going to blacken a greater part of mankind that one imagines. Not just Ethiopians and other African Negroes, but also Egyptians, Arabs, Syrians, Assyrians, Chaldeans, etc. would all become Negroes—since all these lands were peopled by descendants of Ham.[9] Moreover, if we may believe the fragments of Berossus that Josephus has conserved, and some other texts of great antiquity, we will find that Italy was first peopled by Ham's descendants, such that the inhabitants of this country would also be Negroes![10]

If we restrict Noah's curse solely to Canaan and his posterity as we should, since Holy Scripture (Gen 9:25) teaches us that it was pronounced against him and not against Ham, then we should not seek Negroes in Africa but instead in the Promised Land, which was peopled by the descendants of Canaan, since it kept this name until its conquest by Joshua.[11] If Noah's curse changed the complexion of the children of Canaan, then the Hittites, Hivites, Amorites, Jebusites, etc. (in short, all the peoples of this cursed posterity) must have been Negroes, which is not the case.

It seems that those who assert that the color of Negroes is a result of Noah's curse ought to prove convincingly from which of these sons they descend and explain why this son's posterity felt this malediction and not the others. The genealogies of Noah's children are only sketchily deduced in the tenth chapter of Genesis; and despite critics' laborious research, it is very difficult to determine to whom the Ethiopians owe their origin.[12] Most people maintain they descend from Cush, but that is easier to suggest than to prove.

[The author speaks at length about the etymology of the Land of Cush, at which point he then refutes two further ideas: the belief that Ethiopians came from Cush and the Curse of Canaan.]

[. . .]

Now I pass to the second opinion, which attributes the color of Negroes to the excessive heat of the climate they inhabit, which was the idea of almost all the Ancients. A dissertation on this subject is found in Strabo; and Aristotle in his *Physics* poses the problem of why the heat of the sun makes men black and that of fire does not.[13] Why does it whiten wax although it blackens the skin? The term *Aethiops* was given to the most memorable nation of Negroes, but actually signifies, as I have already said, blackened or burnt. The Fable of Phaeton again illustrates the common opinion that Negroes only became black due to the sun's action.[14]

1) I do not disagree that the heat of the climate where Negroes live might contribute to maintaining and perpetuating their color as long as they live there, yet this could not have sufficed on its own to change them from white to black. If that were so, then other animals ought to have been affected just like men, and this is not so. All animals in these climates keep the same color they have elsewhere.

2) If the excessive heat of the climate were the sole cause of this complexion, at least this effect ought to extend to all men, such that Whites would become black there, or at least engender children of that color. But long experience constantly undermines this idea; the Whites who have settled in the countries of Negroes have always conserved their color there and they produce children that are perfectly similar to them.

3) If the ardor of the sun were the sole cause of this complexion, it would be reasonable to conclude that all those who lived at the same latitude (just as near the sun and its fervent rays) would also be the same color, which is definitely not true. Look at the inhabitants of Cambodia, Java, Sumatra, Borneo, etc.; or at the inhabitants of America. Although this habitat is between the two Tropics and at the same latitudes as the countries of Negroes, still the color black has never been natural or original among these peoples. It is true that we find a great number in these places today, but everybody knows that they were transported from Africa, that there were never any present when Columbus and the first Navigators to the West made the discovery of this new world.

Another reason that the sun's proximity cannot be the sole cause of this complexion is that in Africa all the peoples living within the Tropic of Capricorn are Negroes, and those who live below or near the Tropic of Cancer are not. [. . .]

To resolve this difficulty, one cannot aver (as some do) that the sun is stronger and more powerful in the Meridional (southern) Tropic than in the Boreal (northern), because when it reaches the Sign of Capricorn, it is at its perigee, or greatest proximity to Earth, and thus this part should feel the effects more sharply. So this explanation is not relevant. [. . .] Indeed, if the color of Negroes were caused solely by the heat of the sun, there should be more of them on our side of the equator than on the other. But as I have just remarked, this is far from being true, as I will point out more particularly now.

Are there Negroes in Africa farther beyond the Tropic of Capricorn? The peoples around the Cape of Good Hope or the Hottentots, who are beyond the 36th degree of southern latitude, are all Blacks, whereas those who live at the same degree of the northern latitude are White, like the inhabitants of the Algarve, Andalusia, Sicily, Malta, Crete, etc.[15]

A similar objection could also be made about the color of the Samoyeds, a few Lapps, and some other peoples from northern Tartary, but they are merely swarthy and not black.[16] If they were black, they would form an incontrovertible argument against the opinion I am examining. Yet these examples do serve to demonstrate that it is not solely from the climate's heat or cold temperature that the whiteness or blackness of skin tone depends. If that were the case, the Samoyeds [who live in frigid climates] would be much whiter than us.

Apart from the heat of the climate, the lack of water and the excessive aridity of the terrain count for something in causing the color of Negroes. But notice that the lands inhabited by these peoples abound in springs and rivers, as much as and maybe even more than any other. On the other side of the Mountains of the Moon, in the great country called Zanguebar [Zanzibar], we find the beautiful rivers of Guamà, Saint Esprit, and several others; and on this side, we find the magnificent rivers—the Zaire, Niger, and Nile— which not only temper and refresh the air by their exhalations, but also humidify and fertilize the land by their yearly inundations.[17] Notice that the part of Africa that is most arid, Libya, is situated between our tropic and the equator and actually has the greatest lack of water as well as having the most burning sand. What is more, Libya is not inhabited by Negroes, but by swarthy people.

From all that I have said, it appears that the opinion that attributes the color of Negroes to the curse pronounced by Noah against Ham is a chimera, and also that this color was not entirely caused by the heat of the climate. I admit that this heat might produce a tendency to acquire this color and contribute to foment it and maintain it once it is acquired, but this cannot be the sole cause. So what are these causes? I am going to offer a few conjectures. If I cannot flatter myself to offer the true causes of the color of Negroes, I will at least try to discover some that might have contributed [to it]. Plausibility, or simple possibility, is all that one may offer in such research.

Before moving on, we must establish the location of Negroes' color, and to understand this, we must have some idea of the structure of the skin of the human body. [To do so], I will use the same terms employed by Alexis Littré, the illustrious historian of the Royal Academy of Sciences in the year 1702.

The skin is composed of three different parts. The inmost is the skin proper. On the inner surface are glands—miliary or glandular nodes, round or oval in shape and the roots of hairs.[18] On the outer surface are the excretory conduits of these glandular nodes, that is to say, the drains for sweat, hair, and an infinity of tiny pores, which anatomists call *papilla pyramidales* because of their shape.[19] They are no larger than the heads of the smallest pins and appear to be the organ of touch. On the skin extends the reticular membrane, pierced like a net with an infinity of tiny holes through which pass the excretory conduits of the glandular nodes, the hairs and the pores of the skin. The reticular membrane is in turn covered with the epidermis or overskin, which is also called the cuticle because of its external thinness. Its external surface is smooth and even, but the inside is full of irregularities that form a quantity of small spaces, where the ends of the nodes enter.

When one seeks the cause of the blackness of Moors, it is found that their body's skin and its epidermis were as white as those in other men, and it was only their reticular membrane that was black. It was this color that appears through the epidermis, which is very fine and transparent. The famous Malpighi believed that the blackness of the reticular membrane came from a thick and glutinous sap that it contained, which was black. We will now see which causes might have contributed to making the reticular membrane of Negroes a different color from that of other men.

Would it not be possible that the use of certain waters or certain drinks of a quite particular nature or quality might have started to produce the effect we are seeking on the first men that partook of them? Aristotle in his *Physics* and Strabo report several phenomena of this kind; Pliny also cites a number of these waters, such as two fountains in Béotie [Boeotia], where the water of one made the sheep white and the other made them black. [He also states that] the water of the Sybaris (a Greek colony, now called the Calabre River) made the cattle black, and somewhat produced the same effect on men, since it made their hair become black and frizzy like those of our Negroes.[20]

[...]

It may be that certain waters or certain concoctions or Infusions, which the Ancestors of Negroes used for their customary beverage, might have caused obstructions in their glands, and especially in their miliary glands or the glandular nodes of their skin. These might have arrested part of their "sap" and thus not permitted the filtration of fluids of a caustic and blackening nature. Their reticular membrane, having been flooded, would have contracted a certain degree of dryness and blackness, which could be the cause of the color of these peoples.

Notice that the inhabitants of hot climates have blood that is much more fluid and glands more dilated than those of more temperate climates. This being so, their bile must be more subject to effusion than that of other men. Their bile cannot fail to be strongly burned. Is it not possible that Negroes are often subject to black jaundice? Is it possible that the first inhabitants of these lands (arriving from more temperate countries) were subject to an epidemic disease of this kind?

If this disease were of long duration, then the glandular nodes of their skin would become engorged with a black and burned bile, and by this means perhaps their reticular membrane contracted several shades of this color. All the children who were engendered at that time must have acquired the indisposition of their fathers and mothers and transmitted this color to their posterity.

I still wonder if this blackness were not produced by a cause like the one Jacob used to multiply the number of his spotted Sheep [Gen 31], that is to say, by the force of women's imagination, which often produces strange effects, as history and experience prove often enough. Hippocrates reports that a woman gave birth to a Negro for having looked too attentively at a picture depicting one.[21] But without resorting to this old story, it appears that a Lady of the most eminent dignity in one of the foremost Kingdoms of Europe gave birth to a Negro girl in the last century, and that this accident led to all Negroes being chased out of Court.[22]

Vagabonds called Bohemians or Egyptians who travel all over the world have their skin darkened by being rubbed during their childhood with a composition made of some fatty matter and the sap of leaves of the walnut tree.[23] In Guinea the Negroes rub themselves every day with fat and sage or other similar lotions in order to moisten the skin and partially to protect themselves against the dryness and heat of their climate.[24] A similar custom might play a share in the color of these people, a color that began with the imagination of women and was continued by the operation of the climate, which was completely suitable for maintaining and continuing the imprinting that the first generations had once received.

All these causes might well have contributed, each playing its part, to producing the bizarre phenomenon we are examining. The Ancestors of Negroes might have by their food and drink altered the nature of their blood and the humors of their body and thus disposed them to receive the imprinting of their climate, to which the extraordinary and copious effusions of a black and burnt bile also contributed. The terrible ardor of this same climate might have required these men to maintain it thanks to the fatty and black unguents. These are still used among the Africans, and make their hair frizzy and their lips thick.

These lips are very tender and spongy and full of an infinity of small glands that can easily imbibe the unguents and swell up. The women are coated with black and fatty materials and when they have [sexual] relations with men in the same state, as well as during pregnancy, they have these objects continuously before their eyes, so their imaginations are vividly struck by them. The reticular membranes of these men and these women are thereby flooded from within by the flow of black bile, and from without by the black matter of the unguents easily transmitted through the cuticle, which is even thinner and more tender among Negroes than other men, because of repeated use of these unguents.

Note that in parts of the body where the cuticle is harder and thicker, like the soles of the feet and the palms of the hands, Negroes are white. All these causes I have just reported might have contributed, each playing its part, to produce a considerable change in the first generations of these peoples and make them acquire gradually and then pass to their posterity the color we see today.

It is useful to note again that the need for unguents persists among newborns as well as among adults; young and old, men and women do not appear in public unless smeared with fats and sage. Their *amour propre* (selfworth) soon leads them to regard as an ornament what was at first just the result of necessity. It is right to say that habit is second nature. Afterward these peoples developed a particular and arbitrary idea of beauty. They regard as perfection what appears to us as dirty and ugly, such that, once it is acquired, they take particular care to conserve and perpetuate this color black as perfect beauty, by all means they can imagine, to the point of suppressing white babies that are sometimes born among them, as I will shortly point out.[25]

Bring an end to such causes and the effects will cease. Transport men and women to temperate lands, give them healthy foods and suitable habits, and then these [corporeal effects] will no longer occur. The glands will contract; the filtrations will take place in a different way than formerly; the nature of the blood and humors will change. The children that will be born from these people (or at least the children of their children) will have reticular membranes that are one or two shades less black than those they came from, and their own children will lose a little more of this color, such that from generation to generation these effects will eventually completely disappear. In a word, the descendants of those black people will become white, in the same way as their ancestors went from white to black. If the causes of blackness in Negroes that I have reported are true, their degeneration when they are transplanted should not surprise us, for this will be a necessary consequence.

It is common that bizarre productions in animal bodies result from some foreign imprinting, either fortuitous or artificial, in their seed or in their bodies themselves. When the causes of these imprintings no longer occur, things return to their natural state. Plants furnish us with many examples of this, if we had the time to pause; bears, foxes and several other animal species are all white in the Far North, whereas everywhere else they are of a very different color.

But without going so far afield, we have here an order of white canaries, which is a very recent phenomenon.[26] They have only acquired this color through artifice. Their natural color is grey-brown on the back and a greenish yellow on the breast. But as soon as we obtained a male and a female of the color white, they did not fail to produce young of this color. It is true that they later degenerated and after a few generations they returned to their primitive color. Nature is always stronger than art.

Canaries seem to reveal to us what happens to Negroes. If we may agree on the external causes I have mentioned (or others of the same kind) that were able to cause the alteration over generations of these peoples, then we may also agree that the descendants of Adam might have been able to commence and to continue a race of Negroes although their Ancestors had been of a very different complexion.

The degeneration of the Negro seems to establish the truth of what I have just said: as soon as one removes the causes, or makes them cease completely, these men will gradually return to their natural state. Negroes do degenerate, meaning that when they are transplanted to temperate climates, they gradually lose the color black and acquire the color white. That fact is certain.[27] I think this obviously proves that the color white is the natural color of Negroes and the color black is purely accidental. It was probably produced by the causes I have reported, or by analogous ones. Moreover, in the lands of Negroes, artifice is used to conserve the color black, even by doing violence to Nature, in order to prevent the color white taking the upper hand over time.

Mangin and some other travelers report that the Emperor of Ethiopia, who claims direct descent from King Solomon and the Queen of Sheba, is proof of this, since he himself is not black like the rest of his people (says Mangin) but mulatto, which are his titles of nobility, and an indubitable mark that his lineage came from a White king and a Black queen.[28] As fabulous as this tale appears and as unfounded as the claims of the Emperor of Ethiopia may be, it is still possible that the Royal family of that country are of a different complexion than that of the people, since among Negroes sometimes white children are born. It even appears that if they were allowed to multiply, their number would increase and that of Negroes correspondingly decrease. To prevent this, these Whites are killed or rendered incapable of generation.

Andrew Battel, a British mariner who was taken captive in the Kingdom of Angola and who remained there and in neighboring countries for eighteen years, gave an account that is included in Purchas's *His Pilgrimage*.[29] Here is this traveler's account of the Kingdom of Longo [Loango]:

> White children are sometimes born in this country, though quite rarely, for all the inhabitants are black. As soon as they are born, they are presented to the King; they are called "Dondos." They are as white as the whitest Europeans. They are trained in Magic and the diabolical arts in order to make them magicians to the King. Nobody dares say anything to these Dondos and if they go to the market, they can take whatever they want without anybody opposing them for fear of displeasing them. Yet this country is in the middle of the Torrid Zone, and inhabitants are so taken with their blackness that they render the Dondos impotent in their infancy, for fear that their race would continue or their number increase. They cannot even bear interring them in their land, they are so averse to Whites.

Other authorities could be used to confirm this fact, but it is time, gentlemen, to finish this discourse, during which I could not avoid discussions that extended it beyond what I first proposed. I am far from convinced that what I have said can be entirely satisfactory on the subject in question. If my *amour propre* might be humbled, this effort has furnished me with the opportunity to pay homage to your Illustrious Academy and to bear witness to the esteem and respect that I have long held for you. As these sentiments do me more honor than they do you, it is not surprising that I desire and seek the means of manifesting them. This desire leads me to address this document to you, more than does the fond hope of being able to win the prize you are offering to the public. [. . .]

**"Make light from smoke"**[30]

# 15 ⌒

# Blackness Classified

This classification-oriented essay is an outlier among the other sixteen submissions. In the first paragraphs, its French-speaking author adopts the division of the world's peoples into six distinct "*espèces*," a term translated here as "species." Species was a polysemic and slippery term in 1741, simultaneously meaning species, line, category, kind, type, and/or race. In this essay, however, the author employs this term to emphasize the real and seemingly racial separations among humankind's various humans; he also emphasizes that there is only one original species of human, "the legitimate one," that is to say the white species. Not surprisingly, the author reserves his most damning and pejorative comments for the fixed and essential black species, for whom he categorically rejects the possibility of climatological origin. His particular theory of degeneration is based on the idea that the original settlers in Africa may have eaten strange foods and animals. At the end of the essay, the anonymous author concludes his essay with a Latin quote: *An mutare potest aethiops cutem suam, aut pardus liuentes maculas suas?* [Can the Ethiopian change his skin or a leopard its spots?] [Jeremiah 13:23]. The answer to this question, from his point of view, was clearly no.[1]

SANSON, IN HIS INTRODUCTION to geography, notes the various ways in which people are divided, either by their location in the various parts of the terraqueous globe or by the nations they form, or by the languages they speak, or by the religions they follow. He ultimately establishes a division of humankind according to the specific differences in their appearance, by the obvious and specific differences in the various body parts that compose all men.[2]

Sanson based this division on the work of François Bernier, the famous traveler and doctor and disciple of the great Gassendi, a man known for his good sense and penetrating thought as much as for his veracity and sincerity.[3] These are rather rare qualities among voyagers. Bernier divides humankind into five categories or species in relation to the exterior appearances, which I am going to explain.

The FIRST CLASS: The first includes all Europeans (except Lapps and little Tartars), and those people who live in the part of Asia that is subject to the Turkish Empire and to Persia, to which should be added Arabia, Georgia, and perhaps some of the lands adjacent to Persia. All these peoples have a notable exterior resemblance, although some are whiter or swarthier than others, but not enough to form a different specification. In fact, I do not intend to explain the [specificity] of these peoples; we may perhaps know this; what I will say about other peoples will show how this first species differs from the following ones.

The SECOND CLASS includes in Europe little Tartary (and particularly the Uzbek Tartars), the Tartar-Mongols, the Manchurian Tartars (in other words, the conquerors of China), the Chinese themselves, the Japanese, the Koreans, and the inhabitants of the Philippine Islands, of the Ganges peninsula, the Sunda Islands, etc. All these peoples have specific characteristics: a very flat face (as if crushed), and eyes of a rather different form from ours; a very small nose, too; and almost no beard, which appears only around the mouth and the chin.

The THIRD CLASS of men comprises the Lapps in Europe, Eskimos in Asia, and other inhabitants of countries in both the arid and cold northern zones. These peoples are smaller than all others; they have an air of being extremely deformed and savage, seeming to have something of the ferocity of the bear; their neck is short, their face is elongated and juts out below in a particular way; their eyes are also somehow different; and finally their stride is accompanied by a certain rocking that is quite extraordinary.

The FOURTH CLASS is that of native Americans, that is to say, the descendants of the inhabitants of America whom the Europeans found there when they discovered it. These peoples are not absolutely white, but they are not black either. They have a certain middling color that is rather difficult to explain and which may vary according to different climates, but which is certainly different from that of all other nations. In addition, their gaze is troubled / shifty, and their manners are fundamentally dissimilar from those of all other species, but what characteristically differentiates them from all the inhabitants of the Old World is that [American natives] have no beard whatsoever, nor any hair on any part of the body except for their head. One could find a thousand proofs [of their difference], but the most obvious is drawn from the name that the natives gave the first Europeans, which was "men who have hair," a term that demonstrates that the Americans had never seen a bearded man.

Finally, the FIFTH CLASS of men according to Bernier are Negroes.[4] Their specific differences include:

The color of their skin, which is sufficiently known;
The somewhat oily softness of this same skin;

Their hair is frizzy and rather similar to wool; their beard is also kinky
and rather different from ours. The hairs are strong but also rough to
the touch.

The thickness of their lips in general; the shape of their nose is always
sunken in the upper part, to which we may add

The whiteness of their teeth, and

The rather general stupidity of this race of men (although in varying
degrees) to the point of some being degenerated (like the Hottentots
and Kaffirs) to the point of being totally useless to others and to
themselves.

As surprising as this list might appear, we have to add a Sixth species of
men, who have something still more extraordinary, since they are different
by the structure of the skull, and the teeth. (Other species differ only by their
color or by their beard or other minor traits.)

Here I am drawing on a paper by the famous M. Winslow of the Memoirs of the Royal Academy of Sciences in Paris (1722). Perhaps the greatest
and most profound anatomist who ever lived, Winslow describes the skull
of a savage of North America living on an island called the Isle of Dogs (in
other words Hound-Eyland).[5] This man has an anatomical structure very different from the ordinary man in many respects, which [Winslow] presents
to us in drawings and description.[6]

I will comment on only one feature [or lack thereof]: what we call *dents
incisius,* or sharp and cutting incisors, are lacking in these men. They have
teeth that are more similar to molars, being short, rather thick, and in no
way sharp. One should not think that this extraordinary anatomical structure is peculiar to the individual whose skull was examined by M. Winslow,
since all the inhabitants of this island eat raw flesh by putting a whole piece
in their mouths, holding it with the front teeth. Now, while holding it with
one hand, they pass a kind of knife with the other hand quite close to their
mouths and thereby cut the meat or, rather, they saw it very crudely with
their mouths. While chewing and swallowing, they also make several extraordinary movements with the jaw and many grimaces.

Here then are the six different species of men on earth; but perhaps these
are not the only ones that exist; others may be discovered as we increase our
knowledge of the globe, which today we know very imperfectly. But whether
there are only these species, or others still found to exist, we must pose as a
principle something indubitable: these differences are not in the essence of
man and his nature. All the men I have just enumerated are equally animated

by an immortal soul; they are spiritual, free, created immediately by God. They are all equally descended from a single man and a single woman, from Adam and Eve, and then from Noah and his wife.

And it is precisely from this that arises the difficulty that today I will try to clarify. For one has to observe that each species of man, as differentiated as I have represented them above, is particularly invariable and inalienable.

To approach more closely the subject of the present essay: a Negro and a Negress will always produce Negroes similar to themselves, in whatever country to which they are transported; reciprocally, a Negro is never produced except by Negroes. This is confirmed by constant experience; the examples claiming to be contrary prove nothing, since when they are profoundly examined, we will find that the [offspring] are monsters, or sick with a particular malady, or a species of runts, that is to say, infants that are imperfectly formed in the womb of their mother. I will touch on this later.

What I say here about the invariability and inalterability of each of these species is very important and can be buttressed by incontestable proofs. I caution the reader that when I speak of this invariability, I always mean that each species is not mixed with another, that they are mating only within the same species.

This stated, we must prove that each species is not changed by mutation, or by a change in climate, or (which amounts to the same thing) by the same species subsisting in a different climate. The experience of Negroes alone proves this, for the misfortune of their condition renders them subject to being transported to many countries. Yet everywhere they always remain Negroes, as much in cold climates as in temperate ones, as well as in the hottest ones.

It is true that Negroes in cold countries do lose the certain luster or tan that they contracted in hot countries, but this luster or tan is very easy to distinguish from the fundamental basis of their black color (as we will easily see when I have reported on the inherent principle of this color). Moreover, it would not be surprising to see Europeans themselves contract a [superficial] luster or tan in hot countries that they do not possess in their native countries.

We have to agree that Negroes do have some differences among them regarding their original blackness: there are Negroes whose black is darker, others where it is lighter, and some where it is mixed with a dark red. We know that in diverse nations, the shades of black differ respectively. Similarly, among individual Negroes there are varieties; the sanguine are blacker, the bilious are less so.[7] Their hair possesses diverse nuances; in some it tends to the blond, in others to the red, but in all of them it is frizzy and similar to wool; this is what accounts for their essential differences.

It is the same with color; one individual is a little less black, the other is more so; but fundamentally they are all black, and everywhere all of them transmit this blackness to their descendants.

Specific differences similarly vary in all other species of men. European Whites are not all equally white, as much with respect to other nations as regarding each individual within the group. The Norwegian is whiter than the Portuguese in general, and this Portuguese man may be swarthier than another from the same country. But they are still equally white men, and it is impossible to confuse them with Negroes. We could—and should—reason in the same way about Asiatics, Tartars, and Chinese etc., who form the second species; and analogously about all the others. Among the differences that compose the species are some slight variations, and there are some between particular individuals. But they all have the characteristics of their species, which makes them able to be distinguished and recognized by others once such particular traits are identified.

This is how I understand the invariability and inalterability of these different men, and now we may prove what I have advanced on this subject by incontestable and detailed facts.

There are some Negroes in Hudson's Bay in northern Canada, which is one of the coldest countries in the world, yet they conserve their blackness there. The Cape of Good Hope is at a southern latitude rather similar to the northern latitude of the Island of Crete; hence the temperature of the air must be quite similar. Yet, the latter is peopled with Whites and always has been, while the former is full of Blacks who are almost brutes.

In all times Negroes have been found in the interior of Africa, that is to say, in the portion of this huge land that lies in the Torrid Zone. However, that part of South America lying in the same zone, when it was seen for the first time, had no Negroes. Today those who are found there were brought by the Europeans; we could say the same thing about the Sunda Islands in Asia, etc. All lands [in the Torrid Zone] that have been found by explorers are full of a single species of people that are different from Negroes.

In addition, the Negroes who have been transported somewhere have not changed; they have always remained Negroes. This is demonstrated by [those] kings of Spain who made laws that established the policing [of Africans] in the large territories they possess in America. We should take note of the lessons to be drawn from the laws and customs of a nation [like Spain]. This country is very political and very attentive to its interests, which gives their actions particular weight.[8]

The Spanish noted that if individuals of different species mate with each other, the infants resulting from these mixed unions derive traits from both of their parents, and they are called *métis* (half castes). If these *métis* continue to mate with the families of European Whites for four consecutive generations, experience shows that by the fifth generation, they totally lose the traces of their barbaric origin and become similar to those Whites who originated in Europe.[9]

There are different sorts of these *métis,* which my subject's brevity obliges me not to explain, and so I must omit them. They have different names according to their various combined origins. But the Spaniards totally exclude all *métis* from the privileges they grant natural Spanish Whites. Moreover, these *métis* can never achieve these privileges for themselves, and their descendants cannot claim them, unless their ancestors—fathers, grandfathers, great grandfathers, etc.—mated for four consecutive generations with White families, in which case they have lost all their specific blackness and have become similar to natural Whites. This is why the Spanish have made a very severe law, which is even more severely enforced: if during the course of these four generations, if only one individual mated with some barbarian family, then all hope is lost and the [descendants] can in no way gain privileges from the preceding alliances with Whites.[10]

Therefore, it is clear that these different species of men always carry within them the traces of their origin, both in their persons and in their descendants, until by a long series of uninterrupted generations within a single one of these species, that species comes to prevail entirely in the children that are born. So it is not the climate, nor the food, that can change a species once it is determined.[11] It is only generation [reproduction] that can have this effect, an act that produces wholly new alliances outside the original species, just as it is only reproduction within one's own kind that perpetuated that species in the first place.

We perceive the truth that these differences (I repeat) are not essential, i.e., they do not reside in basic human nature. If these divergences were fundamental, one species could not mate with another, and their union would never lead to one species changing into another, regardless of the number of successive generations [of mixing]. Thus, although such variations are not essential, they are still considerable and merit the whole attention of philosophers.

So the question is how from a single man there came to be several diverse species. How did a single species degenerate and change several of its individuals, or even a large number of them? Why did only a portion of these individuals conserve their original state?

But I could be asked: among these six species, which one actually conserved its primitive state? How can we distinguish the veritable species from bastard and degenerated versions?[12] This question can be considered under two aspects, the physical, and that of religion.

On the physical side, it seems that the best means of making this distinction is to consider the species that contains the greatest number of individuals, since it appears that this must be the one that has best conserved its first origin, since a species that degenerates is always weaker and less capable of resisting foreign imprintings.

But on this level, if we exclude Lapps and the savages of the Isle of Dogs, this would return us to a difficult choice between Europeans, Chinese, Negroes, and Americans. Perhaps we should even note that the Europeans are the least numerous of all these species.[13]

We can scarcely determine the number of individuals [in each species], either by means of great industry or a great aptitude for the sciences. We have heard it said that a species that has not degenerated must be one that has the most strength to resist foreign imprintings, and is therefore most able to maintain itself in its primitive and natural state. Consequently, a degenerating species must have been enfeebled, at least to a certain point. The brain and the nerves must be sensitive to such weakening and degeneration.

It must follow that in bastard species, there is less industry, less capacity for the arts and sciences. And depending on the various degrees of this weakening in the organs of internal sensations, the result might even be a kind of stupidity in a few of these human species that would render them inept in civil society.

Therefore, there is no doubt that the first species (the one we ourselves are from) is the primitive and legitimate one, so to speak. All the others have degenerated, but diversely according to [their particular] susceptibility. If you want to know in which order I place them in this respect, I'll say that the Chinese seem to me the closest to us; I put the Americans in second place; next, the Lapps and the inhabitants of the Isle of Dogs; finally, I put the Negroes in last place because of their general stupidity and the almost bestial barbarity of some of them.

[The author refutes at great length various biblical explanations related to the origin of Africans, including the Myth of Ham. These reasons are not valid since, as he puts it, this "would greatly embarrass our savants, since we cannot see why this color became perpetual in this race, and this assertion is not based on any testimony either from Scripture or tradition. Moreover, we would have to find other men who were similarly and miraculously changed in order to become the fathers of the other species of men we are talking about. This is why we should abandon this idea."]

There are numerous other hypotheses put forward by various writers to explain the difference of Negroes from other men. If I wanted to report and refute them all, I would need a hefty tome. Here I have reported the most famous and the oldest and I have posed some general principles that could be applied to all these various opinions, were we not suddenly struck by the total absurdity of this procedure, for it is impossible for this discussion to satisfy every point. What I am going to say going forward will shed more clarifying light on the shadows commonly obscuring this matter.

I assert that one cannot explain the blackness of Negroes and their degeneration without posing general principles that might explain the diversity of colors that differentiate men. One must also explain not only the various degenerations that have occurred up to now (and to what portions of humankind), but also all those that might occur later.

There are three matters that I will take up:

FIRST, THERE IS the current state of the skin and hair of Negros, which is related to how their skin and this hair are structured. We therefore have to understand the conformation [anatomy] of the Negro, to settle this first point.

The second is the immediate cause for some individuals having this skin; this can only be generation [reproduction], as we have already proved, and we will linger no longer on this subject.

The third question is: what is the original, primitive (and certainly distant) cause for the first members of the black race being thus shaped? Why did the ancestors of Africans, previously similar to us, come to change and to degenerate into this bastard form? This is the most difficult point.

### FIRST QUESTION

The current conformation of the Negro can be easily demonstrated in the discoveries of the celebrated anatomists Malpighi, Littré, and Winslow.[14] There is nothing in the world as difficult as perfectly deciphering the secrets of nature. Therefore, we should not be surprised that it took three of the greatest men who have ever fleshed out our knowledge of the human [body] to solve this mystery, with each one [of these savants] contributing something [quite important].

The human skin is composed of three parts. The First is the outer skin or epidermis. It has been claimed that it is perfectly white in Negroes, as in us, but this is not exactly true. M. Winslow had demonstrated that it is like a very thin layer of black horn, which has the effect of looking dirty-white.

The Second is called the reticular membrane, the cutaneous network, the reticular plexus, or the Malpighian network; in Latin, *plexus reticularis.* These are all synonyms for one and the same thin membrane that is pierced by an infinity of small holes like a reed; it is located immediately underneath the epidermis, to which it is attached. This membrane is above the skin proper, and it gives passage through the tiny holes with which it is pierced to nerve tufts that come out of this skin; and which are the organ of the sense of touch. It keeps them in a state of constant firmness.

The third is the skin, properly speaking, which is immediately below the reticular membrane. But since this is not an anatomy lesson, I will not give a more ample description because this does not serve my goal. I will merely note that this skin in no way contributes to the exterior and apparent color of the human body because it is absolutely the same in all of us, and it is covered by the reticule and the epidermis, which alone produce and characterize any particular color.

It is true that the skin contributes very little in Negroes to their blackness; this is not the physical and inherent principle of this color, as we shall see. The reticule just described is the seat and constant principle of color in all human bodies, whatever that color may be. This is a certain fact, and should be taken as axiomatic on this subject.

The color of this membrane differs not only in various individuals, but also in the same man according to the various parts of his body, for example the tongue, palate, cheeks, etc. These variations are known by everybody.

Generally speaking, this reticular membrane (which was discovered and demonstrated for the first time by [Marcello] Malpighi) is black in color in Negroes, like charcoal; but this color is softened by the diaphanous quality of the epidermis, which resembles the color of grease. In other men the reticular membrane has a different color. It is white among all Europeans, and among all Asians, except for some slight differences indicated above. It is a lively red among natural Americans, with various nuances of shade and several other modifications.

Now we need to know from whence comes this different quality of the reticular membrane; why it is black in some, and white or red in others. This can only be from a particular sap with which it is impregnated and which has different effects in diverse subjects.

But what is this sap? Malpighi believed it is a sticky, mucous, and glutinous sap. Littré tried to extract and separate this liquor from the vessels that contained it; he also macerated a portion of the skin of a Moor for seven days in warm water, and another strip [of skin] in wine spirits. Even when boiled, these powerful solvents could not extract this sap. This led Littré to conclude that this liquor is chimerical and that the black color of the reticular membrane of the Moor came from this particular tissue and from its original structure.

But it appears that Monsieur Littré was wrong. If his opinion were correct, he might have concluded that the color of Moors was merely a simple degeneration, a change that occurred since the first creation of man. But on the contrary [given his opinion], this conformation could not come from a primordial structure that would be particular to those men, since ultimately the intimate tissue of a body's membranes cannot change [suddenly] due to some accident that occurs without the subject perishing. Instead this change must have taken place over many centuries and have been perpetuated from race [viz., lineage] to race, without our seeing that the life and health of subjects suffered in any way. I do not see how the consequences of M. Littré's opinion could be reconciled with the principles of our religion.

It is true that M. Littré also attributes to this membrane the effects of hot air as a cause of the effect we see in Negroes, but I have already gone over what we ought to think about this way of reasoning.

For my part, I think that although it cannot be drawn out by long maceration, this sap must still exist. It must lend its color to the skin and to the epidermis, according to the judicious remark of Monsieur Winslow. If there were no sap in this membrane, we would never see this effect.

[The author maintains that this dark sap comes from the blood and the lymph, which are carried to this reticular membrane by ordinary blood vessels.]

It cannot be reasonably doubted that it is the fluctuation of this mucous sap that, in its most delicate parts (which sweat removes from the body), must communicate a soft and oily quality to the skin of Moors that distinguishes them so remarkably. I cannot see to what other cause this effect could be attributed, as something that always accompanies the skin's blackness.

Nor do I doubt that the thickness of lips, the flatness of the nose, the whiteness of the teeth, which are also remarked among Negroes, are all distant effects of this sap in the reticular membrane. It is true that the link among these features is not easy to find, but one may plausibly conjecture about it due to the union of all these effects in the same subjects, which shows that these traits must follow from each other. I think this is all we may say on the subject, for this point is very obscure.

We should reason the same way about the specific quality of the hair of Negroes. But since this subject was posed in our topic as a problem to be resolved, I cannot be content with mere generalities.

The origin of all the hair on the human body is under the skin, in the fat; in order to reach the air outside, as we can observe, every hair must traverse and pierce the skin, so to speak, including the Malpighian reticular membrane and the epidermis.

Every hair leaves from certain oval corpuscles [follicles] that are called onions because of their shape. The celebrated M. Chirac has described them; Heister thinks the hairs come from nerves, and Ruysch, along with Leeuwenhoek, thinks they are a continuation or an expansion of nerve crests.[15] It is agreed that they are vascular and their roots are bathed in some kind of humor.

From this, we conclude that this type of hair must vary in nature, strength, and color, according to the quality of the land (terroir, if it is permitted to use this term) where they grow; according to the liqueur that waters them, and the sap with which they are surrounded.[16] This is visible in daily experience; the hair of children is softer than that of adults, the beard becomes tougher as one advances in age; finally, hair whitens in old age in all men, generally speaking.

So if hairs encounter a foreign sap in the terrain that bears them, they will be obliged to pass through a membrane impregnated with a sap that is thicker and more tenacious than it is in other men. This kind of hair will respond to this [circumstance] and will take less nourishment, so it will be shorter and finer, as is observed in Negroes.

With respect to the curliness, hairs take the shape of the pores through which they pass; if they grow out of tortuous and irregular pores, they take the same configuration. When they are exposed to air, the hair fibers maintain the same form they received during their passage. So it must be said that the reticular membrane in Negroes affects the pores through which their hairs and their beard pass. It seems this is all that can be said on this obscure and difficult point, since to attribute (along with Pliny) the curliness of this beard and this hair to the heat of the climate would be extravagant.

### SECOND QUESTION

On the immediate cause of the blackness in each Negro individual: we said above that this cause can only be generation, inasmuch as this individual was generated by Negroes who always produce something similar to themselves.[17] We have given sufficient proof of this fact, and therefore we have nothing more to say on this point. The general question is why all animals produce something similar to themselves, which is outside my subject. Suffice it to say that I have proved (apparently incontestably) that Blacks are engendered by Blacks, and that they are produced by them alone. Vice versa, Negroes always produce only Negroes in whatever part of the world they are conceived, and this suffices to answer the second question.

THIRD QUESTION

What is the cause of the degeneration of Negroes; and more generally of all other men, who are different in some accidental ways from the primitive and original state of humankind? Above I pointed out that this cause could not be air or climate. For such a singular effect, we could point to food or to something else that in the degenerated men has caused their blackness and made this astonishing change in them.

But first we must formally exclude the ordinary food consumed by all mankind without risk or danger in all countries of the world. Experience has shown that Negroes transported to various countries, very different as they may be from each other, have eaten the common and ordinary goods of each region, without their being altered in any way, for better or for worse. The same must be said of all the other human species without exception.

So we must look at the extraordinary foods that famine, necessity, and poverty have forced people to eat. These foods may nourish the body at the instant they are consumed, when their harmful effects are not immediately perceived. But over a long period they may produce surprising effects. We need to find a period and circumstances in which these strange foods might have been more abundant and more avidly consumed.

This is what I propose to do. But in order to be better understood, I must prove by several examples the truly marvelous consequences that certain singular foods may have, for better or worse. The experiments conducted for several years by M. Belchier in England show that the roots of madder mixed into the [diets] of several kinds of animals soon reddens the bones of these animals, but without making any impression on the cartilage and other neighboring parts.[18]

The Dutch who have remained in Batavia on the Island of Java (one of the Sunda Islands) cannot nurse their infants when they have consumed the food of this island; their milk becomes salty and infants cannot bear it. The infants must be nursed by women native to these islands.[19]

Busbecq (an eminent scholar) reports as an eyewitness that there is a certain canton in Anatolia where the goats produce beautiful hair that makes very prized textiles.[20] If one transports these animals elsewhere, their hair changes nature as soon as the goats taste the grass of another region. Our dogs, when they are transported to Guinea and when they have tasted the food of this region, cease to bark; their hair becomes rough, and in a word, they degenerate so much as to become unrecognizable.

[The author describes several examples of maladies being communicated by eating particular foods, e.g., horsemeat producing matted hair among the Polish; a Sicilian fish that gives mange to all who eat it; certain Alpine waters producing goiters.]

The most beautiful blood in the world, we are told, is that of the Georgians and the Colches.[21] We can attribute this fortunate singularity only to their principal nourishment, which is particular to that country. It is a sort of small grain they call *gom*, a kind of mush or nourishing dough, though a little cold, which can be corrected by adding the local wine, which is excellent. The result is a very healthy and agreeable food, as tested by those who have been forced to get used to it over time.[22]

[The author goes on to attribute the origin of venereal disease to eating a certain iguana found on Saint-Domingue. This becomes the point of departure for a food-based theory of degeneration.]

Could one not conclude that it is precisely this extraordinary and pernicious food [iguana] that produced such an effect with respect to Negroes, which is the subject of the present study?

We cannot yet determine this, because the interior of Africa is little known to us; the matter could only be perfectly clarified by organizing expeditions that we will not be able to conduct in a land inhabited by such ferocious and unsociable tribes.[23] But do not doubt that we would discover this if we had the ability to conduct such searches.

[. . .] Even though [my belief that blackness was caused by food] cannot yet be confirmed in this way, this does not entirely destroy my hypothesis. Indeed, the singular and evil food that produced this effect has perhaps disappeared. Perhaps this [poisoning] occurred only in a fleeting manner, as one of the momentary effects that followed the universal Flood.

[The author speculates at length about what happened after the Flood, when humankind moved across the world.]

During the time the earth was softened and soaked with this salty water, the great humidity (especially combined with the heat of the Torrid Zone) may have given rise to innumerable unknown insects and new plants. Later these insects and plants did not find similar circumstances in which to grow and vegetate, and so they utterly disappeared, or else today they appear only very rarely.

Therefore after the Flood there must have appeared over the whole surface of the earth (and particularly in Africa and all other warm lands) many new and singular things; for example, in London in the last century, after the awful fire that desolated that city, one was surprised to see on more than 200 acres (arpents) of land a kind of plant called *erysimum latifolium,* of which there had been no vestige before and which has not appeared since then.[24]

Now shortly after the Flood, men by their multitude and due to the confusion of languages could not remain in the same place and so went in search of distant places to settle. And since they found everywhere only deserted and uncultivated lands, ravaged by the horrible scourge they had just undergone, they were obliged to eat everything they found that appeared to be edible. Certainly, they could not have had enough provisions to carry so far, and if they did, not enough wagons and animals to transport them. So the life of these wandering men must have been the literal experience of what we read in the poets (Ovid and Plutarch) of the miserable times when people ate acorns and wild fruits and berries, if they were lucky enough to find them. In these extremities, even serpents and the most extraordinary plants were not overlooked. So it was that a few of these poor unfortunate people found one of these foods, in appearance innocent and useful, but pernicious and dangerous on the inside, which caused in them a marked degeneration; and then perhaps this food disappeared. Or at least it would have diminished, as the bad leavening that sea water communicated to the earth also diminished, and the remaining waters dried up. This required a certain amount of time, during which degeneration reached its final stage.

Note that this might be a general explanation of all the degenerations that occurred in various parts of the world, which must have been diverse, since each area has its particular salts [and minerals] and its specific qualities. There must have been born in different parts of the world diverse plants and insects, which must have caused varied degenerations, since [such changes] continue to exist today.

But even so, this does not explain the principle for the bastardization of Negroes. We must consider the miserable life that Pliny, Diodorus of Sicily, and Strabo attributed to Negroes twenty centuries after the Flood. To be convinced that these poor people were in the same state then as they still are today, look at the Hottentots and Kaffirs, of whom it has been said that "it would seem that their land had just been created, given the small number of inhabitants with which it is peopled, who dress in animal skins, eat roots and whale blubber and dead or half-cooked fish, and often totally raw carcasses."[25]

The [contemporary] authors I cite do not describe the Hottentots and Kaffirs in better terms. Some eat only serpents, others only locusts, but they can never live longer than forty years, and they all perish from the winged lice that this kind of food causes to emerge from their bodies. Some of them live only on the flesh of panthers and lions, but others find better meat. They may eat elephants, but they are not any luckier. They are reduced to living on roots and even more unfortunate ones are forced to eat whatever they can find, whom Pliny and Diodorus call *panphagi*.[26] Some of these tribes did not even know the use of fire in the time of King Ptolemy Lathyrus.[27] This should not surprise us, since in southern America we found the Amicouanes who were not familiar with fire, either.[28] When Magellan discovered the islands that are now called the Marianas, the inhabitants had never seen fire.[29] But to come back to the ancient Ethiopians, the most civilized of them in the time of Pliny knew no other grain than millet and barley, while Strabo also describes their lives as poor and miserable, and Diodorus of Sicily (a wise man) depicts them in these terms: "With regard to food, some live on a certain fruit that grows without cultivation in ponds and swampy places, others eat the tenderest offspring of trees whose shade guarantees them from the heat of the noon, some sow sesame and lotus. Some live only on reed roots."[30]

Thus Diodorus depicted [Africans] who live in total nudity, and who use women in common like beasts; others who graze on the grass that grows in shady places.[31] Among the Troglodytes, they drank the sap of brambles, but only the ordinary people did so. The great lords feasted on the juice of a certain flower, which was something execrable.[32] This is the miserable state of Negro societies around the end of the reign of Augustus, almost two thousand five hundred years after the Flood. So it is easy to conclude that this bad food and deep poverty, combined with a bestial way of life, necessarily made them degenerate.

But you will say that since that time things must have changed and that although those societies are not yet on a level that approaches our to own, still they live much more comfortably than formerly, and they no longer eat anything out of desperation, except for those who live in indolence and shameful idleness, and are good for nothing, either for themselves or for others.[33] But perhaps any changes among these peoples since Augustus' century have only returned them to their primitive state, or only slightly improved the barbaric deterioration from which they had initially suffered.

I respond that the changes once introduced into a species do not correct themselves like that; a pure and simple change in [diet] will never serve as antidote against a secret and hidden venom once these uncommon and insidious foods have been introduced into the body. If a man has contracted venereal disease on account of having eaten the flesh of the iguana serpent, in vain will we nourish him with excellent meats. We will never cure his sickness, nor prevent him from communicating this venereal plague to all the women he approaches, and with which he infects his posterity. If you want to cure him radically, resort to the great and sole remedy.[34]

We have to reason the same way about what has produced all these degenerations in men: it is like a bad leavening that has invaded the interior of the body and which will never fail [. . .] to change its nature, or to assimilate everything that is susceptible to this change; thus this leavening continually augments over time. It communicates its [nature] to the seed of the degenerated body, and so its offspring is born degenerated like its father.

[To substantiate his thesis, the author provides several more examples of how the physical "vices" of a certain population are handed down to subsequent generations: these include examples from the animal kingdom, royal "maladies," and the birth of albinos among black populations.]

"Can the Ethiopian change his skin or a leopard its spots?" [Jeremiah 13:23]

# 16

## Blackness Dissected

Essay 16 is unique for being purely *naturalist,* meaning its arguments derive not from metaphysics or Scripture but from human anatomy. The author, Pierre Barrère (1690–1755), was a doctor from Perpignan (near the Spanish border). In 1722, he was appointed to the post of "King's botanist" in Cayenne. He spent roughly three years in this French colony, practicing medicine as well as botany, and took a keen interest in the dissection of African slaves, an extremely rare practice at the time. His most notable work was *Observations anatomiques tirées des ouvertures d'un grand nombre de cadavres* (Anatomical Observations Taken from the Openings of a Great Number of Cadavers), 1751 and 1753. Barrère was the only "contestant" to publish his submission, which he did in the summer of 1741. This was quite unusual, but he claimed the authority to do so after being encouraged by the Bordeaux Academy. As it turned out, this published essay had an enormous influence on racialized thinking during the eighteenth century; by identifying the source of blackness in African bile and blood based on anatomical observations, Barrère inspired a new generation of thinkers to conceive of what we now call *race* as something that was much more than skin deep.

W ERE I TO EXAMINE in detail the various phenomena related to this question, a long dissertation would result. Given the limits prescribed [by the Bordeaux Academy], however, I will concentrate on what is most essential and try to demonstrate the most probable cause of the color of Negroes, the quality of their hair, and the degeneration of both, based on facts, reasoning, and [the] structure of the human body.

There is almost as much variety in men's hue as there are nations: it is olive-green among some Asians, white among Europeans, reddish among southern Americans, and black among Africans. Whence comes this blackness of Negroes; what is its cause? Here is what the anatomy of the Negro skin teaches us.

After long maceration of the Negro skin in water, the epidermis or outer skin may be detached and examined attentively. We find it black, very thin, and appearing transparent when peered through in daylight. This is what I saw in America, a fact that has also been noticed by one of the most expert

Anatomists of our day, M. Winslow: "Examining the epidermis of Moors, we find there no whiteness other than that of a thin and transparent slice of a black horn" (*Exposit Anatom.* 489).[1] Through dissection we find the hide, properly speaking, i.e., the skin with all its features, including cutaneous nipples, and a reticular body of a blackish red.[2]

It is obvious that the color of Negroes is not borrowed, so to speak, and thus the apparent color of their epidermis does not come from a mucous body (as some have called it) or from the reticular body, as has been previously believed.[3] The epidermis or the outer skin of the Negro derives its black color directly from its own tissue.

Moreover, since the epidermis of Negroes is naturally of a blackish shade, its color should be made even darker by the skin above this same layer, which is of a reddish-brown approaching black.

But since the epidermis of Moors, like that of Whites, is a tissue of vessels, they should necessarily contain a sap, which it is appropriate to examine. It seems certain that this sap is analogous to bile, and observation seems to support this: 1) When I had occasion to dissect the cadavers of Negroes in Cayenne, I noticed that their bile is always as black as ink; 2) It was more or less black in proportion to the Negro's color; 3) I also noticed that their blood is blackish red, according to the tint of the Moor; 4) It is certain that bile enters along with chyle into the blood, and flows with it to every part of the body, that it is filtered in the liver, and that several of its parts escape through the kidneys and other parts of the body. Why, then, could this same Negro bile not be displaced into the tissue of the epidermis?

Experiments prove in fact that bile is separated in the Negro epidermis into small individual pipes [i.e., capillaries] since, if one touches a Negro's skin with one's fingertips, an oily and fatty humor detaches, somewhat soapy and with a disagreeable odor, which no doubt is what gives the luster and softness that is remarked in their skin; if one rubs the skin with a white cloth, it is sullied with brown. All these qualities are specific to Negro bile.

Note what is observed among us in cases of jaundice: an abundance of bile in the blood tints the whole skin yellow; the inflammation of this same bile (for whatever reason) becomes blackish, which also turns the skin black, as noticed by specialists in black jaundice. In Moors it is also probable that a black humor similar to bile, which is always black in their case and naturally separated in the epidermis due to its abundance, gives it a blackish color.

Bile seems naturally abundant in the blood of Negroes by the strength and quickness of the pulse, by the extreme lecherousness and other frisky passions, and especially by the heat of their skin.[4] Moreover, experiment shows that hot blood produces much bile, just as milk turns yellow in white women when a woman who is nursing has a fever.

Finally, could we not consider the Negro color as a form of natural black jaundice? Hippocrates, that genius of Medicine, said [as much] in his book of humors: *qualis humor, talis color in cute efflorescit* [as the humor, so its color comes out into the skin]. And Hippocrates was not relying on feeble reasoning.[5]

From what has been said here, we see: 1) that the humor forming the Negro color seems to be the same as bile, and perhaps what is separated in the liver differs only in quantity; 2) that it is very probable that the bile separates not only in the Negro liver but also in the almost imperceptible vessels of the epidermis, where, disengaged from the red parts of the blood, it may well resume its first form and consequently reveal its natural blackness; 3) that the larger parts of this bile, given their location in the epidermis, must give them a black tint. But the parts retained for discharges of blood are exhaled through the skin pores like a vapor that is not at all black and almost free of bitterness. These parts gather on the skin, thicken there, and spread a disagreeable odor.

Something very similar happens when one heats the bile of a Negro in a small vessel covered with a sheet of parchment pierced with holes. One notices the sides of the vessel tinged with black, and after a while through the cover's small holes one notes a kind of smoke that condenses into visible drops (when one fits the lid with a goblet like a cone), which have neither the color nor the taste of bile.

These are the corollaries and proofs of the most probable cause of the color of Negroes. The bile seems to separate more in the liver and epidermis than in other parts of the body, no doubt in relation to whether the secreting vessels are more or less large and to the greater or lesser movements of the matter that it filters, as demonstrated in the mechanism of secretions—but this is not the place to speak of this.

The hairs of Negroes, in addition to their blackness, are fine, short, and curly, and when closely examined their natural shape appears spiral, somewhat resembling flocking hooks; they might also be compared to plant trachea.

It seems the color has the same cause as the blackness of the skin, which is to say that it stems from a kind of unctuous black humor or medullar humor, that being filtered through each hair root, passes to the end of the strand.[6]

Negro hair, which might be called a kind of wool, has almost no consistency at the level of the [follicle]. On the contrary, the hairs are very supple and fine and, as such, there is no doubt that the [capillaries] and fluids forming the whole structure must be prodigiously fine. It follows from this extreme fineness of hair, which presupposes capillary diameters that are very narrow and tight, that these hairs seem unable to furnish enough nourishment to give them longer length. This must be the same reason that hair becomes white, since the restriction of the vessels that form hair tissue increases with age as the body progressively dries out. In fact, hair does whiten in old Negroes.

Finally, their hair is curly and each strand forms little circumvolutions, which the great Anatomists who have carefully studied the structure of the human body presume to depend solely on the pathways or pores from which the stem of each hair grows, and so probably the hair of Negroes passes through tortuous pores from which they take this configuration.

But the color of Negroes, like the quality of their hair, degenerates in their natural state, as is the case with Americans, Europeans, and other men of different shades: how and by what mechanism does such a change occur? I admit that I find this question very vexing: bodies change only through the action of a foreign cause, and so we must necessarily examine what happens in the formation of an animal, knowledge of which must advance in order to discover the true cause of this degeneration.

It has already been accepted in the scholarly arena and is a generally received opinion that in the seed of animal bodies is found (as if concentrated) all the parts that compose it, with shape and color [already] determined.[7] These parts develop, grow, and blossom as soon as they are put into play; they are penetrated by a very fine and spirited fluid, which is the seed of the male. This seminal liquor imprints its character on the matter that concentrates all these parts in its own seed.[8] The evolution and development of all parts of the animal occur thanks to this arrangement; there must be a proportion between the solids and the fluids that penetrate these body parts and shape them into an animal machine that under ordinary conditions is always similar [to others], always the same in its original parts. Finally, if the order and the relationship among these same parts is no longer maintained, as must be the case during generation [reproduction], then the body of the Animal must undergo a new modification of the original parts, and must consequently find itself disfigured.

By following these reliable principles, the following points may be conceived: 1) Since the seed of animal bodies relates to the male and to the female, it must receive the traits of both; 2) The enclosed seed within the female naturally contains all the traits of its resemblance; and it receives its resemblance to the male only through the intrusion of the seminal liquor that determines the parts that receive animation; 3) The animation that reaches the parts of the seed in animals of the same species must always be almost uniform as to degree, yet less great in comparison with what occurs in the coupling of animals of different species.[9] In this case, the animation must be violent, as if forced, such that fluids must escape their natural line of direction and deviate, so to speak, judging by the considerable disruption of the original parts of the seed; 4) The production of monsters is one of the most convincing proofs of this surprising disruption; 5) It follows that a Negress who has relations with a white or European man must produce a *mulatto,* who, due to the new modification that this child receives from its mother, loses the original nature of its skin and hair and so must appear different from a Negro; 6) This new modification in the mulatto presupposes the filtration of a humor through a less black epidermis and [different] pathways or pores [follicles], all of which results in less winding strands of hair.[10] Every day in the Americas we see both mulattoes and other people with various blood mixtures whose skin has become less dark and whose hair has become straighter and longer, depending on the distance from the natural tint of Negroes; 7) Finally, one must conclude that the cause of degeneration of the color of Negroes and of the quality of their hair should plausibly be related to the action (and more or less disruption) in the seminal fluid with the seed that it penetrates in the first moments of the evolution of its parts.

All these consequences appear quite natural and seem to prove that the seminal fluid must contain within itself (as in an abbreviated version) the whole character of the animal from which it takes its origin, which it then engraves (so to speak) on the seed during generation. And how can that possibly not be the case? Proof lies in the resemblance of the child to the father, the maladies and very manners that the child usually inherits from the father. By what manner could they be transmitted to children, if not by generation? We may now perceive the cause of the degeneration of the color of Negroes and the quality of their hair.

Is this same cause not recognized in plants that degenerate entirely when grafted onto other plants of different species, from which they receive a totally different seed? Above all it is perceptible in animals of diverse species that mate every day.

Finally, one should simply reflect that from the mating of animals of two different species there must come animals that relate to both species because the male and the female communicate their traits to them, which the male could do only by the intrusion of the seminal liquid. So we get an idea of what causes degeneration in animals—and therefore in the case of the color and hair of Negroes.

There can be no doubt that different air and foods cause some change in the color of the skin, and every day we notice this not only among Europeans but in *négrillons* of both sexes.[11] At birth they have nothing black other than the natural parts, but their bodies become all black a few days after birth—no doubt because the blood's circulation accelerates after birth and it filters through the epidermal vessels (which at birth were not yet sufficiently developed) the bilious humor that makes all blackness.

Certainly, the [maternal] imagination may have an influence on matter, [which we see in cases where] swarthy parents produce very white infants. Such traits most often appear in infants whose mothers desired some particular food, demonstrating the imagination at work. But I do not see a real and immediate cause of the degeneration of Negroes and the quality of their hair other than what I have just established; all other causes are merely mediate and accidental.[12]

There are many people who imagine that Negroes are a species of degenerate and (as they say) bastardized men and consequently that they are different from others, that what comes from their blood mixed with a different kind of blood may be compared with male and female mules.[13] But this notion is contradicted by the fact that if this were so, then mulattoes [and] Saccatros, which is to say those issuing from a Negro and an Indian, (and other men of different shades all originating with Negroes), would become sterile and unable to generate, just like mules. . . . [14] This, however, is not consistent with what we see every day.

The search for the cause of the degeneration of the Negro's color and hair quality requires us to speak of various changes they may both undergo during the process of degeneration. To get a general idea, we must recall that all degenerations are produced by the various inconsistencies between the seminal fluid and the [maternal] seed being penetrated. These divergences depend on the animation of the shape, the size, and the liquidity of the parts that compose them; the combinations that result from different degrees of movements in the liquidity, size, and configuration—all surely produce strong examples of degeneration. Thus, it is evident that the blood of a Negro when mixed with that of a White, of an American, or an Asiatic, even with that of Africans of a different hue, must produce a prodigious quantity of [pigments] and modification to the skin and hair. Therefore, the degeneration in the color and hair quality of Negroes must vary infinitely.

A more thorough examination of how the color of Negroes and the quality of their hair are modified through degeneration would demand a work of an entirely different extent than this dissertation. I therefore believe it necessary to stop at what seemed to me the most essential points related to the question, and to focus upon a certain number of reasons supported, above all, by experience. Given the prodigious enigma [of blackness], I hope that my essay conveys a semblance of proof for everything that I have just said about the physical cause *of the color of Negroes, and the quality of their hair, and the degeneration of the one and the other.*

**"Laziness slackens and dulls the body, but labor strengthens and makes it firm."**[15]

# INTRODUCTION

# The 1772 Contest on "Preserving" Negroes

THE BORDEAUX ACADEMY's published program for January 1772 announced attention-grabbing news: a "zealous friend of humanity" concerned with the disease-ridden state of "Negroes" on board French slave ships was sponsoring the year's annual essay contest. The subject of the competition—"What are the best ways of preserving Negroes from the diseases that afflict them during the crossing to the New World?"—reflects a significant shift in Enlightenment history, a time when the rational quest for progress finally turned its attention to the horrors of the slave trade.[1]

The members of the academy behind this 1772 competition were not abolitionists by any stretch of the imagination. In fact, these men made sure to let potential contestants know that the academy was not interested in antislavery tirades. To that end, they added two pages of telling desiderata stipulating that the winning essay should strictly limit itself to the symptoms and causes of diseases. The call for papers also seemed to ventriloquize what might be useful for a Bordeaux shipowner, insisting that essay submissions should propose only *economical* and *simple* solutions to the problem of African suffering, including modified stowage layouts, a more suitable diet for enslaved Africans, and new regulations to ensure that experienced surgeons were present during the crossing. In the final two paragraphs of this bulletin, the academicians also reiterated a desire for certifiable facts and clarity, as well as systematic ways to diagnose, treat, and cure the tropical diseases

*Programme de l'Académie Royale des Belles Lettres, Sciences et Arts de Bordeaux,* January 13, 1772. The first page of the published call for papers addresses the health of slaves during the trans-Atlantic slave trade. The three essayists suggested improvements in the stock of medicinal plants and accommodation, as well as the implementation of mechanical devices for the ventilation of the *entrepont,* or 'tween deck of the ship.

that were causing African "depopulation" on board French ships. As an addendum to the contest, the academy also called upon all captains and surgeons serving on slaving vessels to keep a scrupulous log related to the slaves' lives on board. Suggested data to be recorded included food intake during the crossing, the daily exterior temperature, the environmental conditions where slaves were shackled on the 'tween deck, the range of diseases that "attacked" the human cargo, and the medical care that the sick slaves received (or did not receive).

Having made this plea for a more fact-driven understanding of the Middle Passage, the academicians ended on a high note by conjuring up a future

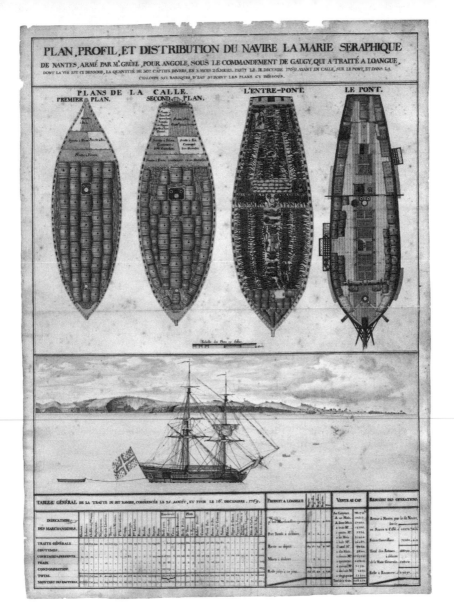

Slave stowage aboard the *Marie-Séraphique*, ca. 1770, watercolor. Nantes, History Museum. The drawing presents a comprehensive account of the voyage of a typical French slave ship of the time. According to the text inscribed at the top of the sheet, the *Marie-Séraphique* was outfitted by the Nantes *armateur* Gruel and sailed by captain Jean-Baptiste Fautrel-Gaugy. The ship picked up 307 slaves as it lay off the coast of Loango, at that time a part of the vast and powerful kingdom of Kongo, now part of the Democratic Republic of the Congo. The voyage across the Atlantic to Saint-Domingue took place during the latter part of 1769 and lasted almost four months. The slaves were stored within the cramped *entre-pont*, or 'tween deck. A ledger at the bottom of the drawing relates the fate of those slaves who perished along the way. Concern over the loss of slaves due to disease, malnourishment, and the lack of exercise and fresh air preoccupy the three essayists of the 1772 contest.

*Nègres à fond de calle* (Blacks in the bottom of the hold). Johann Moritz Rugendas, *Voyage pittoresque dans le Brésil* (Paris: Engelmann, 1835), hand-colored lithograph. The print affords a more realistic view of the interior of the *entrepont* than the slave ship diagrams of the eighteenth century, although the height of the slave quarters has been increased by the artist, possibly for greater clarity of detail. According to the testimony of the artist, he had personally witnessed this scene of a slave ship in distress in the vicinity of Brazil. He further states that the slaves were suffering from a lack of potable water. This dire circumstance was a major concern of the essayists who competed in the 1772 Bordeaux contest.

shipowner who, in the best of worlds, would benefit from all this new information and put these practices into place. Such a man, they concluded, would become someone "who deserves to share in the gratitude of humanity."[2]

### THE ESSAYS

The sponsor of this distressing Bordeaux Academy contest is unknown to us. We can easily surmise, however, that he was a wealthy man since the prize he offered was 1,200 livres, three times what the academy usually awarded and more than double the annual salary of a journeyman worker in 1770. Despite the lure of this prize, by the time that his contest closed in 1777, the academy had received only three submissions. Some scholars have assumed that the paltry number of essays submitted to this contest can be attributed to a lack of interest in slavery or the slave trade at the time.[3] In fact, the opposite was probably true. During the 1770s, a new generation of abolitionists, philosophers, and physiocrats had begun clamoring for the end of both the slave trade and slavery itself. A number of scientific and literary academies—at least those in cities not tied to the slave trade—had begun taking a stand on this question as well. In 1775, the Académie Française itself accorded "first honors" to a poem that conjured up a young enslaved African asking the new king, Louis XVI, to abolish slavery.[4] Three years later the Academy of Nancy also awarded a prize to an author named Nicolas who published an antislavery essay entitled *A Philosophical Essay on the Slavery of Negroes*.[5]

If there is one antislavery text that best exemplifies the shift in mentalities taking place during the era of this contest, it is abbé Raynal's runaway best seller, the *History of the Two Indies* (1770, 1774, 1780).[6] Raynal's stinging indictment of the slave trade (and those who facilitated it) in this book was so violent and well known that it may have even convinced potential participants in the Bordeaux contest to think twice about submitting an essay. After all, one of Raynal's most famous *cris de coeur* against the slave trade at this time was, "Whoever justifies the system of slavery merits a contemptuous silence from the philosopher, and a stab of a dagger from the Negro."[7]

Two of the three essayists who took up the pen for the 1772 contest acknowledged the political climate of the 1770s in their submissions. The first contestant, a ship's surgeon with a tremendous amount of experience on board slave ships and on colonial plantations, began his essay by painting a gruesome portrait of the pestilential existence led by the slaves on board the ships on which he sailed. Though a willing participant in the trade—he was either hired by the shipowner or a state-appointed royal doctor en route to the colonies—this medical practitioner nonetheless hoped that he might number among those who could be a champion of this miserable "branch of humanity" (Part II, Essay 1, p. 200).

The second essay, which was submitted by an anonymous Parisian writer, reflects a more philosophical point of view. Conceivably written by someone who had never even seen the sea—this was quite common among Parisians—this contestant nonetheless drew on other primary sources in order to accuse slavers of subjecting Africans to a life that was "abject, odious, inflexible, hard, cruel and in all respects no better than the condition of an animal" (Part II, Essay 2, p. 211). Stopping short of calling for an end to slavery, however, this same author ultimately advocates for a more progressive form of bondage both on the ship and on the plantation, proposing better food, clothing, recreation, and housing.

The final essay provides a useful counterpoint to the moral ambiguity found in the first two submissions. This essay was authored by a prominent Bordeaux master apothecary by the name of Louis Alphonse who took the unusual step of having his manuscript *printed* before submitting it. Unlike the other submissions, Alphonse's essay studiously avoids any ethical quibbling, and sticks to a description of the specific medical and especially pharmacological treatments that might lessen the loss of human cargo during the crossing. In particular, Alphonse emphasizes the efficacy of the same type of mercury-based medicines and salves that he presumably concocted in his shop.

### THE FATE OF THE CONTEST OF 1772

By the end of 1777, the Royal Academy of Bordeaux had finally read through the three submissions. Several weeks later, on January 13, 1778, a spokesman for the academy announced that the institution would not be awarding a prize.[8] Not only had the academicians been disappointed by the small number of entries; they had found little among the submissions that had drawn their attention. One can also imagine that the academy was probably less than pleased with the antislavery digressions found in the first two essays.

Though the 1772 competition failed to elicit a suitable answer to the challenge of preventing Africans from falling ill during the Middle Passage, the academy had nonetheless drawn attention to a subject of increasing national concern. Indeed, the contest announcement had presumably inspired a royal physician named Jean-Barthélemy Dazille (1738–1812) to take up the question of slave-based "medicine" far more completely than the three contestants who had actually entered the competition.[9] In 1776, a year before the contest closed, Dazille published a 334-page book whose title, *Observations on the Diseases of Negroes, Their Causes, Their Treatments, and the Means of Preventing Them*, seems to have been directly inspired by the academy's call for essays.[10]

Dazille's experience in the French colonial world—he served as a doctor in Mauritius (Île de France), Réunion (Île Bourbon), Cayenne, and finally Saint-Domingue—gave him a global perspective on the numerous diseases that afflicted African slaves in French colonies. In addition to associating blackness with certain pathologies, his writing on smallpox, scurvy, scabies, tetanus, fevers induced by various tropical diseases, pneumonia, Guinea worm and hookworm infestations, sexually transmitted diseases, urinary blockages, and yaws amounts to an unsettling register of the medical horrors related to forced migration and enslavement.

Dazille obviously felt a certain amount of ambivalence about the tremendous economic expansion that had occurred in the colonies during his lifetime. By the 1780s, more than 10 percent of France's population was employed in a job related to the colonial trade.[11] In the preface to his book, the doctor acknowledged that sugar and other colonial commodities had become necessities, both for the nation's inhabitants, but also for the overall "commerce of the nation."[12] He concluded by admitting that this economic reality had been terrible for Africans; it had transformed them into "the most unhappy and neglected members of the human species, despite their utility."[13]

Very much like the Bordeaux Academy of Sciences, whose links with France's colonial empire also ran deep, Dazille was not calling for an end to the plantation system itself. Indeed, his book promoted the same sort of compromise that the academy had called for in its 1772 contest: the shocking oxymoron known as "enlightened slavery": the hope that France's slave traders and planters could make better use of the era's increasingly *medicalized* understanding of Africans in order to simultaneously decrease mortality rates and increase profits on their disease-ridden ships and plantations.[14]

# I  ⌒

# A Slave Ship Surgeon on the Crossing

This essay was written by a surgeon who had years of firsthand experience witnessing the horrors of the slave trade. In addition to the voyages he made between Africa and the Caribbean, the author spent time on plantations in Guadeloupe, Martinique, Saint-Domingue, and Cayenne, the main city in the South American colony Guiana. Although this medical practitioner earned his living as a willing participant aboard slave ships, he nonetheless reveals that he is deeply affected by the suffering he witnesses on board slave ships and in the colonial hospitals where he worked. Indeed, the sum of the initial sentences in the essay have an abolitionist feel to them that was presumably unappreciated by the Bordeaux Academy. The vast majority of the essay, however, enumerates specific medical treatments that might help mitigate the threats of the diseases that afflict the "cargo," including changes in diet, living conditions, and even dress code. The details that he reveals about the Middle Passage are often shocking. Note that we have both redacted this essay and added rubrics to make its thrust clearer.

### INTRODUCTION

There is a species of men whom the yoke of ignorance and barbarism renders miserable in their homeland, and still more miserable in the irons of Europeans whose thirst for wealth transplants [these same Africans] to America. Some of these people are sold at home by their relatives to foreigners, while others are nourished and held in kinds of pens, where they are fed and grow in order to be sold.

Oppression to such an extent by any branch of humanity results from an indifference to the lives of such men. Interested parties, in trying to combat such apathy, become the sole champions of these unfortunate people. The academy, by proposing as a subject the means of preserving Negroes from the frequent, serious, and often dire illnesses to which they are exposed during the passage between Africa [and] America, will teach these inhuman [Europeans] that these reviled slaves not only deserve their own place among mankind, but that we must be concerned with their happiness.

Without neglecting anything that might be of interest in the proposed sub-ject, I will deal succinctly with the dangerous illnesses to which these same Negroes are exposed after their arrival in the colonies of America. Because these maladies go on to harm all who live there [in the Caribbean colonies], I will then proceed to a second part, which will also interest humanity as a whole. The benefits offered by commerce and cultivation seem to me capable of fulfilling the views of the academy and the generous citizen who [will] share the glory and merit of pleading in favor of these unfortunates.

### FIRST PART

In the Kingdom of the Congo [Kongo] and almost all of Loango, Negroes are raised in the same way we raise livestock in Europe; this barbarity is all the more odious because the Negroes are persuaded that the Europeans are buying them in order to eat them.[1]

The Negroes that we purchase from the Gold Coast are laborious, used to hard labor, and accustomed to the hardships of war. They nourish themselves with livestock, game, rice, vegetables, potatoes, bananas, and other fruits. These are the most robust Negroes; those that we prefer for agriculture.[2]

Those that we take from the Angolan coast, known as "Congos," are of an entirely different temperament; they are soft, cowardly, indolent, and lazy, and have their women work the soil. Vegetables are more common here than among [other Negroes]. These Negroes are more dexterous, and better adapted to the mechanical trades in which they are trained.[3]

### THE TWO MAJOR ILLNESSES THAT THREATEN THE HEALTH OF NEGROES DURING THE TRANSATLANTIC VOYAGE

There are really only two major illnesses [that threaten the lives of enslaved Africans]: smallpox and scurvy. The other illnesses are rare, accidental, or of little consequence. Most of them are [actually] symptoms of scurvy, which is to say dysentery, diarrhea, open wounds, infestation of worms, fevers, or dropsy.

### SMALLPOX

Smallpox, whether spread out over the body or localized, causes harm. Yet it is less dangerous in the warm African and American climates than in

Europe. Despite this, smallpox causes ravages that are more of an afflic-
tion among these savage peoples, where medicine is still in its infancy. Most
treatment is limited to poultices, and the healing of the illness itself is left to
chance. Sometimes the sick are abandoned, or else confined to remote places
in order to prevent the spread of contagion.[4]

It is common to see this malady aboard vessels that trade on the Guinea
coast. By preference [captains] try to load young Negroes who have not had
this sickness, but they then take no care to avoid contagion. In order to make
what would be a more circumspect decision in this regard, our captains have
only to consider the wishes of the Negroes themselves.

The bad quality of air on board ship combines with the bad quality of the
food to give this disease a degree of malignity that is rarely seen elsewhere
under such climes. Ordinarily our ship surgeons do not follow the [advice
of] expert doctors, such as Thomas Sydenham, who had experience treating
Negroes [illegible].[5]

### THE MANNER IN WHICH THE NEGROES ARE KEPT ON BOARD THE SHIPS

The Negroes are all lodged in the 'tween deck of the ship; they are usually
so cramped that they can barely lie down. The sick Negroes occupy a specific area within the 'tween deck; they suffer and are constricted; they only
get air from the porthole and the hatches. Outdoor [air] never really gets
down here. The ocean is usually too rough to leave the portholes open; it is
also sometimes true that the hatches need to be battened down as well.

Once air has been breathed once, it is no longer good. It must be circulated. The more people there are in the 'tween deck, the more the danger
increases. Perspiration, be it cutaneous or pulmonary, considerably befouls
the physical quality of the air that is so sealed in.[6]

### SMALLPOX CAUSED BY UNSANITARY CONDITIONS IN THE HOLD

Smallpox, which is almost always non-life-threatening in other situations, often becomes deadly on a ship. Both the smallpox virus and the
movement and the disturbance of [the body's] humors—the latter occa-
sioned by fevers, poor air quality, the heat of the climate and that in the
'tween deck, and the breathing of air close to sick people—produces a
putrid and gangrenous necrosis in the sick person's humors, which is almost always followed by death.[7] Badly conceived medicines and methods

of treatment are not capable of countering the dangerous course of this disease.

### NECESSITY OF CLEAN WATER FOR THE PREVENTION OF SCURVY

[Negroes with scurvy] need abundant liquid; this must have a refreshing [. . .] unspoiled, quality. One can boil about two ounces of millet or rice, that has been lightly grilled in a pan in two pints of water. Each pint should have forty-five grains of saltpeter, or [illegible] just a tisane by itself, with vinegar dosed to a pleasant acidity. Millet and rice are plentiful on board, but one could substitute a piece of bread or grilled biscuit, that one can [dip and serve along with] two pints of water.[8]

### ON THE SIZE OF SLAVE TRADING SHIPS

The ease with which small slaving vessels are able to approach the coast, to sail up rivers, has convinced ship owners and their captains to prefer them to all others. One only needs a small crew; the expeditions take less time; and [one loses fewer lives] if one takes on Negroes in proportion to the size of the ship. The costs of financing a voyage for a smaller ship, however, are more costly than those of a larger one.

### IDEAL CONDITIONS FOR THE ACCOMMODATION OF
### SLAVES BELOW DECKS

The 'tween deck must be kept very clean, well deodorized, and as high above the water as possible, if the ship is big. Having the 'tween deck at a high level allows the hatchways to remain open, either partially or entirely, either on one side of the ship or the other without danger; this is the case at least for the normal hatches.

The 'tween deck should be empty of any extraneous objects, such as the sailors' equipment and belongings, in order to provide as much space as possible, and so that the air is not infected by the sailors' dirty and foul laundry.

Every morning one should make the Negroes come up on deck, where they should remain as long as the weather permits. This can be at night or during the day.[9] The best practice is to leave them as little as possible in the 'tween deck. This 'tween deck should be raked out and washed down every day; it should be deodorized with a good vinegar that one has simmered over a stove, and with which one sprays both sides of the 'tween deck.

### ESSENTIAL ROLE OF VENTILATION FOR HEALTHY AIR IN THE HOLD

Sea water corrupts food of all sorts, such as salted meats in the hold, as well as the water in barrels. It [also] contributes to the corruption of the air in this part of the ship. The bad air then arrives in the 'tween deck and cannot help but cause illness.[10]

The ventilation system of Stephen Hales, who is a pioneer in the hygiene of ventilation, and whose invention is described in a book by Monsieur Duhamel, confirms all of the advantages of such an interesting machine.[11] Monsieur Poissonnier Desperrières relates in detail the experiments undertaken in the hold regarding the treatment of diseases suffered by seafarers.[12] Slave ships could use this method even more effectively since there is no lack of manpower to operate this machine. The exercise afforded the slaves would be a further advantage which should not be taken lightly.

### ISOLATION OF SICK SLAVES

There should be an area designated within the 'tween deck for an infirmary. One should select the airiest part, so that the healthy slaves are isolated from the sick. I would suggest that there be large hammocks in the infirmary which could easily be installed in the 'tween deck.

### AMELIORATION OF OTHER THREATS
### TO THE HEALTH OF THE SLAVES

Other than the infection produced by the breathing of the slaves in the 'tween deck, which spreads throughout the entire ship, the Negroes urinate and defecate in pots during the night. The receptacles are neither covered nor emptied in the morning.

The bad odor can spread dangerous infections. To remedy such a frightful situation, twelve *close stools* [portable toilets] with open bottoms can be fitted with ceramic pots. In the morning the pots can be brought up to the top deck to be emptied, and cleaned thoroughly for reuse.

The Negroes are quite used to bathing themselves. It is very easy to provide enough water every day for this purpose.

I have said that the slaves must be left on the top deck during the day for as long as possible. There they may amuse themselves with games of their own type as well as songs that they love so much. By this means one can deter the bad effects of the somber sadness produced by the uncertainty of their fate. Nearly all of them have the idea that they are being taken [to be eaten].

## SECURITY ABOARD SHIP

For security reasons, Negroes are not permitted to remain free on board. Since there is little to fear from the women and children, they should be excepted from this precautionary measure. The men, however, should be double shackled in irons.

Five or six slaves and up to ten (which is far too many) are to be left free in accordance with the size of the ship, the number of the crew, and slaves on board. The ship's [African slave overseers] are known as quartermasters; they are the most skillful and least feared.[13] They keep a watch over the others, empty the waste pots, and care for the sick. They also help to steer the ship, and to man the guns in times of war.

## EFFECT OF HUMANE TREATMENT
## ON THE MORALE OF THE SLAVES

All care should be taken to dissuade the slaves that Whites want to drink their blood, and that they have been bought only to be eaten.

English slave traders are in the habit of having Negroes on board who are native to the African lands where they trade. They serve as interpreters, and dissuade their countrymen of their groundless beliefs.

It is also very worthwhile to treat the Negroes with kindness and humanity. Their spirits will be raised and less alarmed by their situation. I maintain, however, that, in general, Negroes are not very grateful for this consideration. Nonetheless, I can cite a few examples [where they were], among those the story of a slave ship that sailed from Nantes to the Guinea coast and on to Saint-Domingue. Three hundred Negroes were on board. Most of the crew had perished. Only the captain, one officer, and five of the crew remained alive. A group of Negroes, realizing that they could revolt, proposed to do so, and massacre the whole crew. [The other Negroes] rebuffed this proposition, however, and informed the captain of the plot. They asked the captain's permission to punish the rebels themselves, to which he agreed. They then whipped them senseless with a rope. If the captain had refused their offer, he would certainly have been killed.

## PROPER NUTRITION OF THE SLAVES

The pythagoricien [vegetarian] diet is strictly followed aboard all slave ships, a practice that I endorse.[14] Many considerations argue in favor of a vegetarian diet: the difficulty of providing meat, the practice that the Negroes have of eating only vegetables, the danger of food spoilage in a very hot and overly humid climate, and the unhealthy conditions [illegible]. Exceptions can be made, sometimes, when fish are abundant during the crossing. This does not happen often, but eating fish is certainly beneficial to the Negroes.

Rice, millet, yams, sweet potatoes, and squash are found in abundance all along the African coast. Slave ships can be amply provisioned with them. Native Negroes depend on them for nourishment. It thus makes great sense that they continue to eat the same food on ship. In every sense they are better than the beans and peas which they are commonly fed.

When the slave ships have boarded their human cargo on the Gold Coast, they put in further south at the island of Principe or São Tomé below the equator.[15] There they take on ample stores of food and water.

The Negroes are put on shore here to refresh themselves. The ship takes on fresh water and wood and then continues its voyage. I believe that [this extra stop] can only be advantageous to all. There are several examples of ships that lack food and water at the end of long crossings and it becomes necessary to throw half of the Negroes into the sea. [To do so], these Negroes are poisoned with arsenic.[16] The Negroes who are the healthiest are made to eat apart, and given separate food bowls. One cannot report such stories without being revolted with horror. Crossings from the Gold Coast are always long, the winds being entirely contrary. It is a principal cause of death.

Some captains feed their Negroes only once a day, at nine o'clock in the morning or four in the afternoon.

Chile peppers, palm oil, and lemons are the only seasonings used by Negroes along the Guinea coast. Our captains only give them salt and sometimes palm oil. Why not also give them lemons, which are found in abundance?

Negroes are big smokers in their country; one must not neglect to provide them with tobacco during the crossing. Failure to do so can be detrimental to them. It is only necessary to take precautions in order to avoid the danger of fire.

### HARMFUL EFFECTS OF CLOTHING

Negroes go about naked in their own country. Children wear very little. They can be left this way on board ships. If they were to wear clothes, the dirtiness, vermin, and humidity which is retained in sweaty clothing could increase the corruption of the air. They will not feel cold [without clothes] during the crossing, indeed quite the contrary.

## PROVISION OF HEALTHY WATER TO THE SLAVES

Water is the only drink given to the Negroes; good water quality helps prevent the diseases to which they are exposed during the crossing to America. This is at least as important as their cleanliness, the purity of the air, the good quality of food, and their tranquility of mind.

Slave ships which trade along the coast of Angola take their water from rivers. It is of good quality. These ships make shorter crossings, since they nearly always sail under a good wind.

I have known English captains who make their Negroes drink a glass of tar-water every morning and evening throughout the crossing.[17] They have assured me that nothing contributes more to their survival. A Spanish slave ship which travels from Acapulco every year across the south sea to [illegible] Africa uses no other kind of water for the several months of the crossing.

## SCURVY

Up to now I have dealt with smallpox. Scurvy and the symptoms caused by it will be the subject of this chapter. These two diseases are responsible for the regrettable catastrophes that befall these people, a fate that exposes them to frightful calamities. Scurvy, more common and more dreadful than the first, is the principal cause of all the misfortunes that the Academy would like to prevent.

The autopsy of dead Negroes invariably reveals inflammation and sphacelous tissue resulting from gangrene throughout the intestinal tract: the last part of the small intestine and the rectum are the most affected parts. The livid covering of the intestines [*epiploon*], the nearly complete dissipation of fat, the inflamed and livid state of the mesentery, the blackish color of the spleen, all tear with slight pressure due to scurvy.[18] The liver itself is pale, and the stomach less affected than the intestines, although a little livid and swollen. The pancreas and the kidneys have very little or no lesions.

The mortality rate is at times so frightful that it rises to more than two or three hundred during the course of the crossing, or more than half. On occasion, I have seen twelve to eighteen Negroes thrown into the sea every twenty-four hours. When the ship drops anchor in America, those who survived the crossing most often suffer the same deplorable fate later, although the disease did not manifest itself when they left the ship.

Scurvy, although stemming from the same disease, does not always produce the same effects. I have often seen a number of Negroes entirely exempt from this condition on ships ravaged by dysentery. Instead, their faces are swollen, pale, their feet and legs also engorged. They quickly die of heart failure brought on by dropsy. Others manifest a considerable effusion in the cavities of the scrotum, which is caused by the infiltration of fluid into the cellular tissue. This produces a subsequent general swelling or general state of hydropsy which soon manifests itself by the collection of fluid in the abdomen or effusion in the interior of the lower abdomen.

### RECOMMENDED TREATMENT OF SCURVY

Yams have large, good tasting roots which can be stored for more than four or five months and are an excellent source of nutrition. I have seen countries where overripe bananas are left to dry in the sun. These also can be kept in barrels for four or five months. They have an excellent taste, similar to how we make jam. Sick Negroes can be nourished with rice, millet, yams, all prepared in a way familiar to them, with palm oil, salt, and chili peppers.

### THE AUTHOR'S PERSONAL EXPERIENCE TREATING SCURVY

I have seen diarrhea and vomitous dysentery that has lasted for several months disappear entirely from this remedy after two or three days of use. [Conversely,] I have seen these illnesses last for three years.

The bark of the yam has a successful effect against worm [infestations]. The Negroes are very subject to worms, both in their own country as well as during the crossing and in America. It is very common for the stomach and the intestines to be full of worms in cases of dysentery. I strongly believe that this quantity of worms is more often the cause of the disease rather than the effect.

In 1757, while on a slave ship, I purchased a young black man of sixteen who was dying of dysentery. His condition approached [illegible]. Empathy and the modest price (which was about one hundred francs) led me to take the risk of buying him. I treated his dysentery with simarouba [cayenne pepper] as the only therapy, along with good nutrition. He went from bad to worse for three days. At the end of this time, one worm came out of him, entirely dead, more than several meters long. Thus commenced the stage of the greatest healing. In very little time this young black man became more vigorous. I have used this remedy with success nearly as often as I have administered it. [...]

Medicine has no remedy that can cure diseases in all cases, but I have witnessed how this yam bark has had a salutary effect on nearly all those attacked by the diarrhea or dysentery that follows fever. This I have seen for myself over the course of several years in the hospitals of Cape Saint-Domingue and Fort Royal in Martinique, where these fevers were putrid or malignant.[19] The pestiferous air of these two hospitals caused by the unhealthiness of the place and the climate, together with the great number of the sick and suffering that were there at those times, caused frequent relapses. Almost all survived the first type of illness or bout of fever, and most everybody also survived from the second. These fevers were sometimes followed by putrid effusions which resisted all treatment. It would have been possible to prevent all such misfortunes through the establishment of a convalescent hospital. This was done in 1762 and 1763 at Cap-François in Saint-Domingue, and at Fort Royal in Martinique in 1765.[20]

### EXPERIENCE AS A DOCTOR ON SHORE

[Most] ships arriving in American ports take their Negroes on shore to sell them. There are some, [however], who sell them on board, as is the case in Saint-Domingue. Those Negroes who are still sick during the crossing, or who have been exposed to disease, are not out of danger, although they may be on shore and have better air, food, and drink.

Negroes, once they have arrived in the islands, are still vulnerable and one must not fail to care for all those who are still slightly ill. Many languish, gain in strength, relapse, and most of these Negroes wind up dead after having fought the disease for three or four years or longer. I have seen cargoes of Negroes where only a few recover, although the number of Negroes who were sick was quite considerable. How many slave merchants, who buy all these sick Negroes—the tail end of the cargo so to speak—have been bankrupted by this profession, for want of being able to know how to treat these afflicted [Negroes]?

Although the treatment of Negroes once ashore is the same as what I have prescribed for the sick during the crossings, the selection and easy application of treatment necessitates great changes: one should avoid lodging Negroes in the street, give them the best nourishment possible, give them some clothing, lodge them in healthy air, have them eat ripe fruit in moderation, amuse them, above all, not crowd them together.

[Other maladies, including eye inflammation, are discussed at length.]

## CONCLUSION

Shipowners can find no better means of saving Negroes from the illnesses to which they are exposed during their transport than by choosing captains and other officers whose experience and vigilance in this trade have been completely verified. It is essential that they are all on good terms with each other. Division among officers has very alarming consequences.

I have considered in great length the treatment of the illnesses in conformance with the aims of the academy, which intends to bring this work to the attention of ship builders, surgeons, and ship officers for their instruction. I have striven to respond with as much clarity and knowledge as I could . . . [21]

# 2

# A Parisian Humanitarian on the Slave Trade

This remarkable essay was written by someone who may never have set foot on a slave ship or a Caribbean plantation. Deriving his information from a variety of written and perhaps oral sources, the author begins his essay by emphasizing the horrors of the slave trade itself. Yet the real thesis of the essay is that the various diseases that afflict Africans aboard slave ships are brought about by their distraught emotional state. This emotionally based theory of illness leads him to argue for a kinder, gentler form of slavery, assuming that chattel slavery must exist in the first place. To do so, he rails against dehumanizing stereotypes associated with Africans, and draws upon "ethnographic information" and economic theory from the era's physiocrats in order to argue that improved living conditions for these generally good people will produce a far more humane, happy, and productive workforce.[1] One of his more "benevolent" suggestions is that plantation owners should hire musicians to play music to soothe and motivate enslaved Africans while they are toiling in the fields.

### MEMORANDUM ON THE MEANS OF PRESERVING NEGROES TRANSPORTED FROM AFRICA TO THE COLONIES

I do not wish to blame or applaud the system of domination that has permitted a few civilized natives of Europe to venture to Africa to purchase slaves, thereby perpetuating the servitude and misery of these people. And yet, if we are to examine this question from a reasonable point of view, it nonetheless appears cruel and unnatural that [slavers] are deliberately subjecting men who share the same [corporeal] attributes with us [. . .] to a servitude that is abject, odious, inflexible, brutal, cruel, and in all respects no better than the condition of an animal.

For a long time, no doubt, people have been concerned with the best means for preserving Negroes from the serious illnesses that ordinarily strike them down, not to mention the other bothers that make their transport from one hemisphere to another so vexing.

We should not be surprised that these slaves, who are subjugated by *force majeure*, then distressed by perpetually revolting and inhumane conditions that contradict Nature . . . should be dominated by the fear of a frightening future; of being chained to overflowing in the bellies of vessels. The way in which they are fed, the mortal fear they must feel about the uncertainty of their fate, the brutal nature of their containment during the crossing in the 'tween deck (under the weather deck, where they are immediately infected by the impure and stifling air they breathe) are all worries that must frighten them when they first encounter a form of commerce that is subject to all sorts of risks.

If Africans are men, it is natural to treat them as such, to disabuse them of the common belief that they must be sacrificed to the voracity of their kidnappers or exposed to a tragic end. If these unfortunate people were warned that, once they have left their homeland, there will be no return, that they will never come back, they would be cured of the dreams and ideas that someone can save them. [Why not explain] who these [white] people are who cross the seas to take them away? Why not explain the specifics to Africans, about why they do not come back and what happened to them? [Enslaved Africans] must wonder if [their predecessors] died of misery or if they were sacrificed. If they believe that they are still alive, they suspect they are unhappy at the very least, and if they are dead, it was because they were unable to prevent some tragic fate.

Such forlorn observations are capable of twisting imaginations weakened by malaise, and might well provoke a suicide among those with the most forceful temperaments. This is all the more likely since most of these unfortunates prefer a precipitous [self-inflicted] death to an agitated and troubled life; they believe this [suicide] would only be hastening what they believe to be a terrible and certain death.

Whatever kind of doctor one may be, it is difficult to prevent and to remedy the maladies that result from life's discouragements or griefs. If one understands this principle, one is easily persuaded that the fact that Africans bemoan the life they left behind may be the cause of the slave revolts during crossings. Slaves must be afflicted with such despair that they can be excited by [instigators]. This often obliges sailors to seize the most determined ones, and to shoot some of the slaves in order to impose discipline on the others, and thereby reduce the cargo by attrition.

Such reprisals for mutiny may end up reducing the shipment by half or even a third of its worth, which gives rise to very high insurance premiums, even exorbitant ones.

Slaves who are subjugated by such inhumane means become even more undisciplinable and more infirm. Nature itself is outraged when everything seems to announce to them the horror of a future that will destroy their very being.

These gruesome consequences destroy the profit of transporting individuals born in their own climate, and sending them to live in another that does not suit them. [. . .] And if one consults the methods by which all successful enterprises operate [illegible] such disadvantages [of the trade] could be understood and anticipated, as is the case in any business speculation whose goal is profit.

BEARING THIS IN MIND, I am developing the following points for the academy.

Part 1:  The measures to take in the market for Negroes in Africa.
Part 2:  On other precautions to take in the crossing from Africa to America.
Part 3:  The necessity of more humane treatment when they arrive in the New World to cultivate the earth.

### PART 1: THE SLAVE TRADE IN AFRICA

[The author discusses how to choose the ideal captain, e.g., someone who knows the best mooring spots in Guinea.]

Once the captain is on shore [negotiating the purchase of slaves] he must, as much as possible, inform himself on the provenance of the Negroes; these precisions can help identify the specific remedies needed to cure them of the sicknesses to which they are exposed. Those who were born in the South of Africa are quite different from those who were born in the North, because the Negroes on the lower part of the equator are subject to smallpox, which does not manifest itself in this people until after the age of eleven. This can be cured using European methods while still at anchor, but if this malady attacks during the crossing, one risks losing the entire cargo.

[The author continues discussions on diseases ashore including virulent abscesses.]

It is through experimentation and the comparative study of diseases that one is able to commonly understand more completely the force, causes, effects, prevention, and cures of these diseases. It is likely that restoring the health of these slaves is counteracted by the disproportionate fear that they have of their fate, by the chains that shackle them, by the treatment they endure, by the infection that suffocates them in a concentrated place, by the food that is ill-suited to their temperament, and by the frightful image of humanity that [is the source] of so much misery. This grating reality can easily disturb the imagination and the constitution of these unfortunate people who are ceaselessly preoccupied by the reality of a condition which is both untenable and humiliating.

It is therefore in the interest of speculators who engage in this branch of commerce to disabuse the Negroes as much as possible of the strong impressions that they have as they leave their homeland to submit themselves to the wave of terror with which they are assailed from the moment they enter our vessels. Would it not be preferable to work against these methods rather than to convince them of their deadly fate? And if the shipowners were to take an interest in this, would it not be apparent that the principal causes of their illnesses stem from their fear and their alarm?[2] [If this were done], the commerce in Negroes could be all the more advantageous and facilitated by bringing together the inalienable rights of Nature with the resources of this trade.

## PART 2: HOW TO TREAT NEGROES DURING THE CROSSING FROM AFRICA TO AMERICA

If we follow the already established principle that the majority of disorders that affect Negroes' disposition stem from the great terror that they feel when they pass under European domination, it must be the case that to avoid the greatest number of troubles, it is imperative to determine the causes, as much as one can, as well as the best ways [. . .] to put an end to the outrageous belief that we want to oppress them or put them in imminent danger. To do so we must either reason with them or show them a convincing example that this is not true. Why would we not seize on this last idea? And put before them a free, well-dressed Negro who would make this trip for this very purpose, and whose job would be to dissuade them from fearing their new masters. This person would let them know that their actual destiny is to work as hard as they can given their respective forces, but they will still benefit from the aid that humanity obliges, because their well-being is intimately linked to the masters' financial interests.

Henceforth these unfortunates would be progressively untroubled by the vexing worries that are by themselves capable of bringing disorder to

Negroes' imagination and their dispositions, both of which are [already] distressed by anxiety. No longer disaffected, and brought back to their senses by plausible arguments voiced by one of their compatriots—that they will be safe and can even flatter themselves with the hope of being free from captivity and, one day, take advantage of the joys of a private, free, and honest life—is it not a real possibility that these Negroes can be mollified and encouraged to adopt a real inclination toward obedience based on their [own] feelings?

If we pay attention to their dispositions, we will no longer delude ourselves regarding the essence of their character, and the deficiencies that we enjoy attributing to them. These shortcomings are not as true as we might believe.

Comparing Africans to brutes is a paradox and an error of pure opinion that can be eliminated by simple reflection. Negroes are capable of reasoning and are susceptible to fears, passions, and other properties of [the human body]. In fact, no doubt we are persuaded of that because we have baptized them and taken great care to inculcate religious faith in them. Finally, they are [considered] human when we set examples for them and want them to express gratitude when they have occasion to applaud our good deeds. They appear stupid to us because we barely allow them the faculty of thinking, and presume that a kind of frenzy or intellectual limitation constitutes, so to speak, the whole range of their sensations. Perhaps they are ignorant because they have been subjected to work that vastly exceeds the scope of their strength? Maybe they steal good food because they are deprived of the food they love and like to eat and which might please them? Instead they are mercilessly refused what would appeal to their taste. They may react against the threatening rod that is always raised against them because they are often tormented or punished without cause. Love of freedom never dies in the human heart; it touches natural existence too closely to be willingly given up. It is in this situation of delirium and outrageous dependence that these unfortunates, once transported to the colonies, prefer a runaway life, as miserable as this may be, to a harsh domestic captivity that is both implacable and painful, and that seems to them to deny them the rights of nature in its most inviolable attributes.

Expediency suggests that we must cure African slaves of the misguided view that they will be prey to the voracity of Europeans or to some other tragic destiny. This will only succeed through an intercession of a Negro that might instruct them in their fate. It should be obvious that this enlightened treatment, in disabusing them [of their misconceptions], must produce a

softening of the organs that are attacked by dark arbitrary vapors. This [treat-
ment should produce] the fruit of sober reasoning, and result in benefits
that should be realized by the shipbuilder who trades, and the colonist who
buys Negroes in the New World.

This measure would facilitate the Negroes' return to the docility that is
suitable to them during the crossing. I would advise those who engage in
this commerce to have in the vessel a *cors de chasse* [hunting horn] which
from time to time would engage the crews: Africans are very taken with the
charms of harmony, and the accents of music, especially when it is lively,
light, and cheerful. [Crews] could flatter them, agreeably awaken and inspire
them in such a way that these expedients, by distracting Negroes via natural
inclinations, should surely have a salutary effect, either by giving birth to a
strong confidence or by preventing the resolutions that might influence
imaginations weakened by the always revolting spectacle of their present
condition and of their future.[3] Again, there is another precaution that is not
to be disdained: giving them food that appeals more to their inclinations,
and to win them over by fresh bread, a little wine, or spirits (*eau de vie*), such
that their predispositions and tastes are satisfied from time to time. This
might gradually inculcate both resignation and trust in them, the lack of
which opens them up to the mortal maladies that destroy so great a number.

### PART 3: ON THE NEED FOR HUMANE TREATMENT ONCE
### NEGROES ARE IN THE NEW WORLD TO CULTIVATE THE LAND

[The author maintains that Negroes must have a good first impression of
their workshop and master in order to avoid revolt.]

Africans are capable of attachment and lofty sentiments, which may even
lead them to heroism; there are verified examples of one African declaring
that he is the guilty party in order to spare his innocent comrade from the
pain of punishment.

Masters who are too demanding or too severe, and are constantly seen
with a rod raised against these unfortunates, will be deprived of these [able]
cultivators, who are exhausted by fatigue and pain, who may kill themselves, desert, or else revolt; others resort to poisons that they know
about from childhood. They know by this means they can escape those
who oppress them outrageously. While apparently cowardly their whole
lives, [they can be] a hero in an instant; what is more, they are unshakeable
under torture and will not admit their crimes; they seem to go to death
without emotion.

## NOTHING SHOULD APPEAR AS DEPLORABLE
## AS THE CONDITION OF BLACKS IN AMERICA

In a stifling and unhealthy hut, the weight [of servitude] is like iron; it is a rope around the body [of the slave]; there is no shelter from the excessive heat during the day, nor from the unbearable coolness at night. His existence [is] only sustained by the minimum: salted beef, codfish, fruits or berries. Deprived of almost everything, he is condemned to harsh and continual labor in a burning climate under the absolute domination of a ferocious slave driver.

The French, especially, rarely consider these slaves as sensitive beings. In allowing them to [illegible], they deny them the means to support the burden of this place, to freely taste its pleasant aspects. The nature of the slave in America seems to be dispensed of the most vital natural rights. Nothing should seem as reprehensible as the excessive work forced upon these unhappy farm workers in America. Without anyone taking into consideration the limits of their strength or their aptitude, they are condemned to continual labor nearly without rest intervals.

Yet we know from experience that it is an economic necessity (and well regarded) to lighten the work of those builders occupied in our transport ships by having [freight] raised by ladders or cranes, and that, if one forced these ships to load these same burdens by hand, the workers would infallibly succumb, for man has only a certain limit to his strength. Moreover, such tasks deprive men of the veritable satisfaction that is practicable and can be completed. So why can we not apply this principle to the slaves, of whom it cannot be said that their strength is extraordinary?

[After speaking about the problems of stomach illnesses among slaves, the author moves on to a discussion of five possible improvements to slavery. This is something of a table of contents for the rest of the essay.]

1. Depression due to the harshness of servitude leads to destruction of slaves' minds, which become agitated. By treating them with humanity in all respects, these slaves would be able to reclaim their tranquility.
2. Regarding the forced labor imposed on slaves, it is necessary to give them periods of rest and relaxation, either as recompense for their docility, or in consideration of a well-accomplished work task.

3. It is necessary to supply slaves with substantial food that is proportional to their labor and that corresponds to their temperament.

4. It is necessary to arrange things such that slaves cannot, out of despair, find poison, the effect of which is known to them.

5. [Allow them] access to humus or manure to increase the poor fertility of the American soil, which is similar to that of Africa.

By evaluating the causes of human maladies, I dare say that one may [not only] understand the changes they may bring about, but prevent their critical and dangerous effects. But if we insist in preserving a system in which Negroes have to be chastised to make them docile, in which impossible work burdens are imposed on them, and in which nourishment is not provided in proportion to the physical effort demanded; if one denies to them any tenderness, and abandons them to the malign influences of a perfidious climate, with no rest, no clothing to cover themselves, with no pallet to sleep on, then [these men are being] outraged in this barbarous regime. And the owners of Negroes wrongly complain when their interests suffer from the loss of so many cultivators.

In order to carry out reform, we have to learn to know the physical and moral man. Let us start with those who seek out Negroes in order to transplant them to America, especially those who claim to oversee their labor, who believe themselves obliged, out of cupidity, to oppress them. These people, it seems, only adopt the tools of terror and violence. If the owners of plantations in America, without ceasing to care for their slaves, would put them into real occupations under their jurisdiction, they would soon abjure their cruel mistakes. The history of all peoples would teach them that one never turns men who are unjustly deprived of their liberties into useful workers, and that one will never prevail over them except by employing the path of persuasion, gentleness, and humanity.

This enlightened policy would entail many resources, since one would realize the necessity of suitably lodging, dressing, and nourishing beings [currently] condemned to the most revolting slavery there has ever been since the first origins of servitude. [Currently], one feels that it is not in the natural order that those who do not reap the fruits of their successful work might have the same intelligence, the same activity, the same zeal, the same attachment, and the same order as the man who enjoys the plenitude of his senses, who receives the entire benefit of his labor. By degrees, via political oration, one would reach a stage where assigning less labor, mitigating punishments, and restoring some rights to men will elicit gratitude. Thereby one would preserve a great number of slaves from the maladies largely caused by grief, by boredom, and by the boundless fatigue among those taken away to the colonies. Instead of making worse the yoke that oppresses them, one would seek to soften it or dissipate its image by fostering a penchant that seems natural to Negroes when one studies deeply their actual character.

For example, their organs are singularly flattered by the sound of music; their ear is so precise and at the same time so true, that in the execution of their dances, the measure of a song makes them leap up and land, a hundred of them at a time, all hitting the ground at the same instant. They seem suspended, as it were, from the singer's voice, or abandoned to the chord of an instrument, the vibration of the earth appears to be the soul of these bodies that are moved by the sounds that animate them, that raise and lead them when elated and when working, the movement of their arms and their feet always in cadence. Among them, music reanimates their courage and awakens sluggishness. Poets and musicians, they invariably emphasize the importance of melody over words.

What the [Italians?] are able to do with their poetry, the Africans do with their music, and when the two [i.e., the people and their art] are combined, the more powerful overwhelms the other; a given object or significant event may soon become the subject of a song, and that air will occupy them all, encourage them at work with dances for whole hours. Among them, musical instruments make joy blossom or augment their sadness.

Such a pronounced penchant could become a great motivator in skillful hands, and one could use it to establish recreations and even prizes; these sorts of amusements when planned with intelligence, would prevent the ordinary stupidity in these slaves, would lighten their working hours and preserve them from the concentrated grief that overtakes them by degrees, and may considerably shorten their days.

Independently of all these reflections, we invite the owners of Negroes in the colonies to engage paid instrumentalists who would be solely occupied in performing cheerful and spirited airs. If one made this suitable and appropriate gesture—a friendly custom that provides a gentle illusion and promotes an active joy among the workers—spirits would rise and the music would easily occupy the Negroes.

According to common knowledge regarding the [physical] constitution of Negroes, these people are just like other men: they are sensitive and delicate beings capable of sophisticated feeling, and if one considers what men who are veritable music lovers are like, then it must be agreed that rarely are truly vicious men found among them. What is more, it must also be agreed that heinous opinions and crude views are being construed about Negroes; one more willingly attributes nature's horrors to Africans than their impulses to tenderness, friendship and attachment, reticence, and love—all the qualities that raise in the human heart the germ of honesty, candor, and moral goodness.

It is not true that Negroes refuse to multiply in the chains of captivity. And yet the cruelty of their masters extinguishes the wishes of Nature. Negresses are required to work too hard after their pregnancies; so often mothers after childbirth will smother their babies in the crib to deprive their barbarous masters of them.

May Europeans open their eyes, and they will reconsider their errors and manage to better combine their economic interests, and so turn their kindness to their advantage; they will realize that by abusing humanity they are losing more than they could win, and if they do not become true benefactors to their slaves, at least they will not become their executioners.

END

> Read, examined, and absolutely rejected from the competition, 16 May 1777.

> Reporter, M. Doazan.

*Sua cuique calamitas tanquam ars assignatur.* (To each his misery is assigned like a skill.)[4]

Seneca

# 3 ⌒

# Louis Alphonse, Bordeaux Apothecary, on the Crossing

The author of this essay is Louis Alphonse, a Bordeaux apothecary, who became a member of the Bordeaux Academy the same year he submitted this essay, in 1777.[1] Unlike the two other submissions, Alphonse's essay is perhaps more indicative of prevailing attitudes in Bordeaux in the 1770s. One finds no invectives against the trade or its "cruel" participants. Instead, Alphonse focused on measures that might make slave expeditions less deadly in the interest of those who organize them. These proposed measures included specific treatments for diseases and recommendations regarding the routes to take when organizing such voyages. Interestingly enough, one might also characterize this essay as a "white lives matter" essay: Alphonse opens his remarks by reminding the academy that white crew members perished at almost the same rate as their African cargo.

T HE ZEALOUS CITIZEN who hopes to improve the survival of Negroes during their transport from Africa to America—a question announced in the Bordeaux Academy of Sciences program—merits our praise. He would draw our greater gratitude if his zeal extended to Whites, whose species [*espèce*] is no less precious than that of Blacks. In truth, proportionally almost as many Whites die as Blacks on the voyages to Guinea.[2] Therefore both groups should merit our attention; the very topic demands it, because it is sometimes one and sometimes the other of these species that communicates a contagion to the other. Both will be the object of my dissertation. I will highlight the maladies to which these two groups are subject and their symptoms, the curative remedies (at least palliative ones), and the precautions necessary to avoid these diseases. I hope by this means to contribute to the good of humanity.

The certificates or attestations that one might require in order to establish the reliability of cures are difficult to come by; indeed, there are scarcely any glimmers of light on this subject, and many of the surgeons who sail to Africa are too mercurial in the way that they conduct their practice. We have very few observers who have established treatments that have been followed consistently; nobody has kept a diary of the diseases or the remedies or successes that have resulted [from their treatments]. Thus, we are obliged to make use of the few rays of light that exist from each source and compare them, choosing those that seem most consequential, and giving credence to them by citing them.

### MALADIES TO WHICH NEGROES ARE SUBJECT

Generally speaking, all Negroes are subject to scurvy, to smallpox, to yaws, to abscesses that form in all parts of the body, to dysentery, and to colds that often become fluxions of the chest. These are almost all the maladies from which Negroes suffer, since they are not febrile by nature, and it is rather rare for them to have fever while they have smallpox.

Negroes are quite subject to worms between the skin and the flesh. The Congolese, on the coast of Angola, have worms in stomach and intestines. The Ardra Negroes are the most greatly subjected to worms, between skin and flesh.[3] The Dangme, who live on the Gold Coast, are subject to hydrocele [swellings].[4] The Gonja and Ibo [Igbo], who live in the lower part of the Gold Coast, having stronger passions than the others, may fold their tongues into their throats and suffocate, or else hang themselves to deliver themselves from suffering.[5]

The Ibo eat no beans and are less subject to scurvy than the others, but they have frequent belly aches instead that kill a lot of them. They owe this malady to yams that are taken onto ships as food. These roots warm up and vegetate in the holds where they are kept. What pernicious effects must such food produce?

Of all these maladies, the most common and harmful is scurvy, both for Whites and for Blacks.

### CAUSES OF SCURVY

Although fresh fish is not harmful, its immoderate use becomes pernicious. Bad food of all kinds—biscuits dipped in beverages, beans and rice, the ordinary foods of Negroes—when eaten too much or in a state of fermentation by humidity (which happens easily due to salty and humid air, mists, and fogs), may all cause scurvy.

It is the same with the bad air that Negroes breathe between decks, if no care is taken to keep [the holds] clear and open them in daytime to circulate the air.

If Negroes get too wet when they are on deck, then they catch cold, and apart from scurvy, they can get colds that often degenerate into chest fluxions.

Whites are subject to the same maladies if they do not take care to change clothes. All Whites that disembark at Luanda, the first port in Angola if one takes the short route, are taken by fever if they repeatedly get their legs wet, but then the scurvy abates, which does not happen in other ports.

[The author goes on to discuss both the symptoms and treatment of scurvy.]

### ON SMALLPOX IN NEGROES

The symptoms of smallpox among Negroes are different from those in Whites. Among Whites, the eruption of the pox ordinarily produces rather violent and continuous fevers, watery eyes, and a desire to vomit. But Negroes have none of these symptoms and rarely a fever, which makes the origin of this malady even more difficult to understand. The eruption of pox among Negroes is very limited; the pustules are the same color as the skin, without any prior symptoms; the spots gradually grow (like those of Whites), and in the end they whiten and rupture. After nine or ten days they start to dry out and after fifteen days they are cured.

Uneducated persons take the start of the eruption to be a heating and so they bleed and purge the sick—and without exception all of them perish. One should neither bleed nor purge victims of smallpox.

With the eruption of this disease among Blacks, we find by passing the hand over their skin that there are many small spots that make [the texture] as rough as a rasp. To accelerate the eruption of these spots, in the first three days they should take a spoonful of hot red wine four times a day in which one has melted a little sugar.[6] With this simple and easy remedy, not one sick person dies. But if some of them have a fever, which is uncommon, one gives them no wine; in such cases, the humors are already agitated enough to facilitate a salutary perspiration that cures the sick. One gives them an herbal tea, a light infusion of Swiss *vulnéraires* [a tea composed of astringent plants].[7] And when the smallpox is cured, one purges them two or three times at eight-day intervals.

By following this practice to the letter, one will not be heartsick at seeing almost entire cargoes of Negroes perish, for want of dealing with the contagion.

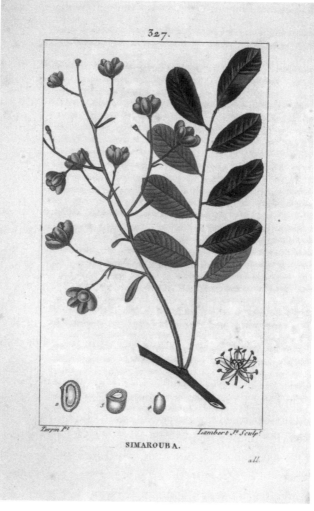

*327.*

SIMAROUBA.

*Simarouba amara.* Pierre Jean François Turpin, designer. Lambert, engraver. Chaumeton, Poiret, and Chamberet, *La Flore Médicale* (Paris: Panckoucke, 1828–1832), pl. 327, hand-colored stipple engraving. The *simarouba* is an evergreen tree native to South America and the Caribbean, including the French colony of Guiana. *Simarouba amara* (also known as *Simarouba glauca*) was carried on board for treatment of a wide range of gastric conditions and other diseases. Extracts from its bark were given to slaves suffering from dysentery, diarrhea, stomach upset, edema, fever, and malaria.

## ON YAWS

It is generally believed that yaws [*framboesia*] is an illness resembling a pox, because it yields to mercury-based medicines.[8] That this is a form of pox does not seem very credible [for other reasons having to do with communicability]. Wet nurses who are afflicted by this disease do not communicate it to their nurslings, nor do they communicate it to Whites who have contact with them, which is, one admits, rather rare.

Be that as it may, the Negroes are all afflicted, just as with smallpox, once in a lifetime with yaws; this illness is all the more dangerous, for it corrupts those who are afflicted with it, putrefying them from head to feet, and causing them to perish if they are not cared for. This said, if a Negro afflicted with yaws is not [treated] appropriately, and even if cured, there remain whitish spots or scars, which greatly reduce the price [i.e., value] of the subject.

The symptoms are from one to five or six spots; once the disease has thoroughly taken hold, they are found all over the body, as with smallpox, but it is rare that they are allowed to reach this point. Yaws manifests itself through large elevated spots, wide like a *liard* [French coin] and of a brown-black color; they cause an itching like scabies; this disease causes considerable harm for the sale of Negroes; but there is a means of curing and ameliorating them externally, without leaving scars.

To heal and externally cure those with yaws, which must always be done before moving on to the great remedies [e.g., mercury], one must cut the pustules down to the base of the skin, then rub them with blue vitriol [a solution of pentahydrated cupric sulphate, a copper salt] [. . .] until the wound no longer bleeds, then cover these with a bit of simple Neapolitan ointment [mercury-based salve], without putting cloth on it.[9]

The same treatment with the vitriol stone and the Neapolitan ointment must be continued every day, once a day, until all the pustules are perfectly healed. One must take care, with each dressing, to lift the crust that has formed.

There remains no scar as if they were never affected by this disease: this is what one calls bleaching the yaws.

During the treatment, the sick are also made to drink a sweat-inducing herbal tea, and are purged three to four times, at eight-day intervals, with a dose of mercury pills or an ordinary medicine.

To thoroughly treat this disease, one must begin by treating the sores without leaving scars, then give [the afflicted slaves] mercury. [. . .]

Many poorly instructed individuals burn the pustules, without trimming them. This burning method is done with silver cautery [one part silver dissolved in three times nitric acid], red precipitate [yellow wax, almond oil, and red oxide of mercury], blue vitriol, or sometimes even with a hot iron without bandaging the wounds with Neapolitan ointment. In such cases, there remain grayish-white scars, which significantly reduce the price of slaves.

[NEGRO ABSCESSES]

[WORMS BETWEEN SKIN AND FLESH]

[ON HYDROCELE (SWELLING)]

PRECAUTIONS TO TAKE TO AVOID SCURVY AND

OTHER MALADIES DURING THE CROSSING

One has to procure a renewal of fresh air between the decks where Negroes are held, which is easy to do, via both sides of the ship, with small windows or vents (*ventouses*) seven feet by seven feet. Without this precaution, the perspiration of these slaves rises and condenses on the deck flooring and falls back on them like rain, which makes them often bathed in this liquid, which must be quite putrid.

Take particular care to keep holds clean, every day have the flooring on which they sleep washed and scrubbed; every day have this place scented, and vary the scents, sometimes with juniper seeds, sometimes with aromatic plants, incense, and vinegar (special or ordinary) to be spread over the flooring to remove the vapors. One can also do this by pouring water on a cannonball heated in a fire, or introducing smoke of cannon powder or, alternatively, a moderate amount of smoke or vapor from charcoal.

If at all possible the Negroes should go up on deck during fine weather to take the air. But if it starts to rain, quickly lock them up because if they get wet they easily catch cold, which often degenerates into fluxions of the chest.

Prevent the crew from eating too much fresh fish, which occasions relaxation [of the bowels] and makes them more susceptible to scurvy.

Biscuits and vegetables must be kept very dry and free from any humidity, for if they contract it, these provisions are spoiled. To remedy that, stick paper in the gaps [in the larder]. By so covering the seams between the boards, the raw air will be prevented from penetrating so much. Dry food well before storing it there, and keep it in a well-enclosed space, or make storage space with calking covered with tarmac cloth.

Negroes have to be given sufficient victuals so they will not lack what is necessary for life, yet their ribs should always show a little, for if they are fattened too much, they will be susceptible of catching scurvy, and we have seen almost entire cargoes of these Negroes who are too fat dying of scurvy. [...]

Separate as much as possible the sick from the healthy because scurvy is more easily communicated than scabies. The prodigious emanation of putrid miasmas raised by these [human] bodies, some of which are already infected, form an immense flux of contagious corpuscles that, becoming airborne, divide and multiply to infinity, causing the most disastrous epidemic.

Prevent the crew from dipping their biscuits to eat them, as this will soften the gums and dispose them to catch scurvy. Keep them away as much as possible from salted meat.

Keep in ships a good supply of lemon and lime juice and make them drink it. As cannot be repeated too often, every day give both Negroes and crew a spoonful [of citrus] on an empty stomach in the morning and let them eat only two hours later. This will infallibly prevent scurvy.

[More such advice]

If possible, have a good provision of tortoises, whose meat is very healthy and has antiscorbutic properties.[10] One may also use cloves, which are good for the stomach, and ginger produces almost the same effect.

### [NAVIGATION]

Make the voyages to Guinea as short as possible in order to avoid the maladies that afflict Negroes, as well as the misfortune of being shut up in the ship during a long crossing. So that the food can be best conserved, only small ships should be sent. Then the trade will barely suffer from delays. This is the maxim of the Portuguese, who lose almost nobody [during their voyages].

When a ship leaves Africa for America, often after several days of being at sea, the Negroes feel considerable cold, which causes serious illnesses. To remedy this, you must heat the hold with a suitable fire, or else you will lose many to fluxions of the chest.

Finally, Providence has provided Africa and America with salutary remedies to usefully prevent or combat the maladies reigning there. They must be knowledgeably used to get the expected benefits.

## [ON SURGEONS]

### IMPORTANT REFLECTIONS

On the coast of Angola or in the Ports of Loango, Malembo, and Cabinda, the Negroes cultivate absolutely all that is necessary for their existence; they live most of the time on fish.[11] This means that it is not possible to stock [the same type of] victuals [that they eat customarily], and that what is carried from Europe must serve for the whole voyage.[12] This necessitates the greatest precautions to take sufficient supplies and the greatest care to conserve them. [. . .]

We invite those who engage in the African trade to follow the example of the Dutch for the conservation of their vegetables. They dry their beans, etc., in ovens; these are so completely dried that they are no longer in a state to vegetate. When the moist parts of these vegetables are thick and close together, the raw air cannot penetrate them as much and spoil them. It is not the same in France, where they are content to dry vegetables in the sun, and so when at sea, the smallest amount of humidity can penetrate and easily spoil them.

### LEAVING EUROPE FOR AFRICA

During this navigation there are two unhealthy practices that should be amended. Those who engage in these voyages commonly make these two major mistakes. First, some shipowners pay attention to the wrong things, paying more attention to the [desired] port [and maps] than to the functioning of their vessels. This necessarily prolongs the voyages, whereas everything ought to invite the shortening of these trips.

The other and even more dangerous inconvenience is the habit of leaving for Africa at any time; the regularity of winds and currents should determine the season suitable for reaching these shores.

This latter unfortunate practice brings up the distinction between the grand and small routes. The small route is the most direct and shortest; it is no more than 1,800 leagues to the most distant ports to find slaves; 35 to 40 days suffice to sail this route, from the beginning of September to the end of November because the most favorable winds and currents occur then. It is even possible to try in December, January, and February, but with less certainty of success.

These shores are no longer practicable from the beginning of March to the end of August since one has to fight continually against violent currents that carry one northward and against the wind from the southeast which is usual. Experience has taught that those who sail at these times have to moor far off shore. [...]

### DEPARTURE FROM AFRICA FOR AMERICA

When ships leave Africa for America and are off the coast of Cayenne [South America], they should sail as far north as possible, and when they are 100 to 120 leagues from this island, they should cross the equator. Here they will find fine seas where it almost never rains and a new strong current. (One should avoid as much as possible being near these shores in August, September, and October, however, because it rains continually these three months at the equator.)

[...]

Another calamity no less annoying in this [humid] climate is that Negroes from north of the equator are subject to smallpox, which, by an aggravating peculiarity, barely develops among these people until after age fourteen. A vessel attacked by this epidemic, if it takes a long route to reach America, finds itself in a situation of losing the whole cargo of Negroes, especially when the surgeons are not sufficiently experienced in treating it.

I think I have satisfied the question proposed by the academy, as much about the efficacy as the simplicity of the remedies, and I have the honor of including a supplement.

[The main text ends here; his supplement is an index of diseases.]

"The principal duty of man in society is to be humane, to be so toward men of all states, all ages, & all that is not foreign to man."

*Dictionary of Anecdotes,* vol. 2, p. 44[13]

1776 Essay 3 (Louis Alfonse)

[Received February 1777]

# SELECT CHRONOLOGY OF
# THE REPRESENTATION OF
# AFRICANS AND RACE

This chronology begins in Antiquity and ends in the 1890s, by which time the foundational ideas associated with racialized thinking had taken shape.

**c. eighth century BCE** In his *Genealogy of the Gods,* the Greek poet Hesiod refers to "the ruler of far-flung Aethiopia" as Memnon, the son of the dawn goddess, Eos. Painted Greek vases made two centuries later clearly depict Memnon with black skin and facial features.

**c. 750–700 BCE** Homer's *The Iliad.* First known reference to the Ethiopians, or "burnt-faced" people, living in the distant lands of the sunrise and sunset.

**c. sixth century BCE–c. fourth century BCE** Compilation of Genesis, the first book of the Bible. Its account of the world's first peoples synthesizes various streams of oral and written material. The story of creation is immediately followed by the "Table of Nations" and the story of Adam and Eve and their descendants. This archetypal genealogy of humankind gave rise to later discussions of 1) the elusive nature of the mark of Cain; and 2) Noah's cursing of his grandson Canaan, as possible explanations for the blackness of African skin.

**c. mid-fifth century BCE** The ancient traveler and historian Herodotus of Samos writes his *Histories.* He expands on the character and location of the black "Ethiopians," and extols them as the most virtuous and handsome of all men in the world.

**c. 400 BCE** Hippocrates II of Kos writes the influential treatise *On Airs, Waters, and Places,* which posits a link between the environment and human health. Harsh climates supposedly challenge their inhabitants, making them sharp-witted and industrious, while those living in less stressful, temperate climates became lethargic and unsuited for physical work. During this era, he also develops a theory of four temperaments, which later came to be associated with the bodily humors. Hippocrates' theories were adopted and modified by generations of successors to suit their own ends; European writers of the early-modern period, for example, characterized the people of the Torrid Zone as living in a fixed state of indolence, stupidity, and superstition.

c. 350 BCE    In the *Politics*, Aristotle describes a natural slave as "anyone who, while being human, is by nature not his own but of someone else" and "he is of someone else when, while being human, he is a piece of property; and a piece of property is a tool for action separate from its owner." Though Aristotle does not refer to African slaves, his writings were often used later to justify the enslavement of Africans.

c. 7 BCE–14 CE    In his *Geographica* (Geography), Strabo, the Greek geographer, philosopher, and historian, attempts to define the coastal contours and inner features of continental Africa. In his view, Africa ends just below the Nile within an area called "Aethiopia," and "Libya" denotes all of North Africa. He also asserts that the blackness of Africans is caused by the intensity of the sun combined with the dryness of the climate. However, he also posits that "seminal impartation" causes children to take on the color of their parents, thus combining hereditary and climatic explanations for physiological differences.

First century    Pliny the Elder, famed scientist of the early Roman empire and author of an exhaustive survey of the natural world, composes his *Naturalis Historia* (Natural History). In Book 7, he embarks on a broad survey of the prodigies and monstrous races of the world and reports that the height of the Syrbotae, a tribe of the Aethiopians, exceeds twelve feet.

c. 150    Claudius Ptolemy of Alexandria, the Greek mathematician, geographer, and astronomer, compiles his *Geography*, with its famous world map. Its reconstruction during the Renaissance provides scholars with a much firmer idea of the location and character of lands found far beyond Europe. He is among the first to use a gridded system of coordinates, and divides the earth into three climate zones: arctic, temperate, and tropical. Ptolemy's map is significant in that it uses the word "Ethiopia" to designate the region roughly corresponding to ancient Nubia (which only took this name much later).

216    Claudius Galen dies. The famed Greek physician of the Roman Empire leaves behind an extraordinary body of work consisting of medical treatises on a great range of topics as well as many works of philosophy. Reintroduced into European culture during the eleventh century through Latin translations from the Arabic, Galen's works took on a central role in the practice of medicine. Among the most important impacts of Galen's legacy was his understanding of *humoralism,* namely, the role of the four key bodily fluids (called *humors*) as the cause of all illnesses.

c. 600    Appearance of Isidore of Seville's magnus opus, *Etymologiae* (Origins). Among a multitude of other topics, this encyclopedic work preserves ancient

Greco-Roman insights into various peoples of the world and their classification. First appearance of the three-part division of the world into continents (Asia, Africa, and Europe), with respective settlement by the sons of Noah, that is, Shem, Ham, and Japheth.

**c. 600**  After more than three centuries, the Bavli, or Babylonian Talmud, is completed. This Rabbinic Jewish text, along with its counterpart the Jerusalem Talmud, asserts that Noah's curse affects Ham's skin color (an assertion not found in the Book of Genesis). This "racialized" version of the "Myth" or "Curse of Ham," which also associates darkened skin with bondage, was also beginning to emerge in early Christian writings, including those of Origen.

**c. 1000**  The Persian scholar and philosopher Ibn Sina, Latinized as Avicenna, writes his highly influential medical treatise, *The Canon of Medicine,* in which he argues that climate produces a slavish mentality in distant areas of the world.

**c. 1150**  The legend of Prester John (*Presbyter Johannes*), the fabled Christian ruler of the East, begins to circulate in Europe. During the Crusades, Europeans seek the "Prester" due to his reputed defeat of the Persian Muslim kings at Ecbatana. Eventually, he will be portrayed as a Black king living in East Africa.

**c. 1200**  In his voluminous *Guide for the Perplexed,* Moses ben Maimonides, the Sephardic Jewish physician and philosopher, reports that due to their hot climate, "black-colored people" are like mute animals, falling between humans and monkeys in the order of creation.

**1271**  Marco Polo, Venetian businessman and traveler, begins a twenty-four-year voyage through the Middle and Far East. Manuscript accounts (many embellished) of his travels bring a much more intimate knowledge of the "outside" world to Europe.

**1315**  Louis X le Hutin, King of France, signs an edict that leads to the "Free Soil" principle, the idea that there are "no slaves in France." This edict formally ends slavery in the kingdom.

**Mid-fourteenth century**  *The Travels of Sir John Mandeville,* a possibly apocryphal travel memoir recounting various adventures throughout the known world (including Libya and Ethiopia), begins to circulate throughout Europe.

**Late fourteenth century**  The beginning of a tradition, which remains in vogue until the eighteenth century, in which paintings of the Adoration of the Magi include an African as one of the three kings, often splendidly dressed with a retinue of Black followers.

**1415–1499**  The Portuguese outthrust into Africa begins with the invasion of the Moroccan city of Ceuta in 1415. By 1499, Vasco da Gama has circumnavigated the entire African continent.

**1449**  Pero Sarmiento issues the *Sentencia-Estatuto* in Toledo, Spain. This invective against Jews is the first example of discrimination on a racialized, rather than religious, basis. It lays the groundwork for the Spanish *limpieza de sangre* (purity of blood) laws, which enforce hierarchical ideas of race based on supposedly intrinsic qualities.

**1452** Pope Nicholas V issues the papal bull *Dum Diversas,* permitting the conquest of disputed land in Africa by the Portuguese king Afonso V, as well as the enslavement of its inhabitants. The Papacy's right to decide the fate of conquered lands and their peoples is further developed in *Romanus Pontifex* (1455).

**c. 1470** Portuguese explorers make landfall in São Tomé and Príncipe, islands off the western equatorial coast of Africa. Settlers (mostly "undesirables" expelled from Portugal) and African slaves are sent to colonize the islands, which become major sugar producers in the sixteenth century.

**1492** A veteran slave trader who had traveled to Africa's west coast, Christopher Columbus makes landfall in the New World, launching the European Age of Discovery. Contact with Amerindians in the Caribbean, who are not mentioned in the Bible, ultimately raises questions about human nature, difference, and origins.

**1494** The Treaty of Tordesillas demarcates lands recently found by the two maritime powers to the east and west of a meridian drawn between Africa and the New World. Spain was allocated all territory in the Americas, except for the eastern part of Brazil, which went to Portugal.

**1520–1525** Titian's portrait of Laura Dianti, a lover of Alfonso I d'Este, Duke of Ferrara, is evidently the first painting to show a person of high rank accompanied by a Black attendant, in this case a small boy. Subsequently male portraits of the nobility often show Black pages who accompanied them into battle. The tradition of such portraits will continue until the late eighteenth century, being revived by Sir Joshua Reynolds.

**1537** Pope Paul III issues the papal bull *Sublimis Deus,* which declares Amerindians to be rational beings and bans their enslavement. Africans do not benefit from such a reprieve.

**1550** First publication of Leo Africanus's *Discovery of Africa,* an account of his travels in sub-Saharan Africa undertaken thirty years earlier, during the 1520s. It is soon translated into several European languages and often reprinted. He provides new information on the Nile River, and his account of the fabled city of Timbuktu in Mali describes a brisk trade in gold, cloth, books, and Black slaves.

**1550–1551** Debate at the Council of Valladolid (Spain) pertaining to military expansion in the Americas, as well as the forced conversion and enslavement of Amerindians. Juan Ginés de Sepúlveda argues, relying on Aristotelian ideas of natural slavery, that Amerindians are inherently inferior to Spaniards and therefore their subjugation is necessary. Bartolomé de las Casas argues in defense of Amerindian rights to self-governance and self-determination without Spanish intervention, as well as peaceful rather than forced religious conversion.

**c. 1560** The term *race,* used to mean a group of people descended from a common root, enters into the English language from the Old French *räiz* or *räis,* which originally referred to families with royal blood.

**1564–1569** Sir John Hawkins initiates British involvement in the slave trade with three expeditions to Africa.

**1566**   First edition of the French historian and political theorist Jean Bodin's *Method for the Easy Comprehension of History,* in which he rejects the theory of the multiple origins of humans. He develops a rudimentary sense of the geographical distribution of the world's people, based solely on skin color and climate theory.

**1571**   First enslaved Africans unexpectedly arrive at Bordeaux. The Parlement of Bordeaux arrests the Norman entrepreneur who brought them and liberates the Africans based on the longstanding Free Soil principle.

**c. 1600**   Giordano Bruno, Italian priest, philosopher, and savant, rejects the biblical monogenist position of universal human descent from Adam. In his opinion, Jews and Ethiopians could not share the same ancestor. The consideration of differences in skin color and geography leads to his proposal of separate Adams or pre-Adamite forebears of the races, which will later be adopted by eighteenth- and nineteenth-century polygenists, often with a toxic racist agenda.

**1612**   Jean Riolan the Younger, anatomist and professor of medicine at the Faculté de Médecine of Paris, performs one of the first recorded vivisections of a black body. His observations lead him to reject the notion that dark humors within the body cause the skin's darkness, instead attributing this quality to the heat of the tropical sun and therefore aligning himself with such ancient Greek writers as Homer and, above all, Herodotus.

**1646**   Sir Thomas Browne, the English physician, polymath, and encyclopedist, publishes his *Pseudodoxia Epidemica, or Enquiries into vulgar and common errors,* in which he discusses the origin of black skin. Browne refutes several explanations: environmental factors, the effect of maternal impression, and the Curse of Ham. Instead, he argues that black skin is inherited and transmitted from generation to generation through sperm, which he asserts becomes "dealbinized" by an as yet undefined internal generative process.

**1650**   Bernhard Varen, the German physician and geographer, produces his *Geographia generalis* (General Geography), in which he expands distinctions among human beings beyond just skin color. His method of classification incorporates a fuller range of physical characteristics, and he also considers dietary habits as a major source of somatic difference.

**1660**   Foundation of the Royal African Company, an English trading company by the royal family and City of London to trade on the west coast of Africa. It is led by the Duke of York, King Charles II's brother, later King James II.

**c. 1660s**   The Italian anatomist Marcello Malpighi dissects a sample of black skin and demonstrates that the African epidermis is as light as that of a European and that the source of blackness is confined to a thin, netlike stratum covering the true skin, or dermis. Malpighi's identification of this anatomical structure, known as the *rete mucosum* or Malpighian layer, ushers in a new era in the scientific community's attempt to define the origin of blackness. It soon becomes a major topic of scholarly discussion, though the source and nature of the coloring agent remains the subject of heated debate.

**1664**   Robert Boyle (1627–1691), famed Anglo-Irish natural philosopher and a pioneer of modern chemistry, proposes in *Experiments and Considerations Touching Colors* that the origin of blackness is "some peculiar and seminal impression," thus rejecting the idea that differences in climate alone determines blackness.

**1672**   The slave ship *Saint-Etienne-de-Paris* sails from Bordeaux, bound for the west coast of Africa. The voyage represents the first involvement in the slave trade by a port hitherto known for its transportation of wines, foodstuffs, and manufactured goods.

**c. 1677–1684**   Antonie van Leeuwenhoek, an amateur naturalist and designer-maker of microscopes, examines African skin under a microscope and affirms that blackness did not come from the blood, but from scales in the deeper tissues of the skin. Among anatomists, his views are perhaps less trenchant since he avoids asserting that there are any essential differences between Whites and Blacks.

**1684**   In an important article published in the *Journal des savants,* the physician, philosopher, and travel writer François Bernier puts forward the first real proto-racial classification of humankind. The title is "New Division of the Earth by the Different Species or Races of Man that Inhabit It." Bernier, who initially hesitates about how to class Amerindians, ultimately divides humankind into four distinct categories.

**1685**   Louis XIV signs an *ordonnance* that will soon be called the *Code Noir.* This document, which is distributed to France's overseas colonies, formalizes the institution of slavery in French colonies by declaring that African slaves are property.

**1691**   John Ray, a priest and biologist whose work is an important precursor to Linnaeus, works out the earliest comprehensive taxonomic system for many parts of the natural world, primarily plants, fish, and insects (in part by making use of the new expression *species*).

**1709**   François Bellet, one of the founders of the Bordeaux Academy of Sciences, delivers a short "Dissertation on the Black Color of Ethiopians" to the members of the academy's institutional predecessor, the Académie des lyriques.

**1710**   The anatomist Alexis Littré publishes *Diverses observations anatomiques* (Various Anatomical Observations), in which he describes his attempt to isolate the fluid contained in the *rete mucosum.* Though his efforts are unsuccessful, his research brings this supposed feature of African anatomy to the attention of a new generation of philosophes and naturalists.

**1711–c. 1820**   *Casta* (lineage paintings) appear in Latin America, primarily in Mexico. These depictions of various admixtures of Amerindians, Africans, and Spanish Whites feature up to sixteen individual portraits and serve to codify specific racialized categories of miscegenation, e.g., a Black and an Amerindian produce a *Lobo.*

**1712**   Founding of the Académie Royale des Sciences, Belles-Lettres, et Arts de Bordeaux (Royal Society of Sciences, Literature, and the Arts of Bordeaux). Its patron, the Duc de La Force, endows a medal of 300 livres to be awarded to the winner of the academy's annual essay contest.

1715   The Treaty of Utrecht ends the long War of the Spanish Succession. Trade with the Caribbean increases dramatically, ushering in a steady rise in the slave trade.

1716   Passage of an edict by Philippe d'Orléans, regent of the French king Louis XV, effectively declaring slavery legal within France itself. The measure puts an end to the long-held principle of Free Soil, which supposedly liberated all enslaved people entering the kingdom.

1733   Voltaire, the French philosopher, historian, and writer, claims that the *rete mucosum* provides irrefutable evidence that Blacks and Whites are separate species (polygenesis) and that Blacks are an inferior type of human being. Voltaire will later become an opponent of slavery, but he will retain these same racist views.

1735   Carl Linnaeus, the Swedish botanist, publishes the first of many editions of his groundbreaking *Systema Naturae* (System of Nature), in which he breaks the genus *homo* into four geographical varieties, including *africanus niger*. In his 1758 of the *Systema*, he will add humoral tendencies and temperaments to the classification of what he now calls *Homo sapiens*.

1737   Bernhard Siegfried Albinus, professor of anatomy and surgery at Leiden University, publishes his *Dissertatio secunda, de sede et caussa coloris aethiopum et caeterorum hominum* (Second Dissertation on the Dwelling Place and Cause of the Color of Ethiopians and Other Human Beings), which cites a comprehensive range of authorities on black skin, from ancient authors such as Strabo and Diodorus of Sicily to more contemporary scholars like Marcello Malpighi. He supports the theory of the effects of the four humors on skin color through dissections of the human body, thus lending the theory greater scientific validity.

1738   The Parlement of Bordeaux votes to accept a royal proclamation that tightens restrictions on the importation and use of slaves by their colonial masters while in France. Those masters found in violation of the proclamation's terms must forfeit their slaves. This same proclamation nonetheless sanctions, under specific conditions, the presence of Africans on French soil.

1739   Announcement by the Académie de Bordeaux of an essay contest proposing to explain the origin and degeneration of black skin and hair. Sixteen essays are received by or just after the deadline of May 1741. The jury finds none to be acceptable and declares the contest closed.

c. 1740–1748   War of the Austrian Succession slows the rise of Bordeaux's involvement in the slave trade.

1741   The Perpignan physician and anatomist Pierre Barrère publishes the influential entry he had sent to the Bordeaux contest on African skin color. Drawing from his own anatomical research undertaken while living on a slave plantation in the French colony of Guiana, Barrère concludes that black bile causes dark skin. It is the only Bordeaux contest essay to appear in print.

1744   Publication of *Dissertation physique à l'occasion du nègre blanc* (Physical Dissertation on the Occasion of the White Negro) by Pierre-Louis Moreau de Maupertuis. Considering the anomaly of white-skinned Blacks (albinos), Maupertuis holds that whiteness represents the primitive state of human skin. This theory is adopted by a number of naturalists as proof of degeneration.

**1748**   Montesquieu publishes his groundbreaking essay *De l'esprit des Lois* (The Spirit of the Laws), in which he both castigates slavery through irony and puts forward a climate-based understanding of slavery.

**1749–1788**   Georges-Louis Leclerc, comte de Buffon publishes one of the most influential books of the eighteenth century, the *Histoire naturelle* (Natural History). A monogenist, Buffon plays an enormous role in disseminating the idea of degeneration caused by variations in climate, food, and lifestyle.

**1750s**   The increasingly scientific study of anatomy is applied to the subject of race, most notably by Johann Friedrich Meckel of the University of Halle in Germany. Meckel claims to have detected a blackish color in the blood and brains of dissected black subjects.

**1756–1763**   The Seven Years' War (called the French and Indian War in North America) greatly curtails the slave trade in Bordeaux and other French seaports.

**1758**   David Hume, Scottish Enlightenment philosopher and essayist, publishes a compilation of his writings in *Essays, Moral, Political and Literary*. In the essay "Of National Characters," first published in 1748 and revised in 1753, he asserts that there are distinct species of men and that he believes Blacks are "naturally inferior to the [W]hites," and incapable of producing their own culture.

**1762**   Anthony Benezet, a Philadelphia Quaker and abolitionist, publishes the first of his many antislavery works, "A Short Account of that Part of Africa Inhabited by the Negroes." Benezet's works influence both French and British antislavery movements. Some years later, Benezet helps found the first antislavery organization, the Society for the Relief of Free Negroes Unlawfully Held in Bondage.

**1764**   Petrus Camper, the Dutch comparative anatomist, zoologist, and surgeon, delivers a lecture entitled "On the Origin and Color of Blacks" in which he highlights the empirical difference between human varieties based on facial angles. Though Camper asserts that these superficial differences had no bearing on intelligence, the published version of his ideas will be appropriated and reinterpreted by European naturalists interested in advancing a racialized physiognomy of human beings.

**1765**   Claude-Nicolas Le Cat, a surgeon from Rouen, announces that he has discovered a dark liquid substance during a human dissection which he calls *aethiops* (essentially, melanin). Following the assertions of the German anatomist Johann Friedrich Meckel, Le Cat suggests that this substance originates in the dark tissue of the black brain, where it flows out through the nerves to all parts of the body, including the skin. In his view, *aethiops* results from the interaction of sulfurous blood with the element mercury bound within the life spirit. This spurious discovery quickly becomes part of the era's raciology.

**1768**   Cornelius de Pauw (1739–1799), Dutch philosopher and geographer, synthesizes the racializing notions found in the works of Barrère, Meckel, and Le Cat in his hugely influential *Recherches Philosophiques sur les Américains* (Philosophical

Research on the Americans). De Pauw asserts that the degenerated character of the brain, blood, and semen of Blacks is such that their very being is pathological.

**1772–1800**  The first real attempts at pseudoscientific biometric theories are published. Early examples include Johann Kaspar Lavater's 1772 theory that a person's physiognomy reveals his or her own inner character, and Franz Joseph Gall's 1798 study of phrenology (craniological bumps), which supposedly determine the entire gamut of intellectual capacity and personality traits.

**1772**  Bordeaux's Royal Academy of Sciences announces two contests related to the health of Africans. The second one solicits insights into improving shipboard conditions during the Middle Passage, an issue of great practical and economic importance for the time.

**1772**  Judgment by Lord Mansfield in *Somersett v. Stewart* is taken to imply that slavery was illegal in England. The Somersett ruling led to the first abolition campaigns.

**1774**  Planter and slave owner Edward Long publishes his unapologetically racist *History of Jamaica,* in which he argues that "the White and the Negroe are two distinct species" as a justification for the enslavement of the latter by the former.

**1774**  The Scottish philosopher Henry Home, Lord Kames asserts in his *Sketches of the History of Man* that climate-based theories for the origins of different human types are false, and that the differences between human groups are so distinct that they must have come from different rootstocks. Home also posits a conjectural history for humankind, according to which certain races or groups are associated with the stages of hunting, pasturage, agriculture, or commerce. This "stage theory" of humankind is also endorsed by fellow Scots Adam Smith, Adam Ferguson, William Robertson, and John Millar.

**1775**  Johann Friedrich Blumenbach, German physician, anthropologist, comparative anatomist, and physiologist, publishes *De generis humani varietate nativa* (On the Natural Varieties of Mankind). Advancing a monogenetic theory of humankind grounded on physical anatomy, he nonetheless gives credence to the notion that humankind can be broken down into useful categories based on empirical data.

**1775–1783**  The American Revolution interrupts the slave trade.

**1777**  The German philosopher Immanuel Kant publishes *Von der verschiedenen Rassen der Menschen* (Of the Different Races of Human Beings), in which he develops a monogenist scheme of essential human categories informed by contemporary ideas about racial degeneration and human anatomy. Kant also asserts that each of the races possesses fundamental attributes endowed by nature. Both his codification of race and his personal writings reflect his disdain for Black people.

**c. 1780**  Rise of the polygenist view of human origin. Although the argument for the descent of human varieties from separate ancestors has already been proposed, only in the latter part of the eighteenth century does the theory of polygenesis begin to challenge the monogenist belief in a single avatar for humanity. Polygenesis will soon become a useful tool for the proslavery lobby in the United States.

c. 1780   The Englishman Sir William Jones pioneers a linguistic theory explaining how Noah's progeny moved across the globe. Historical linguistics will later flourish in Germany.

1784–1788   A three-way exchange of ideas on race between Kant, Johann Gottfried Herder, and Georg Forster is provoked by Herder's *Ideen zur Philosophie der Geschichte der Menschheit* (Ideas toward a Philosophy of the History of Mankind).

1784   Samuel Thomas Soemmerring, a German anatomist, theorizes in his *Ueber die köperlich Verschiedenheit des Negers vom Europäer* (On the Physical Differences between the European and the Negro) that brain size is directly related to the thickness of the nerves attached to the rest of the body. In his view, these spurious anatomical differences determine if a race is low or high functioning.

1785   Christoph Meiners, an anatomist at the University of Göttingen, publishes *Grundriß der Geschichte der Menschheit* (Fundamentals of the History of Mankind), one of several works in which he puts forward both a racial hierarchy and a polygenist theory of humankind. It is he who coins the description *Caucasian* in this year, which Blumenbach later popularizes. Meiners will later become one of the spiritual ancestors of the Nazi movement.

1787   The Society for Effecting the Abolition of the Slave Trade forms in London. Several months later, the French equivalent, the Société des amis des Noirs, is also established.

1787   The institution of slavery is upheld in the Constitution of the United States, inscribing the assumption of black inferiority into the very fabric of the new country. Failure to eradicate slavery at this crucial point in America's experiment in democracy is considered the nation's "original sin."

Early 1780s–c. 1790   This period of relative peace in Europe allows the exponential rise in the slave trade in Bordeaux and Europe in general. In 1789 alone, thirty-four ships left the harbor of Bordeaux, bound for the slave pens of the African coast.

1791   Beginning of revolts in Saint-Domingue (Haiti).

1791   First motion to end the slave trade defeated in the British Parliament.

1794   Publication in English of *The Works of Professor* [Petrus] *Camper on the Connexion between the Science of Anatomy and the Arts of Drawing, Painting, Statuary etc.*, containing Camper's hugely influential anatomical charts of the "racial angle," which compare facial features from the Apollo Belvedere to the ape.

1794   During the French Revolution, slavery is legally abolished in the French colonies by a decree of "Universal Emancipation" issued by the National Assembly of the revolutionary government. The following year the national constitution codifies the emancipation of French slaves.

1799   In *An Account of the Regular Graduation of Man*, Charles White, reinterpreting Petrus Camper's charts, suggests that Africans' supposedly lowly nature situates them in the "Great Chain of Being" at a point just after the great apes. The notion of a concatenation of "races" will continue unabated during the nineteenth century.

1801   The one-time pharmacist Julien-Joseph Virey publishes his very influential
       *Histoire naturelle du genre humain* (Natural History of the Human Genus), in which
       he posits that Africans are closer to animals and can be considered a distinct
       species. His later works are even more overtly polygenist.

1801–1804   The final years of the Haitian Revolution. Freedom for all enslaved
       peoples is proclaimed by the brilliant military strategist Toussaint Louverture. In
       1802, Napoleon attempts to reimpose slavery and retake Saint-Domingue, as Haiti
       was called then. In 1803, French armies are resoundingly defeated. In 1804 the
       Empire (later Republic) of Haiti is declared by Jean-Jacques Dessalines. Slavery is
       nonetheless re-imposed in France's other Caribbean colonies.

1807   Abolition of the British transatlantic slave trade by act of Parliament, but not
       slavery itself in the British colonies.

1808   Abolition of the US transatlantic slave trade, but not slavery itself.

1808   Abbé Henri Jean-Baptiste Grégoire publishes his *De la littérature des Nègres*
       (An Enquiry Concerning the Intellectual and Moral Faculties, and Literature of
       Negroes), a major antislavery work that begins by refuting the era's increasingly
       race-based views of Africans. He will be castigated as a *negrophile*.

1809   In his *Philosophie zoologique* (Zoological Philosophy), the naturalist Antoine de
       Monet, Chevalier de Lamarck posits that primates transformed into humans, and
       that Africans were the logical missing link between Whites and primates.

1811   Spain abolishes slavery in most cases in its colonial possessions, but definitively
       ends the practice only in 1867, followed by Portugal two years later.

1816   The French naturalist Georges Cuvier publishes *Le Règne animal* (The Animal
       Kingdom). A proponent of the single origin of all human types (monogenesis), he
       nonetheless espouses the theory of catastrophism, which posits that traumatic
       natural events isolated certain human populations from their forebears 5,000 years
       before his own day. In his view, this gave rise to the inferior Mongolian and Black
       Ethiopian races.

1818   The United Kingdom establishes treaties with Spain and Portugal. The terms
       greatly restrict their participation in the slave trade.

1819   Simón Bolívar issues his address to the Congress of Angostura, where he calls
       for the abolition of slavery in liberated territories.

c. 1830   Georg Wilhelm Friedrich Hegel, the German philosopher and proponent of
       German idealism, posits a philosophy of history around the concept of race. Hegel
       believes that Black Africans are an undeveloped people who have been left out of
       history due to their geographical isolation from the rest of the world and their
       supposed failure to form political states. These ideas infuse the work of later racist
       scholars. Hegel is nonetheless an ardent abolitionist: "in rational states," he
       proclaims, "slavery no longer exists."

1833   The Slavery Abolition Act is passed by British Parliament. Reparations are to be
       paid to former slave owners. The measure is to take effect in British West Indian

colonies one year later, but only after passing through a transitional system of unpaid "apprenticeships." Complete freedom came only in 1838.

**1839–1849** Samuel George Morton, an American ethnographer, publishes a series of books, including *Crania Americana* (American Skulls), in which he asserts that he could determine the intellectual potential of a given race simply by measuring the typical size of its brain.

**1839** Fifty-three enslaved Africans aboard the Spanish slave ship *Amistad* take control of the vessel off the coast of Cuba.

**1840** Chemical analysis of the dark coloration of the eye by the Swedish scientist Jöns Jacob Berzelius ultimately leads to the coining of the term "melanin." Today it is used more broadly to describe the pigmenting material responsible for the wide range of human skin and hair color.

**1840** J. M. W. Turner's painting *Slave Ship (Slavers Throwing Overboard the Dead and Dying, Typhoon Coming On)* (Boston Museum of Fine Arts) is exhibited at the Royal Academy, London.

**1848** Slavery definitively abolished in all French colonies by the revolutionary government of the Second Republic. Slaves are first bought by the government from their owners, then formally liberated.

**c. 1850s** Rise of the racist American School of Ethnography. Among its proponents is the aforementioned naturalist Samuel George Morton. Morton's views, which uphold racial hierarchy (and thus white superiority) as scientific fact, are codified in Josiah Nott and George Gliddon's widely read *Types of Mankind* (1854).

**1850** The Scottish abolitionist and anticolonialist Robert Knox publishes *The Races of Men*, in which he advances the existence of fixed racial types, asserting that each group can only flourish in its own environment, hence his belief that the native inhabitants of countries will always repel settlers. Knox even believed that native Americans would eventually expel White settlers. His scorn for nonwhite races extended not only to the "negroid" but also to the loathsome Celts.

**1851** The American physician and racial polemicist Samuel A. Cartwright attributes the tendency of slaves to run away from their masters to a mental illness known as *drapetomania*. His hypothesis becomes a spurious but nonetheless important part of the proslavery argument leading up to the American Civil War.

**1853–1855** Joseph Arthur, Comte de Gobineau publishes his *Essai sur l'inégalité des races humaines* (Essay on the Inequality of the Human Races), which asserts that race is the most important explanatory criterion in understanding the human species. Excerpts from the book, which castigates racial mixing and posits the existence of an "Aryan" master race, would later be taught in schools in Nazi Germany.

**1859** Charles Darwin publishes *On the Origin of Species*, the foundational text in the history of evolutionary biology. The theory of natural selection will soon be appropriated by race theorists in order to explain the supposed primacy of the white race. Later, in his 1871 *The Descent of Man*, Darwin debunks the concept of polygenesis to emphasize the fact that differences among human groups are superficial and come about through the indiscriminate process of sexual selection. He is not immune to the prejudices of his era, however. He claims that Australian Aboriginal people and Black Africans are closer to the great apes.

**1864**   The German scientist Carl Vogt asserts in his *Lectures on Man* that there is a kinship between Africans and apes, and that Whites are a separate species.

**1861–1865**   American Civil War. Southern secessionists, asserting the principle of states' rights to justify slavery, are ultimately defeated by the Union. Slavery is legally abolished in the United States with ratification of the Thirteenth Amendment to the Constitution.

**1879**   José Antonio Saco publishes *Historia de la esclavitud de la raza africana en el Nuevo Mundo* (History of the Enslavement of the African Race in the New World), a monumental history of New World slavery that traces slavery's origins back to Egypt and other civilizations. Although an abolitionist and intellectual leader of Cuban independence, Saco saw Africans as a threat to Cuba's future national identity.

**1883**   Francis Galton coins the term *eugenics* to describe selective breeding for human beings. His idea is to encourage the procreation of the "fit" (educated White people) over the "unfit." His concern with the "betterment of the [white] race" has a detrimental effect on African Americans in particular, leading in many cases to sterilization and confinement.

**1880s**   Slavery is abolished in Cuba (1886) and Brazil (1888), the last strongholds of the "peculiar institution" in the New World.

**1890s**   Alfred Binet, a French psychologist, opens a new chapter in the history of racialized thinking when he devises tests to measure the mental abilities and learning habits of schoolchildren. His methods are adopted by American psychologists, leading to the creation of the Stanford-Binet Intelligence Quotient (IQ) test. The standardized survey purports to measure innate intelligence but fails to account for external conditions that influence children's exposure to intellectual enrichment. Results are detrimental to Blacks due to prejudiced assumptions of "white" cultural norms.

# NOTES

Abbreviations

ENC   *Encyclopédie, ou dictionnaire raisonné des sciences, des arts et des métiers* [1751–1780, 28 vols.], ed. Denis Diderot and Jean le Rond d'Alembert
TRV   *Dictionnaire universel françois et latin (Dictionnaire de Trévoux)* [1771, 8 vols.]

## Part I

## *Introduction: The 1741 Contest on the "Degeneration" of Black Skin and Hair*

1. See Daniel Roche, *Le siècle des Lumières en province: Académies et académiciens provinciaux, 1689–1789*, 2 vols. (Paris: Mouton, 1978), and Christine Adams, *A Taste for Comfort and Status: A Bourgeois Family in Eighteenth-Century France* (University Park: Pennsylvania State University Press, 2000), 195–196, on the role of provincial academies.

2. Adams, *A Taste for Comfort and Status*, 196.

3. See Jeremy L. Caradonna, *The Enlightenment in Practice: Academic Prize Contests and Intellectual Culture in France, 1670–1794* (Ithaca: Cornell University Press, 2012), for a broad contextualization of academy culture and scientific competitions.

4. The first traces of a "scientific" interest in the source of African "blackness" occurred in 1709, when the medical doctor (and future member of the Bordeaux Academy) François Bellet delivered a paper on the origins of "Ethiopian" skin. Writing as a physician, Bellet first debunked both biblical and environmental explanations of blackness before putting forward his own physiological theory, namely, that one of the interior layers of black skin had a sap of sorts that became activated when mixed with certain

body salts. See Éric Saugera, *Bordeaux port négrier XVIIe—XIXe siècles* (Paris: Karthala, 1995), 322.

5. Several essays had been eliminated from the competition because they had arrived after the final deadline.

6. *Mercure de France dédié au Roi* (Paris: chez Guillaume Cavalier et al., October 1741), 2257; Pierre Barrière, *L'Académie de Bordeaux: Centre de culture internationale au XVIIIe siècle (1712–1792)* (Paris and Bordeaux: Éditions Bière, 1951), 117.

7. *Mercure de France,* October 1741, 2257.

8. Shifts in scientific focus or methodology were taking place at about the same time that deep-seated color prejudice and notions of "blood purity" were emerging in the slave colonies of the Caribbean. For an assessment of how this transpired in Guadeloupe, see Mélanie Lamotte, "Color Prejudice in the French Atlantic World," in *The Atlantic World,* ed. D'Maris Coffman, Adrian Leonard, and William O'Reilly (London: Routledge, 2014), 151–171. See also Guillaume Aubert, "'The Blood of France': Race and Purity of Blood in the French Atlantic World," *William and Mary Quarterly* 61, no. 3 (2004): 439–478.

9. On the subject of race during the French Enlightenment, see Michèle Duchet, *Anthropologie et histoire au siècle des Lumières* (Paris: Albin Michel, 1995); Laurent Dubois, "An Enslaved Enlightenment: Rethinking the Intellectual History of the French Atlantic," *Social History* 31, no. 1 (2006): 1–14; Nicholas Hudson, "From 'Nation' to 'Race': The Origin of Racial Classification in Eighteenth-Century Thought," *Eighteenth-Century Studies* 29, no. 3 (1996): 247–264; Pierre H. Boulle, "La construction du concept de race dans la France d'Ancien Régime," *Outre-mers* 89, nos. 336–337 (2002): 155–175; and Andrew Curran, *The Anatomy of Blackness: Science and Slavery in an Age of Enlightenment* (Baltimore: Johns Hopkins University Press, 2011).

10. Jacques Savary des Brûlons, *Dictionnaire universel de commerce* (Universal Dictionary of Commerce) (Paris: chez la veuve Estienne, 1741), 1:39.

11. For detailed, comparative information on French ports, see Silvia Marzagalli and Hubert Bonin, eds., *Négoce, Ports et Océans, XVIe–XXe siècles* (Bordeaux: Presses Universitaires de Bordeaux, 2000). See also Silvia Marzagalli, "The French Atlantic World in the Seventeenth and Eighteenth Centuries," in *The Oxford Handbook of the Atlantic World, c. 1450–c. 1820,* ed. Nicholas Canny and Philip Morgan (Oxford: Oxford University Press, 2011), 235–251.

12. See Robin Blackburn, *The Making of New World Slavery: From the Baroque to the Modern, 1492–1800* (London: Verso, 2010), 432, and Robert Louis Stein, *The French Sugar Business in the Eighteenth Century* (Baton Rouge: Louisiana State University Press, 1988), 111. See also Savary des Brûlons, *Dictionnaire universel de commerce,* 1:39.

13. The French began colonizing Saint-Domingue in 1665; the country acquired the western third of Hispaniola officially from the Spanish in 1697.

14. The above numbers come from *Colons de Saint-Domingue sans propriété foncière* (Colonists of Saint-Domingue without Land Ownership, 1750–1800), a compilation of the six-volume *Royal Indemnity Report,* which enumerates what was lost during the Hai-

tian Revolution. The original citation is: F. de Barbé de Marbois: "État des finances de Saint-Domingue," Bd. 2 (1790).

15. Jacques de Cauna, "Les Aquitains à Saint-Domingue: Une approche quantitative globale du phénomène de la colonisation régionale aux Antilles françaises (fin XVIIIe siècle)," *Proceedings of the Meeting of the French Colonial Historical Society* 22 (1998): 31.

16. Saugera, *Bordeaux port négrier,* 219.

17. For more on eighteenth-century European visual depictions of Africans, see David Bindman and Henry Louis Gates, Jr., eds., *The Image of the Black in Western Art: From the "Age of Discovery" to the Age of Abolition, Part 3: The Eighteenth Century* (Cambridge, MA: Belknap Press of Harvard University Press, 2011).

18. Silvia Marzagalli, "Bordeaux, la traite négrière, l'esclavage: Le point sur la question," *Lumières: Revue du CIBEL* 1 (2004): 98. Note: in an online re-evaluation of this article, Marzagalli writes that some records were presumably lost, which means that there were perhaps 500 slave-trading expeditions leaving from Bordeaux and perhaps 150,000 captives taken to the Caribbean from the port.

19. The breakdown of known slave voyages sailing from Bordeaux is as follows: c. 330 to the major French colonies in the New World; 38 to Île-de-France (Mauritius) and Bourbon (Réunion); 16 to Cuba and Puerto Rico; 2 to Surinam; 1 to Saint-Thomas. See Saugera, *Bordeaux port négrier,* 218.

20. Robert Louis Stein, *The French Slave Trade in the Eighteenth Century: An Old Regime Business* (Madison: University of Wisconsin Press, 1979), 137.

21. Saugera, *Bordeaux port négrier,* 351–362.

22. See Marzagalli, "Bordeaux, la traite négrière, l'esclavage," 96. One of the reasons that Bordeaux's slave trading expeditions increased after 1784 was that the government modified the *Exclusif,* a trade monopoly that had helped assure Bordeaux's domination of the colonial trade. The specter of foreign competition and decreasing profitability of trading with the islands, in short, led Bordeaux's business people to look for other ways to make their fortunes, including the slave trade. After Napoleon reestablished slavery in the French Caribbean, Bordeaux achieved the dubious honor of overtaking Nantes as the largest French exporter of enslaved Africans in 1802 and 1803.

23. The term *négrillon* simply means young *nègre,* quite literally, and was used as a descriptor in the colonies. Yet this term functioned quite differently in Europe, where these children had the particular social function described in the essay.

24. Michel Roussier, "L'Éducation des enfants de Toussaint Louverture et l'Institution nationale des colonies," *Revue française d'histoire d'outre-mer* 64 no. 236 (1977): 308–349.

25. Érick Noël, "Être noir à Nantes," *Dix-huitième siècle* 35 (2003): 344.

26. Léo Elisabeth, "The French Antilles," in *Neither Slave nor Free: The Freedmen of African Descent in the Slave Societies of the New World* (Baltimore: Johns Hopkins University Press, 1972), 158–159. See also Érick Noël, ed., *Dictionnaire des gens de couleur dans la France moderne* (Geneva: Droz, 2011), xviiii. Noël estimates that perhaps 15,000 people of color passed through France during the Ancien Régime.

27. Jacques de Cauna, "Aux origines du peuplement des 'Isles de l'Amérique,'" in Marzagalli and Bonin, *Négoce, Ports et Océans,* 211. Among the families attached in some way to the parlement, Marzagalli cites Ségur, Cazaux, Dupaty, Dubourdieu, Saint-Arroman, and Saintout; Jean-Baptiste Mercier Dupaty and Alexandre de Ségur were both in the academy.

28. François-Armand de Saige was mayor of Bordeaux three times; he was also a supporter of the rights of *les gens de couleur* during the Revolution. Paul-André Nairac was admitted to the Bordeaux Academy once it was re-established as the Société des Sciences, Belles-Lettres et Arts after the Revolution. We are indebted to David Eltis for supplying us with a treasure trove of information on the companies, ship captains, and individuals involved in the slave trade in Bordeaux. This information will soon be available as part of a Mellon Foundation–funded project entitled PAST (People of the Atlantic Slave Trade) whose specific URL will be located on the website www.slavevoyages.org.

29. Paul Butel and J. P. Poussou, *La Vie quotidienne à Bordeaux au XVIIIe siècle* (Biarritz: Hachette, 1980), 211.

30. Guyenne is a term used to refer to the old French province and archdiocese of Bordeaux, which extended far beyond the city limits. Guyenne had a governor, a provincial intendant, a *jurade* (a small municipal council), a maritime and a commercial court, as well as financial courts. The Parlement of Bordeaux, which was at the summit of the hierarchy, was one of twelve sovereign courts in France. See William Doyle, *The Parlement of Bordeaux and the End of the Old Regime, 1771–1790* (New York: E. Benn, 1974), 5–9.

31. The Royal Academy of Sciences of Bordeaux, as the saying goes, was actually the *daughter* of the Parlement of Bordeaux. At any given time there were generally at least a dozen members of the academy who also held positions in Bordeaux's parlement. The most famous member of the Bordeaux Academy of Sciences, Charles-Louis de Secondat, Baron de La Brède, better known as Montesquieu (1689–1755), was typical in this respect. Like many of his colleagues, he had effectively inherited his father's position as *parlementaire* in 1716, and in 1734 he too made sure that his own son would occupy similar positions within the parlement as well as within the academy. François Cadilhon, "Jean-Baptiste de Secondat," in *Dictionnaire électronique Montesquieu,* http://dictionnaire -montesquieu.ens-lyon.fr/en/the-dictionary.

32. On the origins of France's "Free Soil" principle, see Sue Peabody, "An Alternative Genealogy of the Origins of French Free Soil: Medieval Toulouse," *Slavery and Abolition,* Special Issue: Free Soil in the Atlantic World, 32, no. 3 (2011): 341–362.

33. Sue Peabody, *There Are No Slaves in France* (New York: Oxford University Press, 1996), 12.

34. The title of this document is *Concernant les nègres esclaves des colonies.* This edict allowed colonists and officers serving in the colonies to take their enslaved Africans with them to France.

35. *Déclaration du Roy, concernant les nègres esclaves des colonies* (Declaration of the King, Concerning the Enslaved Negroes of the Colonies) (Bordeaux: chez Jean-Baptiste Lacorne, 1739), 1.

36. "Compagnie des Indes" was a catchall phrase referring to a series of monopolies. See Patrick Villiers and Jean-Pierre Duteil, "Les Compagnies des Indes au XVIIIe siècle," in *L'Europe, la mer et les colonies (XVIIe–XVIIIe siècle)*, ed. Patrick Villiers and Jean-Pierre Duteil (Vanves: Hachette, 1997), 188–205.

37. Jean-Claude Nardin, "Encore des chiffres, la traite négrière pendant la première moitié du XVIIIe siècle," *Revue française d'outre-mer* 209 (1979): 425. In the vast majority of cases, the Company granted permission to individual shipowners rather than chartering its own ships.

38. Jean-François Melon, *Essai politique sur le commerce* (Amsterdam: chez François Changuion), 61. The English title in the text comes from the translation by David Bindon; it was published in Dublin in 1738.

39. See Catherine Volpilhac-Auger, "La Dissertation sur la différence des génies: Essai de reconstitution," *Revue Montesquieu* 4 (2000): 216–237.

40. Montesquieu attempted to go beyond a purely mechanical understanding of this phenomenon in an abandoned project, *Essai sur les causes qui peuvent affecter les esprits et les caractères* (Essay on the Causes that Can Affect the Spirit and Character), which he fleshed out between 1735 and 1737.

41. Montesquieu, *De l'esprit des lois* (Paris: Garnier frères, 1973), 1:248.

42. Montesquieu, *De l'esprit des lois*, 1:248.

43. Montesquieu, *Pensées et fragments inédits de Montesquieu* (Bordeaux: G. Gounouilhou, 1889), 167. My emphasis.

44. Montesquieu, *De l'esprit des lois*, 1:255.

45. Curran, *The Anatomy of Blackness*, 176–215.

46. *Programme de l'Académie Royale des Belles-Lettres, Sciences et Arts de Bordeaux, du 13 janvier 1772* (Program of the Bordeaux Royal Academy of Belles-Lettres, Sciences, and Arts of 13 January, 1772) (Bordeaux: chez Michel Racle, 1772), 4.

47. André-Daniel Laffon de Ladébat, *Discours sur la nécessité et les moyens de détruire l'esclavage dans les colonies* (Discourse on the Necessity and the Means of Ending Slavery in the Colonies) (Bordeaux: Michel Racle, 1788), 4–5.

48. In February 1794, the French government in Paris had also endorsed the emancipation of all its enslaved populations.

49. Bordeaux merchants nonetheless shipped another 9,000 captives to the New World during and after the Revolution, most of them before 1826. The final Bordeaux ship to carry slaves to the Caribbean left West Africa for Martinique in 1837. See Saugera, *Bordeaux port négrier*, 351–362.

50. Butel and Poussou, *La Vie quotidienne à Bordeaux au XVIIIe siècle*, 322.

51. "'Out of Africa' Hypothesis," *Encyclopedia of Race and Racism*, https://www.encyclopedia.com/social-sciences/encyclopedias-almanacs-transcripts-and-maps/out-africa-hypothesis.

52. The relationship between providentialism and slavery was a topic of conversation in the New World as well. In 1765, John Adams evoked God, black skin, and human bondage in the same breath, arguing that Providence essentially guaranteed Whites from

slavery by dint of their light pigmentation and "superior" morphology: "Providence never designed us for negroes, I know, for if it had, it wou'd have given us black hides, and thick lips, and flat noses, and short wooly hair, which it hadn't done, and therefore never intended us for slaves." John Adams, *Boston Gazette,* October 14, 1765, quoted in Vincent Carretta, *Phillis Wheatley: Biography of a Genius in Bondage* (Athens: University of Georgia Press, 2011), 70–71. Several years later, the American patriot and physician Benjamin Rush found this conflation of the Black body and slavery to be foolish: "Nor let it be said," he wrote, "that their black color (as it is commonly called), either subjects them to, or qualifies them for slavery. The vulgar notion of their being descended from Cain, who was supposed to have been marked with this color, is too absurd to need a refutation. Without enquiring into the Cause of this blackness, I shall only add up on this subject, that so far from being a curse, it subjects the Negroes to no inconveniences . . ." Benjamin Rush, *An Address to the Inhabitants of the British Settlements in America, on the Slavery of Negroes in America* (Philadelphia: John Dunlap, 1773), 3.

53. Scripture's most powerful assertion that all humans are related is found in the New Testament, in Paul's *Letter to the Athenians.* Here Paul affirms quite categorically that all humans are part of an extended, although implicitly multicolored, family. As he put it, God had "made of one blood all nations of men for to dwell on the face of the earth"; Acts 17:26.

54. David M. Goldenberg's study of the complex history of the Myth of Ham, particularly as it relates to perceptions of Black Africans, demonstrates that the racialized version of this "curse" probably emerged from a variety of sources and related facts, first among them a Hebrew Bible in which darkness symbolized evil or sin. Demographics, he also argues, may have had an effect on the revising of this myth since "there was probably a greater proportion of Black Africans among the slaves," which presumably "created a ready association of Black and slave" (p. 196) Most importantly, Goldenberg points out that there was a properly etymological source for the conflation of Ham and blackness because the Hebrew words for "dark, brown, black" were mistakenly associated with the word "Ham" (p. 197). These phenomena surely contributed to a more "gradual introduction of blackness into the retelling of the biblical story, which was originally colorless." David M. Goldenberg, *The Curse of Ham: Race and Slavery in Early Judaism, Christianity, and Islam* (Princeton: Princeton University Press, 2005), 7. An early example where Ham is described as having black or dark skin can be found in the Babylonian Talmud (c. third century CE–fifth century CE). In this case, however, Ham was cursed for having sex while on board the ark (copulating in the dark) and was "smitten in the skin." Later rabbinic commentary in the Bereshit Rabbah (c. 500 CE) actually affirms that Ham emerged from the ark with black skin. See Werner Sollors, *Neither Black nor White Yet Both: Thematic Explorations of Interracial Literature* (Cambridge, MA: Harvard University Press, 1999), 86–87. Two of the earliest Christian sources that specifically mention the "blackening" of Ham and the resulting inevitability of servitude and slavery include the Alexandrian theologian Origen (c. 185–c. 254 CE) and Ephrem the Syrian, the latter who

specifically mentioned the slavery of Abyssinians in his *Cave of Treasures* (c. fourth century CE). Other interpretations of the Myth of Ham or Canaan (several of which show up in the essays in this book) went further than this Old Testament allegory, extrapolating from the Bible's genealogy that Ham's grandson, Cush, went on to populate "Ethiopia."

55. Joseph L. Graves, *The Emperor's New Clothes: Biological Theories of Race at the Millennium* (New Brunswick: Rutgers University Press, 2003), 25.

56. Richard H. Popkin, *Isaac La Peyrère (1596–1676): His Life, His Work, and Influence* (Leiden: E. J. Brill, 1987), 35.

57. Popkin, *Isaac La Peyrère*, 74.

58. "Nouvelle division de la terre," *Journal des Savants* (Paris: Académie des inscriptions et belles-lettres), April 1684. This was the same periodical in which the Bordeaux Academy would later announce its contest.

59. Siep Stuurman, "François Bernier and the Invention of Racial Classification," *History Workshop Journal* 50 (2000): 2. Technically, Bernier was a monogenist, but this did not really come out in his breakdown of humankind.

60. Voltaire, *Traité de Métaphysique* (Metaphysical Treatise, 1734), ed. Helen Temple Patterson (Manchester: Manchester University Press, 1937), 5.

61. See Edward B. Rugemer, "The Development of Mastery and Race in the Comprehensive Slave Codes of the Greater Caribbean during the Seventeenth Century," *William and Mary Quarterly* 70, no. 3 (2013): 429–458.

62. The unnamed ancestor of the Bordeaux essayist was presumably taken back to Germany in the aftermath of the conquest of Tunisia in 1535 by Charles V, Holy Roman Emperor. His subsequent success and integration into European society, while not common, was not entirely extraordinary. Other famous people of color in this category include Juan Latino, the sixteenth-century Spanish scholar of classical Latin at the University of Granada; Abram Petrovich Gannibal (c. 1696–1781), who not only served at the court of the reformist czar Peter the Great, but was the great-grandfather of the renowned novelist and poet Alexander Pushkin; the philosopher Anton Wilhelm Amo (c. 1703–c. 1759), who held important teaching posts at the universities of Jena and Halle, in Germany; Jacobus Elisa Johannes Capitein (c. 1717–1747), who studied at the University of Leiden, and produced with no little irony a dissertation on the Christian defense of slavery; and Angelo Soliman, born Mmadi Make (c. 1721–1796), who became an upper-class member of Enlightenment Viennese society. The problems that might arise when an African is taken to Europe and raised in elite European society was the subject of the best-selling short novel *Ourika* (1823), written by Claire de Duras.

63. Buffon was nonetheless very much aware that an enormous amount of information related to sub-Saharan or Black Africans seemingly gave credence to not only the possibility of a separate taxonomic category, but also a separate origin. He responded forcefully to these ideas by emphasizing the *interfecundity* of all humans, the idea that all *varieties* of humans can produce children with the members of other *varieties*. As he

put it, the spurious idea that the "White and the Negro do not have a common origin . . . is invalidated by the fact that all humans who can communicate with each other and reproduce with each other come from the same stock and are of the same." Georges-Louis Leclerc, comte de Buffon, *Histoire naturelle, générale et particulière* (Natural History, General and Particular) (Paris: Imprimerie royale, 1749–1788), 4:388–389. My translation.

64. Buffon, *Histoire naturelle*, 3:530.

65. Other writers had asserted that African blood was black as well. These included Dr. Thomas Towns in a letter sent to the Royal Society from Barbados in 1675. *Philosophical Transactions* 10, no. 117 (1675): 399–400.

66. This is an obvious, updated anatomical version of humoral theory, which had a long history that began with Hippocrates, but reached its apogee with Galen of Pergamum (130–200 CE), who explained differences between character (even national character) in terms of the composition and balance of the four primary humors: *sanguis* (blood), *flegma* (phlegm), *chole* (bile), and *melanchole* (black bile). Negroes, who were supposedly born with an abundance of black bile, were described as *melancholic*.

67. See Curran, *Anatomy of Blackness*, 125.

68. Before the 1770s, Carl Linnaeus was the only naturalist who was still putting forward racialized taxonomies. In the tenth and most famous edition of his *Systema Naturae* (1758), Linnaeus continued to divide the continents by color; this time, however, he added the curious addendum that the black race anointed itself with "grease" as one of the salient points. While later classifiers tended to distance themselves from his methods, Linnaeus's decades-long push toward animal and human taxonomies had certainly been prescient.

69. Thomas Jefferson, *Notes on the State of Virginia* (Boston: David Carlisle, 1801), 204.

70. See Justin E. H. Smith, *Nature, Human Nature, and Human Difference: Race in Early Modern Philosophy* (Princeton: Princeton University Press, 2015), 32–38, for a related discussion of this so-called *liberal racism*. Paradoxically, Blumenbach also drew on his comparative anatomy expertise to downplay anatomical differences among human varieties, defending the "Negro race" as equal to any other and advocating for an abolition of slavery.

71. Johann Friedrich Blumenbach, *The Anthropological Treatises of Johann Friedrich Blumenbach* (London: Longman, Green, et al., 1865), 106–107.

72. Blumenbach, *Anthropological Treatises*, 265–267.

73. The full title of this section is "Of National Characteristics, so far as They Depend upon the Distinct Feeling of the Beautiful and the Sublime." David Hume, *Political Essays*, ed. Knud Haakonssen, Cambridge Texts in the History of Political Thought, 78–92 (Cambridge: Cambridge University Press, 1984), 86. See John Immerwahr, "Hume's Revised Racism," *Journal of the History of Ideas* 53, no. 3 (1992): 481–486. Voltaire's 1756 tirade against Africans in his *Essai sur les mœurs et l'esprit des nations*, translated into English as *An Essay on Universal History: The Manners and Spirit of Nations*, resembles Hume's. In speaking of Africans, Voltaire writes, "their round eyes, their flat noses, their invariably fat

lips, the wool on their head, even the extent of their intelligence reflects prodigious divergences between them and other species of men." Voltaire, *Oeuvres Complètes,* ed. and illus.
Jean Michel Moreau et al. (Paris: Garnier frères, 1877–78), 11:6.

74. Immanuel Kant, *Observations on the Feeling of the Beautiful and Sublime* (Berkeley:
University of California Press, 2004), 110. For a larger contextualization of Kant's race
thinking, particularly as it relates to theories of skin, see Nina G. Jablonski, "Skin Color
and Race," *American Journal of Physical Anthropology* 175 (2021): 437–447, and *In Living
Color: The Biological and Social Meaning of Skin Color* (Berkeley: University of California
Press, 2012). See also Robert Bernasconi's seminal article "Who Invented the Concept of
Race: Kant's Role in the Enlightenment Construction of Race," in *Race,* ed. Robert Bernasconi (Malden, MA: Blackwell, 2001), 11–36.

75. Kant, *Observations on the Feeling of the Beautiful and Sublime,* 113. Kant's reference
to Labat was taken from Jean-Baptiste Labat, *Nouveau Voyage aux Îsles de l'Amérique*
(Paris: chez Pierre-François Giffart, 1722), 4:161–162.

76. Immanuel Kant, "Of the Different Human Races," 1777. Although Kant's essay was
published in 1777, he composed it in 1775. For a discussion of Kant and the construction
of *whiteness,* see Nell Irvin Painter, *The History of White People* (New York: W. W. Nor-
ton, 2010), 48–49. The notion of "unchanging and unchangeable" comes from Emmanuel
Chukwudi Eze, "The Color of Reason: The Idea of 'Race' in Kant's Anthropology," *Buck-
nell Review 38* (1995): 219.

77. Immanuel Kant, *Kant and the Concept of Race: Late Eighteenth-Century Writings,*
ed. Jon M. Mikkelsen (Albany: State University of New York Press, 2013), 44.

78. See Kant, *Kant and the Concept of Race,* 60: "*Negroes* and *Whites* are certainly not
different kinds of human beings, [but] they do constitute two different races. [This is]
because each of them perpetuates itself in all regions [of the Earth] and both, [when they
interbreed with each other], necessarily produce half-breed children, or *hybrids.*" Kant
was far from the last thinker to assert that the product of miscegenation was the exception that proved the rule. Legally speaking, the stiff penalties for miscegenation in the
United States, which forbade marriage between Blacks and Whites, only further solidi-
fied these categories in the minds of many people.

79. This contradiction had certainly been present in Buffon's and Blumenbach's
thought. Neither had really figured out how to distinguish between the categories of *race*
and *variety* since degeneration, by their own accounts, produced an uninterrupted con-
tinuum of colors from an original root stock.

80. Voltaire, *Candide, ou, l'optimisme,* ed. André Morize (Paris: Librairie E. Droz, 1931),
146.

## 1. Blackness through the Power of God

1. The word comes from "Nigritia," which the period defines vaguely in texts and letters as the "country of the Negroes." According to Diderot's *Encyclopédie,* "Nigritia is

confined in the north by the Barbary deserts, in the east by Nubia and Abyssinia, in the south by Guinea, in the west by the Atlantic Ocean. This country contains several small kingdoms, as much to the north of Niger as to the center, and from both sides of this grand river." ENC, vol. 12, 140.

2. The Latin manuscript of this essay is very difficult to read; the meaning of many words and expressions has been inferred from the context. Here the author's assertion is unusual given that the Bordeaux Academy did not establish a page limit and that this essay is remarkably short relative to others from the competition.

3. Genesis 11:7–8. All biblical quotations are from the King James Version.

4. Catholic orthodoxy upheld the idea of a miraculous occurrence and disagreed with Enlightenment philosophers who doubted or even denied the authenticity of the Genesis episode. See, for example, Paul Sadrin, *Nicolas-Antoine Boulanger, 1722–1759, ou Avant nous le déluge* (Oxford: The Voltaire Foundation, 1986).

5. To our knowledge, the author is alone in claiming an association between language and skin tone as produced by this miraculous event.

6. In the event that one physical cause (generated by God) may explain blackness, the author contends that his hypothesis remains valid; the key being that God, according to His goodwill, has made it so.

7. The author here devises an experimental method informed by both the natural sciences and a colonial ideology of African deportation. It does not occur to him to propose a reverse experiment, wherein Europeans are forcibly taken to Africa so that Africans may study changes in their skin color. This suggestion is characteristic of the period in that it shows an increasing interest in concrete experimentation, with the African as a test subject.

8. The author here recalls Michel de Montaigne, who in the first book of his *Essais* (1580) explains through a humanist metaphor of knowledge that students must develop themselves via "knocking off [their] corners by rubbing [their] brains against other people's." Montaigne, *The Complete Essays,* trans. M. A. Screech (London: Penguin Books Ltd, 2003), 172.

## 2. Blackness through the Soul of the Father

1. The geographical boundaries of Ethiopia in this period are ill-defined and tend to divide Ethiopia into two parts, upper and lower Ethiopia. It is worth noting that in the eighteenth century, scholars still sometimes followed the Greeks, who labeled Ethiopians those people in possession of "black or dark skin." Article "Éthiopie," ENC (1756), vol. 6, 54.

2. The era's geographers describe Guinea as a "vast African country," encompassing "numerous kingdoms both big and small," situated "between Nigritia to the north, Abyssinia to the west, and Caffraria in the south." It was also divided between "lower Guinea, which is the same state as the Congo" and "upper Guinea," which was "demarcated to

the south by the Ocean," which "comprises diverse countries." Article, "Guinée (géographie)," ENC (1757), vol. 7, 1009.

3. The manuscript mentions *ingeniique crassioris*, literally "thick humor."

4. African and American cannibalism fascinated Europe, starting in the Renaissance era. To the extent that it existed, its frequency or occurrence was generally exaggerated in the minds of Europeans in travel narratives, scientific treatises, and works of literature.

5. Here I choose to translate *in commercio* as "enslaved." *Commercium*, in addition to its first meaning of "trade, exchange," also means, secondarily, "sexual relationship." Because the words *conjugali, conjugis*, and *conjugio* (conjugal, spouses, marriage) appear three times in the same sentence, it is more likely that *commercio* is here used literally as "traded" Ethiopians, hence slaves, since Ethiopians living in their own land would normally marry from within their own people.

6. The Dominican missionary, explorer, botanist, ethnographer, soldier, engineer, and slave owner Jean-Baptiste Labat (1663–1738) never set foot in Africa. His works *Nouveau Voyage aux îles de l'Amérique* (New Voyage to the Islands of America, 1722) *Voyage du Chevalier Des Marchais en Guinée* (Voyage of the Chevalier des Marchais in Guinea, 1730), *Nouvelle relation de l'Afrique occidentale* (New Account of Western Africa, 1728), and *Relation historique de l'Éthiopie occidentale* (Historical Account of Western Ethiopia, 1732) were of great interest both to general audiences and to planters eager to obtain firsthand technical information. In the Antilles, where he held slaves, he remains a controversial figure. See Andrew Curran, *The Anatomy of Blackness: Science and Slavery in an Age of Enlightenment* (Baltimore: Johns Hopkins University Press, 2011), 58–67.

7. This is the literal Latin translation. It may be, however, that the author meant to say the infant's body, once out of the womb, is capable of further developing blackness as a result of the harsh environment.

8. The *Dictionnaire universel françois et latin (Dictionnaire de Trévoux)* defines the epidermis, or "*Cuticula summa cutis*," as the "very fine membrane" situated "atop the skin, and to which it is strongly attached. It is also called the *cuticle*, the *first skin*, or the *top-skin*." "Épiderme," TRV, vol. 3, 277. Such terms as *epidermis* and *cutis* had not yet become unequivocal in their meaning. The article "Cuticule," for example, gives the term as a synonym of epidermis. TRV, vol. 2, 1090.

9. The Italian physician and naturalist Marcello Malpighi (1628–1694) is the founder of microscopic anatomy. The Malpighian layer distinguished among various cellular layers in the epidermis. The *corpus reticularis* to which the author refers is a separate membrane which would be pale in white skin and dark in black skin.

10. The *Dictionnaire de Trévoux* describes smallpox as a "contagious disease," covering "the body with scabs, or pustules, which thicken the skin" and "leave scars or cavities." "Vérole," TRV, vol. 6, 627. The disease plagued all strata of society, and notably affected slave ships and plantations; this became the subject of much European scientific research.

11. During the eighteenth century, there was great interest in fibers, threads, or filaments as elements of internal human anatomy. These were discussed and debated by such diverse figures as the philosopher Nicolas Malebranche (1638–1715) and the doctors Herman Boerhaave (1668–1723) and Albrecht von Haller (1708–1777). See Diderot, article "Fibre," ENC (1756), vol. 6, 662–675.

12. In his *Book of Prognostics* Hippocrates, the founder of medicine, advises first the observation of the face to diagnose an illness. The further from healthy the face appears to be, the more severe the illness.

13. Hippocratic medicine distinguishes four humors or liquid substances of the body, causing phlegmatic, sanguine, bilious, and melancholic temperaments. This categorization was a subject of debate in the eighteenth century.

14. Also called *uvea,* the choroid is "the second coat of the eye." Dotted with vessels, it is "pierced in the front to let light through," and its opening is called "the pupil"; see article "Choroïde," TRV, vol. 6, 488.

15. Although in ancient philosophy, starting with Aristotle, *anima* referred to the animating spirit or vital principle of all animate beings, in this essay the word is generally translated as "soul," as the author clearly writes from within a Catholic perspective in which the word has an added religious and moral connotation, being created by God in His own image and infused in the human body at the time of conception.

16. The author expounds on the fundamental Christian belief that the body was created to serve as the dwelling of the soul and the embryo is endowed with the soul in the very moment and act of conception. (According to Aristotle, on the other hand, the soul entered the embryo at quickening—about forty days from conception for males, ninety for female embryos).

17. This too is not terribly clear in the original argument. In addition to being partially innate in the father's soul, blackness is also transmitted by impression as the mother looks at the father. Or as the father looks at the mother's blackness.

18. Monstrosity, and its possible explanations, had a huge impact on what would become race theory. Indeed, François Bellet, one of the founders of the Bordeaux Academy of Sciences, wrote both a "Dissertation sur la couleur noire des Éthiopiens" (1709) and a memoir "Sur la génération des monstres" (1713). On the subject of the monster, see Patrick Tort, *L'ordre et les monstres. Le débat sur l'origine des déviations anatomiques au XVIIIe siècle* (Paris: Le Sycomore, 1980), and Andrew S. Curran and Patrick Graille, "Faces of Eighteenth-Century Monstrosity," *Eighteenth-Century Life* 21, no. 2 (May 1997): 1–15.

19. The chyle (or juice) is the product of digested foods which "improves in the intestines by mixing bile and pancreatic juice" to then enter "into the milky veins," "mingle with the blood" "and all the other parts of the body," article "Chyle," TRV, vol. 2, 502.

20. The German doctor, naturalist, historian, and polygraph Christian Franz Paullini (1643–1712) provides numerous examples of how maternal imagination could affect the fetus in the *Observationes medico-physicae* (Medical-Physical Observations, 1706).

21. The Portuguese doctor and humanist Amatus Lusitanus (1511–1568) mentions numerous cases of intrauterine influences in his *Curationum medicinalium centuriae quinque* (Five Centuries of Medicinal Cures, 1557).

22. "One unquestioned instance is that of the famous boxer Nicaeus, born at Istanbul, whose mother was the offspring of adultery with an Ethiopian but had a complexion no different from that of other women, whereas Nicaeus himself reproduced his Ethiopian grandfather." Pliny the Elder, *Natural History, Volume II: Books 3–7*, trans. H. Rackham. Loeb Classical Library 352 (Cambridge, MA: Harvard University Press, 1942), 539–541.

23. The use of the word "aberration" occurs three times, which was unusual given that the term was generally reserved for astronomy, indicating the distance and declination of the fixed place of a star.

24. Classical dictionaries and theology distinguish "the human species" from "the animal species" (itself comprising diverse species) in order to uphold the theory of monogenism (the idea of a single species of human, diversified after the biblical flood). In his article "Humaine espèce (Histoire naturelle)," Diderot nevertheless develops several more nuanced considerations: "Man considered as an animal, offers three types of categorization; one is color; the second is size and form; the third is the nature of different peoples," ENC (1765), vol. 8, 344.

25. This is a curious moment in the manuscript since this very biblically oriented essayist seems to be flirting temporarily with polygenism.

26. The French pastor Samuel Bochart (1599–1667) was known throughout learned Europe. One of his major works is the *Geographia sacra* (Sacred Geography, 1646), which discusses the peoples of the Bible and the Phoenicians, and in which he employs a remarkable number of sources of various languages: Latin, Greek, Hebrew, Arabic, Aramaic, Syriac, Samaritan, Ethiopian, and so on. All of the references in the manuscript refer to this work.

27. The term *Moor* initially indicated a North African, Berber, or someone living in Barbary. It came from the Old French *More*, from Medieval Latin *Morus*, and from Latin *Maurus*. This term was sometimes used, as above, to indicate sub-Saharan Africans.

28. The famous Andalusian Berber diplomat and author Joannes Leo Africanus (al-Hasan ibn Muhammad al-Wazzan al-Fasi, c. 1494–c. 1554) is best known for his *Descrittione dell'Africa* (Description of Africa, 1550).

29. Horace, *Satires, Epistles, Art of Poetry*, trans. H. Rushton Fairclough. Loeb Classical Library 194 (Cambridge, MA: Harvard University Press, 1926), 475.

## 4. Blackness as a Moral Defect

1. The author is not to be confused with his homonym and more well-known countryman Ericus Molin, co-author with Johannes Palmroot of the *Dissertatio philologica* (Philological Dissertation, 1703).

2. Though we know very little about him, Molin represents an interesting case. In addition to the fact that he was sent to trial, imprisoned, and eventually exiled for his religious views, Molin was an intellectual who came from a low social class.

3. A Hanseatic port on the Baltic Sea, in today's Germany.

4. Regarding the term "founded," throughout this essay the author prefers to use *condire* (to found, establish) and *Conditor* (Founder), uncharacteristic choices (coming from a clergyman) for "create" and "Creator." As for the Gordian knot, this was also known as the Alexandrine (Alexander the Great's) knot.

5. The noun *discrimen* did not have today's judgmental meaning of "discrimination": it literally meant dividing line, hence difference, distinction.

6. *Indoles* is a key term in this essay, signifying innate nature or innate quality, characteristics or predisposition.

7. The Batavians were an ancient people of lower Germany (now known as the Netherlands). See "Bataves," TRV, vol. 1, 918. Diderot confirms: "One understands today that by Batavians one means the Dutch," article "Bataves," ENC (1751), vol. 2, 140.

8. The use of these mythological references to justify marital equality does not address the incest that characterizes these unions: Jupiter and Juno are the children of Saturn, Mars and Venus those of Jupiter, Pluto and Proserpina are the son and granddaughter of Saturn.

9. The story of Jacob's sheep serves as a precedent for the author's argument.

10. Inspired by Aristotle and theorized by Saint Augustine's *De libero arbitrio* (On Free Choice of the Will, 388–c. 395), the notion of free (voluntary) will tends among Christians to exonerate God from all moral evil and to hold man accountable, particularly with regard to his sins. For Spinoza and many philosophers of the Enlightenment, free will is a complete illusion because man is conscious of his actions but not of the reasons which cause him to act.

11. The reasoning in this paragraph is anything but clear in the original.

12. On this subject, read Patrick Graille, "Portrait scientifique et littéraire de l'hybride au siècle des Lumières," *Eighteenth-Century Life* 21, no. 2 (May 1997): 70–88.

13. This is the author's central premise, that physical ailments or conditions (including blackness) originate from a defect in the vital force, i.e., from sin.

## 5. Blackness as a Result of the Torrid Zone

1. *Natural* in this context is a synonym of indigenous.

2. The French term was *camard,* which means "someone with a flat nose set around the root." See "Camard," TRV, vol. 2, 65.

3. The article "Hale" from the *Dictionnaire de Trévoux* defines this word as the "hot and dry quality in the still air that blackens and spoils the skin," TRV, vol. 3, 1558.

4. A key word of the Bordeaux Academy competition, *degeneration* was a major scientific and naturalist idea of the period. In the proper sense, the term means "to reduce in value or merit"; in the figurative sense, it recalls "all which turns or changes from bad to worse." "Dégénérer," TRV, vol. 2, 1216. Unlike many authors of the second half of the

century, notably Georges-Louis Leclerc, Comte de Buffon and Jacques-Christophe Valmont de Bomare, the author does not here claim that Africans are the result of climatic degeneracy from a white prototype.

5. This hypothesis recalls the ideal of whiteness among nobility, wherein pallor, sometimes artificially produced with talc, visually and socially contrasts with the sun-darkened skin of the subjugated laboring classes.

6. Aristotle claims that "Nature does nothing which lacks purpose." Aristotle, *Generation of Animals*, trans. A. L. Peck, Loeb Classical Library 366 (Cambridge, MA: Harvard University Press, 1942), 207 [Book 2, 741b]. Christian theologians often adopted this idea to their worldview. The French priest, theologian, philosopher, and mathematician Antoine Arnaud (1612–1694), one of the principal Jansenist thinkers of the era, writes for example: "God does nothing useless. He does what he pleases: and as he has no need of anything, it is not uselessness that makes him act. One does not know, furthermore, what is useful or useless." *Œuvres de Messire Antoine Arnaud, Docteur de la maison et société de Sorbonne* (Works of Mister Antoine Arnaud, Doctor of the House and Society of the Sorbonne) (Paris and Lausanne: Sigismond d'Arnay et Compagnie, 1780), 38:652.

7. The author here affirms his monogenism.

8. The dissection of the human body became commonplace during the Renaissance. By the eighteenth century, the practice was encouraged by doctors, naturalists, and philosophers, in the name of scientific progress as well as curiosity. Some *savants* began dissecting the black body in order to solve the "mystery" of its coloring. In the *Histoire de l'Académie royale des sciences de Paris* (History of the Paris Royal Academy of Sciences, 1702), the French anatomist Alexis Littré presents his theories on the dissection of the sexual organ of a black man. In Essay 16, Pierre Barrère, a doctor and native of Perpignan, offers in-depth investigations of the dissections of slaves in Cayenne, where he lived for three years. Several years later, the German Johann Friedrich Meckel would present his work on the subject in his *Mémoires de l'Académie royale des sciences et des belles-lettres de Berlin* (Memoirs from the Berlin Royal Academy of Sciences and Belles-Lettres, 1755).

9. This phrase is taken (more or less) from the English astronomer and engineer Edmund Halley (1656–1742), in praise of the English physician, mathematician, philosopher, alchemist, astronomer, and theologian Isaac Newton (1643–1727). In a Latin poem introducing Newton's *Philosophiae naturalis principia mathematica* (Mathematical Principles of Natural Philosophy, 1687), Halley extols the idea that the gods now invite us to discover the hidden laws of the world via Newton. On this subject, see R. Lavalle, "Newton, nuevo Prometeo," *Byzantion Nea Hellás* 31 (2012): 259–268.

10. *Sapiens naturae effectibus suas opiniones non opinionibus suis.*

## 6. Blackness as a Result of Divine Providence

1. On the subject of Armenia, Diderot's brief article "Arménie" explains that "earthly paradise was situated there," ENC (1751), vol. 1, 695.

2. This is a theory that is unique to the author and is not found in any major texts of the time to our knowledge.

3. We have not found the source for this vague reference.

4. In addition to reflecting the political rivalry between France and Portugal at this time (the latter had previously been the premier European colonial power), the author's words describe a historical reality. From the sixteenth century on, the Portuguese presence in Africa yielded mixed-race societies through marriage or affairs with local women. On this subject, read Luís Filipe Thomaz, *L'Expansion portugaise dans le monde, XIVe–XVIIIe siècles: Les multiples facettes d'un prisme*, trans. Xavier de Castro and Émile Viteau (Paris: Éditions Chandeigne, 2018). The author fails to acknowledge that in the seventeenth and eighteenth centuries, the colonial authorities of the plantations in the French Caribbean (Saint-Domingue, Guadeloupe, and Martinique) did not prohibit the intermarriage of Blacks and Whites. On the subject of mixed-race offspring in the French Caribbean, see Chantal Maignan-Claverie, *Le Métissage dans la littérature des Antilles françaises, le complexe d'Ariel* (Paris: Karthala Éditions, 2005). See also Doris Garraway, *The Libertine Colony: Creolization in the Early French Caribbean* (Durham: Duke University Press, 2005). On the history and legacy of Africans in Latin America, see Henry Louis Gates, Jr., *Black in Latin America* (New York: New York University Press, 2011).

5. Based on Jean-François Regnard's *Voyage en Laponie* (Voyage in Lapland, 1681), the article "Renne" from the *Encyclopédie* confirms that the Lapons "nourished themselves with the flesh of these animals, which are fatty and very succulent, and that their milk is their "common drink," ENC (1765), vol. 14, 109.

6. The *Encyclopédie* defines Batavia rather tersely as an "Asian city on the island of Java, in the kingdom of Bantan," which was occupied by the Dutch. See "Batavia," ENC (1752), vol. 2, 140. The same book described Bengal as an "Asian kingdom of the Indies, on the gulf of the same name" which is "crossed by the Ganges." According to the author, Diderot, Bengal had two defining characteristics: the libertinism "of the Gentiles and the Muslims" and great wealth. See "Bengale," ENC (1752), vol. 2, 204.

7. Biledulgerid is a former country in North Africa, south of Mount Atlas, bounded on the north by Tunis, on the west by Algiers and the Sahara, and on the east by Tripoli. Absent from French dictionaries, this term was used by the Dutch.

8. The duc de La Force is Jacques Nompar III de Caumont (1714–1755), marquis and later duke of La Force (1730), peer of France.

## 7. Blackness as a Result of Heat and Humidity

1. The idea that an anthropomorphic nature would "amuse itself" by producing an "infinite variety" of flora and fauna was a commonplace notion during the eighteenth century. See, for example, Louis de Jaucourt's article "Jeu de la nature [Games of nature]," ENC (1765), vol. 8, 532–535. Previously reserved for botany, the word "variety" came increasingly to be applied to humans in the eighteenth century. Georges-Louis Leclerc, comte de Buffon, wrote about the "Varieties among the human species" in his *Histoire naturelle* [Natural History] (1749–1789).

2. The polysemic term "quality" is here a synonym of "attribute" or "equivalence"; that is, cold corresponds to white and heat to red. Whiteness appears in this text, as for many others, as the "original quality."

3. "Corruption" in this context designates "the state by which something ceases to be what it was." Corruption is the exact opposite of "generation" and suggests degeneration. See Jean le Rond d'Alembert, article "Corruption (philosophie)," ENC (1754), vol. 4, 278.

4. The comparison of African skin with coal pores is made all the more curious by its presentation as a proven scientific experiment.

5. Along with the color of the skin and the texture of the hair, the lips and nose are the key organs of the anatomical, naturalistic, aesthetic, ideological, and therefore political distinctions of the time.

6. Temperament, in this era, "means more particularly the natural constitution of the human body, or the state of the humors in each subject." The blood is thus not "a simple liqueur" but a "concoction of several other liquids," of "four simple and primitive qualities," which are mixed from secondary humors, called "bile, phlegm, melancholy and blood proper." Article "Tempérament. Médecine," ENC (1765), vol. 16, 56.

7. Like the rest of this essay, the conclusion remains unclear, especially given its references to teeth.

## 8. Blackness as a Reversible Accident

1. "The blood vessels," writes Louis de Jaucourt in the *Encyclopédie*, "are comprised of arteries and veins. One calls arteries the vessels which receive blood from the heart, to distribute throughout the parts of the body," and "veins the vessels which draw from all the parts to the heart a portion of the blood which had been distributed to those parts by the arteries." "Vaisseau sanguin (physiologie)," ENC (1765), vol. 16, 800.

2. The author of Essay 8 annotated his text, hereafter marked as author's notes. AN: Carl Linnaeus, *System. Natur.* [*Systema Naturae*, 1735].

3. AN: Or any kind of skin veneer, as illustrated in Winslow [anatomist Jacques Winslow (1669–1760)].

4. AN: Frederik Ruysch, *Advers. Anat.* [*Adversarium anatomico-medico-chirurgicorum*, 1717], decad. Vol. 3, 26.

5. AN: Lorenz Heister [Heisterus], *Comp. Anat.* [*Compendium Anatomicum*, first edition 1721], edit. 3, 197, not. a.

6. AN: See [Herman] Boerhaave, *Elem. Chem.* [*Elementa Chemiae*, 1732], Part. 2. proc. 116, 117, 118 and especially 119, num. 3, 4, 5. See also Johann-Friedrich Schreiber, *Elem. Med. phys. mathem.* [*Elementorum medicinae physico-mathematicorum*, 1731], tom. I. physiol. L. 1, cap. 2 experim. 20, 227, 229.

7. The author here again cites Boerhaave, *Elementa Chemiae*.

8. AN: *Epist.* 128 A.D. perill. [The source has not been identified.] See also Johann-Friedrich Schreiber, *Elem.*, vol. 1, *Physiol.*, L. 1, chap. 2, and separately, para. 220, and L. 2, chap. 2.

9. AN: Linnaeus, *Critic. Botan.* [*Critica Botanica*, 1737], 266.

10. Charles V (1500–1558) was king of Spain from 1516 and Holy Roman Emperor from 1519 to 1556. By using the word "Mauritanico," the author seems to indicate the "Moors," perhaps Muslim slaves captured by the army of Charles V during the conquest of Tunis in 1535.

11. The author's monogenism rests on a triple argument: biblical, climatic, and anatomical.

12. Sequelae are abnormal conditions resulting from a previous disease.

## 9. Blackness as a Result of Hot Air and Darkened Blood

1. Doubtless the best-known of the novels introducing a wider public to the ideas of Spinoza, the anonymously published *Voyages et Aventures de Jacques Massé* (Voyages and Adventures of Jacques Massé, 1714) tells the tale of a Catholic surgeon who embarks on a ship in search of adventure. Jacques then begins a journey that will bring him from Catholicism to deism, and then atheism. This book, which claimed that human races have separate origins (!), was written by the Huguenot philosopher Simon Tyssot de Patot (1655–1738), who settled in the Netherlands after being banned from his city and community in Normandy.

2. According to the author, the variety of climates would produce a diversity of skin color but also a range of "quality of minds"; even if the author does not prioritize this range here, he suggests that the minds of Blacks are of lower "quality."

3. This mechanistic analogy aligns with Cartesian physics, wherein comparisons of the human body to hydraulic machines are frequent.

4. This is a Hippocratic notion.

5. The Latin name of the balsam plant used to make this balm is *Commiphora gileadensis*. Diderot describes this balm "of such great value that it is part of the heritage of the great lord," article "Baume de Giléad," ENC (1752), vol. 2, 163–164.

6. There were two opposing scientific schools on this subject in the eighteenth century: the *animalculists*, who believed that the sperm contains preformed beings (*homunculus*) and that the ovum is merely a chamber for development; and the *ovists*, who believed that the sperm only serves to activate the ovum, the latter being the operative element.

7. Whether the African nose was innate or created through intervention was a topic of debate at the time. One theory was that African women who carried their young children on their backs flattened their noses. Others maintained that Africans flattened their noses on purpose. The author of the *Encyclopédie* article hesitates between several theories, including the belief that African noses and lips were a natural feature. He did conclude, however, that since this flat shape was seen as the norm in Africa, "the first task of the mother after childbirth is to flatten the noses of their children, so they may not be deformed in their eyes. So strange are the ideas about beauty of the people of the earth." See "Nez (anatomie)," ENC (1765), vol. 11, 127.

8. Thus the supposed normalcy of the temperate climate and of the white body justify the inertia, and the inferiority of body, blood, and mind, of the African (which the author relates, a few lines after, to the equal-but-opposite condition of the Nordic people).

9. Despite the proto-raciological elements of this essay, the author chooses Acts 18:26 as the "key" to his identity as a contestant. This maxim, which the author repeats, was one of the primary foundations for monogenesis and human *sameness*.

## 10. Blackness as a Result of a Darkened Humor

1. The name in the title of the essay reads Matthew Hicks. At the end of the essay the name seems to read Hickis (genitive, rendered in Latin), and in the English address at the bottom it is spelled Hickes.

2. The belief in *effluvium,* which literally means "outlet, a flowing out or exhalation of vapor," was prevalent during the era. In the article "Émanations," the co-editor of the *Encyclopédie* compares these "flows or exhalations" to "a kind of sweat" emanating continually from all the "bodies which surround us." This theory was adapted from the work of the Irish physician and chemist Robert Boyle (1627–1691), whose *Essays of the Strange Subtilty Great Efficacy Determinate Nature of Effluviums* (1673) affirmed that the respective volume and form of these emanations can produce great movement in the human machine, and thereby induce great changes in the body. See ENC (1755), vol. 5, 545.

3. The *Encyclopédie* briefly mentions this "large country situated in the southern part of Africa, bordered to the north by Abyssinia and Nigritia; to the west by Guinea and the Congo; to the south by the Cape of Good Hope; to the east by the Ocean. The inhabitants of this country are Negroes and infidels. This land is little known by Europeans, who have not yet been able to enter it: however, the inhabitants are accused of being cannibals." "Cafrérie (Géographie)," ENC (1752), vol. 2, 29. The *Dictionnaire de Trévoux* offers a far more disparaging article: "The Kaffirs are the people of the world known to be the most rude and the least human. [. . .] They are naked, black, ill-made, filthy, brutal, savage almost as beasts. [. . .] Their language is nearly unintelligible, and more closely resembles the sounds of beasts than those of humans," article "Cafre," TRV, vol. 2, 32.

4. Bitumen is "a kind of thickened and creamy fat, of a highly flammable nature, like sulfur," article "Bitume." The article also specifies that "there are various soils and minerals of a bituminous and sulfuric nature." See article "Bitumeux," TRV, vol. 1, 1054.

5. Æthiops, so called because of its color, was a medicament made by grinding "equal parts of pure mercury and flowers of sulphur into a mortar, till the mercury disappears, and a very black powder is formed." "Æthiopis Mineralis," George Motherby, *A New Medical Dictionary; or, General Repository of Physic* (London: J. Johnson, 1785), 32.

6. This is a curious use of the theories of the paternal and maternal imagination, alongside heredity, to justify his climatic and mineralogical theory.

7. Uninterested in or unaware of actual geography and climatology, the author ignores the fact that numerous African countries are climatically divided into a dry season and a rainy season.

## 11. Blackness as a Result of Blood Flow

1. A slip of paper found within this document revealed its author. The paper reads "Doctor Physician Andreas Nyvert, alumnus of the University of Montpellier, made this attempt to elucidate the question on the 3rd day of April in the year 1742," well after the contest was over.

2. This psychosomatic vision of color draws heavily from Hippocrates.

3. The Dutch scholar Antonie van Leeuwenhoek (1632–1723) is known for his improvements to the microscope. One of the pioneers of cellular biology and microbiology, he discovered the existence of spermatozoa in 1677, thereby challenging scientists who favored the idea of "spontaneous generation."

4. Herman Boerhaave, *Institutiones rei medicae in usus annuae exercitationis domesticos digestae* (Medical Principles Divided into the Domestic Uses of Annual Training, 1708), 416. Numerous editions of this book, which was translated into French by Julien Offray de La Mettrie (*Institutions de Médecine* [Institutions of Medicine], 1738), were printed in Europe.

5. *History of the Paris Royal Academy of Sciences* (1702), 32.

6. On this subject, see Jacques Roger, *Les Sciences de la vie dans la pensée française au XVIIIe siècle. La génération des animaux, de Descartes à l'Encyclopédie* (Paris: Albin Michel, 1963 and 1993).

7. Pierre Louis Moreau of Maupertuis refuted the theory of preformation in 1745, noting that the child of a black person and a white person will have an intermediate color. He also studied the transmission of polydactyly over multiple generations, concluding that it is carried by both men and women.

8. Leeuwenhoek's discovery of spermatozoa popularized the theory according to which the embryo preexists within the sperm. In crossbreeding gray male rabbits with white female ones, he observed that the offspring were gray, suggesting that characteristics are passed down from the male, with the female serving only as the receptacle.

9. The author uses the word *glans*, which modern dictionaries define as the head of the penis.

10. Despite being an *animalculist*, the author nonetheless introduces the idea of a type of "double seed" to justify hereditary resemblances.

11. This author's use of the word *degeneration* implies how Africans change once they leave Africa.

12. With this vague, unique, and final reference to the Flood, the author implies that prior to this event the Earth did not have Torrid Zones, but rather only a moderate climate, yielding white skin.

## 12. Blackness as an Extension of Optical Theory

1. A merchant in the service of the Dutch East India Company, Willem Bosman (1672–after 1703) is known for his *Voyage de Guinée, contenant une description nouvelle*

*et très exacte de cette côte où l'on trouve et l'on trafique l'or, les dents d'éléphant, et les es-claves* (Voyage in Guinea, Containing a New and Very Accurate Description of this Coast Where One Finds and Transports Gold, Elephant Tusks, and Slaves, 1704, translated into French in 1705). In twenty letters, he recounts his experiences and observations from seven years on the Gold Coast, the Ivory Coast, and the Slave Coast.

2. The author is correct in his first assertion, the Devil being systematically associated with blackness from the Middle Ages onward. His second claim, however, is incorrect; historians have determined that the Devil, properly speaking, did not exist in African cultures during this period, and the color white, according to region and context, was sometimes associated with positive rites and spirits or sacred animals such as the whale or manatee.

3. Johannes-Ludovicus Hannemann (1640–1724) was a Dutch doctor. *Of the Appearance and Color of Ethiopians* (1677) was by Johann Nicolas Pechlin (1646–1706), a Swedish professor of medicine.

4. In this domain as in others, the influence of Antonie van Leeuwenhoek was ambivalent during the first part of the eighteenth century: sometimes cited approvingly, sometimes rejected.

5. The famous anatomist Marcello Malpighi identified the reticular membrane within the epidermis; a clear "sap" is found in this membrane in Whites and a dark one in Blacks. In the *Histoire de l'Académie royale des sciences de Paris* (History of the Paris Royal Academy of Sciences, 1702), the French anatomist Alexis Littré denied the existence of this dark sap by expounding his theories on the dissection of the sexual organ of a black man.

6. The article by the surgeon and doctor John Belchier (1706–1785) is "A further Account of the Bones of Animals being changed to a red colour by Aliment only," *Philosophical Transactions of the Royal Society of London* 442 (October 1736): 287–288.

7. See Charles François de Cisternay du Fay (1698–1739), "Observations physiques sur le mélange de quelques couleurs dans la teinture," in *Mémoires de l'Académie Royale des Sciences de Paris* (1737), 253–268. Du Fay was the first chemist to study the subject of dyeing and to propose a theory of the binding of dye to fabric.

8. The philosopher René Descartes (1596–1650), the philosopher, priest, and theologian Nicolas Malebranche (1638–1715), and the mathematician, philologist, and theologian Isaac Barrow (1630–1677) each proposed and published their own theories of light and visual perception during the seventeenth century.

9. Isaac Newton, a student of Barrow, concluded from his studies of light that "colors are not qualifications of light derived by reflection or reflection on natural bodies," but "original and connate properties," which in diverse rays are diverse. From 1672 to 1676, he shared his research at the Royal Society through his teachings at Cambridge (*Lectiones opticae*, 1670–1672), later synthesizing them in *Opticks: or, a Treatise of the Reflexions, Refractions, Inflexions and Colours of Light* (1704), in which he considered light to be composed of corpuscles or subtle particles, unlike the ordinary matter formed from larger corpuscles.

10. In *Les Météores,* Descartes establishes his law on refraction, where "the angle of incidence" equals "the indication of the center" and the "angle of refraction."

11. Possibly "Des éléments de la matière" (Elements of Matter), the seventh chapter of *Institutions de physique* (Institutions of Physics, 1740), an anonymously published essay by the marquise Émilie du Châtelet, French translator of Isaac Newton and a scientist and woman of letters in her own right. The essay was republished under the title *Institutions physiques* in 1742.

12. The Jesuit scholar, mathematician, physicist, and journalist Father Louis Bertrand Castel (1688–1757) published a book on the idea of synthesizing color and sound: *Clavecin pour les yeux* (Harpsichord for the Eyes, 1728). This proposed ocular harpsichord, which was never realized, would have been capable of affecting the eye through a succession of colors, just as the harpsichord affects the ear through a succession of sounds. In 1740, Father Castel's essay *L'Optique des couleurs* (The Optics of Colors) addressed the relationship of painting and music.

13. The doctor and anatomist Pierre Tarin (1725–1761) observes that black bile "resembles old blood, which corrodes, burns, destroys, dissolves, causes inflammations, gangrenes, necroses, sharp pains, and violent fermentations." Herman Boerhaave identifies "three types of black bile," the first being "the sweetest, coming from a violent movement of the blood;" the second of a "bigger degree of alteration;" and the third "a corrupt and burnt bile, which, if it becomes greenish or pale in color, is the worst of all." "Bile, dans l'économie animale," ENC (1752), vol. 2, 252.

14. "Why does the sun burn (*the skin*), whereas fire does not? Is it because the sun is finer, and so is more able to penetrate the flesh? But fire, even if it does burn, produces only on the top of the skin what are called blisters; but it does not penetrate within." Aristotle, *Problems, Volume II: Books 20–38,* ed. and trans. Robert Mayhew and David C. Mirhady, Loeb Classical Library 317 (Cambridge, MA: Harvard University Press, 2011), 429.

15. The author refers to upper-class women.

16. Cambaïa (also called Cambia or Cambodia) was an Indian city and kingdom situated beyond the Ganges River. The Dutch navigator Jan Huygen van Linschoten (1563–1611), trading in service of the Portuguese in the Indian Ocean, claimed the opposite: "None of their women surpass the Portuguese in whiteness, closely resembling the Europeans in form and stature." Jan Huygen van Linschoten, *Histoire de la navigation de Jean Hugues de Linscot Hollandois et de son voyage es* [sic] *Indes orientales* (History of Jean Hugues de Linscot's Navigation and his Voyage in the East Indies) (Amsterdam: l'Imprimerie de Henri Laurent, 1610), 103.

17. Abyssinia, populated according to Judeo-Christian tradition by the descendants of Chus, son of Cham, was curiously disregarded by intellectuals during the first part of the eighteenth century. This empire, known since Antiquity and often confused with Ethiopia, was understood only via myths of the Great Negus and Prester John, and through the memoirs of the Portuguese Jesuit missionary Jerónimo Lobo (1595–1678). These memoirs, from 1622 to 1640, were compiled in his *Itinerario* and translated into French under the title *Voyage historique d'Abissinie* (Historical Voyage of Abyssinia, 1728).

18. If the word *Abyssinia* possibly means *mixture* in Arabic, the etymology of the word nonetheless remains uncertain. According to the 1771 edition of the *Dictionnaire de Trévoux* (the term did not appear in earlier editions), the name of the country, also called *Æthiopia superior* or *interior,* came from the Latin *Abassia* or *Abyssinia* (country of Abyssins), related to the Arabic *al-habacha,* article "Abyssinie ou Abissine," TRV, vol. 1, 51.

19. On the subject of the Cape of Good Hope, Linschoten writes, "Although this location is 35 degrees from the line, and in the same climate there are cold mountains covered with snow, namely the mountains of the Moon, the inhabitants are also Black, such that it is necessary to attribute the cause of such blackness to some property of the country, rather than the heat of the sun." Linschoten, *Histoire de la navigation,* 269.

20. Popular understanding of Canada at this time came from the *Histoire et Description générale de la Nouvelle France* (General History of New France, 1722) by the Jesuit historian, professor, and traveler Pierre François-Xavier de Charlevoix (1682–1761), as well as the *Mœurs des sauvages américains comparées aux mœurs des premiers temps* (Mores of the Savage Americans, 1724), in which the Jesuit missionary, philosopher, and anthropologist Joseph-François Lafitau (1681–1746) appraises the customs of the Iroquois, seeking to prove the common origin of Amerindians and Europeans to uphold the theory of monogenism found in Genesis.

21. The consensus of the time was that "various savage nations of America, due to poor treatment that they experienced, and that they still fear," secluded themselves "in forests and mountains" in order to preserve "their freedom" there. Jaucourt, article "Sauvage (géographie moderne)," ENC (1765), vol. 14, 729. However, the authors differed in describing the complexion of inhabitants, as the article "Caraibe ou Cannibales" by Diderot reveals: "Island savages of America, who inhabit part of the Antilles islands. They are naked; their complexion is olive," ENC (1752), vol. 2, 669.

22. The first-century BCE Greek historian, geographer, and ethnographer Diodorus of Sicily was the author of a forty-volume *Bibliotheca Historica.* Following Herodotus and Strabo, he described the "Troglodytes" or Troglodyti (literally "cave-lovers").

23. In *Pseudodoxia Epidemica, or Enquiries into vulgar and common errors* (1646, translated into French in 1733), the English writer and doctor Thomas Browne (1605–1682) attacked the arguments of the period which claimed that Blacks were well suited to manual labor in the context of slavery due to the color of their skin. His essay drew much discussion at the time because the slave population of Barbados grew from 500 to 4,000 people between 1640 and 1645 with the establishment of the first major sugarcane plantations.

24. French merchant and pharmacist Pierre Pomet (1658–1699) wrote the *Histoire générale des drogues, traitant des plantes, des animaux et des minéraux* (General History of the Drugs Treating Plants, Animals, and Minerals, 1694). The book, considered the most complete and correct of the period, was translated and disseminated throughout Europe. On the quality of natural sulfur, Pomet writes: "The first and most beautiful is that of Quito, which is the color of gold," and the second "that of Nicaragua which is "a yellow-gray."

Pierre Pomet, *General History of the Drugs Treating Plants, Animals, and Minerals* (Paris: Jean-Baptiste Loyson & Augustin Pillon, 1694), chap. 9, 90.

25. The *Dictionnaire de Trévoux* confirms that the pulp of the areca, a "species of palm common in the East Indies" is "of a reddish color," article "Aréca," TRV, vol. 1, 554. The whitish juice of junipaba, a "tree from the Antilles islands, which is also called junipa or junipapa," is good for dyeing black: "as soon as it is rubbed on some part of the body, the stain cannot at first be rubbed away," "but it goes away on its own, in six or seven days," article "Génipa," TRV, vol. 3, 1248.

26. The Dominican historian and botanist Jean-Baptiste Du Tertre (1610–1687) is best known for his *Histoire générale des Antilles habitées par les Français* (General History of the Antilles Inhabited by the French, 1667–1671), which Jean-Baptiste Labat would incorporate into his chronicle of the Antilles in 1722. The author transforms the particular case described by Du Tertre of a Brazilian slave charged with finding deserter slaves threatening to "bring the whole island to fire and blood" into a generalization applying to all Blacks: his "sense of smell was so subtle that it could distinguish the remnant of a Black and of a Frenchman by smelling the ground upon which they had walked." Du Tertre, *Histoire générale des Antilles,* vol. 1, 501.

27. The author cites in the margin the *Nouvelle anatomie raisonnée, ou les Usages de la structure du corps de l'homme et des autres animaux, suivant les lois des mécaniques* (New Reasoned Anatomy, or the Uses and the Structure of the Body of Man and Other Animals Following the Laws of Motion, 1699) by the French doctor and anatomist Daniel Tauvry (1669–1701).

28. The naturalist and doctor Louis Jean-Marie Daubenton (1716–1799) describes this "material used for scarlet and purple dyeing" from America: the most sought-after color is "the gray dye of slate color, mixed with reddish and white. Cochineal is preserved as long as desired, without changing quality. For a long time it was not certain whether this material pertained to the plant kingdom or the animal kingdom: it was formerly believed to be a seed of what are called berries; but there is no doubt now that the cochineal is a dried insect," article "Cochenille, histoire naturelle," ENC (1753), vol. 3, 559.

29. In the remainder of the paragraph, the author defines the common Latin words that are used to describe chyle. This is part of his argument that people who suffer from melancholy are clogged with imbalanced humors or substances.

30. *Institutiones medicae* (Principles of Medicine, 1655), by Lazare Rivière (1589–1655), professor at the Faculty of Montpellier, adviser and doctor of King Louis XIII.

31. Browne explains this in his book *Pseudodoxia Epidemica.*

32. *De morbis internis libri duo, auctoris scholiis et observationibus illustrati* (Two Books Concerning Internal Diseases, 1571), by the doctor and humanist Jacques Houllier (1498–1562), famous leader of the "Parisian hippocratists."

33. On this subject, read Hélène Prigent, *Mélancolie. Les métamorphoses de la dépression* (Paris: Gallimard, 2005).

34. The author cites Diodorus of Sicily, translated by Terrasson, in the margin.

35. *Réflexions nouvelles sur les causes des maladies et de leurs symptômes* (New Reflections on the Causes of Diseases and their Symptoms, 1687), by the king's physician François de Saint-André (1649–1700).

36. The references to Hippocrates and to doctors of the previous century reveal the author's unfamiliarity with contemporary research, theories, and hypotheses on the subject.

37. The author cites the anatomist Littré, *Histoire de l'Académie royale des sciences de Paris* (1702), in the margin.

38. The author cites Jean Riolan the Younger (1577–1657), *Anthropographia et osteologia* (Anthropographia and Osteology, 1618), and Thomas Browne, *Pseudodoxia Epidemica: or, Enquiries into vulgar and common errors.*

39. Herodotus writes that the semen of the black people of India "is not white like other peoples', but black like their own skins; the same is to be found in the Ethiopians." Herodotus, *The Histories,* trans. Aubrey de Sélincourt (London: Penguin Books Ltd, 2003), 215 [Book 3, 101]. This assertion is refuted by Aristotle, partisan of the uniqueness of the human species: "Herodotus is incorrect when he says that the semen of Ethiopians is black." Aristotle, *Generation of Animals,* trans. A. L. Peck, Loeb Classical Library 366 (Cambridge, MA: Harvard University Press, 1942), 163 [Book 2, 736a].

40. The Italian astronomer, mathematician, and geographer Giovanni Antonio Magini (1555–1617) was a collaborator in the writing of the *Histoire universelle des Indes orientales et occidentales, divisée en deux livres, le premier par Camille Wytfliet, le second par Antonio Magini et autres historiens* (Universal History of the East Indies, 1605).

41. A long tradition traces the kings of Abyssinia to the marriage of Solomon and Makeda, Queen of Sheba.

42. Bosman describes this physical and behavioral transformation of dogs exported to Guinea: over generations, their ears become "long and stiff, like those of foxes, and more or less the same color; such that in three or four years, they have such a hideous appearance that they can scarcely be looked at. After they have multiplied three or four times, they entirely lose the ability to bark; thus the bark of a dog which is then brought to this country resembles a dreadful shriek." *Voyage de Guinée* (Voyage in Guinea) (Utrecht: Antoine Schouten, 1705), 240–241.

43. The doctor and ship surgeon Alexander Stuart (1673–1742) published various articles in the *Philosophical Transactions of the Royal Society of London.*

44. These prejudices anticipate the phrenology promoted at the beginning of the nineteenth century by the German doctor Franz Joseph Gall, which sought to determine characteristics of individuals via the shape and composition of the skull.

45. The author refers to *The Canon of Medicine* by the great Persian philosopher and doctor Ibn Sina, called Avicenna (980–1037).

46. The author refers to the *Physiologia barbae humanae, in tres sectiones divisa, hoc est de fine illius philosophico et medico* (Physiology of the Human Beard Divided in Three Sections, that is, Concerning its Philosophical and Medical Purpose, 1602) by the Italian doctor and philosopher Marco Antonio Olmo (1575–1622).

47. The Roman satirical poet Juvenal (alive from the end of the first century to the beginning of the second century) describes Messalina "with a yellow wig concealing her raven locks." Juvenal, "Satire 6: Roman Wives," in *Satires of Juvenal*, ed. William Barr (Cambridge: Oxford University Press, 1999), 40.

48. This is a common topos of scholarly and fictional literature of the period.

49. "Nigra Sum Sed Formosa." This phrase appears at the beginning of the biblical Song of Songs: "I am black, but comely, O ye daughters of Jerusalem, / as the tents of Kedar, as the curtains of Solomon / Look not upon me, because I am black, because the sun hath looked upon me." Song of Songs 1:5–6.

## 13. Blackness as a Result of an Original Sickness

1. "Conjunctivitis" is *lippis*, literally, bleary-eyed, in the original Latin.

2. *Trifolium Hermeticum, oder Hermetisches Kleeblat* (On the Hermetic Cloverleaf, 1629, 127), by Johann Baptist Großschedel (1577–1630s), a German alchemist and esoteric author.

3. The German mathematician, philosopher and scientist Ehrenfried Walther von Tschirnhaus (1651–1708), author of *Medicina mentis* (1687), and the French student of natural history, flora, and numismatics Pierre Le Lorrain, abbé de Vallemont (1649–1721). The author most likely refers to the abbé's *Curiosités de la nature et de l'art par la végétation, ou l'Agriculture et le jardinage dans leur perfection* (Curiosities of Nature and Art by Vegetation, 1705).

4. On this subject, see Patrick Graille, "Portrait scientifique et littéraire de l'hybride au siècle des Lumières," *Eighteenth-Century Life* 21, no. 2 (May 1997): 70–88.

5. Aristotle writes that "Resemblances of this sort recur after many generations, as the following instance shows. There was at Elis a woman who had intercourse with a blackamoor; her daughter was not a black, but that daughter's son was." Aristotle, *Generation of Animals*, trans. A. L. Peck, Loeb Classical Library 366 (Cambridge, MA: Harvard University Press, 1942), 53–55 [Book 1, 722a].

6. "And Miriam and Aaron spake against Moses because of the Ethiopian woman whom he had married: for he had married an Ethiopian woman." Numbers 12:1.

7. Lilith is a figure in Jewish mythology, first developed in the Babylonian Talmud. She is often depicted as a dangerous, sexually wanton night demon. In rabbinic literature, Lilith is sometimes referred to as the mother of Adam's demonic offspring following his separation from Eve, or as his first wife. Whereas Eve was created from Adam's rib (Genesis 2:22), some accounts hold that Lilith was the woman implied in Genesis 1:27 and was made from the same soil as Adam.

8. Theophrastus von Hohenheim (1493–1541), called Paracelsus, was a Swiss-German physician, alchemist, and astrologer. The hypothesis of two Adams was a precursor of polygenism.

9. Titus Flavius Josephus (37–c. 100 CE) was a Jewish historian born in Jerusalem who became a Roman citizen, and the author of *Antiquities of the Jews* (c. 93). Gaius Julius

Solinus, an early third-century Roman author, wrote *De mirabilibus mundi* (*Collectanea rerum memorabilium*) (The Wonders of the World: Collection of Curiosities) and *Polyhistor.*

10. The manuscript is not clear: could be read as *Odyssey* A., line 23; and Pliny 5.8.

11. In Greek, *Ethiopia* means "burnt face" (Αἰθιοπία / Aithiopía, from αἴθω / aíthô "to burn" and ὤψ / óps, "face"). The word refers to the legend of Phaeton, son of the sun god Helios and of Clymene, wife of Merops, king of Ethiopia. In his route across the sky in his father's chariot, Phaeton steered too close to the land, and the populations living where he neared were therefore burned; the myth thus explains the dark skin of certain peoples.

12. In Genesis, the wife of Lot becomes a pillar of salt after looking back while fleeing Sodom (Genesis 19:26). Nameless in the Bible, she is sometimes given the name "Ado" or "Edith" in Jewish traditions.

13. The word used is *spiritus*, however, in its literal, nonspiritual meaning. The author is evoking the mother's feelings, mood, spirits.

14. Georg Ernst Stahl (1659–1734) was a German chemist, physician, and philosopher. In his *Theoria medica vera* (True Medical Theory, 1707), he promoted an animistic medical system that anticipated medical vitalism, and a chemical theory that explained combustion by postulating the existence of a "flame-element" called phlogiston, a fluid present in combustible bodies.

15. Thus the feminine imagination punctually influences the body of the fetus without modifying the essence, the fixity of the human species.

16. Aristotle, on the unfertilized eggs of pigeons, writes that "all such are wind-eggs." Aristotle, *History of Animals, Volume II: Books 4–6*, trans. A. L. Peck, Loeb Classical Library 438 (Cambridge, MA: Harvard University Press, 1970, 233 [Book 6, 561a].

17. This is in line with the Christian belief that the soul, being immortal, is not created at the time of conception, but has existed [in the supernatural realm] from the origin of creation, and that God places it inside the egg at the moment of conception.

18. *Palingenesis* is the term used by Stoic philosophers to designate the reconstitution of the world after its destruction by fire, in an eternal return. In Greek the word means "birth anew," or "regeneration."

19. On the subject of African animals, Aristotle notes that "the origin of the proverb about Libya, to the effect that 'Libya is always bringing forth something new,' is said to be that there animals of different species unite, owing to the fact that as there is very little water they all meet together at the few places where springs are to be found, and so animals of different species unite." *Generation of Animals*, 245 [Book 2, 746b]. Hence the Latin words: *Quid novi sert Africa?* and *Semper Africa quid novi gignit.* Citing the cross-species coupling of animals, Pliny the Elder (23–79 CE) similarly notes: "Africa is always producing some novelty." Pliny the Elder, *Natural History, Volume III: Books 8–11*, trans. H. Rackham, Loeb Classical Library 353 (Cambridge, MA: Harvard University Press, 1963), 33 [Book 8, 17].

20. Franciscus Baco (1561–1626) de Verulamio. Verulamium was located within contemporary St. Albans, and Bacon was made Viscount St. Alban (sometimes written Albans), a title exclusive to him, near the end of his life. See "Experiment Solitary, touching the coloration of Blacks and Tawney Moores," in *Sylva Sylvarum, or A Natural History in Ten Centuries* [1626–1627] (London: W. Lee, 1631), Experimenta 399, 103–104.

21. Aulus Cornelius Celsus (c. 25 BCE–c. 50 CE), who wrote the famous *De Medicina*.

22. To define *smegmatic* see, for example, Louis de Jaucourt's article "Smegma (*médecine ancienne*)." Jaucourt informs us that its provenance is σμήχειν, "to clean by rubbing," and that it consists of a composition of "softeners, or detergent powders, such as bean flour, melon seeds, deer horn, antimony, dry bones, shells, sulfur, different types of salts," etc. These powders can be used "alone, or incorporated into honey, wine, oil, barley cream, and made into a composition of the consistency of a poultice, with which part or all of the body would be anointed." ENC (1765), vol. 15, 239.

23. Writings of the period rarely reference this "city and port on the Persian gulf," as Diderot describes it in "Benderick, géographie," ENC (1752), vol. 2, 201. *Dictionnaire de Trévoux* mentions its modern name of "Bender Gamron" and references "Mandeslo, *Voyage aux Indes*," TRV (1638), vol. 3, 1151.

24. Charles de Rochefort (1605–1683), a Netherlands-based French shepherd and writer who traveled to the Antilles, is the presumed author of the aforementioned work, which was translated into Dutch (1662), English (1666), and German (1668), and republished several times. The author of the manuscript refers to the "Junipa apples" whose "sap, dyed deeply violet, although yet crystal clear," "seemed black" upon the "second dyeing." [. . .] "The swine who eat it have entirely purple flesh and fat. [. . .] It is the same with the flesh of parrots, and other birds, who consume it." Rochefort, *Histoire naturelle et morale des îles Antilles de l'Amérique* (Natural and Moral History of the Antilles) (Rotterdam: Reinier Leers, 1681), chap. 6, 70–71.

25. Diderot's *Encyclopédie* describes this climbing plant as growing "in all of the West Indies, and above all on the coasts of the sea," clarifying that "the Indians chew their leaves at all hours" and "spit after the first chew a red liquid, which is colored by the areca nut," article "Betele, horticulture," ENC (1752), vol. 2, 261.

26. Rochefort describes this wax "of a color so black that no 'trick' is capable of whitening it: but in return, the honey is much whiter." Rochefort, *Histoire naturelle*, 161.

27. "Medical term, which refers only to blood that has left the ordinary vessels, namely, the arteries and veins, and remains in the body; thus the blood which leaves the body, or is drawn by bleeding it, is not called 'extravasated,'" article "Extravasé," TRV, vol. 2, 612.

28. The author is sometimes mistaken about the location of the reticulum.

29. Lorenz Heister (1683–1758) was a German anatomist, surgeon, and botanist, author of the *Compendium anatomicum* (Anatomical Compendium, 1721).

30. Johann Nicolas Pechlin (1646–1706), born in Leyden (Netherlands), published *Of the Appearance and Color of Ethiopians* (1677) and was made a Royal Society fellow in 1688.

31. *Canesco, canitia, canus,* refer to hair that grows gray or white as a person ages.

32. "When, therefore, the outer pores contract, the moisture contained in the thing cannot escape, but is trapped inside when the pores shut." Aristotle, *Meteorologica,* trans. H. D. P Lee, Loeb Classical Library 397 (Cambridge, MA: Harvard University Press, 1952), 309 [Book 4, 3, 381b].

33. See Bacon, "Experiment Solitary, touching the coloration of Blacks and Tawney Moores," *Sylva Sylvarum,* 104.

34. Jan Baptist van Helmont (1580–1644), a Dutch alchemist, chemist, physiologist, and physician, was considered the "father of pneumatic chemistry." In his *Opuscula medica inaudita* (New Medical Opusculum, 1644), he writes: "The Egyptians, who generally have almost completely black blood, and mostly without water, in lieu of being melancholic, are almost entirely choleric; and the extravasated blood of the body blackens immediately because it has left the veins, because the heat hastens its corruption," *Les Oeuvres de Jean-Baptiste Van Helmont traitant des principes de médecine et de physique, pour la guérison instantanée des maladies* (The Works of Jean-Baptiste Van Helmont Concerning the Principles of Medicine and Physics, for the Instantaneous Recovery from Illnesses) (Lyon: Jean Antoine Huguetan et Guillaume Barbier, 1670), part. 3, chap. 1, 169.

35. "Some animals have, and some have not, a gall-bladder up against the liver. The deer is an example of a viviparous quadruped which has none: other examples are the roe, the horse, the mule, the ass, the seal, and some kinds of pig." Aristotle, *History of Animals, Volume I: Books 1–3,* trans. A. L. Peck, Loeb Classical Library 437 (Cambridge, MA: Harvard University Press, 1965), 237 [Book 2, 15].

36. Pierre Tarin defines these *capsulae atrabilariae* or "renal glands" as two glands "situated between the aorta and the kidneys [. . .]" and whose "true use is unknown. It is believed that they serve to separate a liqueur of the arterial blood before it reaches the kidneys." See "Glande, anatomie," ENC (1757), vol. 7, 702.

37. On the subject of albinos (given various names in French including white moors and more commonly white *nègres*), see Andrew S. Curran, "Rethinking Race History: The Role of the Albino in the French Enlightenment Life Sciences," *History and Theory* 48, no. 3 (October 2009): 151–179.

38. The author's monogenism reconciles an *accidentalist* explanation (i.e., blackness caused by illness), a climatic one, and a preformationist one (hereditary blackness).

39. The author of the manuscript in some ways anticipates the experiments of the physician and naturalist René-Antoine Ferchault de Réaumur (1683–1757), who was one of the first to popularize attempts to mate pairs "contrary to the ordinary rules of nature," notably between a duck and roosters, a hen, and a rabbit. See *Art de faire éclore et d'élever en toute saison des oiseaux domestiques de toutes espèces, soit par le moyen de la chaleur du fumier, soit par le moyen de celle du feu ordinaire* (Art of Hatching and Raising Domestic Birds) (Paris: de l'Imprimerie royale, 1751), vol. 2, 337.

40. Esau, son of Isaac and Rebecca, older brother and twin of Jacob, was born "red, all over like an hairy garment; and they called his name Esau," (in Hebrew: hairy) Genesis

25:25. "And Esau said to Jacob, Feed me, I pray thee, with that same red *pottage;* for I *am* faint: therefore was his name called Edom" (in Hebrew, red-colored), Genesis 25:30.

41. The southern lands [*terres australes*] were largely unknown to the Europeans at this time, as the brevity of the articles on the subject attests. Following the *Histoire de la découverte des régions australes* (History of the Discovery of the Austral Regions, 1595–1606) by Pedro Fernández de Quirós (1565–1614), Portuguese explorer in the service of Spain, the historian and writer Charles de Brosses (1709–1777) reported that sailors saw "a large number of inhabitants of three colors: some entirely black, others extremely white with red hair and beard, and others mulatto," *Histoire des navigations aux terres australes* (History of the Navigations of the Austral Lands) (Paris: Durand, 1756), vol 1, Book 2, 325.

42. Jean François Fernel (1497–1558) was a French physician who introduced the term *physiology* to describe the study of the body's function. The *Therapeutice* is the third part of his *Universa Medicina* (1567).

43. Reference to the famous parable of the lily: "And why take ye thought for raiment? Consider the lilies of the field, how they grow; they toil not, neither do they spin: / And yet I say unto you, That even Solomon in all his glory was not arrayed like one of these. / Wherefore, if God so clothe the grass of the field, which to day is, and to morrow is cast into the oven, *shall he* not much more *clothe* you, O ye of little faith? / Therefore take no thought, saying, What shall we eat? or, What shall we drink? or, Wherewithal shall we be clothed? / [. . .] Take therefore no thought for the morrow: for the morrow shall take thought for the things of itself. Sufficient unto the day *is* the evil thereof." Matthew 6:28–34.

44. The *Encyclopédie* does not mention this use of the plant but underscores the fact that "in medicine, it makes a mucilage with rose water, purslane, plantain, which is used to ease inflammation of the eyes, excoriations of the palate, of the uvula, and of any other part; it is a refreshing and soothing mucilage." "Psyllium, botanique," ENC (1765), vol. 13, 45.

45. Lucius Annaeus Seneca, *Natural Questions,* trans. Harry M. Hine (Chicago: University of Chicago Press, 2010), 92 [Book 6, 5.3].

## 14. Blackness Degenerated

1. The Irish physician and chemist Robert Boyle (1627–1691) published his *Experimenta et considerationes de coloribus . . . ceu Initium historiae-experimentalis de coloribus* (Experiments and Considerations of Colors . . . or the Beginning of a Historical Experiment Concerning Colors, 1676).

2. *Histoire de l'Académie Royale des Sciences* (1702) (Paris: Gabriel Martin and Jean-Baptiste Coignard, 1743), observation 13 (on the epidermis of "Mores"), 30–32.

3. The different branches of the Chaigneau family had established a prosperous wine trade network in Ireland and served numerous high-ranking army members (in large part because the family owned several gunpowder factories). We have not identified the

uncle belonging to the Royal African Company (1672–1752, successor of the Guinea Company), a company integral to the European slave trade.

4. The author refers to the Royal Academy report, which notes that "they have at the head of the penis a small black mark," and contradicts the observation of Alexis Littré that "the children of the Moors are born white." *History of the Paris Royal Academy of Sciences* (1702), 32.

5. Pre-Adamism is a belief which opposes the theory of Adam as the ancestor of all humans. The theory was articulated by the French philosopher Isaac La Peyrère (1596–1676) in his heretical work *Prae-Adamitae* (1655).

6. Condemned by God to perpetual exile for killing his brother Abel, Cain received a mark in order to protect him, "lest any finding him should kill him." Genesis 4:15. Though Cain's bloodline ostensibly would have ended with the Flood, certain thinkers speculated on the nature of the mark, which they theorized was black skin that he passed to his descendants. See Genesis 4:1–15.

7. On the association of Noah's descendants with the first Black by certain Muslim thinkers, read Ida Zilio-Grandi, "La figure de Caïn dans le Coran" (The Figure of Cain in the Qur'an,) *Revue de l'histoire des religions* 216, no. 1 (1999): 31–85.

8. Samuel Bochart (1599–1667), French scholar and Protestant minister, supported the theory of the curse of Noah upon his son Ham, who was condemned to wander the countries where the sun is harshest, which thus darkened his skin and that of his descendants. *Geographia Sacra, seu Phaleg et Canaan* (Sacred Geography, or, Peleg and Canaan) (Caen: Pierre de Cardonel, 1646), Book 4, chapter 1.

9. The author writes in a note: "Objections against the opinion that the blackness of Blacks is an effect of the Curse of Noah." Still in the note, he references the tenth chapter of Bochart's *Sacred Geography, or, Peleg and Canaan*.

10. The priest, astronomer, and historian Berossus, called Berossus the Chaldean, is the author of the *Babyloniaca* [History of Babylonia] (c. 280 BCE), also called *Chaldaika* [History of Chaldea]. Several fragments of the work were published by the Roman Jewish historiographer Flavius Josephus (37 or 38–c. 100 CE) in his *Antiquities of the Jews* (c. 93).

11. Note that Noah himself made no mention of the blackening of the skin when cursing his son.

12. "Now these *are* the generations of the sons of Noah, Shem, Ham, and Japheth: and unto them were sons born after the flood. / The sons of Japheth; Gomer, and Magog, and Madai, and Javan, and Tubal, and Meshech, and Tiras. / And the sons of Gomer; Ashkenaz, and Riphath, and Togarmah. / And the sons of Javan; Elishah, and Tarshish, Kittim, and Dodanim. / By these were the isles of the Gentiles divided in their lands; every one after his tongue, after their families, in their nations. / And the sons of Ham; Cush, and Mizraim, and Phut, and Canaan." Genesis 10:1–6.

13. The historian and geographer Strabo (c. 60 BCE–20 CE) attributes the color of Blacks to both the sun and humidity: "But better is the opinion of those who lay the cause to the sun and its scorching, which causes a very great deficiency of moisture on the

surface of the skin." Strabo, *Geography,* Volume XII: Books 15–16, trans. Horace Leonard Jones, Loeb Classical Library 241 (Cambridge, MA: Harvard University Press, 1930), 39–41. Aristotle writes: "Why does the sun burn (the skin), whereas fire does not? Is it because the sun is finer, and so is more able to penetrate the flesh? But fire, even if it does burn, produces only on the top of the skin what are called blisters; but it does not penetrate within." Aristotle, *Problems,* Volume II: Books 20–38, ed. Robert Mayhew and David C. Mirhady, Loeb Classical Library 317 (Cambridge, MA: Harvard University Press, 2011), 429.

14. Phaeton steered the chariot of his father, the sun god Helios, too close to the land and thus burned its inhabitants, a myth that explains the existence of dark-skinned peoples.

15. The so-called Hottentots, a South African people now known as the Khoikhoi or Khoisan, were almost universally denigrated in the eighteenth century. The German naturalist Peter Kolb (1675–1726) in *Caput Bonae Spei Hodiernum* (Description of the Cape of Good Hope, 1719), which was translated throughout Europe, introduced the Dutch colony of the Cape by describing its inhabitants as close to animals. One of few writers to challenge these prejudices, Jean-Jacques Rousseau (1712–1778) transformed the Hottentot into the model of the "noble savage" uncorrupted by the artifices of European civilization in his *Discours sur l'origine et les fondements de l'inégalité parmi les hommes* (Discourse on the Origin and Basis of Inequality among Men, 1755). On the subject, see François-Xavier Fauvelle-Aymar, *L'Invention du Hottentot: histoire du regard occidental sur les Khoisan, XVe–XIXe siècle* (Paris: Publications de la Sorbonne, 2002).

16. "The races of the Samoyeds and the Hottentots seem to be two extremes of our continent," writes Louis de Jaucourt in the article "Samoyèdes ou Samoiedes, géographie moderne," ENC (1765), vol. 14, 603. This seminomadic Siberian people, who lived largely self-sufficiently and supposedly without religion, fascinated Europeans in this period.

17. The mountains of Rwenzori, identified as the legendary Mountains of the Moon of ancient Egypt, form a mountain chain on the border of Uganda and the Democratic Republic of the Congo. It contains the few glacial mountains in Africa, along with Kilimanjaro and Mount Kenya. Receiving plenty of rainwater, it produces numerous waterways, several of which feed the Nile.

18. According to the *Encyclopédie,* miliary glands are the organs allowing sweat to be separated from the blood. Jaucourt, article "Miliaires, glandes miliaires, anatomie," ENC (1765), vol. 10, 504.

19. Name given to "a membrane or tunic of the tongue, which is called papillary tunic, papillary membrane, or papillary body." Jaucourt, article "Papillaire, anatomie," ENC (1765), vol. 11, 872.

20. Pliny writes: "Eudicus tells us that in Hestiaeotis are two springs: Cerona, which makes black the sheep that drink of it, and Neleus, which makes them white, while they are mottled if they drink of each. Theophrastus says that at Thurii the Crathis makes oxen and sheep white, and the Sybaris makes them black. He adds that men too are affected

by this difference; that those who drink of the Sybaris are darker and more hardy, and with curly hair, while those who drink of the Crathis are fair, softer, and with straight hair. He also says that in Macedonia those who wish white young to be born lead their beasts to the Haliacmon, but to the Axius if they wish the young to be black or dark." Pliny, *Natural History: Volume VIII: Books 28–32*, trans. W. H. S. Jones, Loeb Classical Library 418 (Cambridge, MA: Harvard University Press, 1963), 387.

21. According to *On Superfetation* from the Hippocratic Corpus, "If a pregnant woman wishes to eat earth or coal, and she does so, a mark will appear on the head of the child at birth as a result." Hippocrates, *Coan Prenotions. Anatomical and Minor Clinical Writings*, ed. and trans. Paul Potter, Loeb Classical Library 509 (Cambridge, MA: Harvard University Press, 2010), 331. The anecdote according to which Hippocrates absolved a white princess accused of adultery for birthing a black child was invented by Saint Jerome; it is found in his *Hebrew Questions on Genesis*. According to this fable, Hippocrates attributed the phenomenon to the imagination of the mother, citing the portrait of a "Moor" resembling her child at the foot of her bed. The story was passed on through literature, notably the *Essais* of Michel de Montaigne (1533–1592).

22. Allusion to Louise-Marie de Sainte-Thérèse (c. 1658–1730), a Benedictine French nun from the Moret convent at Moret-sur-Loing. She was widely believed to be an illegitimate child of the royal family, whether by Queen Marie-Thérèse (1638–1683) or King Louis XIV, or a woman baptized and sponsored by the royal couple. She received a pension from the king as well as visits from the royal circle, both of which fueled rumors, and was described by Voltaire in his work *Le Siècle de Louis XIV* (The Age of Louis XIV, 1751). According to Serge Bilé, the nun's royal heritage was concealed to prevent scandal in the royal court, either of the queen's adultery or of the king's affair with a servant or black actress, the latter being more likely given the king's propensity for liaisons irrespective of social class. On the subject, see *La Mauresse de Moret. La religieuse au sang bleu* (Saint-Malo: Pascal Galodé Éditions, 2012).

23. This practice, artificial darkening of the face, is also mentioned in the early seventeenth-century pamphlet *Lanthorne and Candle-Light* by the Englishman Thomas Dekker (c. 1572–1632). Diderot's *Encyclopédie* was critical of these "vagabonds who read fortunes as a profession, whose talent is to sing, dance, and fly," known pejoratively as Gypsies. The dictionary makes no mention of the skin-darkening practice but notes that they have "black and crimped hair," article "Bohémiens, histoire moderne," ENC (1752), vol. 2, 295–296.

24. Jaucourt notes: "Their skin is very black; their hair is a veritable wool. [. . .] They are entirely naked for the most part; and those who are reasonably wealthy" "rub themselves in oil and paint," article "Guinée, géographie," ENC (1757), vol. 12, 1009.

25. The doctor, pharmacist, and chemist Gabriel François Venel (1723–1775) underscores the apparent dirtiness and ugliness of the practice: "It seems, however, that the custom of greasing the body is quite useless, and is most certainly very filthy and smelly, greatly decried even when these anointings are done with perfumes," article "Onguent," ENC (1765), vol. 11, 482. Depending on the region, albinos were sacred, mutilated, or even

sacrificed. On the subject, read Tsevi Dodounou, *Le Mythe de l'albinos dans les récits subsahariens francophones* (Berlin: Lit Verlag, 2011).

26. The canary was introduced to European nobility at the end of the fifteenth century, leading to a high-society passion: the keeping of caged canaries.

27. This curious conviction of the author is not supported by any fact.

28. In the first Book of Kings (chapter 10), the Queen of Sheba visits the king and prophet Solomon, son of David. Anecdotes of this meeting in Jerusalem vary, depending on the source. Supposedly Black, this sovereign mentioned in biblical, Koranic, and Hebrew accounts would have governed the kingdom of Sheba, which extended from Yemen to the north of Ethiopia and Eritrea. We were unable to identify the traveler Mangin mentioned by the manuscript author.

29. During his eventful stay in Angola and surrounding regions (from 1589 to 1610), the English sailor Andrew Battel (c. 1560–1613), forced into the service of the Portuguese, lived for two months as a hostage of the Imbangala of Jaga warriors and mercenaries. His description of albinos (Dondos) was cited by numerous compilers of travel and medical narratives from the seventeenth to the nineteenth centuries. Read *The Adventures of Andrew Battel of Leigh in Essex, sent by the Portuguese prisoner to Angola,* in Samuel Purchas, *Hakluytus Posthumus,* or *Purchas His Pilgrimes* (London: H. Fetherston, 1626), vol. 2, 974–977.

30. The quote is from Horace: "Non fumum ex fulgore, sed ex fumo dare lucem / Cogitat, ut speciosa dehinc miracula promat" ("Not smoke after flame does he plan to give, but after smoke the light, that then he may set forth striking and wondrous tales"). Horace, *Ars Poetica,* trans. H. R. Fairclough, Loeb Classical Library 194 (Cambridge, MA: Harvard University Press, 1926), 462–463. According to him, it is not smoke which follows fire, but rather smoke which provokes a vibrant flame.

## 15. Blackness Classified

1. These quotes were used to identify the authors. Contestants signed their essays with such aphorisms and sent a separate letter to the academy with the same aphorism and their name and address.

2. The author refers to the work of two people, Adrien (1639–1718) and Guillaume (1633–1703) Sanson, who wrote *Introduction à la géographie des Srs. Sanson, géographes du Roi* (Introduction to the Geography of Messrs. Sanson, Geographers to the King, 1690) (Paris: Durand et S. Landry, 1743).

3. The philosophe and doctor François Bernier (1625–1688) was the anonymous author of the "Nouvelle division de la Terre, par les différentes espèces ou races d'hommes qui l'habitent, envoyée par un fameux voyageur à M. l'abbé de la ***** à peu près en ces termes," (A New Division of the Earth According to the Different Types or Races of Men who Inhabit it) *Journal des Savants* (24 April 1684): 133–140.

4. Globally, the "human species" is divided thus, according to Bernier: 1. Europe, North Africa, Egypt, "a good part of Asia," and America. 2. "All of Africa." 3. "Part of the kingdoms of Arakan and Siam, the island of Sumatra and Borneo, the Philippines, Japan,

the kingdom of Pegu, Tunkin, Cochinchina, China, the part of Tartary between China, the Ganges, and Muscovy, Uzbek, Turkistan, Zaquetay," and some other lands. 4. "The Lapps." 5. The Blacks of the Cape of Good Hope, who "seem to be of another species than those of the rest of Africa," "Nouvelle division," 134–136. The author of the manuscript disregards Bernier's order, modifies the content of the "classes," and establishes a hierarchical scale of dominance where the fifth "species" becomes "that of the Negroes" (and not "the Blacks," who are second in Bernier's list). Whereas for Bernier the words species and race are synonymous, for the manuscript author, the terms "species" and "class" accentuate, singularize, radicalize the differences between the groups so as to consolidate the idea of "race" (a word only used in the body of the text).

5. Jaucourt notes: "This island, in the sea of the South, found in 1616 by Jacques Le Maire, is none other than the island of Sharks, which Magellan had discovered in 1520," article "Isle des chiens, géographie," ENC (1765), vol. 8, 922.

6. See Jacques-Bénigne Winslow, "Conformation particulière du Crâne d'un Sauvage de l'Amérique septentrionale." (Particular Structure of the Skull of a Savage from North America) Observation II, *Histoire de l'Académie royale des sciences. Avec les Mémoires de mathématique et de physique* (History of the Royal Academy of Sciences with Memoirs on Mathematics and Physics) (Paris: l'Imprimerie royale, 1722), 322–324.

7. The author adapts Hippocratic humoral theory to explain the nuances of black skin color.

8. The Spanish laws may be found in *Las siete partidas del rey D. Alfonso el Sabio glossadas por . . . Gregorio Lopez . . . Partida quarta corregidas y publicadas por Joseph Berni y Catalá* (Seven Records of King D. Alfonso the Wise Annotated by . . . Gregorio Lopez . . . Record Four Corrected and brought before the public by Joseph Berni y Catalá (Valencia: Printed by Benito Monfort, 1767). On the subject, read Bernard Grunberg, "L'esclave noir dans la législation de l'Amérique espagnole des XVIe et XVIIe siècles" (The Black Slave in Sixteenth and Seventeenth-Century Legal Codes in Spanish America), in *Esclaves: Une humanité en sursis*, ed. Olivier Grenouilleau (Rennes: Presses universitaires de Rennes, 2012), 141–160.

9. In colonial societies, the term *métis* refers to the descendants of Europeans and Amerindians or Africans. From the Latin *mixticius*, the term means mixed, or "people born of two different nations." Europeans referred to individuals of mixed origins with euphemisms from the animal world such as *mulâtre, loup*, or *coyote* [mulatto (from the Spanish for mule), wolf, or coyote]. Many of these words were employed in *pinturas de casta*, or casta paintings, a genre of painting that documented degrees of racial admixture among the inhabitants of New Spain (Mexico).

10. In New Spain, accusations of miscegenation were used to restrict individuals' access to certain institutions: the accused would be deemed a member of a "bad race" (*mala raza*), and could have their marriage authorization request denied (*disenso matrimonial*) in addition to prohibition from corporations and institutions.

11. In the margin of the manuscript, the author notes: "The foods of which I speak here are the ordinary foods of each region, and not certain extraordinary foods which

entail unique effects; this remark is absolutely necessary to make in relation to what follows."

12. The manuscript author here identifies degeneration with *bastardism,* a term to which he gives a racial meaning not found in dictionaries.

13. Human demographics was anything but an exact science during the eighteenth century.

14. These three authors, particularly the first two, are frequently cited in the manuscripts: Marcello Malpighi, Alexis Littré, and Jacques Winslow.

15. Superintendent of the Royal Garden of Medicinal Plants (1718) and first doctor of Louis XV (1730), Pierre Chirac (1657–1732) notably wrote the *Extrait d'une lettre écrite à M. Regis l'un des quatre Commis pour le Journal des Sçavans, sur la structure des cheveux* (On the Structure of Hair, 1688) (Paris: Durand, 1744), wherein he compares the roots of these delicate threads to those of bulbous plants and specifies their mode of nutrition and growth, as well as their deterioration. The German anatomist, botanist, and surgeon Lorenz Heister (1683–1758) is the author of the *Programma anatomicum quo inquiritur an sanguis circulus veteribus fuerit incognitus* (Anatomical Program in Which it is Inquired Whether Blood Circulation was Known to the Ancients, 1714). The Dutch doctor and professor of anatomy and botany Frederik Ruysch (1638–1731) is the author of the *Epistolae anatomicae problematicae* (Letters of Anatomical Problems, 1696–1701) and *Thesaurus anatomicus* (Anatomical Thesaurus, 1701–1716). Antonie van Leeuwenhoek (1632–1723) was a self-taught microscopist.

16. "Terrain, or land space considered according to its qualities: one says good *terroir* [soil], thankless terroir, terroir which is humid, dry, swampy, stony, sandy, fatty, lean, barren, fertile, vineyard, wheat, etc." Diderot, "Terroir, agriculture," ENC (1765), vol. 16, 186. On the subject, see Thomas Parker, *Tasting French Terroir: The History of an Idea* (Oakland: University of California Press, 2015).

17. The exact term highlighted by the manuscript author is "progénéré" [progenerated]. It is a neologism of his own making, evoking the "old word" *progeny,* which the dictionary cites as a synonym of "race." Article "Progénie," TRV, vol 5, 1124.

18. The author alludes to two articles by the physician, botanist, and agronomist Henri Louis Duhamel du Monceau (1700–1782), a member of the Academy of Sciences from 1738 onward and its three-time president: "Sur une racine qui teint les os en rouge," *Histoire de l'Académie royale des Sciences* (History of the Royal Academy of Sciences, 1739) (Paris: Imprimerie royale, 1741), 26–29, and "Sur une racine qui a la faculté de teindre en rouge les os des animaux vivants," *Histoire de l'Académie royale des Sciences,* 1–13.

19. The *Encyclopédie* warns against "the excessive use of gelatinous, austere, acidic, etc. foods. It is inconceivable how quickly the vices of food are communicated to the milk, and what impression they make; it is a known fact to all that the milk of a nanny becomes purgative when she takes any medicine which has this property. Article "Lait, maladies qui dépendent du, médecine, pathologie," ENC (1765), vol. 9, 212.

20. The author refers to the Flemish diplomat and botanist Ogier Ghiselin de Busbecq (1522–1592), author of *Epistolae ad Rudolphum II. Imperatorem e Gallia scriptae* (Letters to Emperor Rudolph II written from France, 1630).

21. Jaucourt confirms: "They are, Strabo says, taller and more beautiful than other men, and the Georgians taller and more beautiful than other women. The blood of Georgia is the most beautiful in the world, says Chardin: nature, he claims, has imbued the majority of the women with graces that are not seen anywhere else; and nowhere does one find prettier faces, nor finer sizes, than those of the Georgians," article "Géorgie, géographie," ENC (1757), vol. 7, 640. For contemporary historians, Colchis constitutes the first Georgian kingdom.

22. The author draws from Jean Chardin (1643–1713), French traveler and writer known for his *Journal du voyage du Chevalier Chardin en Perse et aux Indes orientales, par la mer Noire et la Colchide* (Journal of the Voyage of the Knight Chardin in Persia and in the East Indies, by the Black Sea and Colchis) (London: Moyse Pitt, 1686), where one learns that *gom*, "ordinary grain" resembling "millet," is a paste as "white as snow." "The Turks call this bread pasta, the Mingrelians" *gom*. [. . .] "It had such a flavor that I had difficulty returning to ordinary bread. I was quite pleased with it, and found my body in better form than before. [. . .] One must drink pure wine when eating it, to correct and temper its cold and laxative quality," 74–75.

23. The author here presents the paradox of an Africa that is unfamiliar, yet somehow known to house "ferocious and unsociable" peoples.

24. The "awful fire" referenced is the fire that ravaged London in 1666.

25. The quote refers to a work by the Dutch compiler Olfert Dapper (1636–1689), *Description de l'Afrique* (Description of Africa, 1668) (Amsterdam: W. Waesberge, Boom and Van Someren, 1686), 387.

26. Used to designate the diet of diverse peoples by Pliny and Diodorus of Sicily, this adjective meaning "omnivore," which according to its Greek etymology means "eats all," is absent from dictionaries of the period.

27. Among the thirteen kings of Egypt bearing the name "Ptolemy" is Ptolemy Lathyrus, king of Alexandria. On the subject, see Jacques Morabin (1687–1762), *Histoire de Cicéron, avec des remarques historiques et critiques* (History of Cicero, with Historical Remarks and Critiques) (Paris: Didot, Saugrin, 1763), ccxiv.

28. The Amicouanes or Amikwanes were encountered first in 1729 by a colonial administrator in Cayenne, Paul Lefebvre d'Albon.

29. The navigator and explorer Ferdinand Magellan (c. 1480–1521) headed the first European visit to this island cluster in the western North Pacific Ocean in 1521.

30. See Diodorus of Sicily, *Library of History, Volume II: Books 2.35–4.58*, trans. C. H. Oldfather, Loeb Classical Library 303 (Cambridge, MA: Harvard University Press, 1935), 107 [Book 3, 8].

31. The author synthesizes extracts from Diodorus originally dedicated to distinct Ethiopian peoples. On the Ichthyophages [fish-eaters] of Asia along the Indian sea, the historian writes: "certain of them go about entirely naked and have the women and children in common like their flocks and herds, and since they recognize only the physical perception of pleasure and pain they take no thought of things which are disgraceful and those which are honourable," Diodorus of Sicily, *Library of History, Volume II*, 107 [Book 3, 15]. Diodorus notes that the Hylophages [wood-eaters], another group named

for what they consume, "gather the fruit as it falls in great abundance from the trees in the summer season and so find their nourishment without labor, but during the rest of the year they subsist upon the most tender part of the plant which grows in the shady glens. [. . .] These men go naked all their life, and since they consort with their women in common they likewise look upon their offspring as the common children of all," 151 [Book 3, 24].

32. "And as a drink the common people make use of juice from the plant Christ's-thorn, but for the rulers there is prepared from a certain flower a beverage like the vilest of our sweet new wines," Diodorus of Sicily, *Library of History, Volume II*, 171 [Book 3, 32].

33. On the subject, read David Diop, "La mise à l'épreuve d'un *régime de véridiction* sur 'la paresse et la négligence des nègres' dans le *Voyage au Sénégal* (1757) d'Adanson," 15–29 in *L'Afrique du siècle des Lumières*, ed. Catherine Gallouët, David Diop, Michèle Bocquillon, and Gérard Lahouati (Oxford: Society for Voltaire and Eighteenth Century Studies, 2009).

34. The author draws his arguments from Jean Astruc's *De morbis venereis libri sex* (Six Books Concerning Veneral Diseases, 1736), for whom venereal diseases depend on a venom or poison that is continuously transmissible.

## 16. Blackness Dissected

1. A black horn is a corneous excrescence, not unlike a wart. Here Barrère's reproduction inverts the order of the anatomist Jacques Winslow's argument, which begins: "It is believed that the color of the epidermis is naturally white, and that the apparent color is rather that of the reticular body. Nonetheless, examining separately the epidermis of Moors, one finds no other whiteness than that of a thin and transparent slice of a black horn." "La surpeau ou l'épiderme," *Exposition anatomique de la structure du corps humain* (Anatomical Exhibition of the Structure of the Human Body) (Paris: Laurent-Charles d'Houry fils, 1732), 489, § 41. On Winslow, see Patrick Tort, *L'Ordre et les monstres: Le débat sur l'origine des déviations anatomiques au XVIIIe siècle* (Order and Monsters: The Eighteenth-Century Debate on the Origin of Anatomical Deviations) (Paris: Le Sycomore, 1980).

2. Johann Heinrich Samuel Formey (1711–1797) reproduces a long excerpt of Barrère in the article "Nègre, histoire naturelle," ENC (1765), vol. 11, 77–78. He found these excerpts in the *Journal des savants* which, after the contest, also addressed Barrère's findings.

3. Note that, according to the disciplines of the period, the reticular body (networks of fibers in the epidermis) fell under the jurisdiction of anatomy while the mucous body (subjects, substances) fell to chemistry.

4. Note the conflation of anatomy and chemistry with the belief in African hypersexuality.

5. Hippocrates, *De humoribus* (On the Humors). On the subject of the four humors, see Antoine Thivel, "Hippocrate et la théorie des humeurs," *Noesis* 1 (March 1997): 85–108.

6. "The medullar humor is the finest and most subtle of the marrow of the bones." It "does not pass through the bones by conduits, but by small vesicles accumulated in dis-

tinct lobules and coated with various membranes that envelop the marrow," article "Médullaire, huile médullaire," ENC (1765), vol. 10, 300.

7. According to the doctor Arnulphe d'Aumont (1721–1800), the term seed [*germe*] is used in the context of generation (about the embryo and its casing), "when it begins to grow," article "Germe, économie animale," ENC (1757), vol. 7, 644.

8. Barrère subscribes to Aristotle (and his Christian successors), for whom "the female always provides the material, the male provides that which fashions the material into shape," and therefore "the physical part, the body, comes from the female, and the soul from the male." Aristotle, *Generation of Animals*, trans. A. L. Peck, Loeb Classical Library 366 (Cambridge, MA: Harvard University Press, 1942), 185 [Book 2, 738b].

9. On this subject see Patrick Graille, "Portrait scientifique et littéraire de l'hybride au siècle des Lumières," *Eighteenth-Century Life*, 70–88.

10. According to *Trévoux*, the word "mulat, mulastre, or mulate" [mulatto] is the name given "in the Indies to those who are the offspring of a Black and an Indian woman, or an Indian and a Black woman." Those born to an Indian and a Spaniard are called *métis*. The Spanish also called "the children born of a father and mother of different religions" *mulates*, and "this word is a great insult in Spain," as it purportedly derives from "mulet, animal born of two different species," or mule. TRV, vol. 4, 1407.

11. *Négrillon* is the French term, often used by slave traders, for young Africans of either sex who have not yet reached ten years of age. Article "Négrillon, commerce d'Afrique," ENC (1765), vol. 11, 85.

12. Barrère's preformationism leaves a narrow but significant space for accidental exceptions produced by the maternal imagination.

13. Note that "mule" refers to any animal produced by two different species.

14. The term "Saccatro" did not appear in dictionaries until the end of the nineteenth century, indicating ambiguously "the colored man who comes closest to the Negro," article "Sacatra," Émile Littré, *Dictionnaire de la langue française* (Paris: Hachette, 1874), vol. 4, 1792.

15. "*Ignavia corpus hebetat, labor firmat.*" Barrère cites Aulus Cornelius Celsus (29 BCE–37 CE), a key figure in the study of the origin of Antique medicine due to the survival of his *De medicina*. (from which Book 1, Chapter 1 is quoted). James Alexander Lindsay, *Medical Axioms, Aphorisms, and Clinical Memoranda* (New York: Paul B. Hoeber, 1924), 2.

## Part II

### Introduction: *The 1772 Contest on "Preserving" Negroes*

1. *Programme de l'Académie Royale des Belles-Lettres, Sciences et Arts de Bordeaux, du 13 janvier 1772* (Program of the Bordeaux Royal Academy of Belles-Lettres, Sciences, and Arts of 13 January 1772) (Bordeaux: chez Michel Racle, 1772), 1.

2. *Programme de l'Académie Royale*, 4.

3. Stephen Auerbach, "'Encourager le commerce et répandre les Lumières': The Press, the Provinces, and the Origins of the Revolution in France: 1750–1789" (PhD diss., Louisiana State University and Agricultural and Mechanical College, 2001), 248.

4. Jeremy L. Caradonna, "Prendre part au siècle des Lumières: Le concours académique et la culture intellectuelle au XVIII^e siècle," *Annales: Histoire, Sciences Sociales* 64, no. 3 (2009): 641.

5. Caradonna, "Prendre part au siècle des Lumières," 641.

6. Ironically, the genesis of France's antislavery sentiment arguably began in Bordeaux itself, under the pen of the city's most famous academician, Montesquieu, who had lambasted the justification of slavery in the 1748 *Spirit of the Laws*. By the 1770s, many of the era's major voices—Helvétius, Voltaire, Bernardin de Saint-Pierre, Saint-Lambert, Raynal, and Diderot—had joined him in castigating the slave trade, especially the "degenerate" colonists who profited from the suffering of enslaved Africans.

7. Guillaume-Thomas Raynal, *Histoire philosophique et politique des établissements et du commerce des Européens dans les deux Indes* (A Philosophical and Political History of the Establishments and the Commerce of Europeans in the Two Indies) (Amsterdam, n.p., 1770): 4:167–168. For a complete list of the antislavery contributors to the very much collaborative *Histoire*, see Ann Thomson, "Diderot, Roubaud et l'esclavage," *Recherches sur Diderot et l'Encyclopédie* 26 (1999): 197–211.

8. Later that year, the *Journal of Medicine, Surgery, and Pharmacy* published an update about the fate of the award money. Since no prize was conferred, the "zealous citizen" who had sponsored the 1772 competition had decided to underwrite a different philanthropic contest: "How to prevent the common practice of breastfeeding abandoned children, and how this is dangerous for both the wet nurses and, more generally, for the general population." *Journal de Médecine, Chirurgie, Pharmacie, etc., Tome L* (Journal of Medicine, Surgery, Pharmacy, etc., Book 50) (Paris: Chez la V. Thiboust, July 1778), 184.

9. Christine Damis, "Le philosophe connu pour sa peau noire: Anton Wilhelm Amo," *Rue Descartes* 36, no. 2 (2002): 115. Damis believes that there is a direct link between Dazille's work and the contest, given the similarity between the two titles.

10. Other examples of this trend in medical literature include Dr. Collins, *Practical rules for the management and medical treatment of Negro slaves, in the sugar colonies, by a professional planter* (London: J. Barfield, 1803); James Thomson, *A Treatise on the Diseases of Negroes, as They Occur in the Island of Jamaica: With Observations on the Country Remedies* (London: Alex Aikman, 1820), and Philip Tidyman, "A sketch of the most remarkable diseases of the Negroes of the Southern states, with an account of the method of treating them, accompanied by physiological observations," *Philadelphia Journal of the Medical and Physical Sciences* 3 (1826): 306–338. See also Rana A. Hogarth's *Medicalizing Blackness: Making Racial Difference in the Atlantic World, 1780–1840* (Chapel Hill: University of North Carolina Press, 2017).

11. See James E. McClellan, III, and François Regourd, "The Colonial Machine: French Science and Colonization in the Ancien Régime," *Osiris* 15 (2000): 49.

12. Jean-Barthélemy Dazille, *Observations sur les maladies des nègres, leurs traitements et les moyens de les prévenir* (Observations on the Diseases of Negroes, Their Treatments, and the Means of Preventing Them) (Paris: Didot, 1776), iv.

13. Dazille, *Observations sur les maladies des nègres,* iv.

14. Dazille's efforts to promote a more "enlightened" form of slavery—one that would actually lead to an increase in slave populations—did lead to a limited number of reforms; after 1784, every French planter was obliged to establish a hospital on his plantation, provide adequate clothing and food, and make sure that slaves had a certain amount of free time. See Karol Kovalovich Weaver, "The Enslaved Healers of Eighteenth-Century Saint-Domingue," *Bulletin of the History of Medicine* 76, no. 3 (2002): 429–460.

## 1. A Slave Ship Surgeon on the Crossing

1. This first sentence was actually a marginal note in the manuscript. The vast Kongo kingdom maintained robust trade relations with Europeans under its Christian kings, enabling greater centralization and expansion, until civil wars broke out in the mid-seventeenth century. After the civil wars, the kingdom was more a politically and commercially motivated alliance than a centralized polity. See Koen Bostoen and Inge Brinkman, eds., *The Kongo Kingdom: The Origins, Dynamics and Cosmopolitan Culture of an African Polity* (Cambridge: Cambridge University Press, 2018), and Jelmer Vos, *Kongo in the Age of Empire, 1860–1913: The Breakdown of a Moral Order* (Madison: University of Wisconsin Press, 2015). The neighboring kingdom of Loango was another centralized polity which benefited economically from the slave trade, mainly selling slaves from inland trade routes. The French understanding of this kingdom at this time came mainly from the publication of Abbot Liévin-Bonaventure Proyart, *Histoire de Loango, Kakongo et autres royaumes d'Afrique, rédigée d'après les Mémoires des préfets apostoliques de la Mission française* (History of Loango, Kakongo, and other African Kingdoms, Taken from the Memoirs of the Apostolic Prefects of the French Mission, 1776).

2. Here the author alludes to the *pièce d'Inde* formula used in the European slave trade calculus, which denoted a specific value for a young, tall African man, who was robust and in "perfect state." The slightest fault, such as a broken tooth, would lower his commercial value. The English equivalent was the "trade ounce" or "bar." For more on this subject, see Karl Polanyi, "Sortings and 'Ounce Trade' in the West African Slave Trade," *Journal of African History* 5, no. 3 (1964): 381–393.

3. On the various geographic origins of African slaves, see David Eltis, David Richardson, and Stephen D. Behrendt, "Patterns in the Transatlantic Slave Trade, 1662–1867: New Indications of African Origins of Slaves Arriving in the Americas," in *Black Imagination and the Middle Passage,* ed. Maria Diedrich, Henry Louis Gates, Jr., and Carl T. Pedersen (Oxford: Oxford University Press, 1999), 21–32.

4. Proposed remedies and treatments for diseases on slave ships varied considerably and were, as the author of the manuscript notes, rarely effective in the eighteenth century. On the subject, read Sowande' Mustakeem, "The Anatomy of Suffering," in *Slavery at Sea:*

*Terror, Sex, and Sickness in the Middle Passage* (Champaign: University of Illinois Press, 2016), 131–155.

5. The English physician Thomas Sydenham (1624–1689) was the author of the *Observationes Medicae* (1676), a work that remained a standard medical textbook for more than two centuries after its initial publication.

6. "The matter of perspiration is separated through the skin, and also from the lungs; it is simply serum." George Motherby, *A New Medical Dictionary; or, General Repository of Physic* (London: J. Johnson, 1785), 577. Pulmonary perspiration, the exhalation of vapors, was a subject of interest for chemists and physiologists during this period; see, for example, William Frédéric Edwards, *On the Influence of Physical Agents in Life*, trans. [Thomas] Hodgkin and Dr. Fisher (Philadelphia: Haswell, Barrington, and Haswell, 1838), chap. 11: "On Perspiration," 99–110.

7. Two types of smallpox are identified in medical dictionaries from the period: distinct smallpox (*variola discreta*) and confluent smallpox (*variola confluens*). The English physician Richard Mead (1673–1754) proposes a different dichotomy, *simple* versus *malignant* smallpox, and observes that in the case of malignant smallpox, "the whole mass of humors is corrupted more or less, according to the nature of the disease; and the blood is in such confusion, that the purulent matter cannot be thrown upon the skin." *A Discourse on the Smallpox and Measles* (London: Printed for John Brindley, 1748), 29. Humors in this case refer to fluids within the body, though the manuscript author's allusion to external influence on the state of the bodily humors echoes the humoral theory of Antiquity and the Middle Ages.

8. The saltpeter (also known as niter) to which the author here refers is potassium nitrate, one of three naturally occurring nitrates given the name of "saltpeter." Potassium nitrate was historically used as both an ingredient in gunpowder and as a treatment for various conditions and diseases, including asthma. On the subject of saltpeter and gunpowder, see David Cressy, *Saltpeter: The Mother of Gunpowder* (Oxford: Oxford University Press, 2013).

9. This recommendation, common among "humanist" authors, was often rejected by shipowners and captains who rightly feared slave revolts.

10. Given the challenges of preserving provisions, less perishable food items such as grains and, more rarely, cured meats predominated in the diets of both crewmen and captives; as the author mentions, these foods were nonetheless susceptible to spoilage. See Sowande' Mustakeem, "'I Never Have Such a Sickly Ship Before': Diet, Disease, and Mortality in Eighteenth-Century Atlantic Slaving Voyages," *Journal of African American History* 93, no. 4 (Fall 2008): 474–496.

11. Stephen Hales (1677–1761) was an English clergyman and self-taught scientist, indeed best known for his ventilators. See Stephen Hales, *A Description of Ventilators* (London: Printed for W. Innys, at the West End of St. Paul's, 1743). Henri Louis Duhamel Du Monceau (1700–1782) was a member of the Parisian Academy of Sciences; he wrote extensively on agriculture and specifically plant anatomy, drawing heavily from Hales. His two-volume *Traité de la conservation des Grains, et en particulier du froment* (Trea-

tise of the Conservation of Grains, and Wheat in Particular, 1754–1765) suggested the use of Hales's ventilation methods in granaries.

12. Antoine Poissonnier Desperrières, *Traité sur les maladies des gens de mer* (Treatise on the Maladies of Sailors) (Paris: Chez Lacombe, 1767).

13. "The quartermasters must, by their example and their diligence, make the sailors act, guide them in the maneuver, and examine, by taking the night shifts, whether the maneuvers [i.e., ropes] are each tied to their mooring cleats, or put in their ordinary place: the quartermasters are particularly responsible for the care and keeping of the vessel," writes Robert de Hesseln in his *Dictionnaire universel de la France* (Universal Dictionary of France) (Paris: Desaint, 1771), vol. 4, 255.

14. The Italian naturalist and physician Antonio Cocchi (1695–1758) published *Del vitto pitagorico per uso della medicina* (Of Pythagorean Nourishment for Use in Medicine) in 1743, introducing the so-called Pythagorean diet (to which he himself subscribed) to Europeans. Cocchi also posited that scurvy was caused by a lack of vegetables in the diet. On French ships, food supplies for slaves and crewmen were stocked differently, and salted meats were generally reserved for personnel. See Angus Dalrymple and Ewout Frankema, "Slave Ship Provisioning in the Long Eighteenth Century: A Boost to West African Commercial Agriculture?," *European Review of Economic History* 21 (2017): 187–188.

15. The islands off the west coast of Africa in the Gulf of Guinea, "discovered" by the Portuguese in the fifteenth century. They were initially a major source of sugar in the sixteenth century, before becoming an entrepôt for the Atlantic slave trade. See Gerhard Seibert, "São Tomé & Príncipe: The First Plantation Economy in the Tropics," in *Commercial Agriculture, the Slave Trade and Slavery in Atlantic Africa*, ed. Robin Law, Suzanne Schwarz, and Silke Strickrodt (Suffolk: Boydell & Brewer, 2013): 54–78.

16. In the eighteenth century, arsenic was both a medical remedy and a toxic poison.

17. Tar-water, a rather self-explanatory concoction, had various applications as a medical treatment in the eighteenth century: "it manifestly promotes the excretions, particularly that of urine; and the same may be presumed to happen in that of others. From all these operations, it will be obvious, that in many disorders of the system, this medicine may be highly useful." Article "Tar-water," Motherby, *A New Medical Dictionary*, 593.

18. "Omentum, called epiploon by the Greeks, and by us the cawl," is found "[b]elow the liver, floating over the intestines," where it is "divided into two borders, one of which is fixed along the great arch of the colon, and the other along the great curvature of the stomach. . . . Its use is, by its fat, to lubricate the parts adjacent, to prevent adhesions of the intestines, and as a preparatory organ for the bile." Article "Omentum," Motherby, *A New Medical Dictionary*, 547.

19. The author may be referring to the Royal Hospital near Cap François known as the Hôpital de la Charité, founded in 1698, or to one of the numerous plantation hospitals found on Saint-Domingue. There were several Royal Hospitals on the island, though many were not built until the second half of the century. The hospital at Fort Royal to which the author likely refers is the naval hospital, completed in 1722.

20. Author's marginal note: The author also recommends treating dysentery with a pharmaceutical composition called *diascordium,* or diascord, which is a kind of electuary, or opiate, made from the dried leaves of scordium. Other ingredients of diascord include red roses, bole, storax, cinnamon, cassia lignea, dittany, tormentil roots, bistort, gentian, galbanum, amber, opium, long pepper, ginger, and malmsey. It was used against malignant fevers, the plague, worms, colic, to promote sleep, and resist putrefaction.

21. The second part of the essay, a long and specific discussion of the diseases themselves, is not included here.

## 2. A Parisian Humanitarian on the Slave Trade

1. The physiocrats were economists whose work addressed the interrelation of nature, morality, and wealth. One of the most important tendencies among members of the school was the idea that the true wealth of a nation can be measured by its agricultural potential and production. Common rhetorical tropes among physiocrats also included the idea that nature itself recoiled at the idea of harsh enslavement. Many physiocrats also claimed, as a corollary argument, that slavery was not an economic necessity; if one simply follows nature itself and frees humankind to achieve its potential, the argument went, happiness and wealth would result. Among primary texts, see Victor de Riquetti, marquis de Mirabeau (1715–1789), *Leçons Œconomiques* (Economic Lessons) (Amsterdam, 1770). For a good summary of the movement, see Liana Vardi, "A Delicate Balance," in *The Physiocrats and the World of the Enlightenment* (Cambridge: Cambridge University Press, 2012), 113–148. On physiocracy and slavery, see Pierre Le Masne, "La colonisation et l'esclavage vus par les physiocrates," *L'Économie politique* 71, no. 3 (2016): 101–112.

2. "The fact that bodily diseases or symptoms are profoundly influenced by mental processes, often partially caused by them, was well known to all great clinicians from Erasistros and Galen to Charcot and Struempell. Psychogenesis, or 'passion-produced disease,' as Galen called it, was thus discussed abundantly until the nineteenth century." Erwin H. Ackerknecht, *A Short History of Medicine,* rev. ed. (Baltimore: Johns Hopkins University Press, 1982), 235. The manuscript author's ideas anticipate William Falconer's (1744–1824) *A Dissertation on the Influence of the Passions Upon Disorders of the Body* (1788), one of several treatises from the period on the supposed effects of "passions" on physical health. See also Erwin H. Ackerknecht, "The History of Psychosomatic Medicine," *Psychological Medicine* 12 (1982): 17–24.

3. The author's proposal is not without precedent: Africans were forced to dance during the Middle Passage, for entertainment of the white crew as well as, purportedly, for exercise. Claims that song and dance were for the emotional benefit of the enslaved Africans belied the cruelty of the practice. See Geneviève Fabre, "The Slave Ship Dance," in *Black Imagination and the Middle Passage,* ed. Maria Diedrich, Henry Louis Gates, Jr., and Carl T. Pedersen (Oxford: Oxford University Press, 1999), 33–46, and Katrina Dyonne

Thompson, "Casting," in *Ring Shout, Wheel About: The Racial Politics of Music and Dance in North American Slavery* (Champaign: University of Illinois Press, 2014), 42–68.

4. "Each has his misery assigned him, like a trade." Lucius Annaeus Seneca, *Declamations, Volume II: Controversiae, Books 7–10. Suasoriae. Fragments,* trans. Michael Winterbottom, Loeb Classical Library 464 (Cambridge, MA: Harvard University Press, 1974), 423.

## 3. *Louis Alphonse, Bordeaux Apothecary, on the Crossing*

1. On apothecaries and the life of this author, read Josiane Cluchard, "Quelques aspects de la vie sociale des apothicaires bordelais au XVIIIe siècle" (PhD diss., University of Bordeaux, Faculty of Pharmaceutical and Biological Sciences, 1982).

2. Note in the manuscript: these figures come from the French Royal Navy in 1773.

3. This ethnicity lived on the Gold Coast, an old kingdom of the Gulf of Guinea (contemporary Ghana and southern Benin). They were among the first to be deported as slaves to Saint-Domingue and Haiti in the seventeenth and eighteenth centuries. See the article "Nègres, considérés comme esclaves dans les colonies de l'Amérique," ENC (1765), vol. 11, 81.

4. A hydrocele is defined as a rupturing of water in the scrotum. Article "Hydrocele," George Motherby, *A New Medical Dictionary; or, General Repository of Physic* (London: J. Johnson, 1785), 408.

5. The ethnicities cited by the author are not terribly clear. On the subject of slave suicide, read David Lester, "Suicidal Behavior in African-American Slaves," *OMEGA— Journal of Death and Dying* 37, no. 1 (1998): 1–13, and William D. Piersen, "White Cannibals, Black Martyrs: Fear, Depression, and Religious Faith as Causes of Suicide among New Slaves," *Journal of Negro History* 62, no. 2 (1977): 147–159.

6. This recipe is mentioned briefly in Louis-Henri-Joseph Hurtrel d'Arboval, *Dictionnaire de médecine, de chirurgie, et d'hygiène vétérinaires* (Dictionary of Medicine, Surgery, and Veterinary Hygiene) (Paris: Chez J.-B. Ballière, 1838), 529.

7. *Vulnéraire Suisse,* also called falltranck, is "an infusion, or tea, prepared with a mixture of the herbs alchemilla, creeping bugloss, betony, periwinkle, philosella, golden rod, vervain, artemisia, mint, and veronica, gathered among the Alps. It is believed to be of great efficacy for removing the effects of falls and blows." "Falltranck," Arnold James Cooley, *A Cyclopaedia of Several Thousand Practical Recipes and Collateral Information in the Arts, Manufactures, and Trades, Including Medicine, Pharmacy, and Domestic Economy* (New York: D. Appleton & Company, 1846), 298.

8. See Niklas Thode Jensen, *For the Health of the Enslaved: Slaves, Medicine and Power in the Danish West Indies, 1803–48* (Copenhagen: Museum Tusculanum Press, 2012), 98–99. Jensen explains that yaws, a very contagious bacteria-based disease that produces suppurating boils for months on end, was often confused with syphilis because their symptoms were very similar.

9. Neapolitan ointment earned its name because it ostensibly cured the "Malady of Naples," or syphilis.

10. The author writes in a footnote that crewmen returning from India and China afflicted with scurvy and other ailments were sometimes treated at islands en route with a diet of tortoise broth and meat.

11. "Angola" referred ambiguously to West Central Africa. Malembo, Cabinda, and Loango were the second, third, and fourth most popular ports for French vessels after Whydah on the Bight of Benin; thus, "West Central Africa formed the main source of captives for the French slave trade." David Geggus, "The French Slave Trade: An Overview," *William and Mary Quarterly* 58, no. 1 (2001): 122.

12. On trade in these ports, read Phyllis M. Martin, "The Conduct of Trade I: Negotiations on the Coast," in *The External Trade of the Loango Coast, 1576–1870* (Oxford: Oxford University Press, 1972), 93–116.

13. Honoré Lacombe de Prézel, *Dictionnaire d'anecdotes, de traits singuliers et caractéristiques, historiettes, bons mots, naïvetés, saillies, reparties ingénieuses, etc. etc. Seconde Partie* (Dictionary of Anecdotes, of Singular and Characteristic Traits, Histories, Good Words, Naivetés, Witticisms, Clever Repartées, etc., etc., Part Two) (Amsterdam: Chez Arkstee & Merkus, & Marc Michel Rey, 1767), 44.

# ACKNOWLEDGMENTS

A multiyear project as complex as *Who's Black and Why?* brought the editors of this book, Henry Louis Gates, Jr., and Andrew S. Curran, into conversation with a wide range of generous colleagues, friends, and students. We would first like to offer special thanks to the people who peered deeply into the project with us: Robert Bernasconi, David Bindman, Jennifer Mayo Curran, Laurent Dubois, David Eltis, Amity Gaige, Jorge Felipe-Gonzalez, Rana Hogarth, Nina G. Jablonski, Mélanie Lamotte, Silvia Marzagalli, Sue Peabody, Kiyo Saso, Éric Saugera, Tiah Shephard, Jack Stewart, and Sophie Dora Tulchin. Conversing with such wonderful colleagues has made this project not only better, but much more exciting and rewarding.

The longer list of dear friends and colleagues who have helped in various ways include Marco Aresu, Michael Armstrong, Martin Baeumel, Charlie Barber, Rowan Beaudoin-Friede, Bruno Belhoste, Elizabeth Bobrick, Cameron Bonnevie, Gregory Brown, Kevin Burke, Jack Canavan-Gossellin, John Charles, Andrew Clark, Lisa Cohen, Sofia Colorado, Robert Conn, Imani Crews, Marlene Daut, Jo Diaz, David Diop, Hamilton dos Santos, Julie Duprat, Demetrius Eudell, Frédéric Fourgeaud, Isis Gaddy, Catherine Gallouët, Nima Ghasoor, Arid Gigi, Carra Glatt, Antonio Gonzalez, Amy Gosdanian, Roger Grant, Judith Gurewich, Paul Halliday, Rob Heinrich, Thierry Hoquet, Maisie Hurwitz, Maddie Ikeda, Joyce Jacobsen, Ethan Kleinberg, Anne Lafont, Sofia Liaw, Walter and Anne Mayo, Elizabeth McAlister,

Mary McAlpin, Michael Meere, Miriam Claude Meijer, Cecilia Miller, Fabienne Moore, Ellen Nerenberg, Michelle Nivar, Chris Parslow, William Pinch, Stéphanie Ponsavady, Mercedes Reichner, Carolyn Roberts, Meghan Roberts, Philippe Roger, Nita Rome, Michael Roth, Scott Sanders, Daniel Smyth, Marguerite Stahl, Joanna Stalnaker, Andy Szegedy-Maszak, Nikki Terry, Melissa Thornton, Jennifer Tsien, Kate Tunstall, Kari Weil, and Courtney Weiss Smith. Andrew Curran would also like to recognize his students at the Cheshire Correctional Institution, who engaged deeply with an early version of this manuscript.

We would also be remiss if we did not single out our friends and tremendously valuable collaborators Sheldon Cheek, Karen C. C. Dalton, and Patrick Graille, all of whom contributed to this project in myriad ways, including during the translation phases. In this latter process they were seconded by the wonderful Susan Emanuel and Rosanna Giammanco, about whom more is written in the Note on the Translations.

While conducting the research for this book, the editors also relied on a number of generous and helpful librarians at Harvard University's Botanical Libraries, Boston Public Library, the Wellcome Collection, the Getty Research Institute, the Cartographic Free Library, the Bibliothèque national de France, and the Bibliothèque municipale de Bordeaux. We are deeply appreciative of the advice, guidance, and images provided by the Musée d'Aquitaine (Bordeaux), the Musée de la Marine (Paris), the Kassel Museumlandschaft, and the Château de Versailles.

As is the case with all such research projects, generous institutional funding allowed it to come to fruition. The Hutchins Center for African and African American Research provided support for the initial research phase of this project, which included trips to France. In particular, we would like to acknowledge the tireless work of the center's executive director, Abby Wolf, for making this possible. The editors would like to recognize contributions made by Wesleyan University's Office of Academic Affairs and the Thomas and Catharine McMahon Memorial Fund of Romance Languages and Literatures.

Harvard University Press has been an excellent partner in this venture, and we would like to thank Sharmila Sen, who, as editorial director at the press, was this project's staunch advocate and is responsible for their decision to publish it, taking our fight into her own hands after our years of lobbying and attempts to raise funds for it had been unsuccessful. Her team, including Heather Hughes, Stephanie Vyce, Kate Brick, Annamarie Why, and Amanda Ice, were excellent partners in the process. John Donohue of Westchester Publishing Services was also an invaluable colleague.

This book grew out of an idea for which Karen C. C. Dalton had long and fiercely advocated. Karen has been dedicated to the maintenance and nurturing of the Image of the Black Archive and Library for over fifty years, growing it at the Menil Collection in Houston and moving it to Harvard University in 1994. It was in her capacity as editor of the Image of the Black series that she became familiar with the collection of documents that we refer to as "the Bordeaux Papers." And it was through the careful research and persuasive—even irresistible!—advocacy of Karen that this project grew into the format it takes today. She and Sheldon Cheek (who continues to serve as the curator of the Image of the Black Archive at the Hutchins Center) brought the idea to Henry Louis Gates, Jr. As the editors of this volume, we owe Karen a tremendous debt of gratitude for being the driving force behind this project, for refusing to see these writings as anything other than absolutely critical to the conversation about how we see race and how we have come to understand it.

Most of all, we are grateful for Marial Iglesias's guidance and knowledge.

# CREDITS

p. ii   Pierre Pomet, *A Complete History of Drugs* (London, 1748, 4th ed.), facing p.
57. Copy in Special Collections Department, University of Virginia Library.
Sugar Works, French West Indies.

p. xii   The first page of Essay 2. Archives Bordeaux Métropole. Ms828.65.2

p. 4   Early photograph of the former home of the Royal Academy of Sciences,
Belles-Lettres, and Arts at Bordeaux. Archives Bordeaux Métropole. Côte XX C
259

p. 5   *Negroland and Guinea with the European Settlements* . . . Herman Moll,
geographer; Thomas and John Bowles, publishers. *Atlas minor* (London, 1729).
Reproduction courtesy of the Norman B. Leventhal Map & Education Center at
the Boston Public Library.

p. 6   Native life in Negroland, from Olfert Dapper, *Description of Africa*, 1668.
The Getty Research Institute / Hathi Trust Digital Library

p. 7   *Les quatre complexions de l'homme* (The Four Temperaments of Man), by
Charles Le Brun, 1670s, pen and ink. Photo © RMN-Grand Palais / Art
Resource, NY

p. 8   *The Conception of Chariclea*, by Karl van Mander III, 1640, oil on canvas.
Kassel, Museumlandschaft Hessen. Shim Harno / Alamy Stock Photo

p. 9   *Vue d'une partie du port et de la ville de Bordeaux, prise du côté des Salinières*
(View of a part of the port and city of Bordeaux, as seen from the wharf of
Salinières), Joseph Vernet, 1758, oil on canvas. Paris, Musée national de la
Marine de Paris. Active Museum / Active Art / Alamy Stock Photo

p. 10    *Une sucrerie dans une habitation à Saint-Domingue* (A Sugar Mill on a Plantation of Saint-Domingue), engraving from Père Jean-Baptiste du Tertre, *Histoire générale des Antilles habitées par les Français* (Paris: Thomas Jolly, 1667–1671). Photo © BnF, Dist. RMN-Grand Palais / Art Resource, NY

p. 11    An African *mascaron* stares out from the former Place Royale, now Place de la Bourse, facing the esplanade along the Garonne River. Langladure / Wikimedia Commons / CC BY-SA 3.0

p. 13    *Prospect of the Coast from El Mina to Mowri*, from John Green, comp., *A New General Collection of Voyages and Travels*, vol. 2 (London: Thomas Astley, 1745–1747), facing p. 589. Reproduction courtesy of The Afriterra Cartography Library.

p. 14    *Africa: A European Merchant bartering with a Black Chief*, from a series of the *Four Continents* by Jean-Baptiste Oudry. 1724, oil on canvas. Christie's Images Ltd. / SuperStock

p. 15    Louise de Keroual, duchess of Portsmouth, by Pierre Mignard, 1682, oil on canvas. London, National Portrait Gallery. Photo © National Portrait Gallery, London

p. 23    *André-Daniel Laffon de Ladébat*, Suzanne Caron, 1763, pastel. Musées de Bordeaux. The Picture Art Collection / Alamy Stock Photo

p. 25    Chronology for the year 1741. From the *Almanach royal* (Paris: Veuve Houry, 1741), p. 4. Private collection

p. 28    *The Drunkenness of Noah*, Luca Giordano, second half of the seventeenth century, oil on canvas. Madrid, El Escorial. De Agostini Editore / age fotostock

p. 34    *Georges-Louis Leclerc, Comte de Buffon (1707–1788)*, Francois-Hubert Drouais. Musée Buffon, Montbard. Heritage Image Partnership Ltd. / Alamy Stock Photo

p. 40    *The Five Races of the World*, Johann Friedrich Blumenbach, *De generis humani varietate nativa* (On the Natural Variety of Humankind). 1795 edition. Wellcome Collection, London

p. 194   *Programme de l'Académie Royale des Belles Lettres, Sciences et Arts de Bordeaux*, January 13, 1772. Archives Bordeaux Métropole

p. 195   Slave stowage aboard the *Marie-Séraphique*, ca. 1770, watercolor. Nantes, History Museum. Musée d'histoire de Nantes / Wikimedia Commons

p. 196   *Nègres à fond de calle* (Blacks in the bottom of the hold). Johann Moritz Rugendas, *Voyage pittoresque dans le Brésil* (Paris: Engelmann, 1835), hand-colored lithograph. The Picture Art Collection / Alamy Stock Photo

p. 224   *Simarouba amara*. Pierre Jean François Turpin, designer. Lambert, engraver. Chaumeton, Poiret, and Chamberet, *La Flore Médicale* (Paris: Panckoucke, 1828–1832), pl. 327, hand-colored stipple engraving. Album / Alamy Stock Photo

# INDEX